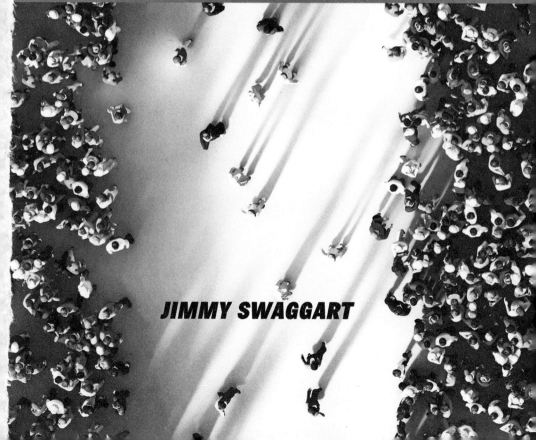

FOOLISH

CHRISTIANS

JIMMY SWAGGART

FOOLISH
CHRISTIANS

JIMMY SWAGGART MINISTRIES
P.O. Box 262550 | Baton Rouge, Louisiana 70826-2550
www.jsm.org

ISBN 978-1-941403-78-5

09-178 | COPYRIGHT © 2022 Jimmy Swaggart Ministries®

22 23 24 25 26 27 28 29 30 31 / Sheridan / 10 9 8 7 6 5 4 3 2 1

TABLE OF CONTENTS

FOOLISH CHRISTIANS

INTRODUCTION

INTRODUCTION

THE SUBJECT MATTER THAT we will address is without a doubt the single most important as it regards the believer's walk with God. I speak of the subject of sanctification. Unfortunately, most Christians simply don't know what sanctification means, much less how to bring it about in their lives.

The word *sanctification* simply means to be set apart from something to something. In this case, it is to be set apart from the world and its spirit and unto God and His Spirit.

The other day, one writer said that the word *sanctification* is so little understood, and that it's not used anymore in most church circles. That's tragic, but it happens to be true.

When we consider how important this is—the single most important aspect of the believer's life and living—we should avail ourselves of the opportunity of trying to find out what it means, and how it is carried out in our lives.

HOW?

One preacher said, and rightly so, "Everyone told me what to do, but no one told me how to do it." That is the tragedy as it regards sanctification.

The modern church has tried to obey this principle in every conceivable way possible, all to no avail. In other words, the modern church has no idea as to how sanctification can be brought about in one's heart and life.

I would pray that the Lord would help us, as it regards this book, to open up this phenomenal subject.

In 1988, the Lord spoke to me and said, "I'm going to show you things about the Holy Spirit that you do not now know." I will never forget that morning so long ago. Yet once that word came, I was somewhat taken aback.

The Holy Spirit is God. Consequently, there are all kinds of things about Him that we do not know. I knew that what the Lord was talking about was our everyday living and the part played by the Holy Spirit, which is all-encompassing.

In 1997 the Lord began to fulfill that promise. He began to show me how the Holy Spirit works within our hearts and lives—He works by and through the cross of Christ. In other words, the cross gave and gives the legal right to the Holy Spirit to do all that He does. In fact, *"the law of the Spirit of life in Christ Jesus,"* which is the most powerful law in the world, is the only law that can overcome *"the law of sin and death"* (Rom. 8:2).

Since that day, the Lord began to open up this all-important subject to me. He has continued to open that door to show me that which the Holy Spirit desires to do and can do—if we will only approach Him in the right way.

THE CROSS

Let me say it again: the Holy Spirit works exclusively by and through the cross of Christ. In other words, it's what Jesus there did that gives the Holy Spirit the legal means to do all that He does. Now that requires one thing on our part, which is so very, very important. It requires of us that our faith be constantly in Christ and the cross—in Jesus Christ and Him crucified. This is imperative!

If the Lord helps me in this book to put down on paper what is in my heart, I personally believe that it will open up to you truths of unparalleled significance—truths that will help you to live for God in a manner that you have never previously known, and truths that will open up this more abundant life that Jesus said we could have, which most believers do not have.

The words *sanctification* and *holiness* come from the same Greek word. At times, the translators translated it *sanctification,* and other times they translated it *holiness.* As stated, both words mean the same thing.

The meaning is one thing and very important; however, what I want to know is, how can I bring about sanctification and or holiness within my heart and life? Paul said a long time ago (and we had better heed his words): *"Follow peace with all men, and holiness* (every effort must be made to live peacefully with all men, but not at the expense of holiness, i.e., 'the compromising of the Word'), *without which no man shall see the Lord"* (holiness cannot be brought about by law; it can only be brought about by grace, which is made possible by the cross) (Heb. 12:14) (The Expositor's Study Bible).

I hear the Savior calling today,
Oh, come unto Me and rest,
I am the life, the truth, and the way,
Oh, come unto Me and rest.

Oh sinner, come, there's mercy for you,
Oh, come unto Me and rest,
Be saved today whatever you do,
Oh, come unto Me, and rest.

Then come today, oh why do you stray?
Oh, come unto Me and rest;
Believe My word, then trust and obey,
Oh, come unto Me and rest.

FOOLISH
CHRISTIANS

FOOLISH
CHRISTIANS

FOOLISH CHRISTIANS

"O FOOLISH GALATIANS, who hath bewitched you, that ye should not obey the truth, before whose eyes Jesus Christ hath been evidently set forth, crucified among you?" (Gal. 3:1).

When I use the term *foolish Christians*, I do not use it in the same tone as did Paul regarding the Galatians. They knew better! He had given them the truth, but they had allowed that truth to slip from them. Modern Christians, and I speak of those who truly love the Lord, simply do not understand the great subject that Paul was broaching—the subject of sanctification.

Sanctification is being set apart from something, namely this world and its spirit, unto something, which is the Lord and His Spirit. As that preacher said, "Everyone told me what I had to do, but no one told me how to do it." That's the problem with modern-day Christians. No one has really told them honestly and scripturally how to be sanctified.

The problem is, as the unsaved cannot save themselves, likewise Christians cannot sanctify themselves. But we keep trying, don't we? Momentarily I'm going to elucidate some particular efforts that are being made in the modern church as it regards sanctification. But first allow me to say the following: sanctification is simply not understood in most modern Christian circles.

For years, one particular Pentecostal denomination taught entire sanctification, which means that one is entirely sanctified, and they will never sin again. The Bible does not teach sinless perfection. It does teach that sin is not to have dominion over us, which, if we study that phrase carefully, we will see that these simple words cradle the seed of our victory (Rom. 6:14).

I would ask you to read the following very carefully, because this is what present believers are attempting to do to be sanctified.

ENCOUNTER SESSIONS

A preacher wrote me the other day. Incidentally, he was a man with whom I was not acquainted.

In his letter he stated that he had found the answer to sin, and then he told me what he had found.

He, along with many other pastors and their wives were invited to this particular meeting where a great truth would be presented as to how victory was to be found in their lives. Several hundred pastors responded.

After the host spoke a few minutes, he told them to take out their pads and pens, which they had been told to bring.

They were to write down all of the sins that they had committed in the recent past. Of course, that within itself is unscriptural because the Bible tells us to forget those things which are behind (Phil. 3:13).

At any rate, the men were told to select a male partner, and the women were told to select a female partner. They were to stand, facing each other, with their papers in their hands on which they had written all of their sins. They were then to read the sins out loud to each other. This man was quick to say that there were others whose sins were a whole lot worse than his own. Sounds familiar, doesn't it?

After they had read aloud their many sins, the participants were to take the sheets of paper on which the accounts of their sins were written and tear them into little pieces. While holding the torn pieces in their hands, they were to put their hands above their heads and then open their hands to let the pieces of torn up paper flutter to the floor. Next, they were to start jumping up and down on the pieces of paper on which their sins had been written while praising the Lord the whole time. This was their victory. Now, they were told, they were sanctified; now they were free from the problems that had beset them in the past.

I don't mean to be unkind, but that is ridiculous.

Did I answer this preacher's letter? Yes, I did, although I did not go into detail knowing that doing so, at that time, would be hopeless. But I did tell him, "My brother, the cross of Christ alone holds the answer for sin, and there is no other answer."

PHYSICAL AND SPIRITUAL TORTURE

This one concerns a Catholic priest.

He was interviewed by a reporter, and I happened to see the interview. The interview took place because this man had set himself on a regimen of self-induced effort to become holy, or an effort of that effect.

The reporter asked what it was that this priest was doing. The priest told how he slept on a mattress each night that was only three inches thick, and he slept without a pillow. He arose at four o'clock every morning to pray. He ate only two meals a day—meals with no meat. He went to town only one time a year, and that was for one hour.

After listening to this litany of self-induced torture, the reporter asked, "So, do you feel God?"

The priest's answer was somewhat startling. He wheeled around, looked at the reporter and, after a few moments, said, "Do I feel God? I've never felt God one single time. I don't even know if there is a God."

That was his regimen of trying to be holy.

THE PENTECOSTAL WAY

The other day, Donnie showed me a book written by a dear brother who I am certain loves the Lord very much, so I do not question his consecration. But in the book, and I read it, this man said that if a person wants victory over sin, he should fast twenty-one days or some such length of time.

Now fasting is scriptural, and it will definitely be a blessing to you. But as someone pointed out, and rightly so, if you're trying to get victory over sin in that fashion, after a while, you're going to have to eat, and then the problem starts again. So while fasting is scriptural, it will not give you victory over sin. There is only one avenue of victory over sin and that is the cross of Christ.

Others have tried to sanctify themselves by the type of clothes they wear or by the way the ladies cut—or don't cut—their hair, and other things that one could name.

I remember years ago—and it still prevails now—if a Christian was having a problem with lust, alcohol, uncontrollable temper, jealousy, envy, etc., then that individual was to look for a preacher who understood these things, and have him lay hands on him or her, and take authority over the demon that was causing the problem. In other words, if it was lust, then the man or woman was bothered by a demon of lust, or a demon of envy, etc.

Once again, this is trying to address the problem without going to the solution which is the cross of Christ. Let me say it again: there is no solution for these things except the cross of Christ.

WHAT DO WE MEAN AS IT REGARDS THE CROSS?

First, the believer has to understand that the only answer for his or her dilemma is the cross of Christ. This means that the believer must do what Jesus said. And what did He say?

"And he said to them all, If any man will come after me, let him deny himself, and take up his cross daily, and follow me" (Luke 9:23).

He also said, *"And whosoever doth not bear his cross, and come after me, cannot be my disciple"* (Luke 14:27).

Paul said, *"For Christ sent me not to baptize, but to preach the gospel: not with wisdom of words, lest the cross of Christ should be made of none effect. For the preaching of the cross is to them that perish foolishness; but unto us which are saved it is the power of God"* (I Cor. 1:17-18).

He also told the church at Corinth *"For I determined not to know anything among you, save Jesus Christ and Him crucified"* (I Cor. 2:2).

The great apostle also said, *"But God forbid that I should glory, save in the cross of our Lord Jesus Christ, by whom the world is crucified unto me, and I unto the world"* (Gal. 6:14).

I could go on in this vein, but I think you get the point.

SO HOW IS A PERSON SANCTIFIED?

Good question!

In the first place, you must understand that there is absolutely nothing that you can personally do to sanctify yourself. To be blunt, the believer, no matter how consecrated, cannot sanctify himself. This means that engaging in rituals or ceremonies, no matter what they are or how scriptural they may be, will not affect sanctification.

Let's use another example: if, as a believer, you set yourself to be sanctified—you want to be set apart from the world unto God; in other words, you love the Lord very much, and you want to be what He wants you to be—so you set out to attain this tremendous position by praying an hour a day. To be sure, praying is scriptural, and you will be greatly blessed, but you won't be sanctified.

Let me say it again: the believer cannot sanctify himself, even as the unsaved soul cannot save himself. It is impossible.

If we try to come by sanctification in that capacity, then, in one way or another, we find ourselves doing the same thing as that Catholic priest did. Yet that's what Christians keep trying to do—sanctify themselves.

So, what do you do? It all comes by faith, but it must be faith in Christ and what Christ has done for us at the cross. Do you understand that?

It is simple faith, but it must be faith in the correct object, and that correct object is Jesus Christ and Him crucified. The moment your faith is in Christ and Him crucified—at that moment—you are sanctified.

The Lord made it very easy for us to do this. Anyone can have faith. And anyone can have faith in the correct object, which is the cross of Christ—that is the means by which one is instantly sanctified.

WHY?

That being the case, why is it that we keep trying to sanctify ourselves, even to the point of going into a regimen of self-induced torture, thinking it will sanctify us? It won't!

The reasons are varied, but the main reason is that the doing of these things speaks to our personal ambition. We feel good about ourselves and think, "Look what I have done!" Doing these things glorifies the flesh, and that is our problem. Even though they are possibly scriptural in their own right and make us feel good while trying to do whatever it is that we've set out to do, still, the result is ugly. It's not Christlikeness but rather self-will.

Let me say it again: it is impossible for the believer, no matter what he does, to sanctify himself. You cannot do it, and you were not meant to do it. Jesus, knowing that we could not do it ourselves, has done it for us. All we have to do is have faith in Him.

PLEASING THE LORD

Read the following very carefully: the Scripture says Enoch *"had this testimony, that he pleased God"* (Heb. 11:5). What was his testimony? What was it that he did that pleased God? The Scripture tells us. It says, *"But without faith it is impossible to please him"* (Heb. 11:6).

We must understand it has to be faith in Christ and the cross. If it's in anything else, then the Lord will not honor it.

Anytime faith in the Bible is mentioned, always and without exception its root meaning is that its object is Christ and the cross. Otherwise, it is faith God will not accept.

And please notice, the Scripture plainly tells us, *"It is impossible to please Him* (God)," any way other than faith in

Christ and the cross. It didn't say that it was difficult or hard, but impossible.

This is man's basic problem, and it is the basic problem regarding the believer. It is impossible for us to save ourselves—most Christians understand that. But it is also impossible for the believer to sanctify himself. You can't do it. You can draw up all types of rules and regulations, but you cannot do it.

GOD'S WAY

When the building of Family Worship Center was finished, we had a meeting with all of our preachers, which possibly numbered about forty. The reason for the meeting was to come to the conclusion as to what we would require of people who wanted to become a part of Family Worship Center.

First one preacher and then another had thus and so to say. They came up with all type of rules and regulations that one had to agree to before he could become a member of our church. I listened to it for quite some time, and then I joined in and asked this question: "What are the requirements for a person to become a member of the kingdom of God?"

Finally, someone said, "To be born again."

I turned, looked at the preachers, and said, "And that will be our requirement as well—and the only requirement."

Many of them agreed with me; others did not.

But let's think about that a moment. The only requirement for a person to become a part of the kingdom of God—to be born again—is to simply trust in Christ. That being done, that person is instantly made a part of the kingdom of God. If the Holy Spirit is satisfied with such, I would certainly think that it should be good enough for us.

Please understand, one cannot improve upon what God has done. Every time we veer from His way and insert our own way we run into trouble, and big trouble at that.

SANCTIFICATION

We have stated and we'll state again, if a person exhibits faith in Christ and what Christ has done for him at the cross, and he maintains his faith in that capacity, then he is instantly sanctified. So then the question must be asked, what about weaknesses and problems in one's life? Do those instantly go away? No, they do not.

But the difference is this: when your faith is in Christ and the cross, the Holy Spirit, who works exclusively within the parameters of the finished work of Christ, will then go to work in your heart and life to rid you of those particulars which are wrong and dragging you down. In fact, the Holy Spirit, who works entirely within the finished work of Christ, will not work any other way. If we try to do it ourselves, we will greatly hinder the Holy Spirit because, in reality, we are actually committing spiritual adultery.

When we come to Christ, we are actually married to Him (II Cor. 11:2-4). As such, the Lord Jesus will meet our every need. In fact, He is the only one who can meet our every need.

So, when we turn to other things, irrespective of how religious they are, we are being unfaithful to Christ. Now think about that for a moment. Unfaithfulness in a marriage can many times cause disruption in that marriage. Thank God, the Lord has great patience with us, so He does not depart immediately. However, this greatly hinders the Holy Spirit. He does not leave us, thank God for that, but we do grieve Him.

The only way is Christ and the cross. When we go in other directions—irrespective as to how religious those other directions may be, or even how scriptural they may be—if it's not faith in Christ and the cross, then it's faith in something else, and we are being unfaithful to Christ, which will cause us great problems. Unfortunately, that's where most of modern Christendom is, being unfaithful to Christ.

God's way of sanctification is faith in Christ and the cross. He has no other way because no other way is needed.

All these efforts we put forth—efforts that might make us feel good for a short period of time as they address our self-will, ego, and personal worth—but in the eyes of God they are sin, and gross sin at that.

Do you mean to say, Brother Swaggart, that if I fast so many days to get victory over sin in my life that I'm sinning? Yes, you are. You are sinning by placing your faith in something other than Christ and the cross. Paul said, *"Whatsoever is not of faith is sin"* (Rom. 14:23).

Does that mean you stop fasting? No. It means that you place your faith where it ought to be placed, which is Christ and the cross as it regards victory over sin. There are many things for which we should fast, and the Lord will bless us abundantly so. However, we must keep in mind that all sin must be addressed at the cross, and when one looks at the situation, almost all of our problems, in one way or another, are caused by self.

GALATIANS

The Expositor's Bible Commentary notes, "This is the first time since 1:11 that Paul addresses the Galatians. Now it is by the impersonal term 'Galatians' rather than by the word 'brothers,' and it sets a sober tone for the formal argument to follow."[1]

The same commentary goes on to say:

Paul cites three things that are inexplicable in regard to the Galatians' conduct. (1) Their conduct is irrational or "foolish," a word that suggests the actions of one who can think but fails to use those powers of perception (cf. Lk 24:25; Ro 1:14; 1 Ti 6:9; Tit 3:3). This term was suggested by Paul by the trend of his thought at the end of the previous chapter—namely, that a doctrine of salvation by works foolishly denies the necessity for grace and declares the death of Jesus Christ unnecessary. A doctrine leading to such a conclusion is irrational. Yet this is what the Galatians were on the verge of embracing. How can such nonsense be explained? Paul suggests facetiously that perhaps they have been placed under a spell by some magician.[2]

Wouldn't that be the same for many modern Christians?

THEIR CONDUCT

The conduct of the Galatians is inexplicable because "the true Gospel has been so clearly preached to them. Undoubtedly, he is referring to his own preaching, arguing that the Gospel has been made as clear by him as if he had posted it on a public bulletin board."[3]

Moreover, he had not obscured it by nonessentials. For "the heart of the Gospel that Paul preached is—and always must be—"Christ crucified."[4]

The perfect tense of this verb is important, for it refers to an act completed in the past, but which has continuing significance, not only in the initial salvation experience, but in our everyday walk with God regarding victory and overcoming power.

HOW MANY BELIEVERS NOW ARE BEING REFERRED TO BY GOD AS FOOLISH?

How foolish are we if we neglect the eternal, spending all our time on the temporal? How foolish are we to lay up treasures here, which are of little worth, and fail to lay up treasures there?

How foolish are we to spend all our time learning about things of earth that will perish, and so little time on the Word of God? How foolish are we to have an improper relationship with Christ, when it is possible to do the opposite?

In fact, such a list is almost endless. I wonder if, in some way, the word *foolish* applies to all of us, even the most consecrated.

A little baby, if given the choice, will grab at a shiny, colored rattle and completely ignore a hundred-dollar bill. To be frank, the analogy is poor. What we as believers so often ignore is of infinite more value than the choice made by the baby. No wonder Jesus said, *"O fools, and slow of heart to believe all that the prophets have spoken"* (Luke 24:25).

One day when we as believers stand at the judgment seat of Christ, we will realize just how important all of this concerning Christ actually was. But then—respecting the consecration and dedication that we should have had—it will be too late. While we won't lose our souls over these things, we will definitely lose reward (I Cor. 3:15).

BEWITCHED

In Galatians 3:1 and the phrase, *"who hath bewitched you,"* theologian Albert Barnes said, "The idea here is, that they had not been led by reason and by sober judgment, but that there must have been some charm or fascination to have taken them away in this manner from what they had embraced as true, and what they had the fullest evidence was true."[5]

In the Greek, the word *bewitched* is from *baskaino*, says Greek scholar Kenneth Wuest, and denoted "either the fascination of an evil eye or some malignant influence akin to it. The infatuation of the Galatians is attributed to the baneful effect of some mysterious power of evil.[6]

FALSE APOSTLES

In essence, when Paul asked the question that starts, *"Who hath bewitched you,"* he excuses the Galatians, at least does so in a sense, and lays the blame upon the false apostles.

It is as though Paul would say, "I see that you are not fallen through willfulness or malice; but the devil has sent enchanting false apostles—his own ministers—among you, and they do so bewitch you in teaching that you are justified by the law that now you think otherwise of Christ than you did before, when you heard the gospel preached by me."

There is a bewitching power and even a sorcery behind false doctrine. It mesmerizes, attracts, pulls, and even seduces. The reason is obvious—seducing spirits are behind all false doctrine (I Tim. 4:1). That's the reason that Satan hates the cross as he does. It was there that he was totally and completely defeated. And if the believer will place his faith exclusively in Christ and the cross, maintain it exclusively in Christ and the cross, not allowing it to be moved elsewhere, then false apostles will not be able to seduce him.

Let's look carefully at the following. It is a strange statement as given by John the Beloved, but it holds a wealth of meaning:

> *And one of the elders saith unto me, Weep not: behold, the Lion of the tribe of Judah, the Root of David, hath prevailed to open the book, and to loose the seven seals thereof. And I beheld, and lo, in the midst of the throne and of the four beasts, and in the midst of the elders, stood a Lamb as it had been slain, having*

seven horns and seven eyes, which are the seven Spirits of God
sent forth into all the earth (Rev. 5:5-6).

Now, what did he mean by seven horns and seven eyes and
seven spirits?

First, the number seven is God's number of perfection, uni-
versality, and totality.

The seven horns denote total dominion, in other words,
that the believer is to have total dominion over the powers of
darkness, and that means total.

As well, the seven eyes pertain to the illumination given
to us by the Holy Spirit, which guarantee that if we keep our
faith in Christ and the cross, that we will not be drawn away by
seducing spirits, and this means that the reason that Christians
keep being pulled away from the true gospel is because their
faith is not in the slain Lamb. Remember, this passage began
with the slain Lamb, and that is the source of all victory. John
saw the Lamb as it had been slain.

The part about the seven spirits does not mean there are
seven Holy Spirits, for there is only one Holy Spirit. The word
seven denotes the attributes of the Holy Spirit, and those attributes are, first of all, *"the spirit of the LORD shall rest upon him, the*
spirit of wisdom and understanding, the spirit of counsel and might,
the spirit of knowledge and of the fear of the LORD" (Isa. 11:2).

In these seven compliments of the Spirit of God, we have at
our disposal all that we need to live this life, hence *"seven spirits."*

The "spirits of darkness" appeal to the believer and do so
in one of two ways: self-will and ignorance of the Word of

God (or both). That's the reason that it is imperative that believers pay careful attention to that which they hear by preachers. Everything must be evaluated according to the Word of God. If it's not scriptural, it must not be entertained. In other words, turn the individual off.

When I say ignorance of the Word, I am not speaking of scholarship. Even though every believer ought to be a Bible scholar, still, God does not require such for scriptural integrity to be maintained, even though He does require a working knowledge. If so, new converts would be at the mercy of Satan.

It requires an honest heart, which actively seeks to do the will of God. If the believer will pray accordingly, asking the Lord to lead Him in the right direction, which, at the same time, keeps him from wrong direction, the Lord will honor that petition. While such a believer may veer off course momentarily, the Holy Spirit—acting upon an honest, seeking heart—will pull the person back to the straight and narrow. However, an earnest seeking desire for the ways of the Lord only must be prevalent in the heart and life of the believer. The Holy Spirit cannot function otherwise.

To humanity the cross itself seems foolish. But this particular foolishness of God is the ultimate wisdom. The cross alone puts the great moral issues of the universe—sin, justice, and salvation—in complete perspective.

You and I must search the Scriptures for God's revelation of His own unique wisdom. Only by looking at our lives from God's revealed point of view can we avoid those notions about life's meaning that distort the lifestyle of the lost.

THE TRUTH

In Galatians 3:1, the phrase, *"that ye should not obey the truth,"* refers to the gospel of Jesus Christ.

The truth of the gospel is obviously the Word of God. The major problem is that some add to the Word of God, take away from the Word of God, or they falsely interpret the Word of God. Whichever way, the results are lethal.

JESUS AND THE PHARISEES

Pulpit Commentary states:

Any one who will be at the pains of reviewing the contents of the four Gospels with an eye to this particular subject, cannot fail to be struck by the frequency with which Christ in his own conduct placed himself in even the sharpest antagonism to the 'traditions of the elders,' and encouraged his disciples in likewise setting them at nought. And this he did in cases in which the contrast of his behaviour to the abject submission to those traditions paraded by the Pharisees must have been most striking, and have jarred, no doubt, very often even painfully, upon the ill-instructed religious sensibilities of those, who had grown up in the belief that to observe the traditions was both seemly and pious and to neglect them unseemly and schismatical. For example, in daily life, neither he nor his disciples would 'baptize' themselves when coming home from the market, nor even apply lustral water to their hands before taking a meal, though there before their eyes stood tire vessels filled with water which had been provided for the guests and which the other guests were punctual in using. It was not without significance that in his first miracle he withdrew the water which had been set apart for such lustrations from one use of it which he would pronounce to be utterly frivolous and vain, to apply it to one which should really be serviceable and beneficent.[7] [See John 2].

This of which we speak had nothing to do with hygiene or cleanliness, but rather that of demon spirits, believe it or not.

The Pharisees believed that a demon spirit called "Shibta," sat upon the hands at night or even at other times.

Consequently, they had a particular belief that the hands were to be washed with water. They were to rub the back with the knuckles of the opposite hand, and this was supposed to get rid of the evil spirit. They taught that this spirit must be washed off or he might be ingested. Jesus ignored this because it contained no scriptural validity.

RESTRICTIONS

Many were the restrictions that the Pharisees placed on a person's daily life and living. For instance, they perfected some six hundred oral laws besides that of the law of Moses. In fact, some of the Pharisees considered these man-devised laws as being more important even than the law of Moses. That's what usually takes place. That which man devises is gradually placed ahead of that which is the Lord, until finally that which is given by the Lord holds no place at all.

That's the reason Jesus said, *"Why do ye also transgress the commandment of God by your tradition?"* (Matt. 15:3).

Furthermore, Jesus ignored these traditions, and did so in the very face of the Pharisees, which angered them terribly so. That's one of the reasons they hated Him—He showed them up as to what they really were.

And yet, man is so bent toward ritual and ceremony, especially of the religious kind, that it was difficult even for the Twelve to keep from falling back into that vortex. Consequently, whenever ritualism and formalism were preached, i.e., "the necessity of works," it seemingly always found a ready audience, even as it does presently.

This readily showed itself in Peter's reluctance to obey the Lord, with the vision accordingly given unto him some three times (Acts 10:9-16).

JESUS CHRIST CRUCIFIED

In Galatians 3:1, the conclusion to the question, *"before whose eyes Jesus Christ hath been evidently set forth, crucified among you?"* proclaims the preaching of the gospel as done by Paul. He had so fully and plainly preached Christ and Him crucified that it might be said, "You have seen Him." It was that clear, that plain. The manner in which Paul preached this great doctrine, and the frequency in which it was preached, was as if Jesus had been crucified before their very eyes.

It was set forth so plainly that it was as if he had carved it in stone, i.e., "a public written tablet."

Barnes said, "There was the utmost clearness and distinctness of view, so that they need not make any mistake in regard to him. The Syriac renders it, 'Christ has been crucified before your eyes as if he had been represented by painting.'"[8]

A CLEAR REPRESENTATION

The representations of the Lord Jesus as crucified, have been as clear and impressive among them as was possible to be.

Barnes added:

> The argument is, that they had so clear a representation of the Lord Jesus, and of the design of his death, that it was strange that they had so soon been perverted from the belief of it. Had they seen the Savior crucified; had they stood by the cross and witnessed his agony in death on account of sin, how could they doubt what was the design of his dying, and how could they be seduced from faith in his death, or be led to embrace any other method of justification.[9]

Actually, that which is said of the Galatians can be said of most modern Christians presently. But I think there is a difference. The Galatians had had the privilege of being instructed in the gospel by none other than the apostle Paul himself. Consequently, they knew the truth, which made their defection even worse.

Presently, most believers have no true teaching whatsoever on the message of the cross. They know "Jesus died for me," and that is the greatest statement that could ever be made. But as it regards our everyday living for God, our present walk before Him, our living of a victorious life—of that they have no understanding whatsoever as it regards the cross.

In other words, they think of the cross only in the manner of salvation and not at all in the matter of sanctification.

Barnes said:

The doctrine taught in this verse is, that a faithful exhibition of the sufferings and death of the Saviour ought to exert an influence over our minds and hearts as if we had seen him die; and that they to whom such an exhibition has been made should avoid being led astray by the blandishments of false doctrines, and by the arts of man. Had we seen the Saviour expire, we could never have forgotten the scene. Let us endeavour to cherish a remembrance of his sufferings and death as if we had seen him die.[10]

In fact, He will bear the scars of the cross forever and forever, and I speak of the nail prints in His hands, etc.

WHAT THE WORD CRUCIFIED MEANT

Wuest writes: "The word crucified is in the prefect tense. This speaks of the fact that the apostle is not speaking of the figure of a dead Christ on a crucifix, but of the risen, ascended

Christ who had been crucified, who was alive, whose glorified body still bore the marks of the nails and the scars of the crown of thorns, and who is the living Saviour by virtue of His atoning work on the Cross."[11] In other words, His work is a finished work.

Galatians 3:1 pointedly tells us that Christ and Him crucified was the primary message preached by the apostle Paul. While He certainly preached other doctrines, this was the foundational doctrine of all doctrines, and it would be the same now, that is if we are preaching the true gospel.

The apostle Paul had preached salvation through faith by the grace of God without the works of the law. Many in the region of Galatia were happy in their newfound redemption and their complete freedom from the curse of the law. But then certain legalistic Judaist teachers, who made a practice of following Paul everywhere he went, also came to Galatia and began to teach these happy new converts that Paul was all wrong in preaching salvation by grace alone. It seems that they agreed with Paul that one is saved by grace without the works of the law, but then after that he must be kept saved by his works and his perfect obedience to the commandments of God. This greatly disturbed the Galatian Christians, who evidently knew that they needed God's grace to keep them, as well as to save them. But these legalists kept hammering away until the churches of Galatia were all confused.

PAUL AND HIS ANSWER

Reports of this confusion reached the ears of Paul while he was preaching in the city of Corinth, and he immediately wrote this epistle under inspiration and dispatched it to the churches of Galatia to correct the error. The error was the teaching that we are saved by grace, and then we are kept saved by our behavior and keeping of the law.

Paul's answer is that salvation is all of grace: we are saved by grace; we are kept by grace. In our first Scripture in Galatians 3, Paul expresses both surprise and indignation at the fickleness of these converts. Then he asks two questions:

1. How are you saved? The answer, of course, was by faith and not by the works of the law.
2. Are you now made perfect by the flesh? (Gal. 3:3).

FOOLISHNESS

How foolish can we be? If we were saved by faith, and we definitely were, then how do we think we can maintain our victory by works? If salvation could not come by works, then victory in our everyday walk with God cannot come by works as well.

Please understand, there is no victory in disciplines. And what do we mean by disciplines? We're speaking of our prayer life, fasting, witnessing—all the good things that every Christian should do. But while there is definitely blessing in those things, which every believer ought to do and must do, at least to a degree, still, there is no victory over sin in that capacity. All victory over sin—and sin really is the problem—must be addressed at the cross. That, and that alone, will give us victory. Unfortunately, there are millions of Christians presently who love the Lord but cannot live a victorious life. Something is dragging them down or causing them problems and the situation, despite their efforts otherwise, is not getting better but rather worse.

Let me say it again: there is no victory in disciplines. That being the case, why are the disciplines so attractive to believers?

They are attractive to us because they address our ego, our self-will, and they make us feel that we have really done something. I was able to do it, whatever it was, but so-and-so was not. We like that! In those cases, we feel good about ourselves, but again, there is no victory in that capacity.

Again, let me make the statement: victory over the world, the flesh, and the devil can come about only by and through the cross of Christ. That means that the cross must ever be the object of our faith, and I mean ever. All victory is found in the cross and no place else.

There are millions of Christians today, who truly love the Lord, and they have an excellent prayer life, which they should have, but to their dismay, they find that despite their prayer life, or their fasting, or their witnessing, or their faithfulness to church, they still cannot walk in victory. Their spiritual life is one of one failure after another, and they really don't know the reason why.

At the same time, it's very difficult for Christians to admit what I have just stated. It's hard for them to admit that they have no victory in their spiritual lives. It's hard for them to admit that despite all the disciplines in which they engage themselves in, they have no victory. It's hard for them to grasp this because they still want to try to do something that will help them have victory.

DEBT

Please read the following very carefully. It's straight from the Word of God, and about as clear as I can make it:

What shall we say then that Abraham our father, as pertaining to the flesh, has found? (Having stated that the Old Testament teaches that God justifies the sinner on the faith principle as opposed to the merit principle, the Holy Spirit now brings forward Abraham). *For if Abraham were justified by works* (which he wasn't), *he has whereof to glory; but not before God* (the boasting of salvation by works which God will not accept). *For what says the Scripture? Abraham believed God, and it was accounted unto him for righteousness* ([Gen. 15:6] if one properly understands this verse, he properly understands the Bible; Abraham gained righteousness by simple faith in God, who would send a Redeemer into the world [John 8:56]). *Now to him who works* (tries to earn salvation or righteousness) *is the reward* (righteousness) *not reckoned of grace* (the grace of God), *but of debt* (claiming that God owes us something, which He doesn't!). *But to him who works not* (doesn't trust in works for salvation or righteousness), *but believes on Him who justifies the ungodly* (through Christ and the cross), *his faith is counted for righteousness* (God awards righteousness only on the basis of faith in Christ and His finished work) (Rom. 4:1-5) (The Expositor's Study Bible).

I am convinced that Galatianism (salvation by faith, which is correct, but then trying to maintain salvation by works) is at least one of the greatest traps or snares for the Christian.

Satan respects only one thing and that is Calvary and the resurrection. He is perfectly content for us to attempt to maintain victory by the works of the law—prayer, fasting, witnessing, and giving money, etc.

In reality, these things we have just mentioned are not laws, but they are extremely helpful exercises, which will definitely prove to be a blessing to any and all believers, and which every believer should engage himself in. The idea is that we oftentimes make laws of that which was never intended by God to be a law.

For instance, if the Christian fails—he sins in some fashion— then he is automatically convicted of such by the Holy Spirit (John 16:8-11). As a child of God with a divine nature, he now abhors sin, and he instantly realizes that the situation must stop, whatever it may be.

THE BIBLICAL COURSE

Upon the event of failure, which is greatly crushing to any believer, he should immediately renew his trust in the finished work of Christ. He should proclaim the fact to himself that when Jesus died on Calvary, He not only paid the terrible sin debt, but also broke the grip of sin for all who believe. The believer is to understand that and realize that it has a definite, positive effect in his heart and life at the present. He must reckon himself *"to be dead indeed unto sin, but alive unto God through Jesus Christ our Lord"* (Rom. 6:11).

No, the Bible does not teach sinless perfection, but it does teach that sin is definitely not to have dominion over us (Rom. 6:14).

However, all of this is done upon our faith in what Jesus did at Calvary and the resurrection. There, our victory was secured, and our victory was guaranteed. At the same time, we must understand that even though we are saved and baptized with the Holy Spirit, we cannot overcome sin within our own ability and strength. Also, this great victory is not an automatic situation. It requires daily faith in Christ and the cross (Luke 9:23).

When faith in the cross is exhibited daily, which is what taking up the cross and following Jesus actually means, the Holy Spirit then steps in with His power, and the problem is solved. What is difficult or even impossible for us is no difficulty with Him whatsoever. However, the Holy Spirit will not work in the realm of our willpower or according to works of the law, etc., but only within the confines of the finished work of Calvary. In those parameters, He works mightily with victory guaranteed—that is if our faith remains in Christ and the cross. The Holy Spirit always spotlights Christ and the cross, so to speak (Rom. 8).

BUT INSTEAD

However, what I have just explained is not usually what takes place. Too many times the believer, upon failure, seeks to overcome such by works of the law. While it is not the law of Moses of which Paul speaks, but rather a law of our own making. Irrespective, the results will be the same. In fact, no matter how hard we try in that capacity, instead of the problem being solved, it gets worse.

Let me say it in another way: no true Christian wants to sin. Sin is abhorrent to the believer. In fact, he can hardly stand it until he confesses it to the Lord and is instantly cleansed, washed, and forgiven (I John 1:9). At least that's the way it is for those who are truly godly. He certainly does not want to repeat the action again; nevertheless, if he tries to overcome any other way—except by faith in the cross—then he is guaranteed of failure again, and again, and again. Satan knows exactly where that believer is placing his trust.

UNDERSTANDING CALVARY

Once the failure happens, if the believer does not fully understand Calvary and his part in that great finished work, then he will resort to other measures. I speak of measures such as more prayer, more fasting, etc. While these things are excellent, and even necessary, they will not serve respecting the overcoming of sin.

Please don't misunderstand, without a proper prayer life, the Christian cannot be what he ought to be or have the relationship with Christ that he ought to have. However, that is different than trying to use prayer to finish out what Christ has already finished at Calvary.

In other words, it is somewhat like trying to make a hammer out of a handsaw. While the handsaw is definitely a proper tool regarding that for which it was made, it will not serve as a hammer, as should be obvious. Likewise, prayer is a proper tool (as are other "tools" we could name), but it will not serve for overcoming sin. That must be done strictly through our faith in the cross.

Let me say it another way: there is no victory in the disciplines. There is blessing, and there is a necessity of these disciplines for our consecration, but there is no victory over sin. And ninety-nine percent of our problems, if we trace them back far enough, we will find that the cause of those problems is sin. And the only avenue of escape—the only solution for sin—is the cross of Christ.

FRUSTRATION

That's what Paul was talking about in Galatians 2:21 when he said, *"I do not frustrate the grace of God."* If we try to use works to overcome sin, irrespective as to how holy those works may be (such as prayer) we are, in fact, frustrating the grace of God. That means the Holy Spirit cannot do for us what He desires to do. God's grace works on the free gift of Calvary, which responds to faith. If we add works to that, we nullify the free gift.

Now please understand, if you think we are teaching against prayer, against Bible study, witnessing to the lost, fasting, etc., then you are completely misunderstanding what we are saying.

Every good Christian will have and should have these disciplines in his life. I have a greater prayer life today than I have ever had before, but now it is for a different purpose and a different reason. I once thought I could pray my way to victory. Such cannot be done, and it is not meant to be done. If it could be done that way, that would mean that Jesus did not finish the work at Calvary's cross.

And please understand, when it comes to sin and everything else pertaining to our Christian walk, Jesus finished the task totally and completely at Calvary.

This was what the Galatians were succumbing to, and why we refer to this problem as Galatianism. It means that these Galatians were saved by trusting Christ, but then trying to live a sanctified life by the means of works. It cannot be done.

To the conscientious reader, it quickly becomes obvious that we are repeating ourselves. But I've done this for a purpose. Paul repeated himself over and over in every conceivable way possible concerning these problems. Actually, the Holy Spirit through him did so because of the propensity of man to drift into error. If the same thing is said in different ways over and over again, then hopefully its potential will eventually connect.

These are spiritual things, and they are spiritually discerned. For that reason, discernment is difficult because of the carnality involved in all of us.

HOW DID THEY BEGIN

"This only would I learn of you, Received ye the Spirit by the works of the law, or by the hearing of faith?" (Gal. 3:2).

Another reason for the incomprehensible nature of the defection by the Galatians is that it was so totally contrary to their initial experiences of Christianity. How did they begin?

This is what Paul would like to hear from them. Did they receive the Holy Spirit by living up to some formal statutes? Or did they enter into the Christian life simply by believing and receiving what they heard concerning the death of the Lord Jesus Christ?

The form of this question (literally), "This only do I wish to learn from you," suggests that so long as they are in their present confused state, Paul does not want to hear anything other than the most basic answer to this most basic question.

ONE QUESTION PLEASE

The phrase, *"This only would I learn of you,"* presents a forcible appeal to the experience of the Galatians. Paul indicates that an answer to the question about to be asked would be a decisive argument. It is as if Paul said, "I will convince you of your error by this one argument."

Barnes said:

The design here, and in the following verses, is, to prove to them that the views which they had at first embraced were correct, and that the views which they now cherished were false. To show them this, he asks them the simple question, by what means they had obtained the exalted privileges which they enjoyed? Whether they had obtained them by the simple gospel, or whether by the observance of the Law? The word 'only' here implies that this was enough to settle the question. The argument to which he was about to appeal was enough for his purpose. He did not need to go any further. They had been converted. They had received the Holy Spirit. They had had abundant evidence of their acceptance with God, and the simple matter of inquiry now was, whether this had occurred as the regular effect of the gospel, or whether it had been by obeying the Law of Moses?[12]

The question, *"Received ye the Spirit by the works of the law, or by the hearing of faith?"* refers to the initial entrance of the Holy Spirit into their hearts when they put their trust in the Lord Jesus—when they were born again. Paul is not here necessarily speaking of the baptism with the Holy Spirit, which is accompanied by the speaking with other tongues as the Spirit of God gives the utterance (Acts 2:4).

Being born of the Spirit and being baptized with the Spirit are two different works of grace.

THE FIRST WORK: REGENERATION

When the believing sinner comes to Christ, he is born again. Jesus said, *"Except a man be born of water* (originally born physically as a little baby; does not speak of water baptism), *and of the Spirit* (the Holy Spirit at conversion), *he cannot enter into the kingdom of God. That which is born of the flesh is flesh* (meaning, born physically as a little baby); *and that which is born of the Spirit is spirit* (referring to the Holy Spirit regenerating the spirit of man) (John 3:5-6).

This takes place automatically at conversion. The Holy Spirit comes into the heart and life of the believing sinner.

Paul also said, *"Not by works of righteousness which we have done, but according to his mercy he saved us, by the washing of regeneration* (regenerating work of the Spirit), *and renewing of the Holy Ghost* (renewing the Spirit of the believing sinner)*"* (Titus 3:5).

This is the impartation of the divine nature which results in the cleansing of the heart by the fact that the new life in God provides the believer with both the desire and the power to do the will of God and to refuse to fulfill the behest of the evil nature whose power has been broken by the identification of the believer with the Lord Jesus in His death on the cross. Actually, the act of regeneration makes believers partakers of the divine nature. This is the basis upon which the Holy Spirit works in the Christian's life.

He (the Holy Spirit) now has in His hands an individual with both the desire and the power to do the will of God. He augments this by His control over the saint when that saint yields to Him and cooperates with Him.

BAPTIZED WITH THE SPIRIT: POWER

Whereas being born of the Spirit takes place at conversion, being baptized with the Spirit is always subsequent to conversion. In other words, one has to first be saved—born of the Spirit—before one can be baptized with the Spirit. Consequently, the two—born of the Spirit and baptized with the Spirit—are two different works altogether, but both are gifts and therefore of grace. As well, there's only one Holy Spirit.

This experience is for power (Acts 1:8) and is always accompanied by the speaking with other tongues (Acts 2:4, 10:44-48, 19:1-7).

To be born of the Spirit takes place at salvation, with the Holy Spirit coming into the heart and life of every believer. But to be baptized with the Spirit takes place after conversion, whether immediately after, as with Cornelius and his household, or at a later time, as with the converts at Samaria (Acts 8:14-17).

This baptism is for power which is desperately needed by every single believer. In fact, unless a person has been baptized with the Holy Spirit with the evidence of speaking with other tongues, they are going to do very little for the cause of Christ. It is that important.

THE REGENERATING WORK OF THE HOLY SPIRIT

You need to read the following paragraph very carefully: there are millions of Spirit-filled Christians who love the Lord supremely and are doing a great work for the Lord, but they cannot live a victorious life despite the fact that they are baptized with the Holy Spirit. What's wrong with this picture? That's a good question! They have been taught that the baptism with the Holy Spirit will guarantee them victory over sin or some such thinking. The Holy Spirit for power is to help us do the work of the Lord, but it does not address itself to the sin question. It's just one Holy Spirit, but He works in two different ways. The first way is what we're discussing here now.

The moment a person gives his heart to Christ, the Holy Spirit is definitely in his heart and life, but he is not *baptized* with the Spirit. However, if he places his faith in Christ and the cross, then the Holy Spirit of regeneration will give him victory over the world, the flesh, and the devil.

Meanwhile, the Spirit-baptized believer, although loving God and doing a great work for the Lord, will not be able to live a victorious life. Why? Because his faith is in the Holy Spirit Himself, regarding His power. Instead of his faith being in Christ and the cross, his faith is in himself or the fact that he has been baptized with the Holy Spirit with the evidence of speaking with other tongues. While that is absolutely necessary (if one is to perform a work for God), the Holy Spirit still demands that our faith ever be in Christ and what He has done for us at the cross. If that's the case, then victory will be the lot of such a believer.

But most Spirit-filled believers have not been taught that their faith must be in Christ and the cross; in reality, their faith is in themselves, etc., and these the Lord cannot bless, and He cannot function, at least properly, in their lives.

The Holy Spirit ever lifts up Christ and ever demands that our faith be in Christ and the cross exclusively. That being done, not only can we work for the Lord as we ought to, but we can also have victory over sin. This is God's way (I Cor. 1:17-18; 23; 2:1-2; Gal. 6:14; Col. 2:10-15; Rom. 8:1-11).

I hope we have made ourselves clear. The faith of the believer—even Spirit-filled believers—must always and without exception be in Christ and the cross. Regrettably, that's where most Spirit-filled believers miss it. As we've stated several times, their faith is in this, that, and the other, but it's not in Christ and the cross. If it were in Christ and the cross, and maintained in Christ and the cross, then there would be victory in that life unparalleled. This is God's way of victory, and His only way of victory. It's the cross, the cross, the cross!

THE HEARING OF FAITH

The words, *"by the hearing of faith,"* refer either to the act of hearing a message, or to the message that is heard. The second meaning agrees more with the statement as given by Paul, because he is contrasting his message of grace with the false doctrine of the Judaizers.

The phrase, *"of faith,"* defines or describes the message. It is a message that announces faith as the means whereby one receives salvation. The only answer the Galatians could give to this question was that they received the Spirit, not by obedience to the law, but through their faith in Paul's message of grace.

THE BAPTISM WITH THE HOLY SPIRIT

Please allow me to go back to Paul's statement in Galatians 3:2 about receiving the Spirit. Even though Paul is here speaking of the born-again experience, we make a great mistake if we feel that the baptism with the Holy Spirit—which can only come after one has been saved and is always accompanied by speaking with other tongues—is optional or not so necessary.

Every evidence is that the early church of which we read about in detail in the book of Acts was comprised of Spirit-baptized believers. In other words, after being saved, they went on to be baptized with the Holy Spirit.

The absolute urgency of this is shown in Acts 8 when many were saved under the preaching of Philip, but not baptized with the Holy Spirit. Evidently Philip, at that particular time, did not preach the baptism with the Spirit as he should have. Consequently, Peter and John went almost immediately to Samaria, praying for these people that they might be baptized with the Holy Spirit, which they were (Acts 8:14-17).

PAUL

As well, immediately upon Paul being saved on the road to Damascus, the Lord sent Ananias to pray for Paul that he might be filled with the Holy Spirit, among other things (Acts 9:17).

As we have already stated, this baptism is for power (Acts 1:8), without which the church is going to do little for God. Consequently, as it regards particular modern denominations which have rejected the baptism with the Holy Spirit, even though there may be much religious activity, there's going to be very little truly done for the Lord. The reason is simple—every single thing done on this earth by God is done through the person, agency, work, and ministry of the Holy Spirit.

Immediately before the ascension, the Scripture says that Jesus, *"Commanded them that they should not depart from Jerusalem, but wait for the promise of the Father"* (Acts 1:4). I might remind the reader that this was a command and not a suggestion. In other words, the followers of Christ, according to His commands, were not to attempt to build churches, evangelize the heathen, or proclaim the gospel in any manner until they were first baptized with the Holy Spirit.

These people were already saved, but to accomplish a work for God, they needed—in fact it was absolutely imperative that they have—the power which could only come about as the result of being baptized with the Holy Spirit. Hence, the command of Christ.

BEFORE CALVARY

Before Jesus paid the terrible sin debt of humanity, the Holy Spirit would come *upon* believers (I Sam. 16:13), and even *in* some believers for particular works (Luke 1:41). But He could not come in to take up abode as He could after Calvary (John 14:17).

Since Calvary, the Holy Spirit literally comes into the believer on a permanent basis and abides constantly for the special purpose foretold by Jesus in John 16:7-15.

Considering the great price paid by Christ at Calvary's cross, and that one of its major benefits is the privilege of being baptized with the Holy Spirit, no believer should shortchange himself by not receiving this experience (Acts 1:4). Not doing so, whether through unbelief or apathy is, in effect, an insult to Christ.

THE HOLY SPIRIT

It is my contention that unless one is baptized with the Holy Spirit (Acts 2:4), the plans they make will be of human origin instead of that of the Spirit. Consequently, God cannot bless such plans. He can only bless that which is authored and instituted by the Holy Spirit.

While it is true that great works of the Lord were definitely accomplished in the past by those who did not claim the baptism with the Spirit; still, this was before the great latter rain outpouring, which is a fulfillment of Joel's prophecy, which would come about in these last days (Joel 2:23, 28-29; Acts 2:15-21).

That which the early church received was the former rain, while that received now is the latter rain.

The men who performed these great works for God in the past were walking in all the light they had; consequently, God blessed them. But it is a different story now.

Light has definitely been given in the twentieth century. But light which has been given and rejected is light withdrawn. That is exactly what has happened to the modern church, which has denied the baptism with the Holy Spirit. Almost nothing is being done in these particular ranks for the cause of Christ, and it will not change, I think, unless the hearts of these people are opened to the Holy Spirit.

Whatever is done for the Lord on this earth must be born and birthed by the Holy Spirit, or else it is not of God but of man. If it is of man, then it cannot be of God and therefore cannot be blessed by God.

Precious few people in those ranks are truly won to Christ, precious few are truly delivered, and precious few truly have a relationship with Christ.

———⊰✕⊱———

There are souls in sin which we fail to win,
Just because we lack desire;
And the thing we need—sorely need indeed—
Is the pentecostal fire.

He will send it down and our lives will crown
With the blessing day by day;
If we truly plead for the thing we need
In the earnest, old-time way.

Let us seek the face of the King of grace,
Let us do His holy will;
Then the fire will come on each heart and home,
For He loves the faithful still.

If your heart is cold, and you've lost the pow'r,
God will give you your desire;
If we seek His face ev'ry day and hour,
He will send the old-time fire.

FOOLISH

CHRISTIANS

CHAPTER 2

THE FLESH

THE FLESH

"ARE YE SO FOOLISH? having begun in the Spirit, are ye now made perfect by the flesh?" (Gal. 3:3).

There are three words or short phrases that describe the Christian way: the Holy Spirit, the cross, and faith.

It must be understood that these three, as powerful as they might be, are all indigenous to the Lord Jesus Christ. In other words, every great doctrine is wrapped up in Him and what He has done for us at the cross.

We must first understand that God cannot use anything that originates in the heart of man, irrespective as to how godly that man or woman might be. That's where all of us go wrong. That's where the church as a whole goes wrong. Everything God has, and everything that God does originates with the Holy Spirit and is made possible by the cross, and we obtain it by faith. In a nutshell, that is the central focus of the great plan of God.

This is where denominations go wrong. They start trying to project that which originates in the heart of man, and it never will work. It has to originate with the Holy Spirit. If it does, and we follow its course, we will find victory and a great work for God carried out.

A PERSONAL EXPERIENCE

It was 2010 when the Lord spoke to my heart about something that He was going to do. He told me: "The Evil One tried to close the door to this ministry in the 1990s, but I kept it open about 10 percent, at least compared to what it had been. But I am about to open that door wide."

No other information was given, just that: "I will open the door wide." The next afternoon while in prayer, again the Lord spoke to me and said, "You misunderstood Me yesterday when I told you I was about to open the door wide. You thought I was speaking only of the programming for television. I was speaking of the programming for television, but I was also speaking regarding everything for which you have sought My face these past years."

Still, outside of that which I have stated, there was not much information given.

A few days later, we had a meeting in the boardroom concerning television. I didn't really pay much attention to what was being said, because I knew it was not the Lord. When our people finished with their statements and left the room, I stayed. I sat there, as I had been feeling it for some time when the Lord spoke to my heart and said, "I want you to start a television network."

It was just that simple and just that abbreviated. I knew it was the Lord, of that I had no doubt, but the monumental effort of the situation was almost beyond comprehension. We had no money, and to start a television network required great sums of money. But if the Lord has said do it, then it will be done. Without going into detail, it got done.

Today, the audience reach of SonLife Broadcasting Network is more than 300 million households, plus untold millions of others around the world. This did not come out of my mind. I had not even thought about a television network. But the Lord originated the direction, told me what to do and how to do it, which made something take place, which was, in the natural, impossible.

The preachers who heard about what we were doing automatically stated, "He'll go broke in thirty days. He'll never make it." If the thought of a television network had originated with me, then that is exactly what would have happened. But if it originated with the Holy Spirit—and that is exactly what happened—then it was sure to be successful in a way that no one could ever begin to imagine.

SO HOW DOES SUCH ORIGINATE?

It must originate in the heart of God if it is to be what it should be. If the Lord is going to lead us and guide us at all, we must have several things in our own disciplines, which include:

- *A concentrated prayer life.* By this I mean a time of prayer each and every day to seek direction from the Lord and, above all, thank Him for all the great things that He is doing for us. That is a must. The tragedy is that not many people, including preachers, have any prayer life at all. With no avenue for God to work, He very seldom, if ever, says anything.

- *A Bible study period.* And I mean reading the Word of God each and every day, completely through, beginning with the book of Genesis. The tragedy is that far too many preachers do not understand the Word, and they very seldom even look at it. That's tragic because the answer for every situation is found in the Word of God.

- *Faith exclusively in Christ and the cross at all times.* This is very, very important—our faith must be exclusively in Christ and the cross at all times. In fact, it would not hurt every believer, when they go to prayer each morning, to tell the Lord, "My faith is in You and the cross. It's not in me or any other human being, and neither is it in the church, or any religious ritual or ceremony. My faith is exclusively in You and the cross" (Gal. 6:14, I Cor. 1:17-18).

Living in a prayerful state and in a state where the Word of God is our foundation provides a fertile ground for the Holy Spirit to move and to speak, and unless those disciplines are prevalent within our hearts and lives, we provide little opportunity for the Holy Spirit to speak to us in any capacity.

ARE YOU SO FOOLISH?

We must remember that Paul is saying this to believers. The truth is, the Galatians were foolish. They had embraced justification by faith, but they had slipped into the mode of sanctification by works, which is impossible. Such will not fall out to Christian victory, but rather the very opposite. That is what they were doing, and that's what most modern believers are doing as well.

Most modern believers do not understand sanctification, which is the single most important aspect for the believer. While justification is the single most important thing for the sinner, sanctification is the most important thing for the believer. Yet most believers have no understanding as to what sanctification is or how they are to be sanctified. To be frank, that falls into the capacity of most preachers also. Sanctification is looked at by something we do or don't do, and to be frank with you, the modern church has pretty well given up on what sanctification really is; it tries one fad after another with all of them failing. In other words, most Christians, sad to say, are being ruled by the sin nature, with sin in some way having dominion over them, despite the fact that they love the Lord very much.

Foolish was the right word to describe these Galatians, and it could probably be said of us at one time or another. If we don't do it God's way, which is the Holy Spirit, the cross, and faith, then foolish we will be.

HAVING BEGUN IN THE SPIRIT

The phrase in Galatians 3:3, *"having begun in the Spirit,"* refers back to the salvation experience of these Galatians, and the same could be said for every believer presently. In fact, the only way that anyone can be saved, then or now, is for the Holy Spirit to have His way within our hearts and lives, thereby allowing Him to convict us of sin and then accepting Jesus Christ as our Savior. That's the way of the Spirit.

The preacher is supposed to be anointed by the Holy Spirit, and to preach directly from the Word of God, with the Holy Spirit then placing the listening sinner under conviction, with the idea being that that person accept Christ as his or her Savior. It's all done by the power of the Holy Spirit—one might say by the convicting power of the Holy Spirit. That's the only way that one can be saved. Unfortunately, far too often other methods are used, which only brings the person into the maw of religion, when they really aren't born again.

ARE YOU NOW MADE PERFECT BY THE FLESH?

First of all, what is the flesh?

The flesh, as Paul uses the term, is anything that is man-devised—our talent, ability, education, motivation—it's what man can do, which God can never accept.

So the idea is this: after these Galatians were saved, which was by the moving and the operation of the Holy Spirit on their hearts and lives, they resorted to the flesh to try to live a holy life.

This is the problem with all of us. We've all tried to do this. So what does living by the flesh mean?

Most of the time, the flesh pertains to that which really is scriptural to begin with. I speak of fasting, our prayer life (which believers must have), plus the hundred and one I haven't named. But if we depend on these things, we are trying to have victory by that method which God can never accept. While the Holy Spirit under such circumstances doesn't leave us, and thank God for that, still, He is greatly hindered in that He cannot help us, because, in a sense, we are living in a state of spiritual adultery.

SPIRITUAL ADULTERY

Let's look at that for just a few moments. What do we mean by spiritual adultery?

Whenever a person comes to Christ, we are married to Him. In respect to this, Paul said, *"For I am jealous over you with godly jealousy: for I have espoused you to one husband, that I may present you as a chaste virgin to Christ. But I fear, lest by any means, as the serpent beguiled Eve through his subtilty, so your minds should be corrupted from the simplicity that is in Christ"* (II Cor. 11:2-3).

To be sure, Jesus can meet our every need, and is, in fact, the only one who can meet our every need. When we resort to other things, such as fasting, witnessing, our prayer life, and try to use these things to overcome sin, that is functioning after the flesh, and is, in effect, spiritual adultery.

One may well surmise that a proper marriage cannot long exist in such an atmosphere. Sad to say, but I fear that is where most Christians are.

SO WHAT ARE WE TO DO?

The believer is to understand that our faith must be in Christ and what He has done for us at the cross—and that exclusively.

When our faith is properly placed in the cross and maintained in the cross of Christ, then the Holy Spirit, who works exclusively within the parameters, of the finished work of Christ, then victory will be ours.

This is God's way, and His only way, because nothing else is needed.

These other things deceive us because, in their own right, they are scriptural—fasting is scriptural, a prayer life is scriptural, witnessing, and a host of other things we might name, are scriptural. So, because they are scriptural, this deceives us.

Concerning this, the apostle Paul said, *"I was alive without the law once: but when the commandment came, sin revived, and I died"* (Rom. 7:9).

When Paul mentions the commandment, He is talking about the Ten Commandments, and to be sure, these definitely are scriptural. So what did He mean by the statement that when the commandment came I died?

He tried to live an overcoming life by keeping the commandments, and he found that he could not do so. Yes, the Commandments can most definitely be kept, but we have to do it God's way. If we think we can keep the Commandments and thereby live a holy life through our own strength, it's impossible. It cannot be done.

That's the same thing as thinking that our prayer life can help us overcome sin or that fasting can help us overcome sin. While those things are desirable, necessary, and will greatly bless us in our engagement, still, if we are trying to use these things to overcome sin—and sin really is the problem—then we will find ourselves failing again and again and again and not really understanding why we are failing.

These things we are doing are scriptural, but what we are doing is trying to use them in the wrong way. Again, it's like taking a handsaw and trying to make a hammer of it. You can't do that; it will destroy the handsaw, as should be obvious. In similar fashion, we try to use these great disciplines to try and overcome sin, and you can't do it that way. So Paul asks, *"Are ye so foolish? having begun in the Spirit, are ye now made perfect by the flesh?"*

SUFFERED?

In Galatians 3:4, Paul asks, *Have ye suffered so many things in vain? if it be yet in vain."*

Every true believer knows and understands that when an individual comes to Christ and is therefore born again, there will be some persecution. In Paul's day, it was the heathen that persecuted believers. Today, it might be those we work with on the job, or it might be members of our own family. Many times, the ones we love the most will turn against us, and I'm speaking of when we come to Christ.

No other religion in the world draws persecution as does Christianity. Actually, Christianity is not a religion, but rather a relationship. And I speak of a relationship with a person—the Lord Jesus Christ.

The animosity is in the heart of people who do not know the Lord. With antagonism they come against those who do serve the Lord, even surpassing blood ties. Many times, our own immediate family will turn against us.

THE MESSAGE OF THE CROSS

I have noticed that individuals who have attended a particular church almost all their lives—individuals who were saved in that church but now embrace the message of the cross—are being told by their church friends that they are no longer desired there. That is hurtful, as one would understand.

What Paul is saying is, that if we go through all of that (the flesh), and every believer does in one way or another, then we will lose, ultimately, our soul. Now think of that. We cannot go against God forever and expect His approval and blessings. It cannot be.

Now let's say this again, because it is so very, very important: if the believer tries to live for God by a wrong method or a wrong way that is not scriptural—outside of the cross of Christ—then ultimately that believer will turn his back on the Lord and walk away. It may not be observable, but that is what happens with such a believer left with virtually nothing in his soul. Then the person loses his loved ones, and he loses his salvation as well.

None of that happens overnight; sometimes, it happens over a period of years. But one cannot disobey the Word of God and thereby try to live for God in all the wrong ways and expect God's approval. While the Lord has and shows great patience with us, and thank God He does, sooner or later, our wrong direction is ultimately going to pull us down, meaning all that we have previously suffered has been in vain. That's a terrible thing for one to realize.

HE THEREFORE THAT MINISTERS
TO YOU THE SPIRIT

He therefore that ministereth to you the Spirit, and worketh miracles among you, doeth he it by the works of the law, or by the hearing of faith?" (Gal. 3:5).

The phrase, *"He therefore that ministereth to you the Spirit,"* has been debated as to whether Paul is speaking here of Jesus or himself. In other words, to whom does the pronoun "he" refer?

It really doesn't matter. In any case, it is the Lord Jesus who is performing the work, and He does so through the Holy Spirit, using Paul, or any other believer for that matter, as the instrument.

The Spirit of God, who alone can bring about the desired results, cannot be ministered to a person unless it is on the basis of Christ and Him crucified. The Spirit of God will function in no other manner, and neither can He be forced to function in another manner (Rom. 8:2).

If the preacher, or anyone for that matter, ministers law, works, or anything else other than Christ and Him crucified, then the Spirit of God simply will not function in that atmosphere. So, if we're going to have the help of the Holy Spirit, without whose help nothing is possible, then we have to go back to Galatians 3:1 where Paul speaks of *"the* truth." That truth is Jesus Christ and Him crucified. That should not be difficult to understand.

AT THE CROSS

It was at the cross where Christ paid the terrible sin debt of man and defeated Satan. There the demands of holy justice were satisfied. Even as I dictate these words, I strongly sense the presence of God. On behalf of sinful man who, incidentally, could not help himself, God accepted payment in full, rendered by Jesus Christ—a payment that can never be demanded again. That's the reason the great canon of Scripture closes out with the words, *"And the Spirit and the bride say, Come. And let him that heareth say, Come. And let him that is athirst come. And whosoever will, let him take the water of life freely"* (Rev. 22:17).

Whenever the cross is held up as the answer to the ills of man, and irrespective as to what those ills may be, the Spirit of God works mightily and even miraculously on behalf of the seeking soul. To be sure, inasmuch as the Holy Spirit is God, no demon from the pit can overcome Him, and no devil can subdue Him. In fact, He has power over all because all were defeated by Jesus at Calvary.

THE CROSS IS NOT POPULAR

The world doesn't care for the cross and, regrettably, neither do many in the modern church. Nevertheless, it is through the cross and the cross alone that salvation and victory are assured.

Please allow me to quote from Martin Luther:

When we first preached the gospel, there were very many that favoured our doctrine, and had a good and reverend opinion of us: and after the preaching thereof, followed the fruits and effects of faith. But what ensued? A sort of light and brain-sick heads sprang up, and by-and-by destroyed all that we had in long time and with much travel planted before and also made us so odious unto them which before loved us dearly, and thankfully received our doctrine, that now they hate nothing more than our name. But of this mischief the devil is the author, working in his members contrary works, which wholly fight against the works of the Holy Ghost.[1]

As stated by the great Reformer so long ago, the same could be said by this evangelist. If the truth be known, and irrespective of the excuses given, it is our preaching of the cross and the moving and operation of the Holy Spirit that are so hated.

The truth is, a person can have the approval of the Lord or the approval of man, but he cannot have both.

THE WORKING OF MIRACLES

In Galatians 3:5, the phrase, *"and worketh miracles among you,"* proclaims the moving and operation of the Holy Spirit, because without Him these things cannot be done (Acts 14:8–10).

The word *therefore* in Galatians 3:5 continues the thought of Galatians 3:2-3, which is further emphasized. In Galatians 3:2 Paul is speaking of the initial entrance of the Spirit into the hearts of the Galatians the moment they placed their faith in the Lord Jesus. In this particular verse, he is not speaking of the baptism with the Holy Spirit with the evidence of speaking with other tongues—an experience to be received *after* conversion. In Galatians 3:3, Paul refers to the sanctifying work of the Spirit in the believer's life.

In Galatians 3:5, the subject of charismatic manifestations of the Spirit is introduced, namely, the act of the Holy Spirit enduing certain members of the Galatian churches with special gifts of the Spirit, which should continue in modern churches as well.

All of these Paul brings to bear upon his contention that the grace way of salvation must be God's way since it is accompanied by the supernatural ministry of the Holy Spirit.

THE WORKING OF THE HOLY SPIRIT

Wuest said:

The construction in the Greek requires us to understand that the One who ministered the Spirit to the Galatians is the same Person who worked miracles among them, namely, God the Father. The word ministereth is from epichoregeo which means "to supply abundantly or bountifully." The word miracles is from dunamis, used in I Corinthians 12:10 (miracles), and it II Corinthians 12:12 (wonders). In each place, the reference is to the Holy Spirit conferring miracle-working power upon certain members of the early Church. In the view of Paul, it was the same Spirit who was performing

His work of sanctification in the lives of the Galatian saints, who was also bestowing miraculous powers upon them. The present tense of the participles here informs us that the work of the Holy Spirit in both respects was continually going on in the Galatian churches, even at the time of the inroad of the Judaizers, although His work was being hindered by the act of the Galatians slowly turning away from His ministrations and depending instead upon self effort. The point however is that these Galatians still had the attesting power of the miracles among them, proving that grace and not works was the way of salvation. Yet in spite of all this irrefutable proof, they were forsaking the place of grace to take their stand under law. Over against all this, the Judaizers had nothing as an evidence that their message was from God.[2]

PROOF?

Galatians 3:5 is an obvious, glaring testimony against most of the modern church world. The manner in which Paul structures these statements proclaims the fact that if the Holy Spirit is present and allowed to work, He will bring about two things:

1. The sanctifying process in the heart and life of the believer
2. Signs and wonders relative to the gifts of the Spirit (I Cor. 12:8–10)

However, in the lives of most believers (and I don't think I'm exaggerating), neither sign nor proof are present.

Most of the modern church world little believes at all in the power of God. They excuse themselves by claiming that the days of miracles are over, that they ceased with the apostles, or that it all stopped when the canon of Scripture was completed with John writing the book of Revelation.

Whatever the excuse, they attempt to cover up the barrenness of their possession with clamoring platitudes of profession.

THE DEVELOPMENT OF UNBELIEF

The main reason for all of this is that these preachers deny the veracity of the doctrine of the baptism with the Holy Spirit with the evidence of speaking with other tongues (Acts 2:4).

The rejection of the abundance of light presently given on this particular subject is, pure and simple, a rejection of God. In this type of atmosphere several things develop:

- Light rejected is light withdrawn, with even the loss of what little light they previously had (Matt. 25:28–29). An even greater tragedy is the abandonment of the Holy Spirit by those who claim to be Pentecostal.
- Without the working, moving, and operation of the Holy Spirit, precious little if anything is done for the Lord, which means all of this energy and effort are, by and large, wasted. The efforts of these preachers, denominations, and churches are, consequently, man-instituted, man-directed, and man-supplied. This means that God has no part in these proceedings, irrespective of all the religious machinery.

- A denial of the Holy Spirit in this fashion, denies, as well, His convicting power (John 16:8–11). Consequently, precious few people are actually saved; rather, they are indoctrinated into a particular religion.

- When the Holy Spirit is denied, Jesus is also denied. Consequently, these denominations deteriorate spiritually until they are presenting no more than an "ethical gospel." In fact, that characterizes almost all of these particular old-line denominations. Without Jesus at its center, Christianity becomes no more than a mere philosophy.

- Consequently, thousands of churches are filled with people (literally millions of people) who actually are not even saved. They have embraced an ethical concept, sort of a "Golden Rule religion," but they have had no true experience and relationship with Christ. In other words, they are not born again.

In all of these denominations and churches, there would be some few exceptions to the things I have listed but, by and large, that given is an apt description of much of the modern church world.

Paul had a striking statement for such. He said, *"Having a form of godliness, but denying the power thereof: from such turn away"* (II Tim. 3:5).

THE BOOK OF ACTS AND THE EPISTLES

The pattern for what the church ought to be is found in the Word of God. It is the book of Acts and the Epistles. If the earmarks of the early church are not present in our modern churches, then the church is not what it ought to be. The Holy Spirit is the same now as He was then. The need now is just as great as it was then. Consequently, if He is present and working, He will do the same things now as He did then. In fact, that's exactly what He does in the hearts and lives of many believers, i.e., "churches."

Every preacher (and every believer for that matter), should strive to follow the Word of God as closely as possible. If they do such, they will be baptized with the Holy Spirit, with the evidence of speaking with other tongues. Thereafter, they should strive to allow Him the latitude in their lives that He desires— latitude He must have—if He is to do the things that He desires to do, as it refers to the sanctifying process and the operation of the gifts.

WORKS OF THE LAW

In Galatians 3:5, the beginning of the question, *"doeth he it by the works of the law … ?"* presents the fact that God's lavish supply of spiritual gifts was not the outcome of law keeping, but of dynamic faith—faith in Christ.

The idea is this: did the act of circumcision, Sabbath-keeping, any other rudiment of the law of Moses, or any ritual or ceremony for that matter, bring about sanctification or produce miracles? Of course, the answer is an unequivocal no.

How could a physical act of circumcision on a little baby boy eight days old (that's what the law demanded) accomplish anything spiritual? How could Sabbath-keeping affect anything spiritual in one's life? In fact, how could any ritual or ceremony, accomplish any positive work?

The answer, of course, is that these things cannot bring forth any spiritual results.

It is the same now with joining a church, water baptism, or the Lord's Supper, etc. While these things are good in their place and should be engaged in, still, within themselves they produce no works of righteousness for the simple fact that they are mere ritual and ceremony, as sacred as they may be.

And yet there are hundreds of millions of people who are trusting in these or similar things to effect salvation, etc., which they cannot do and were never intended to do, even as the law of Moses was never intended to save anyone.

THE GREAT NEED OF THE
HUMAN HEART AND LIFE

Man has a distinct need summed up in a fallen nature. It breeds all type of sin, and in fact, that's all it can breed, at least within itself (Rom. 3). To climb out of that, there must be a power, a force, a strength, that is greater than the power of sin and death. Mere rituals and ceremonies have no such power. In fact, they have no power at all; however, the Holy Spirit, who is God, does have that power. He alone can do the required work.

However, He does not function, does not operate, does not move on rituals and ceremonies, but only on the instrument of faith. As well, it must be faith in Christ and what He did for us at the cross. That always must be the object of the believer's faith. That and that alone is the parameter in which He works (Rom. 6:1-5, I Cor. 1:17-18, 23, 2:2; Gal. 6:14, Col. 2:10-15). Can it be any clearer than that?

Faith is the key, but it must be faith in the correct object, and that correct object always is Jesus Christ and Him crucified (I Cor. 1:23).

In fact, the only way that the believer can be sanctified—live a sanctified life, which means to be set apart from the world unto God, and unto God exclusively—is to place his or her faith exclusively in Christ and what He did for us at the cross. That being done, and the moment it is done, that person, in the eyes of God, is sanctified. It cannot be any other way, yet this seems to be so difficult for the church to see and believe. We keep wanting to try to do something ourselves, which never brings sanctification as it cannot bring sanctification.

In the first place, God cannot use anything that man concocts or thinks up out of his own mind. God can only use that which is breathed and birthed by the Holy Spirit, and this is where the church so often goes wrong. It tries to ignore the Word of God and insert its own plans, means, and ways, which God never accepts.

Everything that God wants from us and desires that we do is all wrapped up in Jesus Christ and Him crucified. In other words, the cross—what was accomplished there—holds the key, but the church seems to be very lax in learning this tremendous truth.

A PERSONAL EXPERIENCE

When the Lord began to open up to me the message of the cross, He first showed me the sin nature—what it was and how it operated. At that time, He did not show me any victory over the sin nature, just what the sin nature was.

Second, He showed me the veracity of the cross. He said these three things to me:

- "The answer for which you seek is found in the cross."
- "The solution for which you seek is found in the cross."
- "The answer for which you seek is found *only* in the cross."

I knew that God had given me a great truth but, to be frank, I did not understand it. First of all, I wondered what part the Holy Spirit played in all of this. I knew that He always played a great part, but the Lord never mentioned to me the Holy Spirit at that time. I continued to seek the face of the Lord. Then, one day, the door finally opened.

We were finishing up our daily radio program, *A Study in the Word,* when all of a sudden, the Lord spoke through me something I had never heard in my life. He said, "The Holy Spirit works exclusively within the parameters of the finished work of Christ and will not work outside of those parameters."

He was telling me that the Holy Spirit works exclusively by and through the cross, and He will not work any other way. In other words, what Jesus did at the cross gives the Holy Spirit the legal means to do all that He does.

When the Lord spoke this through me, I was spellbound. I didn't know what to say or do. He had spoken something through my lips that I had not read, had not heard, and did not know, but I realized how important it was.

Loren Larson was with me on that program, sitting across from me on the other side of the table. When I made this statement about the Holy Spirit and the cross, Loren asked, "Can you give me Scripture for that?"

I thought, *How can I give him Scripture for this when I've never heard of it in my life until it was uttered a few minutes ago?* All of a sudden, I looked down at my Bible, which was open to Romans 8:2. That passage seemed to leap out at me: *"For the law* (the legal means) *of the Spirit of life* (the Holy Spirit) *in Christ Jesus* (what Jesus did for us at the cross), *hath made me free from the law of sin and death."* Even though it opened up to me tremendous amounts of understanding, still, I didn't quite understand how the cross played such a part.

A short time later, we were in campmeeting, and I was to preach that night. I went to prayer to seek the face of the Lord about the service, when the Spirit of God came over me and stated, "The cross of Christ is the means by which all of these wonderful things are given to us." The Spirit of God then said, "As I told you, I will not work outside of the cross of Christ. It is the cross that provides all that is needed, whatever the need might be." In other words, it's what Jesus there did. And what did He do?

CHRIST AND THE CROSS

First, Jesus atoned for all sin—past, present, and future—at least for all who will believe (John 3:16). At Calvary, He satisfied the demands of the broken law, of which every human being was guilty. Remember, justification gives us victory over the penalty of sin; sanctification gives us victory over the power of sin.

Second, Jesus broke the grip of sin on the human race. We must understand that sin has a power to it that is far stronger than any power we may come up with within ourselves. That's the reason the Lord is displeased with us when we try to do that which cannot be done and ignore that which has already been done. I speak of Christ and the cross.

Let me say it again: when the believer places his or her faith exclusively in Christ and what Christ has done for us at the cross, at that very moment that believer is sanctified—and sanctified totally and completely. And yet, the sanctification process is something that continues on and on, which we refer to as "progressive" sanctification.

Many think that they must become perfect before they can call themselves sanctified. That's not the case at all. When one's faith is placed exclusively in Christ and the cross, the perfection of Christ is granted to that individual. That's what God looks at and sees. But when the believer starts to look to things other than Christ and the cross, that is actually spiritual adultery, with that believer serving another Jesus, by another spirit, producing another gospel (II Cor. 11:1-4).

DECEPTION

Deception is one of Satan's strongpoints. He deceives people, and he is so good at it simply because he is deceived himself.

How can a Christian guard himself against deception? What can we do to not accept that which is erroneous, which will cause us all type of problems?

That's a good question, yet not difficult to answer. Christians are deceived by Satan when they place their faith in something other than Christ and the cross. When this is done, it will take them down a wrong path and eventually destroy them, unless they finally make their way back.

As a believer, you must understand the following:

- Every blessing we have comes by and through the Lord Jesus Christ (John 1:1-5, 9-12, 29; 3:16; 14:6).
- All these wonderful things are made possible to us by the means of the cross. In other words, it's the cross that opened the door (I Cor. 1:17-18, 23, 2:2; Gal. 6:14).
- Understanding that Jesus is the source, and the cross is the means, the cross of Christ must ever be the object of our faith. This is immeasurably significant (Phil. 3:17-19).
- With Christ as the source, and the cross as the means, and the cross of Christ the object of our faith, then the Holy Spirit, who works exclusively within the parameters of the finished work of Christ—and will not work outside of those parameters—will then go to work for us and rid us of the things that are displeasing to the Spirit, things that we are not able to dislodge ourselves.

If the believer functions in this way, he will not be deceived. Unfortunately, most of the modern church functions totally opposite of what we have stated.

THE HEARING OF FAITH

In Galatians 3:2, the conclusion of the question, *"or by the hearing of faith?"* proclaims to us the only manner in which the Holy Spirit can come into our hearts and lives, and the only manner in which He works.

The *"works of the law"* and *"the hearing of faith"* are contrasted as sharply as possible. Right here is the problem of the child of God. We claim to be exercising faith in Christ and the cross or the Word, but in reality, we are not. The faith of most Christians is in themselves whether they understand it or not. When we try to explain the cross of Christ to many, their instant answer is, "Well, what is there for me to do?" Why is it that the believer is so set on *doing* something? That's the reason he will set out to try and fast for twenty-one days, or something else similar—anything that enables him to say, "Look what I've done."

Why is that so important?

It's important to the believer simply because it appeals to the believer's ego, his self-will; it makes him feel good. He's done something that others have not done or cannot do.

The cross of Christ is the very opposite. It is trusting what Jesus Christ has already done. All we have to do is simply put our faith in that which He has done, and I speak of the cross, and maintain it accordingly. That being done, the Holy Spirit will do everything else.

If our faith is in anything except Christ and the cross, always and without exception it leads to self-righteousness. That's the reason the modern church presently is more self-righteous than maybe it has ever been in its history. The answer for that, and the only answer, is Jesus Christ and Him crucified.

Many times my soul is overburdened,
Many times I'm prone to disobey,
But to Thee, dear Jesus, I am praying,
Keep me in the straight and narrow way;
Precious Jesus, ever linger near me,
Help me stem the battles that are met,
Keep me ever in Thy blessed keeping,
Precious Jesus, don't forget.

There are times when I am disappointed,
Sorely tempted by a wicked race'
But I love the precious name of Jesus,
And I cling to God's protecting grace;
Don't forget me, Jesus, don't forget me!
Be my guide through sorrow and regret,
Keep Thy Spirit daily watching o'er me,
Precious Jesus, don't forget.

Be my guide through life's uneven journey,
Lead me safely to the journey's end,
There's no other one so true and faithful,
None on whom, in need, I can depend;
I would ever labor in Thy harvest,
Till at last the harvest sun is set,
And when I walk that lonesome valley,
Precious Jesus, don't forget.

FOOLISH

CHRISTIANS

CHAPTER 3

RIGHTEOUSNESS

RIGHTEOUSNESS

"Even as Abraham believed God, and it was accounted to him for righteousness" (Gal. 3:6).

The Expositor's Bible Commentary explains this in greater detail:

Paul now turns to the first section of the alternating argument. The issue is scriptural, for he is concerned to show that not only the experience of the Galatians but also the words of the OT support his teaching that the means of entering into salvation is faith. Abraham is his example. Paul's statements presuppose a knowledge of Abraham by the Galatians, and it is not difficult to imagine how the Christians of Galatia had come by it. If Paul had preached among the Galatians for any length of time, he would undoubtedly have taught Christian doctrine in part on the basis of Abraham's life. Furthermore, if … the churches of Galatia were the churches of the south, there was undoubtedly a large Jewish population in the area with which Christians must at least have had some contact and with whose history they must have been familiar. Most significant, however, is the probability that the obligation to become 'children' Abraham through circumcision formed the central argument of the legalizers' teaching. This argument would have focused on Ge 12 and 17; they would have claimed that no one could be blessed by God who was not a part of the company to whom God's promises were made, and one entered this company solely through circumcision. These arguments Paul encounters head on, for he shows that even Abraham was blessed through faith, not circumcision. Paul begins his argument by linking his OT example to the Galatians' spiritual experience, showing that what they had known to be true in their own lives (salvation by faith alone) was also true for others and is confirmed by Scripture. To appeal to Abraham is more than to appeal to just any historical example, because Abraham was the acknowledged father and prototype of Israel. He was the man God started with. He had come from a pagan ancestry beyond the river Euphrates (Jos 24:1-2), but God had called him and had made a covenant with him. From Abraham the Jewish people came, and all Jews looked back to him as their spiritual father and example. How then, did Abraham receive God's blessing? How was he justified? Paul answers by a quotation from Ge 15:6, noting that Abraham 'believed God' and it was credited to him as righteousness. What does Paul mean by faith being imputed to Abraham as 'righteousness' (GK 1466)? The answer depends on the definition of 'righteousness.' he is using. This may be either a forensic term (denoting a right standing before the law) or a term denoting a right relationship (in this case to God). If the latter definition is taken, Paul's point is that Abraham's trusting attitude toward God was accepted by God as righteousness. But if the forensic use predominates, then it must be God's own personal righteousness that was imputed to Abraham in place of his own, which was inadequate. If there was nothing else to go on than Gen. 15:6, the second of these two uses might be preferable. But in view of Paul's development of the doctrine elsewhere, the first must be adopted. It is only by thinking of God's righteousness actually being credited to our account that Paul can say (II Cor. 5:21): 'God made Him [Christ] who had no sin to be sin for us, so that in him we might become the righteousness of God.' These two views are not in opposition, of course, for justification does bring one into a right relationship with God out of which ethical changes follow. The changes result from one's being placed 'in Christ,' as Paul has shown (2:20).[1]

In a most simplistic form, one might say that righteousness is simply that which is right. However, it is God's definition as to what is right and not man's.

Justification is a legal declaration that one has a proper standing before God. It is all done through Christ, and more importantly, faith in Christ and what He did for us at Calvary.

One might say the following:

- Justification is deliverance from the penalty of sin.
- Sanctification is deliverance from the power of sin.

The penalty of sin is eternal hell—a place where there is weeping, wailing, and gnashing of teeth—and, above all of that, it is forever and forever. It is so awful it is beyond compare. Justification before God delivers us from this penalty.

Sanctification is power to overcome sin. Sin is far more powerful than people realize. There are millions of alcoholics in America today who are trying to quit drinking, but they can't. That's the power of sin. Sin has dropped untold millions, even billions, into the horrors of hell where they will burn forever and forever. That's the power of sin.

What Jesus did at the cross totally and completely eliminated the terrible bondage of darkness and gave man eternal life, at least those who will believe.

ABRAHAM BELIEVED GOD

In Galatians 3:6, the phrase, *"Even as Abraham believed God,"* proclaims the fact that the Patriarch was justified by faith, not works. Therefore, the true children of Abraham are justified in the same way.

Wuest writes:

Paul demonstrates that salvation is by grace and in answer to faith, and not by works. His first proof was based upon the fact that the supernatural ministry of the Spirit which accompanied the act of faith on the part of the Galatians, is a proof that his message of grace was of divine origin, and that the message of the Judaizers which in character was diametrically opposed to it, was of human origin. Now, in these verses, he adduces proof from the fact that Abraham was saved by faith and not by works. The occasion for his argument is found in the fact that the Judaizers taught that the natural descendants of Abraham were his children, and thus accepted with God. All of which meant that only the circumcised could be saved. Thus, circumcision was a prerequisite of salvation. This teaching was based on a misapprehension of Genesis 12 and 17. They argued that no one could participate in the blessings of God's covenant with Abraham, and so in the Messianic salvation which was inseparably connected with it, unless he was circumcised. The mistake they made was in failing to distinguish between the purely Jewish and national covenant God made with Abraham, which had to do with the earthly ministry and destiny of the Chosen People as a channel which God would use in bringing salvation to the earth, and that salvation which came through a descendant of Abraham, the Messiah. Circumcision was God's mark of separation upon the Jew, isolating him in the midst of the Gentile nations, in order that He might use the nation Israel for His own purposes. It had nothing to do with the acceptance of salvation by the Jew. Over against this contention, Paul argues that Abraham was justified by faith, not by circumcision. In Romans 4:9, 10, he proves his case conclusively when he shows that Abraham was declared righteous before he was circumcised, which demonstrates that his circumcision had nothing to do with his acceptance of salvation.[2]

Paul's contention is that Abraham believed God and was justified, even before the law of Moses was given. Therefore, the law of Moses could not have had anything to do with his salvation. If the law of Moses was necessary to salvation, then it would not have been possible for Abraham, or anyone else at that time, to have been saved. It could not, therefore, be pretended that the law was necessary to justification. And if not necessary in his case, then it wasn't necessary for others as well, and this instance demonstrated that the false teachers among the Galatians were wrong even according to the Old Testament.

MODERN CLAIMS

As these Judaizers of old, so do many now contend in the same manner, which, I suppose, has always been the case. They hold up their church as a necessary requirement for salvation, but just as Paul proves with Abraham, how were people saved before their particular church came into being? Others contend that speaking in tongues is necessary for salvation.

But again, how were people saved before tongues were given on the day of Pentecost? Abraham did not speak in tongues, and he was saved. Others claim that water baptism is necessary for salvation. Again, Abraham was not baptized in water. All of these arguments fall down when approached by Scripture. Faith is the only requirement for salvation, and more particularly, faith in Christ and what He has done for us at Calvary (John 3:16).

BELIEVED WHAT?

What does it mean when it says, *"Abraham believed God"*?

Was it the mere fact that he believed there was a God? Was it his believing Him regarding the leaving of his home in Ur of the Chaldees and moving to Canaan? More particularly, was it his believing God relative to he and Sarah having a child, even though they were long past age?

All of this, of course, entered into his believing—his faith. His faith involved God's salvation plan for humanity.

In regard to this, Jesus said, *"Your father Abraham rejoiced to see my day: and he saw it, and was glad"* (John 8:56).

What did Abraham see?

- He saw the plan of God in sending the Messiah for His people to redeem them and guarantee to them the land of Canaan as an everlasting possession, and he was happy (Gen.12:1-3; 17:1-22).

- He saw the plan of God in the Messiah being sent through his natural seed, in other words, the incarnation for the whole world (Rom. 4:13-22; 9:4-7; Gal. 3:16). And he rejoiced by faith (Rom. 4).

- He saw the second person of the Trinity in visible form (Gen. 18:1-8; 19:1-20, 24).

Abraham saw all of this, and he believed God. He put his faith and confidence in the coming Redeemer, the Lord Jesus Christ, and what He would do as it regards the redemption of man, namely His death on Calvary's cross. Abraham believing God as it is recorded in Genesis 15:6, and here in Galatians 3:6, is no different than what Jesus said: *"For God so loved the world, that he gave his only begotten Son, that whosoever believeth in him should not perish, but have everlasting life"* (John 3:16).

ACCOUNTED TO HIM FOR RIGHTEOUSNESS

In Galatians 3:6, the phrase, *"and it was accounted to him for righteousness,"* presents one of the cardinal passages of the Bible. It is quoted likewise in Romans 4:3, 9, 21-22, and in James 2:23.

Wuest says:

The word accounted is from *logizomai*. It deserves careful study. The word is used in the papyri as a business term: for instance, "put to one's account.[3]

He goes on to say:

Thus Abraham believed God, and his act of faith was placed to his account in value as righteousness. He believed God and his act of faith was credited to him for righteousness. He believed God and his act of faith was placed on deposit for him and evaluated as righteousness. He believed God and his act of faith was computed as to its value, and there was placed to his account, righteousness. He believed God, and his act of faith was credited to his account for righteousness. Finally, he believed God, and his act of faith was credited to him, resulting in righteousness.[4]

NO MERIT

Wuest continues:

All this does not mean, however, that Abraham's act of faith was looked upon as a meritorious action deserving of reward. It was not viewed as a good work by God and rewarded by the bestowal of righteousness. That would be salvation by works. But the fact that Abraham cast off all dependence upon good works as a means of finding acceptance with God, and accepted God's way of bestowing salvation, was answered by God in giving him that salvation. Abraham simply put himself in the place where a righteous God could offer him salvation upon the basis of justice satisfied, and in pure grace. God therefore put righteousness to his account. He evaluated Abraham's act of faith as that which made it possible for Him to give him salvation.[5]

RIGHTEOUSNESS

In the Greek, the word *righteousness* is *dikaiosume*, with its adjective being *"dikaios,"* both with the same root.

Wuest said:

Righteousness in the biblical sense is a condition of rightness the standard of which is God, which is estimated according to the divine standard, which shows itself in behavior conformable to God, and has to do above all things with its relation to God, and with the walk before Him. It is, and it is called dikaiosune theou (righteousness of God) (Rom. 3:21, 1:17).[6]

One might say that it is moral perfection, but only in Christ.

GODLIKE RIGHTEOUSNESS

Wuest continued:

[W]ith this righteousness thus defined, the gospel (Rom. 1:17) comes into the world of nations which had been wont to measure by a different standard. Righteousness in the Scripture sense is a thoroughly religious conception, designating the normal relation of men and their acts, etc., to God. Righteousness in the profane mind is a preponderatingly social virtue, only with a certain religious background.[7]

One might say that righteousness is simply that which is right. But the definition of righteousness must be that of God and not man.

So God is the standard of righteousness, not man. That's where the problem comes in. God will not accept man's righteousness. Not on any terms. He will only accept His righteousness, which should be understandable.

Man, at his best, cannot even remotely come close to God's righteousness. Even the best of us—whoever that might be—fall short of the righteousness that God demands. The beautiful thing about it is, all we have to do to receive the righteousness of God is simply accept it. It's a free gift. There is one thing—we must admit to ourselves that what God demands, we cannot do. That seems to be a problem with many people. Most in the world today label their righteousness according to so-called good deeds. I call it the brownie point system. They get so many points in their own minds for the good things they do, or whatever it is they think is good, and then no points at all for the bad things that are done. In their minds, the good always comes out best, so that means they are saved. But it means no such thing. God cannot accept our righteousness. In fact, He refers to it as self-righteousness.

In order for this righteousness of God to be had, the Christian must understand, or have at least some understanding of the cross of Christ, which is what it took for God's righteousness to be granted to us. The cross made it all possible and makes it all possible. It's what Jesus there did, the price that He paid, the great work that He accomplished at Calvary's cross by simply atoning for all sin—past, present, and future—at least for all who will believe (John 3:16).

JUSTIFICATION: A RESULT OF THE RIGHTEOUSNESS OF GOD

Wuest said: "Justification is the act of God removing from the sinner his guilt and the penalty incurred by that guilt, and bestowing a positive righteousness, Christ Jesus Himself in whom the believer stands, not only innocent and uncondemned, but actually righteous in point of law for time and for eternity. This is what God did for Abraham when he believed Him. This is what the Judaizers were attempting to merit for themselves by their own good works."[8]

Of course they were unable to do so, but at the same time would not accept what Paul taught about righteousness, using Abraham as an example.

Abraham received this righteousness of God even though he was not circumcised, did not keep the Sabbath, did not keep any of the feast days, and did not do anything described in the law of Moses simply because that law had not yet been given. In fact, it would be more than four hundred years down the road, so to speak, before that law would be given to Moses.

Paul proves by using Abraham, as a perfect example, that righteousness does not come—and cannot come—by means of the law, works, self-effort, or self-will. It is a free gift, and it is bestowed upon anyone, instantly, if that person will give himself over to Christ.

THAT WHICH IS RIGHT

Righteousness carries the idea of that which is right. However, what man declares as right and what God declares accordingly are two different things altogether.

Man, in his morally depraved state, cannot begin to imagine a righteousness that will be acceptable to God. In other words, it is impossible for pure water (righteousness) to come from a polluted source, which is man. Consequently, this—the standard of righteousness—is the great contention between God and man.

Man claims that his righteousness—humanly-devised and constantly changing—is satisfactory, which God rejects hands down.

Inasmuch as God could not accept man's righteousness, if man was to be received in the presence of God, a way had to be found for man to come up to the standards imposed by God; but this was something that man simply could not do.

THE INCARNATION

Therefore, God would become man, would perfectly keep the law, which was God's standard of righteousness, at least in written form, and thereby accrue the righteousness of the law, which no man had ever done.

It was not that Jesus needed righteousness, for He was already perfectly righteous. That which He did by His perfect life was done strictly for fallen man, in other words, He did for man what man could not do for himself. He did this as our representative man, i.e., "the last Adam."

He then died on Calvary, offering up Himself as a perfect sin offering, which God would accept, thereby paying the sin debt and breaking the grip of sin. He did all of this as our substitute.

Consequently, faith exhibited in Him and what He did guarantees the believing sinner a perfect, pure, spotless righteousness—a righteousness which God will accept, because, in effect, it is the righteousness of God.

KNOW

"Know ye therefore that they which are of faith, the same are the children of Abraham" (Gal. 3:7).

Paul used a very strong imperative, "know," to remind the Galatians that all who believe in the certainty of God's promises are true descendants of Abraham, regardless of their ethnic origin. The idea is that all who derive their position in the Lord from faith belong to faith and are, above all things, characterized by faith.

The Expositor's Bible Commentary says:

One example does not make a case, however. So Paul continues his argument with a sentence linking the situation of Abraham to the present. He means, "Since Abraham was saved by faith, his true children are, therefore, even now, those who are saved by faith, as he was." The background is undoubtedly the claim of the Judaizers that one became a genuine child of Abraham by circumcision and subsequent obedience to the law. This verse is an important one for linking the two covenants, that of the OT and that of the NT, for Paul stresses that Abraham's faith was of the same kind as Christian faith.[9]

This places the phrase "those who believe" or "those who are characterized by faith" in the first and prominent position.

THEY WHICH ARE OF FAITH

The phrase, *"Know ye therefore that they which are of faith,"* presents faith and faith alone as the foundation.

Wuest said, "The argument is, Since faith was the way Abraham was justified, it follows that those who exercise like faith, are his true followers.'"[10] He adds, "The expression 'they which are of faith,' refers to those who have exercised faith for salvation, and whose standing and character are consequently determined by that faith."[11]

THE CHILDREN OF ABRAHAM

The phrase, *"The same are the children of Abraham,"* presents Paul lowering the boom, so to speak, by specifying the authentic posterity of Abraham. He is saying that the legitimate sons of Abraham are those who respond to God in faith as Abraham did.

In fact, John the Baptist lambasted the Pharisees and Sadducees who claimed to be the children of Abraham but did not believe God enough to repent of their sins (Matt. 3:7-10; Luke 3:7-9).

Jesus was even more blunt when He called them the children of the devil (John 8:33-47). Paul concluded that the physical descendants of Abraham are not his authentic seed; his spiritual posterity are.

Wuest said, "The phrase 'sons of Abraham,' is not to be understood in a genealogical sense but rather in the ethical sense of the term. Abraham was accepted by God on the basis of faith, and God deals with all men on the same moral basis. God is no respecter of persons. Thus the faith exercised by Abraham is declared to be the fundamental condition of acceptance with God."[12]

CIRCUMCISION

The Jews argued that the privileged relationship of being "sons of Abraham" necessitated the seal of circumcision, and thus could not be claimed by any uncircumcised person.

This Paul rejected arguing that if the basis of Abraham's acceptance with God was his faith, then the men of faith today are the true sons of Abraham—exclusive of circumcision. Consequently, there is here an important distinction. The significant relationship with Abraham is not racial through outward circumcision but ethical on the basis of inward faith.

Luther said:

For this was the greatest confidence and glory of the Jews: "we are the seed and children of Abraham." He was circumcised and kept the law: therefore, if we will be the true children of Abraham, we must follow our father, &c. It was no doubt, an excellent glory and dignity to be the seed of Abraham; for no man could deny but that God spake to the seed, and of the seed of Abraham. But this prerogative nothing profited the unbelieving Jews.[13]

ABRAHAM

Let us come to the Patriarch himself and see by what means he was justified and saved.

It was not for his excellent virtues or holy works. It was not because he forsook his country, kindred, and father's house. It was not because he was circumcised and observed the law; there was no law of Moses then given.

It was not because he was about to offer up in sacrifice, at the commandment of God, his son Isaac, in whom he had the promise of posterity. In fact, none of this counted. He was saved simply because he believed God (Gen. 12:1; 15:6; 17:24; 22:1, 3). Wherefore, he was not justified by any other means than faith alone. Paul therefore concludes with this sentence: *"They which are of faith, the same are the children of Abraham."*

As an example, when a Catholic monk imagines that his shaved head and vows do please God, and that grace and everlasting life is given unto him for the same, he has no true opinion of God. As well, when a Protestant thinks that his membership in some church accomplishes the same, he, too, has no knowledge of God or what God requires. God demands a spotless, pure righteousness—a righteousness that man cannot produce.

How can joining some earthly organization such as a church effect a pure, spotless righteousness? It cannot.

Why is it that men will use good common sense when it comes to worldly things, and then go completely off the deep end when it comes to things about the Lord?

THE GOSPEL PREACHED TO ABRAHAM

How were people saved before Jesus died and rose to justify the believer? How was Abel saved? How was Abraham saved?

Were they saved by the law of Moses? This was impossible; all of them lived before the giving of the law. Abraham knew absolutely nothing about the Ten Commandments given to Moses upon Mount Sinai. Clearly the Bible declares that the law was not given to Israel until four hundred and thirty years after Abraham was saved (Gal. 3:17).

Certainly, Abraham was not saved by keeping the law, nor was he saved by it. How then was Abraham saved?

The Bible takes great pains in telling us. In the first three chapters of Romans, Paul goes to great lengths to prove that no one was ever saved by works but by grace. He comes to conclusion and says, *"Therefore we conclude that a man is justified by faith without the deeds of the law"* (Rom. 3:28).

This was a difficult truth for his legalistic listeners to accept, and so Paul refers them to Father Abraham, revered and honored by all. He asks, "How was Abraham saved? By the law or by grace?"

Listen to Paul:

What shall we say then that Abraham our father, as pertaining to the flesh, hath found? For if Abraham were justified by works, he hath whereof to glory; but not before God. For what saith the scripture? Abraham believed God, and it was counted unto him for righteousness. Now to him that worketh (attempts to earn salvation) *is the reward not reckoned of grace, but of debt. But to him that worketh not, but believeth on him that justifies the ungodly, his faith is counted for righteousness* (Rom. 4:1-5).

HOW WAS ABRAHAM SAVED?

Abraham was saved by believing long before the Ten Commandments were written upon tables of stone. How then was he saved? Paul answers this way: *"What saith the scripture?"* (Rom. 4:3).

That is the final word. What does the Scripture say? Was Abraham saved by the law? Listen to the answer: *"Abraham believed God, and it was counted unto him for righteousness"* (Rom. 4:3).

Note carefully, Abraham believed God.

It does not say, Abraham believed *in* God, but he believed God. Now, of course, Abraham believed in God. He could hardly believe God until he first believed in God. Hebrews 11:6 says, *"For he that cometh to God must believe that he is* (this is fundamental)*, and that he is a rewarder of them who diligently seek him."*

A person may believe in God and be lost forever, and indeed he will be, if all he does is believe in a god. Only the fool says in his heart, "There is no God." But simply believing in a god, some kind of a god, is not enough.

These days there is much flippant talk about God. Everyone today talks about God, praying to God, returning to God, and putting God back into our nation's life. But we do well to remember that all this talk about faith in God is not enough.

Abraham believed God. He believed what God said, he believed God's Word, and he acted upon that Word by putting his trust and confidence in that which the Lord said.

WHAT DID ABRAHAM BELIEVE?

Not only did Abraham believe that God existed, but he also believed what God said. In other words, Abraham believed the gospel. He believed the entire gospel—the good news of the virgin birth, the atoning death, and the resurrection of the Lord Jesus Christ.

Paul contrasts faith and the law and proves that Abraham was saved by believing the gospel. What did Abraham believe to be justified? The answer is, he believed the gospel.

To understand what Abraham believed, we must define what we mean by the gospel. In the Greek, the word is *evangelium* or *good news*. Usually the gospel is defined as the good news of the death and resurrection based on Paul's words in I Corinthians 15: *"How that Christ died for our sins according to the scriptures. And that He was buried, and that he rose again the third day according to the scriptures"* (I Cor. 15:3-4).

This definition is usually accepted for the gospel, but there is more to the good news than that. The good news also includes the virgin birth, the incarnation of the Lord Jesus Christ. The birth of Jesus was declared to be the gospel by the angel on the hills of Judaea: *"And the angel said unto them, Fear not: for, behold,*

I bring you good tidings of great joy... For unto you is born this day... a Saviour" (Luke 2:10-11).

The word translated *good tidings* is the gospel. Yes, the supernatural birth of Jesus is part of the gospel. Concerning this very thing, Jesus Himself said, *"Your father Abraham rejoiced to see my day: and he saw it, and was glad"* (John 8:56).

ABRAHAM AND THE GOSPEL

God revealed to him the message of the gospel of the miraculous conception and birth, substitutionary death, and the glorious resurrection of the coming Redeemer.

Abraham believed in the supernatural conception and miraculous birth of a promised son. God had promised to Abraham a seed, and the birth of a son. Concerning Abraham's wife, Sarah, God said, *"I will bless her, and give thee a son also of her... and she shall be a mother of nations."* (Gen. 17:16).

But the years dragged on and on, and this promise remained unfulfilled until Abraham and Sarah had both long passed the age at which either one, in the natural course of nature, could become parents of a son. Abraham was impotent, and Sarah was sterile. Abraham was one hundred years old, and Sarah was ninety, when we read, *"Now Abraham and Sarah were old and well stricken in age; and it ceased to be with Sarah after the manner of women"* (Gen. 18:11).

Sarah had passed the age of childbearing and Abraham was impotent (Rom. 4:19; Heb. 11:11). It was at this time God came and told Abraham that he and Sarah would become parents of the promised son: *"Sarah thy wife shall have a son"* (Gen. 18:10).

ABRAHAM BELIEVED WHAT GOD SAID

And Abraham believed this word from God, even though, in the course of nature, it was impossible. It would take a miracle, a supernatural act, to make these two old people parents of a son. Although it was naturally impossible, we read, *"And he* (Abraham) *believed in the* LORD; *and he* (God) *counted it to him for righteousness"* (Gen. 15:6).

Abraham believed the gospel, the good news of the birth of a promised son by a supernatural birth. The birth of Isaac was as great a supernatural miracle, in a sense, as the virgin birth of Jesus Christ, and Abraham believed it. In the natural, both the birth of Isaac and the birth of our Savior were, in every sense of the word, impossible. But God is the God of the impossible.

There is more to the gospel than the virgin birth. The next step is the substitutionary death of this promised Son. This part of the gospel also was preached to Abraham and he believed it.

When the miraculously-born son, Isaac, had reached maturity, Abraham was commanded to take him to Mount Moriah and sacrifice him upon the altar. Some believe that Isaac was thirty-three years old at that time—the same age as Christ when He was crucified.

Abraham again believed the gospel, and in Genesis 22, we have a detailed account of Abraham (type of the Father), taking the son (type of the Lord Jesus Christ) up the mountain, and there potentially and typically offering his son upon the altar.

Yes, Abraham believed the gospel, the good news of the miraculous birth and the substitutionary sacrifice of that same son. For God provided a substitute for Isaac when Abraham took the ram from the bushes and offered him up *"in the stead of his son"* (Gen. 22:13).

ISAAC

There is, however, another part of the gospel of good news. It is the resurrection of the miraculously-born son, who was sacrificed on the mountain. While Isaac was not literally killed, nevertheless God reckoned it as though it actually occurred. Isaac was only a type of the Lord Jesus, for he himself was in need of a Savior, and so God provided for him a substitutionary ram to die in his stead.

But as far as God was concerned, He reckoned it as though Isaac was actually slain. So Abraham potentially sacrificed his son.

To Abraham, Isaac was as good as dead for three whole days, from the time of the command to sacrifice his son until God spared him. When God suddenly intervened, it was a potential resurrection of the son. Abraham, therefore, believed the gospel—the miraculous birth, the substitutionary death, and the victorious resurrection after three days.

Yes, Abraham believed that while he would have to put his son to death, God would also resurrect him. It had to be that way. How else could God fulfill His promise of the seed?

God had promised that in Isaac would His seed be called. But Isaac had no seed; he was not even married when he was to die. If God was to keep His word, Abraham reasoned, then He would have to raise Isaac from the dead after his sacrifice.

THE BIBLE CONFIRMS

This is confirmed by the Word of God. Abraham understood that the death and resurrection of Isaac pointed to the death and resurrection of the greater Son, the promised seed, of whom Isaac was only a type. In Genesis 22:13, after he had offered his son and saw him restored, Abraham called the name of that place Jehovahjireh, which means "the Lord will provide," and, *"as it is said to this day, In the mount of the LORD it shall be seen"* (Gen. 22:14).

Abraham looked ahead and saw in this the gospel of the supernatural birth, the atoning death, and the resurrection of the greater Son of Isaac.

If any would doubt this, then read Hebrews 11: *"By faith Abraham, when he was tried, offered up Isaac: and he that had received the promises offered up his only begotten son… Accounting that God was able to raise him up, even from the dead; from whence also he received him in a figure* (type)*"* (Heb. 11:17, 19).

This was the gospel that Abraham believed and by which he was saved. It had nothing to do with keeping the Ten Commandments, for they were not yet given, and God's plan has never changed. Salvation today is still believing what God says about His only Son—virgin born, crucified, and risen again.

Referring to Abraham's faith, Paul said:

"Now it was not written for his (Abraham's) *sake alone, that it was imputed to him; But for us also, to whom it shall be imputed, if we believe on him that raised up Jesus our Lord from the dead; Who was delivered for our offenses* (the cross), *and was raised again* (resurrection) *for our justification"* (Rom. 4:23-25).

Salvation is not merely believing in God, or a god, but believing *"the record that God gave of his Son"* (I John 5:10).

Salvation is not by the law or by works of man, but by faith in the virgin-born, crucified, risen Savior. The law is bad news for the sinner, but the gospel is good news—the good news of salvation by faith in Jesus Christ and what He did for us at the cross, of which Isaac was a type.

I can see far down the mountain,
Where I wandered weary years,
Often hindered in my journey
By the ghosts of doubt and fears;
Broken vows and disappointments
Thickly scattered all the way;
But the Spirit led unerring
To the land I hold today.

FOOLISH

CHRISTIANS

CHAPTER 4

FAITH

FAITH

"AND THE SCRIPTURE, foreseeing that God would justify the heathen through faith, preached before the gospel unto Abraham, saying, In thee shall all nations be blessed" (Gal. 3:8).

The Bible—the Word of God—is the single most important work on the face of the earth, and that a thousand times over. Due to the fact that it is the Word of God, and there is no other publication in the world like it, every believer should do whatever he can do to master its contents as much as possible. In fact, every believer should read the Bible completely through at least once a year.

The Bible is without error meaning that there are no contradictions in it. That's why Jesus said, *"Man shall not live by bread alone, but by every Word that proceedeth out of the mouth of God"* (Matt. 4:4).

God spoke through the great prophet Isaiah concerning the Word of God: *"For all those things hath mine hand made, and all those things have been, saith the LORD: but to this man will I look, even to him that is poor and of a contrite spirit, and trembleth at my word"* (Isa. 66:2).

Many people claim they cannot understand the Word of God, and that's the reason that they do not too often read it. I would advise such a person to get a copy of The Expositor's Study Bible. Virtually every Scripture is explained in this rendition. As well, it is the King James Version, and this translation is correct.

Incidentally, the Word of God is inspired, meaning that it is of God and thereby without error or contradiction.

INSPIRATION

Concerning the writing of the Word of God, the Scripture says:

> *Knowing this first* (harks back, as stated, to the Old Testament, which, in effect, was the Bible of Peter's day) *that no prophecy of the Scripture is of any private interpretation.* (This refers to the fact that the Word of God did not originate in the human mind.) *For the prophecy* (the word *prophecy* is used here in a general sense, covering the entirety of the Word of God, which means it's not limited merely to predictions regarding the future) *came not in old time by the will of man* (did not originate with man): *but holy men of God spoke as they were moved by the Holy Spirit.* (This proclaims the manner in which the Word of God was written and, thereby, given unto us) (II Pet. 1:20-21) (The Expositor's Study Bible)

Inspiration means that when God wanted something written, He searched through the vocabulary of the writer—whoever that prophet or apostle was—and selected the words in each sentence. In other words, the Word of God is not the mere thoughts of those who wrote it, but it is actually the Word of God. That's why, in a sense, the Word of God is so very, very important; it is actually the single most important thing on the face of the earth. As someone well said, the Bible is the only revealed truth in the world today, and in fact ever has been.

TRANSLATIONS

There are many and varied translations of the Bible, with only two or three of them worth having. Personally, I like the King James Version, and I'll tell you why.

When the scholars, under the direction of King James, set out to translate the Old and the New Testaments, they had no idea of trying to promote a pet doctrine. They only wanted to get the translation as close to the original Hebrew and Greek as humanly possible, and I believe the Lord helped them to do that.

Now it must be understood, from the time it was first finished, the King James translation has been edited several times and rightly so. I have in my office a copy of the first printing of the King James Version, and the English is so Elizabethan that you simply cannot read it. It was necessary for the King James Version be edited to bring the words up to date. It was not changed as far as its meaning was concerned, but words that were no longer used were replaced with words used presently.

Satan is attacking the Word of God today in a different fashion than he has in the past. Once, he tried to deny it, but of course that would be impossible. Now he is bringing out scores of religious books, calling them Bibles, which, if followed, will cause great problems for the believer.

For example, the book *The Message* is not a Bible. It may be referred to as such, but it isn't a Bible. In fact, it is anything but.

There are a good many editions that are similar. I would advise that the believer use the King James Version. As a result of reading and studying the King James Bible, more people have been saved, baptized with the Holy Spirit, delivered, and healed by the power of God than all other renditions and translations put together. I personally believe that the King James translation is closer to the original Hebrew and Greek than anything else.

I love the Word of God. I have read the Bible completely through nearly sixty times, and I never tire of its power and prestige, simply because it is the Word of God. That's the reason I don't want most of these translations, but rather that which is the closest to the original text. Yet, to all devotees to the King James, you must understand that the prophets and apostles did not write in Elizabethan English.

THE JUSTIFICATION OF THE HEATHEN

The Lord always intended that the gospel would go to the entirety of the world. Yet for many hundreds of years, the only people on the face of the earth who knew anything about God at all were the Jews. They were the only monotheistic nation, meaning that they believed in one God, Jehovah. Every other nation in the world was polytheistic, meaning that they believed in many gods (actually, demon spirits).

If a Gentile wanted to serve God (this is before the cross), then he had to, in essence, become a proselyte Jew. He had to enter into the sacrificial system and do his best to keep the law of Moses. But the law of Moses did not save anyone; it was never designed to save anyone. Rather, it was designed to show man how inadequate he was, and to portray God's standard of righteousness, which man could not keep.

The sacrificial system was meant to portray the coming Redeemer, who would give Himself as a sacrifice, making it possible for "whosoever will" to be saved.

Even after the cross, the presentation of the gospel to the world really did not gather speed until the time of the apostle Paul. Paul was called of God as the master builder of the church, and as well to be the spearhead for the presentation of the gospel to the Gentiles, which referred to the entirety of the world. While Paul preached to the Jews constantly, still his heavy and great burden was for the Gentiles. The cross of Christ opened all of this up. It made it possible for "whosoever will" to come and take of the water of life freely. Once again it was the cross, the cross, the cross! The cross put everything on an equal footing, meaning that anyone could be saved, and all would be saved in the same manner, which was faith in Christ and what Christ did for us at the cross.

Man must recognize himself as the sinner and recognize Jesus Christ as the Son of God, who gave Himself on the cross, and He did so as a ransom to pay a debt to God the Father that He did not owe—a debt we did owe but could not pay.

THROUGH FAITH

By the time of Christ, the Jews had come to think that the keeping of the law saved them. The tragedy of it was, despite their claims, they did not keep the law. Irrespective, the law was never meant to save. It was only meant to show man how inadequate he was, and what God demanded. In fact, the sacrificial system, which looked forward to the coming time of Christ, was brought about by God in order that Israel could be saved—by faith in what the sacrifices represented. The blood of bulls and goats could not save anyone, and it was never intended to save anyone. Always it was what the sacrifices represented and faith in that representation that saved man.

From day one, and I speak of the time of Adam and Eve, individuals have always been saved by faith, and when I say that I am speaking of faith in Christ and what He did for us at the cross.

The sacrificial system was instituted at the very dawn of time, which was a representation of Christ and what He would do at the cross on behalf of sinners, making it possible for men to be saved. So man has always been saved by faith in Christ and what Christ did for us at the cross. There was no other way, as no other way was needed. It has always been by faith, but it had to be in the correct object. And that correct object was Jesus Christ and Him crucified.

PREACHED BEFORE THE
GOSPEL UNTO ABRAHAM

In Galatians 3:8, Paul was speaking of the account given to us in Genesis 12.

The Scripture says:

Now the Lord had said unto Abram (referring to the revelation which had been given to the Patriarch a short time before; this chapter is very important, for it records the first steps of this great believer in the path of faith), *Get thee out of your country* (separation), *and from your kindred* (separation), *and from your father's house* (separation), *unto a land that I will show you* (refers to the fact that Abraham had no choice in the matter; he was to receive his orders from the Lord and go where those orders led him)*: And I will make of you a great nation* (the nation which God made of Abraham has changed the world and exists even unto this hour; in fact, this nation *'Israel'* still has a great part to play, which will take place in the coming kingdom age), *and I will bless you, and make your name great* (according to Scripture, *'to bless'* means *'to increase'* the builders of the tower of Babel sought to *'make us a name,'* whereas God took this man, who forsook all, and *'made his name great'*)*; and you shall be a blessing:* (concerns itself with the greatest blessing of all. It is the glory of Abraham's faith. God would give this man the meaning of salvation, which is *'justification by faith,'* which would come about through the Lord Jesus Christ, and what Christ would do on the cross. Concerning this Jesus said of Abraham, *'your father Abraham rejoiced to see my day: And he saw it, and was glad'* [John 8:56]). *And I will bless them who bless you* (to bless Israel, or any believer for that matter, guarantees the blessings of God), *and curse him who curses you* (to curse Israel, or any believer, guarantees that one will be cursed by God): *and in you shall all families of the earth be blessed* (It speaks of Israel, which sprang from the loins of Abraham, and the womb of Sarah, giving the world the Word of God and, more particularly, bringing the Messiah into the world. Through Christ every family in the world who desires blessing from God can have that blessing, i.e., *'justification by faith.'*) (Gen. 12:1-3) (The Expositor's Study Bible).

SAYING, IN THEE SHALL ALL NATIONS BE BLESSED

That has come to pass in totality. Every nation in the world that hears and receives the gospel of Jesus Christ—that which the Lord showed to Abraham some four thousand years ago—has been a blessing to the entirety of the world and in an unprecedented manner.

For instance, our television network, SonLife Broadcasting Network, covers almost the entirety of the world, whether by TV stations, cables, satellites, etc. Of course, we are not the only one preaching the gospel. The Lord said He would do it, and I'm speaking of the presentation of the gospel over the entirety of the world, and that He has done. The parts of the world that have accepted the gospel (and other regions have, at least to a degree), have been blessed beyond measure. The parts of the world that have opted to embrace false religions have been cursed, and they will be until Jesus comes back and sets the record straight, and He shall.

JUSTIFICATION BY FAITH

One can only be justified by God. No individual can justify himself. We are all guilty. But when the believing sinner comes to Christ and evidences faith in Christ, the Lord then totally and completely—through and by that person's faith— justifies him, which means that he is declared by God as perfect.

Of course, we all know that we are not perfect, but God judges us on the basis of His Son and our Savior, the Lord Jesus Christ. And so, whenever we come to Christ, a pure, spotless, righteousness is given to us, which affects our justification.

It is all done by faith, which means to have faith in Christ and what Christ did for us at the cross. Man cannot be justified in any other manner or by any other way. It is all in Christ and His atoning, vicarious, efficacious sacrifice, in the offering up of Himself as a ransom to God.

Unfortunately, millions try to justify themselves by their good works, by this, that, or the other. They cannot do such; actually, it is impossible. But by simple faith—and we speak of faith in Christ and the cross—anyone, even the vilest of sinners, can be instantly justified and is, in fact, instantly justified upon accepting Jesus Christ. It is that which comes with the born-again experience. And it can come no other way.

BLESSED

"So then they which be of faith are blessed with faithful Abraham" (Gal. 3:9).

If you want the blessings of God, and there is nothing greater than that, then do what the Lord commands us to do. It's not difficult. It's not hard. It's just laying the flesh aside, and that's not a pleasant experience for most believers.

WHAT DOES IT MEAN TO BE OF FAITH?

The answer to that question is just as acute now as it was some two thousand years ago with the apostle Paul. The people heard Paul preach this over and over, but somehow it was difficult for them to understand it and abide by what he was saying.

It is a problem today as well. We keep wanting to do something ourselves—something, incidentally, which we cannot do. Yet we keep trying, don't we?

To be "of faith" is to place your faith exclusively in Christ and what Christ has done for you at the cross. That's the key.

Everyone in the world has faith; unfortunately, most of the time, it's not in the right object. The right object is Jesus Christ and Him crucified.

Every human being in the world has faith. God created this planet with sheer words of faith. And His creation of man is in the same capacity. Man is to be a faith object, so to speak. Really, that is what makes free enterprise so advantageous. It operates on the principle of faith. That's the reason that communism and socialism will not work, because it bypasses faith altogether.

The world has no interest in the faith that God demands, so it will not receive its benefits. Unfortunately, most Christians fall into the same category. We keep trying to do what we cannot do and what God alone can do. God gave His Son, the Lord Jesus Christ, as a ransom on the cross of Calvary that man might be saved and blessed beyond measure. All that is required of us is that we place our faith exclusively in Christ and what He did for us at the cross and maintain it accordingly.

CRUCIFIED WITH CHRIST

Listen again to Paul:

I am crucified with Christ (as the foundation for all victory; Paul, here, takes us back to Rom. 6:3-5): *nevertheless I live* (have new life); *yet not I* (not by my own strength and ability), *but Christ lives in me* (by virtue of me dying with Him on the cross and being raised with Him in newness of life): *and the life which I now live in the flesh* (my daily walk before God) *I live by the faith of the Son of God* (the cross is ever the object of my faith), *who loved me, and gave Himself for me* (which is the only way that I could be saved). *I do not frustrate the grace of God* (if we make anything other than the cross of Christ the object of our faith, we frustrate the grace of God, which means we stop its action, and the Holy Spirit will no longer help us): *for if righteousness come by the law* (any type of law) *then Christ is dead in vain* (if I can successfully live for the Lord by any means other than faith in Christ and the cross, then the death of Christ was a waste) (Gal. 2:20-21) (The Expositor's Study Bible).

That's what it means to be "of faith." It is the correct object that is so very, very important. And of course, that correct object is Jesus Christ and Him crucified.

Software developer Bill Gates had faith—faith that he could devise computer programming that would change the way we live. He was right, but that type of faith is not recognized by God.

Tragically so, most of the faith evidenced by Christians is not recognized by God, because it is faith in self instead of Christ and Him crucified.

BLESSED WITH FAITHFUL ABRAHAM

All Abraham did was simply have faith in God, which means he believed what God said to him. He did not argue about it but accepted it readily. He believed God, and God accredited it to him for righteousness. In reality, that's the only way that people have ever been saved. Which means we continue to be saved that way today.

Inasmuch as Abraham set the standard—actually doing what God wanted him to do—everyone now who is born again, and I mean everyone, is looked at by God as a child of Abraham.

Paul said concerning this, *"Know you therefore that they which are of faith* (presents faith, and faith alone, as the foundation; but the object of faith must ever be the cross), *the same are the children of Abraham* (the legitimate sons of Abraham)" (Gal. 3:7) (The Expositor's Study Bible).

As well, we must understand that Abraham was no simpleton. His home before coming to Canaan was Ur of the Chaldees, which was one of the most sophisticated cities in the world of that day.

Jewish targums state that Abraham's family was idol makers and made idols out of gold, silver, wood, stone, etc. They were also very wealthy and well-educated, at least up to the standards of that day. So this man was not a simpleton who believed whatever he saw or heard. He was a very intelligent individual, yet very godly.

Hold that thought as we look again at what the apostle Paul said regarding Enoch of old: *"By faith Enoch was translated that he should not see death; and was not found, because God had translated him: For before his translation he had this testimony, that he pleased God. But without faith, it is impossible to please him"* (Heb. 11:5-6).

He didn't say that it was hard or difficult to please the Lord without faith; he said it was impossible.

As we've already said, it is the correct object of faith, which is so very, very important. As we've also previously said, everybody in the world has faith, but it's not faith that God will recognize. The faith that He recognizes, and that alone which He recognizes, is faith in Christ and the cross.

Many are fond of saying that their faith is in the Word of God, and that's exactly where it ought to be. However, what one must understand is, the entirety of the story of the Bible is the story of Jesus Christ and Him crucified. So if we have faith in anything else as far as the object of faith is concerned, our faith is misplaced.

I read the other day where a young man had written a book wherein he stated, "If you want victory over sin, fast for twenty-one days," or words to that effect. While fasting is most definitely scriptural and helpful (if it's done in the right way), trying to use fasting to overcome sin won't work. If sin could be overcome by fasting, then Jesus did not have to come down here and die on a cross, but rather just teach people how to fast.

Paul said, *"I do not frustrate the grace of God, for if righteousness come by the law, then Christ is dead in vain"* (Gal. 2:21).

The modern church is fond of coming up with one fad after another, trying to have victory over sin. But there is only one way that this can be done, and that is faith in Christ and the cross.

Sanctification—how we live for God on a daily basis—is the story of the book of Galatians in your Bible. That's how important it is. I'm speaking of how we have victory over the world, the flesh, and the devil. How we grow in grace and the knowledge of the Lord. How we have victory over Satan. How we order our behavior. All of this has to do with our everyday living for God. But the sad fact is that the modern church, and I speak of those who truly love the Lord, simply do not know how to live for God.

HOW TO LIVE FOR GOD

The words I've just used are fighting words. When you tell a Christian that he doesn't know how to live for God, he will look at you a little bit askance simply because he doesn't understand the question. If you were able to get him to answer, he would say that we should be more faithful to church, we should pay our tithe, we should witness to people, etc. All of those things are good and right, at least in their own capacity. But that's not the way to live for God.

Let me tell you how: as a believer, you must place your faith exclusively in Christ and what He has done for you at the cross and maintain it exclusively in Christ and what Christ has done for you at the cross. That being done and being continually done is the way to live for God.

Have you ever stopped to think why the sacrifices of the Old Testament were offered constantly? Because the blood of bulls and goats could not take away sin. Furthermore, those sacrifices could not help people live for God as they should. Yet those sacrifices were necessary and necessary continuously because without the shedding of blood, there is no remission of sin. So, to have some relief from sin, the sacrifices had to be offered continually. That was all a picture of the cross. Every time an animal was offered (which numbered into the millions) that was a picture of Christ and the price He would pay at Calvary's cross.

Thank God that now, the one sacrifice of Calvary is all that is needed. It atoned for all sin—past, present, and future. That's why the cross is so very, very important, simply because there is no other way that sin can be overcome, cleansed, washed, or done away with—only by the cross.

When we do away with the cross, ignore the cross, or do not believe in the cross, we close the door to forgiveness of sin. That spells tragedy for anyone who is foolish enough to try to function in such capacity. Somebody has said, and rightly so, that the cross of Christ is never forsaken or denied, because of a theological problem, meaning that the cross is too difficult to understand. It is never denied on those principles. Every time the cross of Christ is denied, forsaken, or ignored; it is always a moral choice. What do we mean by that? It means there is pride, self-will, or hidden sin that we do not want to part with, and this causes one to deny the cross. I used to think it was ignorance in totality, and while ignorance definitely plays a part in all of this, that's really not the problem. The problem is unbelief.

ARE BLESSED

We are told plainly in Galatians 3:9 that when we embrace the cross—that which Jesus did at Calvary—we will be blessed. The full passage is, *"So then they which be of faith are blessed."*

Do you want a blessing from God? Well, He has plainly and clearly told us in this text that blessing will most definitely follow simple faith in Christ and the finished work of Calvary.

A short time after the Lord began to give to me the great meaning of the cross, He said that I should teach the cross, preach the cross, and proclaim the cross until He told me to stop. That has been over twenty years ago, and He hasn't told us to stop yet.

I have watched this great promise come true in my own life and ministry, and I'm speaking of the blessings of God. Just a few weeks ago, the Lord spoke to me and said, "Tell the people that all who support this work and ministry, this proclamation of the cross of Christ, and who will be faithful in that which they do and say, I will bless them abundantly so." Now I believe that, and I believe it in totality.

WITH FAITHFUL ABRAHAM

Abraham was referred to as faithful because he believed God. What did he believe? He believed that one was coming who would redeem fallen humanity. He believed that this one would be the Son of the living God. He believed that this Lord of Glory would perform miracles even to the raising of the dead. He believed that at Calvary's cross, this Redeemer would pay the ransom owed to God by man, who was unable to pay. God would pay it, and Abraham was faithful to believe this. This was some four hundred years before the law was given, but he never wavered in his faith, and he is referred to as "faithful Abraham." We must understand that it is the Holy Spirit who gave Paul these two words to say about Abraham. What an honor, to be referred to as "faithful."

THE WORKS OF THE LAW

"For as many as are of the works of the law are under the curse: for it is written, Cursed is everyone that continueth not in all things which are written in the book of the law to do them" (Gal. 3:10).

Most Christians reading these words as given by Paul automatically think that they belong to another time, some two thousand or more years ago. They reason in their minds that Jesus fulfilled all the law, and that's exactly right. It must be understood in this fashion. If we try to live for God by any means, which means to have righteousness by any means other than Christ and the cross, then we are putting ourselves under law. It's not the law of Moses that bothers most Christians today, but laws they devise themselves, or laws somebody else devises, or laws other preachers will formulate. Whatever it is, God looks at it as law.

Let's say it again: if our faith is not in Christ and the cross and that exclusively, then whatever it is that we are looking to, no matter how scriptural it may be in its own right, the truth is we have just devised a law, which God cannot bless. So it's not only the law of Moses, it is also laws that we devise ourselves, or that others devise, thinking somehow that by the doing of these things it will bring victory to our lives. It won't.

Let me say it again: anything that we devise, no matter how good it may sound, and no matter how scriptural it may be, if it's not Christ and the cross, then we have turned it into a law, which God cannot bless.

ARE UNDER THE CURSE

It's bad enough to go in the wrong direction, but to be guaranteed of a crash, which the curse of the law will bring about, is something else altogether.

Again, if our faith is not in Christ and the cross exclusively, that means we are under law of some manner, which always brings a curse.

It must be understood that all law has a penalty attached to it if that law is broken. And some may think, "Well, simple laws that we devise have no penalty, because they're just stipulations that we try to bring about." It's not that it has no penalty. The penalty is that we are not placing our faith in Christ and the cross, which opens the door for Satan to steal, kill, and destroy. Yes, there is a curse that is attached to every law. The only law that doesn't have a curse to it is that which is devised by the Godhead.

Paul said, *"For the law of the Spirit of life in Christ Jesus hath made me free from the law of sin and death"* (Rom. 8:2).

These are laws devised by God, and they will work exactly as God has designed them to work. When it comes to laws that we devise ourselves—laws of our own concoction—we will find a penalty attached to those laws, and to be sure that penalty will take its effect.

It's tragic, but virtually the entirety of the modern church world is under a curse because they are trying to function under law—whether the law of Moses or laws devised by themselves or someone else. Irrespective, a curse is attached to it, and that is the cause of most problems with most Christians.

Christians are plagued with all kinds of problems, and most of them are from being under law. They are put under law by teachers in their churches or of their own devising, but law it is, and a curse it is. It's the cause of much sickness (not all, but much), it's the cause of difficulties of every kind. It's the cause of a lack of peace, a lack of faith, a lack of victory in our hearts and lives, which causes all types of problems. It's because the person is under the curse of the law. The only way you cannot be under that curse is to place your faith exclusively in Christ and what He has done for you at the cross and maintain it exclusively in Christ and what He has done for you at the cross.

FOR IT IS WRITTEN

In Galatians 3:10, the full passage says, *"For it is written, Cursed is every one that continueth not in all things which are written in the book of the law to do them."*

Man cannot keep laws, whether the law of Moses or laws that he or others have devised. It's simply not in us to do it.

Paul said there is a reason for that: *"And if Christ be in you, the body is dead because of sin; but the Spirit is life because of righteousness"* (Rom. 8:10).

What did he mean by the statement, *"the body is dead because of sin"*?

He is speaking of the fall in the garden of Eden as it regards Adam and Eve. When Adam fell, it weakened every part of his being—his soul and spirit as well as his physical body. We are too weak to do what God wants us to do, so Jesus had to do it for us. He does whatever we need only because of and through the cross. If we try to place our faith elsewhere, we are then left on our own, which means that whatever we're trying to do can't be done. In this case we are trying to live for God victoriously, but it simply cannot be done if we are trying to do it outside of the cross.

This is the reason that willpower simply will not accomplish the task. While the will is very important ("whosoever *will*"), it within itself will not give us the power we need to do what is needed. And yet the modern church is trying to live for God exclusively by the means of willpower. It will not work simply because it cannot work. As I've already stated, the will is important, but if we think we can live for God by that fashion, we make a terrible mistake. We cannot. We live by faith, not by physical or mental strength.

Many Christians believe that the Lord greatly strengthens willpower when we come to Christ. He doesn't. Our will is the same now as it was before we were saved. We are not meant to live for God in this fashion. We are meant to live for God by faith—and that faith must be in Christ and the cross. That's the way it should be simply because the body is dead because of sin.

Have you been to Jesus for the cleansing power?
Are you washed in the blood of the Lamb?
Are you fully trusting in His grace this hour?
Are you washed in the blood of the Lamb?

Are you walking daily by the Saviour's side?
Are you washed in the blood of the Lamb?
Do you rest each moment in the Crucified?
Are you washed in the blood of the Lamb?

When the bridegroom cometh, will your robes be white,
Pure and white in the Blood of the Lamb?
Will your soul be ready for the mansions bright,
And be washed in the blood of the Lamb?

Lay aside the garments that are stained with sin,
And be washed in the blood of the Lamb!
There's a fountain flowing for the soul unclean,
Oh, be washed in the blood of the Lamb!

FOOLISH

CHRISTIANS

CHAPTER 5

JUSTIFIED

JUSTIFIED

"BUT THAT NO MAN *is justified by the law in the sight of God, it is evident: for, The just shall live by faith*" (Gal. 3:11).

To prayerfully help us understand this a little better, I would suggest that anything in which we place our faith other than Christ and the cross, is judged by God as being law, which can never be accepted in His sight. To be frank, this is the problem with Christian man. We try to be justified by things we do or things we don't do. Let's again state what justification actually is: it is God declaring an obviously guilty sinner as justified and doing so on the basis of faith, but it must be faith in Christ and what Christ did at the cross. It is that and that alone that God will recognize.

Let us say it again because it is so very, very important: we have a guilty sinner standing before God, with his guilt undeniable. But when that guilty sinner evidences faith in Christ—even though he may not understand very much, if anything at all, about the Lord—still, at the moment of his faith in Christ and what Christ did for him at the cross, he is instantly justified in the sight of God. A perfect, spotless righteousness is awarded him and done so immediately.

To be justified is to be declared not guilty, but it goes a step further in declaring one as innocent; however, it goes even further than that. In the mind of God, not only is the person, according to his faith, declared not guilty and declared innocent, but he is also declared perfect. God can accept nothing less than perfection. Of course, we all know that there is no perfection in mankind. All perfection is in Christ. But our faith gives us the perfection of Christ.

THE OLD TESTAMENT SACRIFICES

Let me explain it this way: the sin offering portrayed the sinner who brought the lamb as placing his hands on the head of the lamb, and thereby transferring his guilt to the innocent victim—the lamb. In other words, the lamb takes all of the guilt, all of the sin, and all of the punishment. That's a type of Christ taking our sin and our punishment.

The whole burnt offering is totally different. Whereas the sin offering has the sinner giving all of his sins to the innocent victim, the whole burnt offering has the perfection of that offering given to the guilty sinner. It is quite a trade, to be frank and plain with you.

Of course, the guilty sinner does not understand any of this when he comes to Christ, but hopefully he will understand it after being saved. It is a beautiful application. Man cannot be justified any other way than by simple faith in Christ and what Christ did for us at the cross.

If man thinks he can be justified some other way, what way is that? And yet, man keeps trying to justify himself. He does so by joining a certain church, thinking that this will justify him. He does so by giving sums of money. He does so by performing good deeds. Good works is now the great vehicle to justification. That's what most of the church presently teaches—good works. While good works are important, such will never justify anyone whatsoever.

SANCTIFICATION AND JUSTIFICATION

Paul catalogs it in the following way: *"And such were some of you: but ye are washed, but ye are sanctified, but ye are justified in the name of the Lord Jesus, and by the Spirit of our God"* (I Cor. 6:11).

When the believing sinner comes to Christ and evidences faith in Christ and the cross, that person is instantly, spiritually washed and sanctified and justified. In reality, it all takes place at the same time.

Justification is a person being declared clean; however, he cannot be declared clean until he has been made clean, which is done by the washing and the sanctification. All of that, as stated, is spiritual and not literal, although it does definitely have a literal application.

However, the sanctification enjoined here is not the progressive sanctification in which every believer must enter into. Unfortunately, most believers do not know what it means to be sanctified. The church has tried to sanctify itself and tried to teach believers to sanctify themselves, which cannot be done.

SANCTIFICATION

Please notice the following very closely: the moment the believer evidences faith in Christ and the cross and maintains faith in Christ and the cross—at that moment—that person is sanctified. This means the Holy Spirit, who is already in the heart and life of the believer, can go to work in that believer's life, bringing about the holiness that is desired. In fact, holiness and sanctification both come from the same root word and mean the same thing.

It is all done by simple faith in Christ and what Christ has done for us at the cross. That's the reason that Paul also said, *"But we preach Christ crucified, unto the Jews a stumblingblock, and unto the Greeks foolishness"* (I Cor. 1:23).

Jesus without the cross is Jesus without salvation and redemption. We must never forget that Christ came to this world for the express purpose of dying on a cross, which was the giving of Himself as a ransom, which satisfied the demands of a thrice holy God. That's the reason we have to evidence faith in Christ and the cross; God will recognize nothing else.

IN THE SIGHT OF GOD, IT IS EVIDENT

In Galatians 3:11, the phrase, *"But that no man is justified by the law in the sight of God, it is evident,"* corresponds to the *"book of the law"* in Galatians 3:10.

While a perfect righteousness is found in the law, providing there is perfect obedience, still the point is moot. It is impossible for fallen man to keep the law; therefore, it is impossible for justification to come from that source.

Even though obedience was demanded by God, as would be obvious, still, perfect obedience was never forthcoming; therefore, the sacrifices were a part of the law, which pointed men to Christ. In fact, the sacrifices were instituted for two reasons:

1. Obedience to the law, which was not forthcoming anyway, could not justify a sinner in that his obedience could not pay for his sin. Only blood can pay for sin, for blood means outpoured life, and death is the wages of sin.

2. The sacrifices pointed to Jesus, but they were only a stopgap measure. However, faith in what and who the sacrifices represented did guarantee salvation. God declares a believing sinner righteous based on the fact that Christ has met the requirements of the law which we broke, with Himself being our righteousness.

JUSTIFICATION

Justification is deliverance from the *penalty* of sin. Sanctification is deliverance from the *power* of sin.

Justification, at least that which God will accept, can only be brought about by the believing sinner exercising faith in Christ, who paid the penalty for our sins on the cross, thereby accepting Him as Savior with an admittance that he is eternally lost without Christ's work at Calvary.

This is the reason the cross of Christ is so very, very important. Without it, man cannot be justified. In fact, man was justified before the cross by placing his faith in the sacrificial system which represented the tremendous price that Christ would pay at Calvary's cross. Even then the blood of bulls and goats could not take away sins. It served as a stopgap measure, but the sin problem remained.

That means that whenever believers died before the cross, they did not go to heaven, but rather went down into paradise, which was referred to as "Abraham's bosom." In other words, their being released from this place and able to go to heaven was dependent totally upon the cross of Christ. That's the reason we emphasize the fact of the cross as we do, for without the cross there can be no justification, but with the cross there can be cleansing from all sin, irrespective as to how bad it might be.

HOW DOES ONE RECEIVE
THIS JUSTIFICATION?

It is all by faith, but it must be faith in Christ and what Christ did at the cross. While the believing sinner coming to Christ does not understand any of the rudiments of the cross, doesn't understand at all what Jesus there did, he just simply believes. And, at the moment he places his faith and trust in Christ and what Christ did for him at the cross—at that moment—that believing sinner is totally and completely justified with a perfect, pure, spotless righteousness granted to him instantly.

At that moment, the believing sinner is transferred from the position of lawbreaker, which means he is doomed, to the position of law keeper, even though he did not keep the law at all.

The truth is, Jesus kept the law on our behalf. He never sinned one time, not in word, thought, or deed, but He walked perfect and pure for the entirety of His life, and He did it all for us as our representative man. When He went to the cross, He paid the price for all the sins committed, that is if the sinner will only place his faith and trust exclusively in Christ and what Christ did for him at the cross. As we've already stated, the believing sinner has no knowledge of the cross, but the moment he is saved, everything changes. He will then begin to realize the tremendous worth of what Jesus there did.

It is appalling when one realizes that the church has almost abandoned the understanding of the cross. Some have relegated it as "past miseries," calling it the greatest defeat in human history. Such constitutes nothing but blasphemy.

There is no way that a person can be saved without the cross. While the believing sinner may not understand anything about it, most assuredly, God does. It was there that the price was paid, the ransom given, and every sin atoned by what Jesus Christ did in the pouring out of His precious blood at the cross of Calvary. As the old song says, "What can wash away my sin? Nothing but the blood of Jesus."

Let us say it again: justification is deliverance from the *penalty* of sin. Sanctification is deliverance from the *power* of sin.

IN THE SIGHT OF GOD

Let us quickly state that it is, as Galatians 3:11 states, *"in the sight of God"* that matters. Nothing else does. Unfortunately, churches are filled with people, even millions of people, who equate the acceptance by the church as acceptance by God. It isn't. In fact, acceptance by man holds no relationship whatsoever with justification by faith. What man says is one thing, what God says is another. Man tries to justify himself by his works, which cannot be done. In fact, it is an impossibility. Man is justified simply by accepting Christ and what Christ did for us at the cross. When that is done, meaning it is *"in the sight of God,"* man is accepted, but only then. Unfortunately, that's not the case with most.

A short time ago, I saw on television an interview of a man who had given many millions of dollars for a particular project in Washington, D.C. When he was being interviewed, something was mentioned about heaven. He went on to say, as many people do, "If there is a heaven, I believe I will make it simply because of the good deeds that I have done with my money."

He didn't realize, and neither do millions of others realize, that none of that has any effect in the sight of God. God recognizes only one thing as it regards salvation, as it regards justification, as it regards regeneration, as it regards the born-again experience, and that is what Jesus Christ did at the cross of Calvary and the believing sinner's faith in Christ and the price that Christ paid on our behalf.

One must understand that Jesus did not go to the cross for Himself. He did not go there for angels or for heaven at all. He went there for sinners. He paid the price that God would accept, and all that man has to do to receive this glorious eternal salvation is to simply have faith in Christ and what Christ did for us at the cross.

Yet, millions upon millions think they will go to heaven either because of their good deeds or by not committing bad deeds. I label it as the brownie point system. Many people think, "I'll go to heaven if I do more good deeds than bad ones." But none of that has anything to do with anything. Millions are in hell today, and other millions are on their way to hell—actually, almost the entirety of the human race—because they believe such a lie. Remember, it is always *"in the sight of God."* It's not in the sight of man. Man may agree and man may not agree, but that holds no court with God. God looks for only one thing and that is faith in Christ and what Christ did for us at the cross. We must never forget that.

THE JUST SHALL LIVE BY FAITH

In Galatians 3:11, the phrase, *"The just shall live by faith,"* was quoted from Habakkuk 2:4. This passage is also quoted by Paul in Romans 1:17.

The word *just* refers to those who are justified in the sight of God.

Again, it is impossible for one to be justified without evidencing faith in Christ and what Christ has done for us at the cross. In coming to Christ, the believing sinner does not have to understand all of that; in fact, he does not understand it; he simply believes. It's just that simple. When one believes in Christ and what Christ did at the cross, everything changes.

We must remember that two things are in vogue here: who Christ is and what Christ has done.

First, who is Christ?

Christ is the Son of the living God. He was and is God manifest in the flesh. He is a man—*the* Man Christ Jesus—and He is also God. That does not mean that Christ is 50 percent man and 50 percent God. In fact, He is very man and very God, meaning completely man and completely God.

His coming into this world by means of the Virgin Mary is referred to as the incarnation, God becoming man. In fact, He was born without the benefit of man whatsoever. Mary was a virgin when Jesus was conceived by an edict of the Holy Spirit, and this means that Joseph had absolutely nothing to do with the birth of Jesus Christ. Jesus Christ came into this world for one purpose, and that was to go to the cross, where mankind, at least those who would believe, would be redeemed. That was His sole purpose in His coming to this world. The believing sinner must believe the things that we have stated—that Jesus Christ was and is God. It is absolutely imperative that he believe this.

Second, what has Christ done?

Jesus had to go to the cross in order for man to be redeemed. His virgin birth was absolutely necessary; however, if it had stopped there, not a single soul would have ever been saved. His absolutely sinless life was perfect, but had it stopped there, not a single soul would have been saved. His miracles were imperative, but had it stopped there, no one would have been saved.

For man to be saved, Jesus Christ had to go to the cross, and there give Himself as a sacrifice, which He did. Jesus did not go to the cross to appease Satan. God owed Satan nothing. He went to the cross to satisfy the demands of a thrice holy God, which man could not satisfy. There was nothing man could do. He was hopelessly lost, due to Adam's fall. But Jesus, as the spotless Lamb of God, would go to the cross and pour out His life's blood, which would be accepted by God, because it was blood that was never tainted by sin. And then, when the believing sinner expresses faith in Christ and what Christ did for him at the cross, in the sight of God that person is totally and completely justified.

LIVE

In Galatians 3:11, the word *live* refers to the believer living his or her life exclusively by faith in Christ and the work carried out at Calvary. We cannot live any other way. If we try to live by works, we will fail. If we try to live by the rudiments of religion, we will fail. We are to live by faith, and what does that mean?

It speaks of us living a righteous life, overcoming sin, Satan, and the world. It speaks of us having victory over the flesh. That's the only way that we can successfully live for God. Regrettably, most Christians, even good Christians, are trying to live by other means. They are trying to live by good works. They are trying to live by not doing bad things. All of that is necessary, but it does not help us to live for God.

The only way, and I want to be emphatic about this statement and say it again: The only way that one can have victory over the world, the flesh, and the devil, in other words, how we live this life, is that we place our faith exclusively in Christ and what Christ did for us at the cross.

FAITH

Whenever we mention faith, what exactly are we talking about?

One will never understand the subject of faith, unless he first understands what the correct object of faith must be. That's the key to everything. Before we tell you what that correct object is, let us address ourselves to something else.

Everyone in the world has faith. Even the atheist has faith. To be sure, it is not faith in God but in himself, but still, it is faith. That's the reason that the capitalist system is the only system that will work in the world and provide a decent standard of living, for those who are privileged to be in its confines. But again, that's not faith that God will recognize.

All believers have faith but for most it is faith in themselves or faith in their good works. And I am speaking of the godliest of the godly. They mean well, but still, it is not faith that God will recognize. There is only one faith that He will recognize, and that is the following: our faith must be in Christ and what

Christ has done for us at the cross. That is to be the focus and the object of our faith.

JESUS CHRIST

Let's say it another way: most every believer will readily agree that every single blessing that we receive comes because of the Lord Jesus Christ. He is the one who has paid the price for everything that we receive from God. We must understand that. We must believe that. Christ is the source of all good things that come our way (John 1:1-5; 14:6).

THE CROSS OF CHRIST

Our Lord is the source; however, the cross of Christ is the means, and the only means, by which all these great blessings come to us (I Cor. 1:17-18, 2:2; Gal. 6:14, Col. 2:10-15).

THE OBJECT OF OUR FAITH

With Christ as the source, and the cross as the means, and the only means, Jesus Christ and Him crucified must ever be the object of our faith. This is of vital significance (Col. 2:10-15).

THE HOLY SPIRIT

With our Lord as the source, and the cross as the means— with that being the object of our faith—then the Holy Spirit, who works exclusively within the parameters of the finished work of Christ will grandly help us (Rom. 8:1-11).

THE LAW IS NOT OF FAITH

"And the law is not of faith: but, The man that doeth them shall live in them" (Gal. 3:12).

The phrase, *"the law is not of faith,"* plainly says that the two have no relationship with each other. Law is not of faith and faith is not of law. And yet virtually the entirety of the present body of Christ, and I speak of those who are truly born again, even Spirit-filled, are living under law instead of grace. We must understand that grace can come only by the rudiments of the cross. In other words, it is the cross that makes it all possible.

How can I say that virtually the entirety of the body of Christ is living under law? How can I know such a thing? I know it simply because the modern church is not trying to live for God by the means of faith, and when we speak of faith, we are speaking of faith in Christ and what Christ did for us at the cross. There is no place for the person to be if he is not abiding by the cross of Christ, but rather trying to live by means of law.

It is law or it is grace, but it cannot be both.

WHAT DO WE MEAN BY LAW?

We'll say it this way: whatever is not faith in Christ and what He did for us at the cross is law. It makes no difference what it is, God constitutes it as law.

Let's take one's prayer life for an example. To be frank, no believer can get anywhere with the Lord unless he has a prayer life. This is an absolute must. However, if his faith is in his prayer life instead of in Christ and the cross, then, despite his prayer life, he will live a life of failure. What do I mean by failure?

I mean that he will fail the Lord, in other words he will sin. To be frank, the real problem with every believer is sin. That's the problem with all of us. It's the problem that every one of us faces—sin. And there is only one place for sin and that is the cross. There is no way to overcome sin unless we do so by faith in Christ and what He did for us at the cross.

While the believer must have an ongoing prayer life, which is so very, very important, his faith must still be exclusively in Christ and the cross and in nothing else. Then the Lord will bless his prayer life as never before. But if his faith is in his prayer life, as valuable as prayer is, he will live a life of spiritual failure, no matter about his prayer life.

Again, the modern church—and we speak of those who are truly born again and who truly love the Lord—is trying to live for God by means of law. While not (in most cases) the law of Moses, it is law that we devise ourselves, law we formulate out of our own minds; we invent such, or we turn into law that which is not law itself. We do this constantly.

That's why I say that the modern church is living in law. It doesn't understand anything about the cross of Christ relative to sanctification, so it tries to live by law. The church doesn't call it law, it doesn't refer to it as law, but if it's not the cross, then that's what it is—law.

SANCTIFICATION AND THE CROSS

Sanctification is one of the most important doctrines of Christianity, yet most believers, even preachers, don't have the foggiest idea as to what it means to be sanctified. Men have tried to sanctify themselves almost from the beginning of time, which is impossible. It cannot be done.

Even though I have already said it in this volume, because of its vast significance, please allow me to say it again: how is one sanctified? That is the question.

A person cannot sanctify himself. It is impossible to do so. Just as the sinner is unable to justify himself, likewise, the Christian cannot sanctify himself. So how do we become sanctified?

Our faith is to be placed exclusively in Christ and the cross. When that is done—at that very moment—such a person is sanctified. He is to maintain his faith in Christ and the cross, which will then give the Holy Spirit latitude to work in his life, thereby making him more and more Christlike.

Sanctification does not mean sinless perfection. In fact, the Bible does not teach such. But the Bible does teach that sin is not to have dominion over us.

The apostle Paul said, *"For sin shall not have dominion over you: for ye are not under the law, but under grace"* (Rom. 6:14). But if our faith is not in Christ and the cross exclusively, then sin will most definitely have dominion over us.

Paul found that the church at Corinth was getting taken up with water baptism, specifically, who baptized who. He said to them, *"For Christ sent me not to baptize, but to preach the gospel:*

not with wisdom of words, lest the cross of Christ should be made of none effect" (I Cor. 1:17). He then said, *"For the preaching of the cross is to them that perish foolishness; but unto us which are saved it is the power of God"* (I Cor. 1:18).

Paul wasn't knocking water baptism. He was telling the Corinthians that the emphasis must always be on the cross of Christ. We must not be drawn away to other things, as important as those other things might be. We must keep our eyes on the Lord Jesus Christ and what He did for us at the cross—and that exclusively.

THE MAN THAT DOETH THEM
SHALL LIVE IN THEM

In Galatians 3:12, Paul is speaking about living for God—how we live this life, how we order our behavior, how we have victory over the world, the flesh, and the devil, and how we grow in grace and the knowledge of the Lord. And that's the question: how do we live for God, at least victoriously?

Sometime back, I was preaching at Family Worship Center during our Wednesday night Bible Study, and I made this statement: "Modern Christians do not know how to live for God." When I said this, an audible gasp went up from the congregation.

What did I mean by that statement? I meant exactly what I said, the modern Christian simply does not know how to live for God. Consequently, there is gross failure in the hearts and lives of many, if not most, believers. It is because they don't know how to live for the Lord. Were you to ask most Christians the question as to how they live for God, most would begin to rattle off particular things they should or should not do. Automatically they resort to law because that's all they know.

Again, the basic problem with living for God is the problem of sin. We don't like to think of it in that fashion; in fact, many Christians claim they have no problem with sin whatsoever. Well, my answer to that is somewhat cryptic: get saved, and you'll find out what sin is.

We must understand that sin comes in many shapes and sizes. We often refer to what we call The Big Five—alcohol, drugs, nicotine, pornography, and gambling. It is sort of the feeling that, if one is not troubled by any of these, and most Christians aren't, then we have no problem with sin.

But sin comes in the form of selfishness, self-will (one of the biggest sins of all), jealousy, envy, and uncontrollable temper. Paul said, *"For whatsoever is not of faith is sin"* (Rom. 14:23).

Think about that for a moment. Every Christian who is under law—and most are—they are living in a state of sin. They don't think of themselves as being such, but in reality they are. In the eyes of God, they're living in a state of sin. Yes, they're saved, and they are justified because their faith is in Christ. Still, they do not live a life of victory because their faith is in something other than Christ and the cross.

Anytime our faith is in anything other than Christ and the cross, that is a spectacle of sin, a constant particular of sin. We don't think of it as such, but it is. That's the reason most Christians never grow in grace. They never get stronger in the Lord. Untold millions who would read this book were it placed before them would automatically think that everything is just fine with them. And it may be, but more than likely, it isn't. How do we live for God? That is the question.

Every morning that I get up; every time I go to prayer, which is very often, I say to the Lord: "My faith is in You and what You have done for me at the cross. My faith is not in me or in any other individual, neither is it in the church with its religious rituals and ceremonies. Rather, my faith is in You and the great price that You paid at Calvary's cross."

That's how you live for God. You understand that what Jesus did at the cross not only guaranteed your salvation, which is the greatest thing there is, but also that what He did at the cross gives you the power to live for God victoriously.

We've already said it twice, but let me say it again: justification is deliverance from the *penalty* of sin. Sanctification is deliverance from the *power* of sin.

That deliverance comes solely and completely from the Lord Jesus Christ and what He did for us at the cross.

THE HOLY SPIRIT

The believer must understand that the Holy Spirit is given His ability to work within our lives by and through the cross.

Listen again to Paul: *"For the law of the Spirit of life in Christ Jesus, hath made me free from the law of sin and death"* (Rom. 8:2).

These are the two most powerful laws in the universe, laws devised by the Godhead in eternity past. The only law that is more powerful than the law of sin and death is, *"the law of the Spirit of life in Christ Jesus."*

Paul is here talking about the Holy Spirit. And when he speaks of the phrase *"in Christ Jesus,"* he is speaking of what Christ did for us at the cross. In fact, he uses that term or one of its derivatives more than a hundred times in his fourteen epistles.

Before the cross, the Holy Spirit could not come into the hearts and lives of believers to abide permanently. In fact, He could only come into the hearts and lives of a select few—prophets, etc. —to help them carry out what He had called them to do. When the work was finished, the Holy Spirit would leave out. Why? Because the blood of bulls and goats was insufficient to take away sins, so the Holy Spirit could not have anything to do with sin (Heb. 10:4).

Before the cross, when believers died, they did not go to heaven. Their souls and their spirits went down into paradise, where they were held captive by Satan. He could not hurt them, but they were confined in that prison house. But when Jesus paid the price at Calvary's cross, and that veil was rent in the temple, He went down into paradise and liberated every soul there.

Since the cross, when a believer dies, his soul and his spirit go instantly to heaven to be with the Lord Jesus Christ.

And, the moment a believing sinner comes to Christ, the Holy Spirit comes into his heart and into his life to abide forever. Jesus said, *"And I will pray the Father, and he shall give you another Comforter, that he may abide with you for ever; Even the Spirit of truth; whom the world cannot receive, because it seeth him not, neither knoweth him: but ye know him, for he dwelleth with you, and shall be in you"* (John 14:16-17).

By the believer maintaining his understanding that all victory is found in the cross—that's how the Holy Spirit works. That being the case, by understanding that our faith must be in Christ exclusively, and what Christ did for us at the cross and not move from that course—that's how we live for God.

And that's the only way one can live for God.

—————◇—————

They who know the Savior shall in Him be strong,
Mighty in the conflict of the right 'gainst the wrong;
This the blessed promise given in God's Word,
Doing wondrous exploits, they who know the Lord.

In the midst of battle be thou not dismayed,
Though the pow'rs of darkness 'gainst thee are arrayed;
God, thy Strength, is with thee, causing thee to stand,
Heaven's allied armies wait at thy command.

Brave to bear life's testing, strong the foe to meet,
Walking like a hero midst the furnace heat,
Doing wondrous exploits with the Spirit's sword,
Winning souls for Jesus, praise, oh, praise the Lord!

Victory! victory! Blessed, blood-bought victory!
Victory! victory! Vict'ry all the time!
As Jehovah liveth, strength divine He giveth,
Unto those who know Him—vict'ry all the time!

FOOLISH
CHRISTIANS

CHAPTER 6

THE CURSE OF
THE LAW

THE CURSE OF THE LAW

"CHRIST HATH REDEEMED US from the curse of the law, being made a curse for us: for it is written, Cursed is every one that hangeth on a tree" (Gal. 3:13).

The very reason for the incarnation—God becoming man—the very purpose was to redeem the fallen sons of Adam's lost race. Redemption would cover it all.

Wuest says there are three Greek words translated by the words *bought* or *redeemed*—*agorazo, exagorazo,* and *lutroo*[1]—and they explain redemption as possibly little else can.

AGORAZO

The first Greek word is *agorazo.* It means, Wuest says, "to buy in the slave market."[2] The idea is that every human being, due to Adam's fall, is actually a slave—a slave to sin with all of its implications. All unsaved people are slaves to sin. They are not actually able to chart their own course, even though they think they can. When Jesus died on Calvary's cross, and when we accept Him as Lord and Savior, He literally purchased us with His own precious blood out of the slave market

In other words, we are no longer slaves, except to the Lord Jesus Christ, and his yoke is easy, and his burden is light (Matt. 11:30). So, every single person who is truly born again is no longer a slave to sin, no longer a slave to Satan, no longer a slave in any capacity except to the Lord Jesus Christ. That is a privilege.

EXAGORAZO

The second Greek word, according to Wuest, is *exagorazo*, and it means "to buy a slave out of the market-place." Wuest goes on to say, "The bondslave of the Lord Jesus is bought not only to be His bondslave, but he is bought out of the slave market, never to be put up for sale in any slave market."[3]

Now think about that because it is phenomenal, to say the least. But it also raises this question: "Brother Swaggart, do you believe in eternal security?" Most definitely I do; however, it is *conditional* eternal security.

No, I do not believe in unconditional eternal security. However, that needs to be explained.

When a person is truly born again, the only way he can lose his soul is to quit believing. In other words, he no longer believes that Jesus Christ is the Son of God, and he no longer believes that Jesus gave Himself on the cross of Calvary, thereby purchasing our redemption. He no longer believes in the Word of God, etc. Such a person is eternally lost irrespective of once being saved.

Paul said:

> *For if we sin willfully* (the *'willful sin'* is the transference of faith from Christ and Him crucified to other things) *after that we have received the knowledge of the truth* (speaks of the Bible way of salvation and victory, which is *'Jesus Christ and Him crucified'* [I Cor. 2:2]), *there remains no more sacrifice for sins* (if the cross of Christ is rejected, there is no other sacrifice or way God will accept), *But a certain fearful looking for of judgment and fiery indignation* (refers to God's anger because of men rejecting Jesus Christ and the cross), *which shall devour the adversaries.* (It is hellfire, which will ultimately come to all who reject Christ and the cross). *He who despised Moses' law died without mercy under two or three witnesses* (there had to be these many witnesses to a capital crime before the death sentence could be carried out, according to the Old Testament law of Moses [Deut. 17:2-7]): *Of how much sorer punishment, suppose ye, shall he be thought worthy, who has trodden under foot the Son of God* (proclaims the reason for the *'sorer punishment'*), *and has counted the blood of the covenant, wherewith he was sanctified, an unholy thing* (refers to a person who has been saved, but is now expressing unbelief toward that which originally saved him), *and has done despite unto the Spirit of grace?* (When the cross is rejected, the Holy Spirit is insulted) (Heb. 10:26-29) (The Expositor's Study Bible).

The great apostle also said:

For it is impossible for those who were once enlightened (refers to those who have accepted the Light of the Gospel, which means accepting Christ and His great Sacrifice), *and have tasted of the heavenly gift* (pertains to Christ and what He did at the cross), *and were made partakers of the Holy Spirit* (which takes place when a person comes to Christ), *And have tasted the good Word of God* (is not language that is used of an impenitent sinner, as some claim; the unsaved have no relish whatsoever for the truth of God, and see no beauty in it), *and the powers of the worlds to come* (refers to the work of the Holy Spirit within hearts and lives, which the unsaved cannot have or know), *If they shall fall away* (should have been translated, *'and having fallen away'*) to renew them again unto repentance ('again' states they had once repented, but have now turned their backs on Christ)*: seeing they crucify to themselves the Son of God afresh* (means they no longer believe what Christ did at the cross, actually concluding Him to be an imposter; the only way any person can truly repent is to place his faith in Christ and the cross; if that is denied, there is no repentance), *and put Him to an open shame* (means to hold Christ up to public ridicule; Paul wrote this Epistle because some Christian Jews were going back into Judaism, or seriously contemplating doing so) (Heb. 6:4-6) (The Expositor's Study Bible).

These passages plainly tell us that a person can be eternally lost, and in fact will be eternally lost if he turns his back on

Christ and ceases to believe. Otherwise, nothing else can separate a person from the Lord Jesus Christ, not even sin.

To be sure, sin will cause all kinds of problems, but if sin separated a person from Christ, there would be no believers left. All would be lost. But they aren't lost due to the mercy and grace of God.

Do not misunderstand. Sin is not a plaything. It is the most destructive power on the face of the earth, and it cannot be engaged in without it causing severe problems for the believer.

LUTROO

The third Greek word is *lutroo.* According to Wuest, it means "ransom money used to liberate a slave."[4]

But the meaning goes even further: In eternity future, angels or demon spirits, or whomever or whatever, will never be able to say that the price paid for our redemption was insufficient.

The word *lutroo* guarantees that irrespective of how many people come to Christ, or how wicked and awful their sins were which were forgiven, it can never exhaust the precious shed blood of the Lamb of God and its effectiveness in cleansing the sinner from all sin. To be sure, the price was and is sufficient, and will ever be sufficient. In fact, if the whole world accepted Christ, what Jesus did on the cross by shedding His pure, spotless life's blood, guarantees the cleansing of all sin and for every sinner. To be sure, the price was far more than sufficient.

THE CURSE OF THE LAW

What was—and is—the curse of the law? It is to be eternally lost and burn in hell forever and forever without parole and without being set free. The soul of man is eternal, and the curse of the law is also eternal.

Every unsaved person in the world is under that curse. It can only be lifted by one accepting the Lord Jesus Christ.

While the unredeemed of the world don't know it (and they wouldn't believe it if you told them), they are under its curse and will answer to the broken law when they stand at the great white throne judgment. They may not know or believe that now, but it is the truth.

The only way this curse can be lifted is for a person to accept the Lord Jesus Christ as his Savior. There is no other relief, no other solution. The only solution is the shed blood of the Lamb.

When the believing sinner comes to Christ, judgment is lifted. He is no longer under the law but under the grace of God. Yet too many Christians insist upon functioning under law. And unless the believer—and we are speaking of the believer—places his faith exclusively in Christ and what Christ has done for him at the cross, he has placed himself under the curse of the law, which will bring judgment.

When Jesus was born of the virgin Mary, He lived a life of perfection, never failing one time in word, thought, or deed. He did it not as God, but as *the* Man, Christ Jesus. And you must understand, His perfect life was lived for you and me. It was not for Himself, for He did not need such. So whenever you accepted Christ, you accepted His perfection.

In other words, we are no longer lawbreakers, no longer living under the curse of the law; but we are now law keepers, not through what we have done, but through what He did and our simple faith in His atoning work.

He then went to the cross to atone for all the times that we have broken the law. We couldn't atone for that; it wasn't possible. But He could atone for such simply because He was perfect in every respect; He never failed even one single time. So when He offered up Himself as a sacrifice, it was accepted by God.

We must understand, what Jesus did on the cross was not to appease Satan, not in any way. God owed Satan nothing. In fact, God owes no one anything. Everything is owed to God. He is the one who had to be satisfied.

When Jesus gave Himself on the cross, He poured out His life's blood, giving Himself as a perfect sacrifice, which satisfied the demands of a thrice holy God. Then we were redeemed from the law. In other words, the law had no more claim on us. Think about that. How did it happen?

THE CROSS OF CHRIST

When Jesus died on that cross, in the mind of God, when we accepted Christ, we died with Him. It was not a physical thing, but rather spiritual. But in the mind of God, it was very real, and it should be real to us. We died with Him. In the sacrifices of old, we gave Him all of our sins and iniquities, and He, in turn, gave us His perfection. What a change! What a bargain!

To think of spending eternity, which never ends, in hell, which will be the case of all Christ rejecters—that is the curse of the broken law.

MADE A CURSE FOR US

Everything that Jesus did He did for us; He did it for sinners.

On the cross He took all of our failures, all of our sins, all of our iniquity, and He became one with that sin and iniquity, even though He never failed, not even one single time.

We have heard people say, "I should have been on the cross," but it would have done no good whatsoever had any of us been on the cross. We were sinful individuals and could, in no way, atone for our sins. The sacrifice that we would produce would be polluted, which means that God could not accept it.

Jesus gave His perfect body, His perfect life, His perfect way, and He died that we might be saved.

Due to the fact that He was the perfect sacrifice, Satan could not hold Him in the realm of death. If Jesus had failed to atone for even one single sin, He could not have been raised from the dead. The Scripture says, *"For the wages of sin is death"* (Rom. 6:23).

So the idea that Jesus died spiritually on the cross is very little short of blasphemy. He could not atone for sin by dying as a sinner, such would not be possible. He atoned for sin by giving Himself as a perfect sacrifice, without spot and without blemish. That's the only sacrifice that God could and would accept.

Man could not furnish such; it simply was not possible, for all men were polluted due to Adam's fall. But Jesus was not a product of Adam's fall. He was a product of heaven, of God, of perfection.

THE CROSS OF CHRIST

I don't believe that Satan fully understood the cross. At the very dawn of time, immediately after Adam's fall, the Lord told the Evil One:

> *And I will put enmity* (animosity) *between you and the woman* (presents the Lord now actually speaking to Satan, who had used the serpent. In effect the Lord is saying to Satan, '*You used the woman to bring down the human race, and I will use the woman as an instrument to bring the Redeemer into the world, who will save the human race*'), *and between your seed* (mankind which follows Satan) *and her seed* (the Lord Jesus Christ); *it* (Christ) *shall bruise your head* (the victory that Jesus won at the cross [Col. 2:14-15]) *and you shall bruise His heel* (the sufferings of the cross) (Gen. 3:15) (The Expositor's Study Bible).

When Jesus stood before Pilate, the religious leaders of Israel screamed for His crucifixion, which Satan had put in their heart to do.

Why did they demand His crucifixion? They knew what was said in Deuteronomy 21:22-23.

Their idea was that Jesus being crucified would say in the mind of the people, *"He was cursed by God."* In a sense, He was, but it was not for His sins, for He had committed no sin. It was for us. He took the curse upon Himself, which was death. That's as far as it went. He did not go down into the burning side of hell, as some claim. There is no record in the Bible of such.

Had the Jews known what the crucifixion meant, how that it would atone for all sin, they would never have demanded that He be crucified. So, I don't think Satan fully understood the cross. He may have had some inkling as to what it meant, but very little. If so, he would not have put it in the wicked hearts of these wicked religious leaders to demand the crucifixion of Jesus.

The truth is the cross did defeat Satan. It overcame the powers of darkness in every capacity.

Concerning the price that He paid the Scripture says:

Blotting out the handwriting of ordinances that was against us (pertains to the law of Moses, which was God's standard of righteousness that man could not reach), *which was contrary to us* (law is against us, simply because we are unable to keep its precepts, no matter how hard we try), *and took it out of the way* (refers to the penalty of the law being removed), *nailing it to His cross* (the law with its decrees was abolished in Christ's death, as if crucified with Him); *And having spoiled principalities and powers* (Satan and all of his henchmen were defeated at the cross by Christ atoning for all sin; sin was the legal right Satan had to hold man in captivity; with all sin atoned, he has no more legal right to hold anyone in bondage), *He* (Christ) *made a show of them openly* (what Jesus did at the cross was in the face of the whole universe), *triumphing over them in it"* (the triumph is complete, and it was all done for us, meaning we can walk in power and perpetual victory due to the cross) (Col. 2:13-15) (The Expositor's Study Bible).

He did all of that by making Himself a sacrifice.

CURSED IS EVERY ONE THAT HANGETH ON A TREE

The Expositor's Bible Commentary says, "If these principles are true and if they support the topic sentence of v.10 [all who rely on observing the law are under a curse] then the condition of humankind under law is obviously hopeless. If there is to be hope, it must come from a different direction entirely. Abruptly, therefore, Paul introduces the work of Christ, through which the curse of the law has been exhausted, and in whom all who believe find salvation."[5]

MODERN LAW

Let's look at this in a little different way. Paul dealt with (but not altogether) the law of Moses. It was that way simply because the Judaizers were attempting to force law (the law of Moses) onto the heads of the believers in the churches in Galatia.

Presently, we are not so much interested in the law of Moses, simply because most believers (but not all) understand that this was all fulfilled in Christ.

Please allow me to venture the following: anything in which we place our faith, and I mean anything other than Christ and the cross, constitutes law. It may not be law within itself, and probably isn't, but we turn it into law when we make it the object of our faith. I speak of fasting, prayer, belonging to a certain church, the giving of money, etc.

Virtually the entirety of modern Christendom is under law— law that they have devised themselves or formed by their own efforts and desires. Why do they do this?

It is done simply because they do not understand the cross of Christ and the part that it plays in the sanctification process— how we live for God on a daily basis. They don't know what this means. They have never really heard anything concerning the cross of Christ as being a part of their everyday living. Salvation, yes, but victory in life and living, no. Consequently, they place their faith—as we all have at one time or another—in things that are good within themselves, but we turn them into law, which God cannot bless. In fact, every one of these believers in some way has placed himself under a curse.

WHAT DOES IT MEAN
TO BE UNDER A CURSE?

It means that nothing goes right anymore. Everything seems to be out of kilter. We labor and toil and do our best to exercise faith, but no good comes from it. That's at least a part of the curse that is upon most modern believers.

However, when the believer places his or her faith exclusively in Christ and the cross and doesn't allow it to meander to other things, that believer is blessed. There is no way that sin can be addressed or handled and no way that victorious life and living can be handled unless one places his faith entirely in Christ and the cross, ever making that the object of his faith.

When that is done, the Holy Spirit, who works entirely within the framework of the cross of Christ, can work mightily within our lives and thereby give us victory (Rom. 8:2). I know what I'm talking about; I've been there.

The Holy Spirit doesn't demand much of us, but He does demand one thing—that our faith ever be in Christ and what He did for us at the cross. Whenever this is done, the Holy Spirit will go to work in our lives, and He will bring forth the victory that we desire.

THE BLESSING OF ABRAHAM

"That the blessing of Abraham might come on the Gentiles, through Jesus Christ; that we might receive the promise of the Spirit through faith" (Gal. 3:14).

The blessing of Abraham, in its short form is, simply put, justification by faith. But it actually includes the entire Abrahamic covenant. What is that?

First, the Abraham covenant incorporates justification by faith, and we must remember that this covenant is still in force today just as much as it was when it was given to Abraham by the Lord.

Regarding justification by faith, the Scripture says, *"And he believed in the LORD, and he counted it to him for righteousness"* (Gen. 15:6).

Without works, without circumcision, without anything except simple faith in Christ and what Christ did at the cross, Abraham believed in the Lord, and He counted it to him for righteousness.

Concerning these things, the Bible says, *"And the scripture, foreseeing that God would justify the heathen through faith, preached before the gospel unto Abraham"* (Gal. 3:8).

That gospel was the good news of the coming of Jesus Christ, who would give Himself on the cross and do for man what man could not do for himself. The Lord preached this to Abraham.

The Abrahamic covenant included a blessing upon all who would bless Abraham and any follower of the Lord: *"And I will bless them that bless thee, and curse them that curseth thee"* (Gen. 12:3).

The Abrahamic covenant also included all the families of the earth being blessed, which happened, and it is still happening. This ministry is just one among many, but our television programming goes out over a great part of the world, blessing all who will accept the gospel of Jesus Christ.

The Abrahamic covenant also included victorious living—victory over the world, the flesh, and the devil. The Lord said to Abraham, *"After these things the word of the LORD came unto*

Abram in a vision, saying, Fear not, Abram: I am thy shield, and thy exceeding great reward" (Gen. 15:1).

Here, Abraham is guaranteed victory in life and living.

When Abraham came back from Egypt where he had failed the Lord and failed miserably, the Scripture says: *"And Abram went up out of Egypt, he and his wife, and all that he had, and Lot with him, into the south."* He went, *"Unto the place of the altar, which he had made there at the first: and there Abram called on the name of the* LORD*"* (Gen. 13:1, 4).

Abraham's life was given over to the building of altars. The altar was a type of Christ and what He would do at Calvary's cross. Abraham was guaranteed victory in his life despite past failures, but it was all found in the altar—in the cross. As well, it includes the Holy Spirit, of which we will have more to say directly.

So we see that the blessing of Abraham covered quite a bit of territory, and that blessing is just as real today as it was when it was given by God to Abraham.

As well, that blessing included tithing. This is the first that we hear of tithing in the Old Testament, when Abraham paid tithe to Melchizedek. Melchizedek was a type of Christ. The Scripture says, *"And he gave him tithes of all"* (Gen. 14:20). If it was a part of the Abrahamic covenant then, it is a part now.

God could have financed His work in a thousand different ways, but He chose tithing. We give, and then He gives back to us, but what He gives to us is so much more than what little we give to Him. Any Christian who neglects to pay his tithe is neglecting himself, his family, and the work of God. In fact, such a person is robbing God, and that is something you don't want to do.

So, in this great covenant of Abraham, include all that the Lord has given us, which includes tithing. You'll be glad that you did.

MIGHT COME ON THE GENTILES THROUGH JESUS CHRIST

This great covenant comes on the Gentiles as well as on the Jews. Unfortunately, the Jews, when they crucified Christ, lost their way. But they are going to be brought back. This will take place at the second coming of the Lord. Then the evidence is that every single Jew on the face of the earth will accept Jesus Christ as Savior and as Lord. In the meantime, this blessing, which is the greatest thing on the face of the earth, has come upon millions and millions of Gentiles, and thank God it has.

Some time back, Frances and I, along with two others out of our office, traveled to the land of Israel, endeavoring to have our programming placed on their television network.

The Israelites had just built new headquarters right beside the Mediterranean Sea, and the meeting they had with us, if I remember correctly, was the first meeting they had in this new headquarters building.

Just a hundred or so yards down from this headquarters building was where Peter was spoken to by the Lord to go to the household of Cornelius, a Gentile, and proclaim the gospel to him and his family, which he did. I sat there thinking about this thing that happened two thousand years ago, when Peter was told by the Lord to take the gospel to the Gentiles. It was the first occasion of such. And here we were now, sitting in the office of the largest cable television network in Israel, asking them to take our programming that the gospel might be preached to the Jews. Thankfully, they did what we asked them to do. So now, twenty-four hours a day, seven days a week, the gospel is going out to the Jews in Israel as well as to the rest of the world, proclaiming the greatest story ever told to both Gentiles and Jews and fulfilling that which the Lord said to Abraham.

It is all through Jesus Christ and what He did at Calvary's cross in order that fallen man might be redeemed.

THE PROMISE OF THE
SPIRIT THROUGH FAITH

In Galatians 3:14, Paul is speaking of the Holy Spirit, who comes into the heart and life of every believing sinner at the moment of conversion. He is not speaking here of the baptism with the Holy Spirit with the evidence of speaking with other tongues, but rather the advent of the Spirit in the hearts and lives of all believers.

Before the cross, the Holy Spirit could not come into hearts and the lives, except for a few, and then, when their work was finished, He would leave out. Why?

It's because the blood of bulls and goats could not take away sins, so that meant sin was still in the heart and life of every single believer, even the great prophets, etc. This greatly hindered the Holy Spirit.

But when Jesus gave Himself on the cross of Calvary, that atoned for all sin—past, present, and future—at least for all who will believe.

Now, when a believing sinner comes to Christ, whether Jew or Gentile, the Holy Spirit immediately comes into the heart and life of such a person, and he becomes a new creation in Christ Jesus. Then that believer can and should go on to be baptized with the Holy Spirit, which will always be accompanied by speaking with other tongues.

When a person is saved—born again—he receives this by faith. What does that mean?

It simply means that the believing sinner *believes* that Jesus Christ is the Lord of glory, and that He gave Himself on the cross of Calvary so that the fallen sons of Adam's lost race can be saved.

At that moment—the moment of conversion—the Holy Spirit comes into that person's heart and life, and He comes to stay forever (John 14:16).

Standing on the promises of Christ my King,
Through eternal ages let His praises ring,
Glory in the highest, I will shout and sing,
Standing on the promises of God.

Standing on the promises that cannot fail,
When the howling storms of doubt and fear assail,
By the living Word of God I shall prevail,
Standing on the promises of God.

Standing on the promises I now can see
Perfect, present cleansing in the blood for me;
Standing in the liberty where Christ makes free,
Standing on the promises of God.

Standing on the promises of Christ the Lord,
Bound to Him eternally by love's strong cord,
Overcoming daily with the Spirit's sword,
Standing on the promises of God.

Standing on the promises I shall not fall,
List'ning every moment to the Spirit's call,
Resting in my Saviour as my All in all,
Standing on the promises of God.

FOOLISH
CHRISTIANS

CHAPTER 7

THE BLESSING OF
ABRAHAM

THE BLESSING OF ABRAHAM

"BRETHREN, I SPEAK AFTER the manner of men; Though it be but a man's covenant, yet if it be confirmed, no man disannulleth, or addeth thereto" (Gal. 3:15).

Paul uses, as an example, the covenant as given by men to buttress his position.

The idea is that most covenants are binding. He is saying, in essence, that if it is binding with men, then a covenant given by God is far more binding—actually irrevocable.

The new covenant is referred to by the Holy Spirit as *"the everlasting covenant"* (Heb. 13:20). This means that the new covenant will never have to be amended, phased out, nor changed in any way, simply because it is a perfect covenant.

THE LORD JESUS CHRIST

Jesus Christ actually is the new covenant. The cross of Christ is the meaning of that covenant, the meaning of which was given to the apostle Paul.

As we all know, a covenant is something between two or more people. Unfortunately, every covenant that God has made with mankind was hurriedly broken by man almost from its inception. So, if man is a party, then the covenant is basically invalid.

So how could this covenant be perfect, and I speak of the new covenant, considering that it is also between God and man?

Here is the way that the Holy Spirit brought it about: Jesus Christ is both man and God. He is very man and very God, meaning 100 percent man and 100 percent God (John 1:1-5).

So Jesus satisfies the demand that man be involved in the process because He is both God and man. While man may fail, Jesus Christ will never fail. The contract is irrevocable, eternal, everlasting, and without blemish.

NO MAN DISANNULLETH OR ADDETH THERETO

The old covenant between God and man was meant to be phased out. It was not meant to be eternal, but rather to serve its purpose, which it did, until the new covenant would come. The reason the old covenant was meant to be temporary is because it was based on animal blood, which was overly inefficient. In fact, all of the old covenant pointed to Christ in one way or another. When Christ came, He fulfilled the law in every respect.

The new covenant is not based on animal blood; it is based upon the precious shed blood of the Lord Jesus Christ. Consequently, it is sufficient in every capacity.

In fact, the new covenant can be summed up in one phrase, "Jesus Christ and Him crucified" (I Cor. 1:17-18, 21, 23; 2:2; Gal. 6:14).

Whereas covenants made by men are not meant to be changed, sadly and regrettably, the new covenant is under attack constantly in order that it be changed. The basic problem with the gospel is the leaven that is introduced—false teaching, divisive spirits, and men's ideas instead of those given by God. When men leave the cross, they have left the gospel. Unfortunately, the cross of Christ, which is the foundation of all biblical doctrine, is little preached anymore. And yet, the only answer for the salvation of man is the cross of Christ. That is the only way that justification by faith can be brought about. As well, the cross of Christ is the only means of sanctification, which gives the Holy Spirit latitude to work within our lives. But man has substituted other things of his own devising, which God can never accept.

SANCTIFICATION

Sanctification is a perfect example. How is it that one becomes sanctified? What is the sanctification process?

While preachers can give a definition of sanctification, most know nothing at all as to how to arrive at this place and position. The great question is, how can one be sanctified?

It's not really as difficult as it seems to be. The moment the believing sinner comes to Christ, at that moment, the believing sinner is born again and also sanctified. I mean the very moment that person is saved—at that moment—he or she is sanctified (I Cor. 6:11).

The way that one maintains this sanctification is for his faith to ever be in Christ and the cross and not allow it to be diverted elsewhere whatsoever. As he maintains his faith in Christ and the cross, the sanctification process continues.

It is the cross of Christ that gives the Holy Spirit latitude to work. In other words, it is the legal means of His work. The Scripture says, *"For the law of the Spirit of life in Christ Jesus hath made me free from the law of sin and death"* (Rom. 8:2).

When one preaches the cross and believes the cross, at that moment the Holy Spirit goes to work in one's life, bringing about the sanctification process, in other words, making us more and more Christlike.

It is impossible for the sinner to save himself. That can only be done as he comes to the Lord by faith. Likewise, it is impossible for the believer to sanctify himself. It cannot be done.

And yet the church has tried every fad one can think of to try to sanctify itself, all to no avail. It is the changing of the new covenant to something it was never intended to be. We can keep the new covenant, and we must keep the new covenant, and it can only be done one way—for our faith to be exclusively in Christ and Him crucified. If we try to live this life any other way, it concludes in spiritual adultery (Rom. 7:1-4), and that is the bane of the modern church—trying to sanctify itself, rewrite the Scriptures, impose its own doctrine, means, and ways. Let's get back to the cross. That's the answer and the only answer. That is the new covenant.

ABRAHAM

"Now to Abraham and his seed were the promises made. He saith not, And to seeds, as of many; but as of one, And to thy seed, which is Christ" (Gal. 3:16).

Everything in the Old Testament pointed to Christ. That includes the great words given to Abraham which we refer to as the Abrahamic covenant, and of course it refers to the entirety of the law. Everything about the Abrahamic covenant, everything about the law, in fact everything done in Old Testament times pointed to Christ and what He would do to salvage the lost souls of Adam's fallen race. That seed was (and is) Jesus Christ.

There is only one who could redeem the fallen race, and that one was (and is) the Lord Jesus Christ. So, whatever the promise was, whatever the covenant was, it all pointed to Christ as it all points to Christ now. He is the one who gave Himself on the cross of Calvary, which was done of necessity if man was to be saved. There is no other way that salvation can come than by the cross.

AND TO THY SEED, WHICH IS CHRIST

The very first prophecy given, which came after the fall of man concerned this seed.

The Lord said to Satan:

And I will put enmity (animosity) *between you and the woman* (presents the Lord now actually speaking to Satan, who had used the serpent; in effect the Lord is saying to Satan, 'You used the woman to bring down the human race, and I will use the woman as an instrument to bring the Redeemer into the world, Who will save the human race'), *and between your seed* (mankind which follows Satan) *and her seed* (the Lord Jesus Christ), *it* (Christ) *shall bruise your head* (the victory that Jesus won at the cross [Col. 2:14-15]), *and you shall bruise His heel* (the sufferings of the Cross) (Gen. 3:15) (The Expositor's Study Bible).

THE INCARNATION

The incarnation speaks of God becoming man. As a man, while Christ never lost the possession of His deity, He did, in fact, lay aside the *expression* of His deity.

I think the incarnation caught Satan by surprise. I don't think he figured that God would become man, but He did. And He did it for the express purpose of going to the cross. This was the only way that man could be redeemed. While God can do anything, still, the cross was the best way, even as horrible as it was.

The cross was not an incident, not an execution, and not an assassination—it was a sacrifice. In other words, God became man for the express purpose of going to the cross. This was the way that God chose that man may be redeemed. And for such redemption to come, all man has to do is simply accept Christ as his Savior. He has to believe that Jesus Christ is the Son of God and that He died to pay for our sins, which He did. That being done, believing in that, salvation instantly comes, which is justification by faith.

I've seen the lightning flashing,
I've heard the thunder roll,
I've felt sin's breakers dashing,
Which almost conquered my soul;
I've heard the voice of my Savior,
Bidding me still to fight on,
He promised never to leave me,
Never to leave me alone!

The world's fierce winds are blowing,
Temptation sharp and keen,
I have a peace in knowing
My Savior stands between—
He stands to shield me from danger
When my friends are all gone.
He promised never to leave me,
Never to leave me alone!

When in affliction's valley
I tread the road of care,
My Savior helps me carry
The cross so heavy to bear;
Though all around me is darkness,
Earthly joys all flown;
My Savior whispers His promise,
Never to leave me alone!

He died on Calvary's mountain,
For me they pierced His side.
For me He opened that fountain,
The crimson, cleansing tide.
For me He waiteth in glory,
Seated upon His throne,
He promised never to leave me,
Never to leave me alone!

FOOLISH

CHRISTIANS

CHAPTER 8

THE COVENANT

THE COVENANT

"AND THIS I SAY, that the covenant, that was confirmed before of God in Christ, the law, which was four hundred and thirty years after, cannot disannul, that it should make the promise of none effect" (Gal. 3:17).

Paul takes the Galatians back to the Abrahamic covenant to prove his point.

He shows that covenants are very important, even with men. As it regards the covenants made by the Lord, they are perfect in that they do what they are designed to do.

He portrays the fact to the Galatians that the Mosaic law, which of course was a covenant, was not meant to be eternal, but only temporary. In other words, when the one would come, who would be the Lord Jesus Christ, He would perfectly keep the law, and then the law would fade into oblivion—fade away. So Paul takes them back to the Abrahamic covenant, which was meant to be eternal.

Actually, the Abrahamic covenant, in a sense, was molded into the new covenant. Even though the Abrahamic covenant is eternal, it only hinted at what the new covenant in Christ would bring about.

CONFIRMED BEFORE OF GOD IN CHRIST

Wuest writes:

The statement of the length of time that elapsed between the giving of the covenant to Abraham and the giving of the law to Moses, implies that the law was something new and different which could not therefore be an element forming part of the promise. The longer the covenant was in force as the alone method upon which God operated in the saving of sinners, the more impressive is Paul's statement. God was saving men on the basis of faith without works since the time of Adam, or 2,500 years before the law was given. The law was in force from Moses to Christ, or for a period of 1500 years. At the Cross it was abrogated. The Judaizers not only attempted to retain the Mosaic institutions for the Jews, but tried to impose them upon the Gentiles, to whom that law was never given. This was what Paul was fighting.[1]

THE MESSIAH

The Abrahamic covenant related to the Messiah and promised that He would descend from Abraham.

According to Barnes, "The word 'in,' in the phrase 'in Christ,' does not quite express the meaning of the Greek .... That means rather 'unto Christ;' or unto the Messiah; i.e., the covenant had respect to him [the Lord Jesus]."[2]

THE LAW, WHICH WAS FOUR HUNDRED AND THIRTY YEARS AFTER

The phrase, *"the law, which was four hundred and thirty years after,"* as stated, was taken by Paul from Exodus 12:40.

The whole of the sojourn was from the seventy-fifth year of Abraham's life when he entered Canaan to this day of the Exodus (Ex. 12:41). The entire sojourning took place in Mesopotamia, Syria, Canaan, Philistia, and Egypt. The sojourn in Egypt was only two hundred and fifteen years—one half of the four hundred and thirty year period. Of course, we're speaking of the time of Joseph.

The four hundred years of Genesis 15:13 and that which Stephen said in Acts 7:6 are to be reckoned from the confirmation of Isaac as the seed when Ishmael was cast out (Gen. 21:12; Gal. 4:30). This was five years after the birth of Isaac.

The four hundred and thirty years, as stated, are reckoned from the departure of Abraham from Haran at the age of seventy-five, twenty-five years before Isaac was born, or thirty years before Isaac was confirmed and Ishmael cast out. There is no contradiction in the statements.

CANNOT DISANNUL

Regarding the phrase, "cannot disannul," Wuest said: "Paul's argument therefore is as follows. If a covenant once in force cannot be changed or rendered void by any subsequent action, God's covenant with Abraham cannot be changed or rendered void by the subsequent law. If this principle holds good in a human covenant, much more is it true when God makes the covenant, since God is more certainly true to His promise than man."[3]

The idea is that if the law was not intended to take the place of the Abrahamic covenant, which it didn't; consequently, the Law must have been given for some purpose entirely different from the promise. Barnes said this:

> It would still be binding, according to the original intention; and the law must have been given for some purpose entirely different from that of the promise. No one can doubt the soundness of this argument. The promise to Abraham was of the nature of a compact. But no law given by one of the parties to a treaty or compact can disannul it. Two nations make a treaty of peace, involving solemn promises, pledges, and obligations. No law made afterwards by one of the nations can disannul or change that treaty. Two men make a contract with solemn pledges and promises. No act of one of the parties can change that, or alter the conditions. So it was with the covenant between God and Abraham. God made to him solemn promises, which could not be affected by a future giving of a law. God would feel himself to be under the most solemn obligation to fulfil all the promises which he had made to him.[4]

These promises were fulfilled in Christ. Consequently, as long as Christ is alive, the Abrahamic covenant will remain in force.

ISRAEL'S PROBLEM

It was intended by God that the law was to be somewhat tagged onto the Abrahamic covenant for a period of time, which it was for some fifteen hundred years. It was then abrogated by Christ on the cross, with the Abrahamic covenant continuing.

Israel's salvation was always in the Abrahamic covenant and never in the law. However, Israel inverted the order, placing the law first, and tagging it with the Abrahamic covenant. By inverting the order, they destroyed the basis of their salvation, attempting to make the law the source, which it could never be.

Millions do the same now, attempting to make the church or particular religious ordinances—water baptism, speaking in tongues, the Lord's Supper, or other various works—with Christ attached onto these things and inverting the order, exactly as Israel of old. Jesus is first and foremost the salvation of mankind. All of these other things must follow Him and should, in no way, be added as a part of salvation, exactly as the law was never meant to be added to salvation.

THAT IT SHOULD MAKE THE
PROMISE OF NONE EFFECT

It is not possible to make the promise of none effect, which refers to evidencing faith in Christ and what Christ did for us at the cross, and maintain it accordingly. The promise is in faith, but it's faith in the cross of Christ. Everybody in the world has faith, but God recognizes the faith that is in Christ and the cross, and that exclusively.

The believer can live for God in one of two ways—law or grace, i.e., the cross. It's not really possible to live properly for God by means of law, but that is the way the majority of modern Christians try to live this life—by law.

Let's go back to the old covenant and look at what the Jews had to do while attempting to live for God.

They had to make certain they kept the Sabbath, not breaking it by going too far from their homes, etc. There were enumerable ways they could break it. The Pharisees had so reworked the law that, on the Sabbath day, it was improper for a woman to run a brush through her hair. There might be a speck of dust there, and the dust would be moved, and that action would be viewed as the task of plowing, which was against the law. A woman could not drag a chair across the floor because, again, a speck of dust might be moved in the process, and she would be guilty of plowing. Ridiculous, yes, but that's what it had come to. It was very hard and difficult.

There were all the feast days that had to be acknowledged. There was the sacrificial system and thank God for that because they would have been totally destroyed had it not been for the sacrificial system.

They even had sacrifices that had to be offered as it regarded priests who had sinned and did not know they had sinned. It was very difficult to live for God in those days. Had it not been for the

CHAPTER EIGHT **THE COVENANT** | **197**

sacrificial system, they would have been totally lost. The sacrificial system was a type of Christ and what He would do at the cross.

At the present time, it is a little easier under law, but not by much.

When we formulate laws of our own devising, to be sure, they are always difficult to keep. But somehow that appeals to our egos as in, "Look at what I have done." And, the harder it is, the greater we think it is. Law appeals to believers. And I'm not necessarily speaking of the law of Moses, although that certainly can be included, but rather laws that we devise ourselves, thinking that the doing of them, whatever they might be, brings victory. It doesn't.

THE CROSS

As it regards the cross, all the believer has to do is place his faith exclusively in Christ and what Christ did for him at the cross and maintain it accordingly, and then the Holy Spirit will work mightily on his behalf.

If the believer is trying to function by law, that ties the hands of the Holy Spirit, so to speak, and makes it difficult, if not impossible, for Him to do what He alone can do. The Holy Spirit is God and, as such, He can do anything. But He will never do things that will impugn His nature of pure holiness.

Whenever we place our faith in anything other than Christ and the cross, that impugns the Holy Spirit, and makes it very difficult, if not impossible, for Him to carry out His work within our hearts and lives.

The Lord has promised us many things in the new covenant, and that is victory over the world, the flesh, and the devil. But to have that we must do it God's way, which is Christ and the cross. In other words, the cross of Christ—and the cross of Christ alone—must ever be the object of our faith. Then the Holy Spirit will work mightily on our behalf and do what He alone can do.

THE INHERITANCE

"For if the inheritance be of the law, it is no more of promise: but God gave it to Abraham by promise" (Gal. 3:18).

Paul labels *"the inheritance,"* which is the Abrahamic covenant, as a promise. The law depended on performance, which man could not do.

That being the case, the Abrahamic covenant must be that on which man depended, which he trusted, because it was eternal. The Mosaic law was temporal, and it was meant to be that way. It had a lifespan which would take in so much time, and which meant it would be dissolved when Jesus came. The Mosaic covenant pointed to Christ in every aspect of life and living.

The feast days pointed to Christ. The Sabbath pointed to Christ. The sacrificial system, of course, pointed to Christ. Again, every single thing about the Mosaic covenant pointed to Christ. So, when Christ came, that covenant—the Mosaic covenant— was no more. That is what Paul is telling the Galatians, and what he is telling us.

MODERN LAW

When reading about law in the writings of Paul, most believers dismiss it because they automatically think, "I know the Mosaic law was fulfilled in Christ, therefore, it holds no attraction for me."

What they don't realize is that anything in which they place their faith other than Christ and the cross, they turn it into law, even though it may not be law within itself.

The truth is that virtually the entirety of the modern church—and I mean on a worldwide basis—is functioning under law. They may not know that; they may not understand that, but that is what is taking place. They have turned fasting into a law, the Lord's Supper into a law, the church into a law, etc.

Let us say it again, because it is so very, very important: anything in which we place our faith—anything that is the object of our faith other than Christ and the cross—is automatically law in the sight of God. This means the Holy Spirit, who works entirely within the framework of the finished work of Christ, will not help us because if He did do so, He would be sinning against His nature, and the Holy Spirit cannot sin. So most modern believers are trying to live this life without the help of the Holy Spirit, which He wants to give, and in fact can give. It is because their faith is in something else other than Christ and the cross.

Every promise is found in the cross of Christ, and when we place our faith in anything else, we *"make the promise of none effect*" (Gal. 3:17). That means the help that God alone can give us is lacking, simply because our faith is in the wrong object.

You must remember, it is all in faith, but it is faith in the correct object. That correct object is Christ and the cross.

THE PROMISE

There is a vast difference between promise and law. Law depended on man knowing and keeping its precepts, which was impossible. The promise depended on God standing behind His promise, which means it cannot fail.

So, the inheritance did not come by law, because it could not come by law. Such was impossible. It came by promise—the promise of God. That is the reason that the Abrahamic covenant is unbreakable, because it is by promise. And it is the promise of God. Such a promise will be carried out to its full power. We are saved today because of that promise. Our names are written down in the Lamb's Book of Life because of that promise. If God gives a promise, it cannot be abrogated.

The inheritance is guaranteed if our faith is in Christ and the cross. Otherwise, we fail. I don't want to fail, and neither do you, so to insure against failure, to guarantee the inheritance, our faith must always be in Christ and what He did for us at the cross.

GAVE

In Galatians 3:18 and the phrase, *"but God gave it to Abraham by promise,"* the verb *gave* is in a perfect tense, which means that

God gave the promise about Christ as a permanent promise, which cannot be superseded.

Wuest said:

> The word gave is from charizomai ... This is a specialized word. It denotes not merely a gift, but a gift which is given out of the spontaneous generosity of the giver's heart, with no strings tied to it. The Greek word grace (charis) ... has the same root and the same meaning. Thus the word refers, not to an undertaking based upon terms of mutual agreement, but upon the free act of one who gives something, expecting no pay for it. This at once shows the difference between law and grace. If salvation were by obedience to the law, that would mean that it would be based upon a mutual agreement between God and the sinner whereby God would obligate Himself to give salvation to any sinner who would earn it by obedience to the law. But the very genius of the word charizomai [gave] ... militates against the teaching of the Judaizers, namely, that salvation is by works ... Furthermore, the verb gave is in the perfect tense here, which tense speaks of a past completed act having present results.[5]

THE LAW

"Wherefore then serveth the law? It was added because of transgressions, till the seed should come to whom the promise was made; and it was ordained by angels in the hand of a mediator" (Gal. 3:19).

In essence, Paul was asking, "What good is the law?"

Of the many reasons the law was given, it was basically given *"because of transgressions,"* meaning that the law defines sin.

Before the law was given, even though sin was committed and committed constantly, still there was no definition for it. The Lord put a face on sin by the law. He told us what stealing was, what lying was, what adultery was, what idolatry was, what covetousness was, etc.

The law was also given to show man God's standard of righteousness. Also, it was given to show man how inadequate, how weak, and how ineffectual he was.

In other words, because of the fall in the garden of Eden long ago, man was so weakened that he could not keep the law. Simple commandments such as *"Thou shalt not steal,"* were beyond the pale of obedience.

When Jesus came, He lived for thirty-three and a half years before going back to glory, and He never sinned one single time—not in word, thought, or deed. He did it as our representative man. In other words, He did it for us.

So, when a person comes to Christ, when he gives the Lord his heart, he is transferred from a position of lawbreaker, which demands death, to the position of law keeper. We should thank God for that every single day because without the cross, we would spend eternity—forever and forever—in eternal hell. The reason? Because man was and is a perpetual lawbreaker. But simple acceptance of Christ, the inheritance one might say, puts man in a totally different position—the position of law keeper instead of lawbreaker.

Yet there remained the law that had been broken, and it had to be satisfied.

So when Jesus went to the cross, He did so to satisfy the demands of the broken law, of which every person was guilty. When He died on the cross and shed His life's blood, our acceptance of Him gives us eternal life and freedom from the penalty of the broken law.

Most Christians don't realize that, but when they gave their hearts to Christ, it involved the greatest work in the annals of human or heavenly history. The salvation of the soul can only be accomplished by faith in Christ and what He did for us at the cross, or else the penalty has to be paid, which is to be eternally lost.

WHY THE LAW IN THE FIRST PLACE?

Paul's question, *"Wherefore then serveth the law?"* reveals the true purpose of the law. It was to make men conscious of the evil that dwelt in their nature. It was necessary that this consciousness should be awakened.

The law not only manifested the presence of evil in human nature, but it also revealed its power; it urged man, immediately, to disobey God's revealed will. The law was therefore introduced between the promise and its fulfillment so that man's true moral condition might be manifested. But its glory was beneath that and subsequent to that of the promise, for it (the law) was ordained by angels in the hand of a human mediator, namely Moses.

THE GLORY OF THE LAW

Barnes said:

Why were there so many wonderful exhibitions of the Divine power at its promulgation? Why were there so many commendations of it in the Scriptures? And why were there so many injunctions to obey it? Are all these to be regarded as nothing, and is the law to be esteemed as worthless? To all this the apostle replies that the law was not useless, but that it was given by God for great and important purposes, and especially for purposes closely connected with the fulfillment of the promise made to Abraham and the work of the Mediator.[6]

Pulpit Commentary says Paul "wishes now show that, while the Law was a Divine ordinance, it was yet not intended to supersede the previously ratified covenant, but rather to prepare for its being completely carried out."[7] And we speak of the Abrahamic covenant.

TRANSGRESSIONS

Regarding the phrase in Galatians 3:19, "because of transgressions," Barnes said:

The meaning is, that the law was given to show the true nature of transgressions, or to show what was sin. It was not to reveal a way of justification, but it was to disclose the true nature of sin; to deter men from committing it; to declare its penalty; to convince men of it, and thus to be "ancillary" to, and preparatory to the work of redemption through the Redeemer. This is the true account of the law of God as given to apostate man, and this use of the law still exists. This effect of the law is accomplished (1) by showing us what God requires and what is duty. It is the straight rule of what is right; and to depart from that is the measure of wrong. (2) It shows us the nature and extent of transgression by showing us how far we have departed from it. (3) It shows what is the just penalty of transgression, and is thus fitted to reveal its true nature. (4) It is fitted to produce conviction for sin, and thus shows how evil and bitter a thing transgression is. (5) It thus shows its own inability to justify and save men, and is a preparatory arrangement to lead men to the cross of the Redeemer. At the same time, (6) the law was given with reference to transgressions, in order to keep men from transgression. It was designed to restrain and control them by its denunciations, and by the fear of its threatened penalties,[8] [but gave no power for man to do so].

THE SEED

In Galatians 3:19, the phrase, *"till the seed should come to whom the promise was made,"* refers to Christ. The promise is said to have been made to Him in whom it is fulfilled, just as Christians are said to "receive the promise," i.e., the fulfillment of the promise "of the Spirit."

Wuest said:

[The law] was brought in alongside until the seed should come to whom the promise was made. Grace flowed full and free from Adam's time to Abraham's, and from Abraham's time to Moses', and from Moses' time to Paul's. And it flows full and free from Paul's time through the present and will be in force as the only way in which God saves a sinner, until the Great White Throne. The law was merely in force from Moses' time to Christ's death on the Cross, and even while it was in force, God saved sinners by pure grace. The covenant of promise is therefore of permanent validity, beginning before and continuing through the period of the law, and afterwards. The law was a temporary provision brought in alongside of grace to show sinners their need of grace, from Moses' time to the Cross. The law was ordained by angels, Paul says. The New Testament refers three times to the interposition of angels in the giving of the law. In Acts 7:53 the fact is mentioned in order to enhance the authority of the law. In Hebrews 2:2 it is contrasted with God's revelation in His Son. Here it is contrasted with God's familiar intercourse with Abraham in which He spoke to Abraham, calling him His friend. At Sinai the law was given through two intermediaries, angels and Moses. The people stood afar off. Grace says, 'Come nigh,' law says, 'Stand off.' The object of showing how the law was given was to indicate the inferior and subordinate position of the law in comparison to the superior position held by grace. The promise was given direct to Abraham, the law through two intermediaries, angels and Moses. Paul shows that the law does not, as the Judaizers claim, have as direct and positive a relation to the divine plan of salvation as does the promise. He also shows that it is only of transitory significance whereas the promise has an eternal value and meaning.[9]

THE LAW OF MOSES AND MODERN CHRISTIANS

Is the Christian under law? This was a burning question in Paul's day and, although the Bible is crystal clear in the answer that was given under inspiration by the Holy Spirit—the believer is not under law but under grace—yet the proud heart of man will not accept God's grace. He would rather try to save himself by his own goodness and works.

That's how it affects the world, which attempts to affect its own righteousness by its own works, which God will not accept, and even how the believer attempts to maintain his place and position in Christ by works instead of by faith.

And that's exactly what Satan wants man to do. Satan, the enemy of our souls, wants us to be religious and morally good. He urges men to strive to improve themselves, to try and obey the law, to work and toil, and be earnest, sincere, and religious in all efforts at keeping the commandments, the Sabbath days, and to make themselves worthy of God's favor—all this instead of accepting His grace.

Paul says this is another gospel and a clever trick of the enemy of our souls to keep us from coming to the Christ of grace as poor, helpless, hopeless sinners. The law, says Paul, was given not to save, but to show the awfulness of sin, and our need of salvation.

GRACE

Paul says that the law was not given until four hundred and thirty years after God made His covenant of grace with Abraham, for that's what it was. When Abraham lived, there was no written law, for Abraham was under pure grace.

There can be no mistaking the words: The law was not given until four hundred and thirty years after God made His covenant promise to Abraham.

The covenant of grace with Abraham was unconditional and then, four hundred and thirty years later, God added the law.

Abraham was under grace, Isaac was under grace, Jacob was under grace, the children of Israel were under grace while they were slaves in Egypt. They were delivered from Egypt by grace. They crossed the Red Sea by grace, and then, when they reached Mount Sinai, God added the law.

The law did not supplant grace. It did not take the place of grace. It did not annul the promises of grace. It was added as a schoolmaster or a guardian until grace would fully come, which it did under Christ (Gal. 3:24). The law was never meant to save. God gave it no power to save, simply because the blood of bulls and goats was insufficient to cleanse from sins (Heb. 10:4). Only the blood of Jesus Christ could cleanse from sin.

Israel placed the law in front of the great Abrahamic covenant when they should have done the very opposite. They should have made the great Abrahamic covenant first in all things, with the law added. But they didn't do that. Instead, they put the law first, which guaranteed their defeat.

MISUNDERSTANDING

If there is a misunderstanding in this capacity, please believe me, it is with most works. No matter how grand they may be, not only will they not help the situation, but they can also make it worse. This is where most believers find themselves—they try so hard, but the situation, whatever it might be, does not improve; it can actually grow worse.

Simply put, the reason for failure regarding the Christian is because of the lack of help by the Holy Spirit. This confuses believers because they know that the Holy Spirit is present with them and even doing great and wonderful things in other areas of their lives.

However, the Holy Spirit will only help us overcome the attacks of Satan through and according to the sacrifice of Calvary and our faith in that sacrifice. He will not increase our willpower. He will not give us His strength respecting all the efforts we make simply because He does not work in that capacity.

He desires for us to know and understand that Jesus not only paid the sin debt at Calvary, but He also broke the grip of sin, which pertains to our everyday walk with God. The way He works is beautiful, simple, and available to every believer, but it does demand an everyday faith. We must take up the cross daily, even as Jesus said, and believe and trust that what the Lord did at Calvary not only sufficed for our salvation, but also makes it possible for us to walk victoriously before Him, despite anything and everything that Satan may attempt to do (Luke 9:23).

THE CROSS ALONE IS THE ANSWER

Again, allow me to emphasize that most Christians would wholeheartedly agree with this subheading: the cross alone is the answer. But the question must be asked, *how* is the cross the answer?

It is the answer because it was there that Jesus not only paid the penalty for our sin, but also broke the grip of sin in our lives that we might live victorious over sin in our daily walk with God. No, the Bible does not teach sinless perfection, but it does teach that sin is not to have dominion over us (Rom. 6:14).

The cross not only pertains to our salvation experience, but also to our sanctification experience—how we live for God on a daily basis.

Believers must first understand that everything we receive from God, and I mean everything, was all made possible by the cross of Christ. When I speak of the cross, I am not speaking of the wooden beam on which Jesus died, but what He there accomplished.

The Holy Spirit works exclusively by and through the cross of Christ. It is the cross that gave (and gives) the Holy Spirit the legal means to do all that He does (Rom. 8:2). So our faith must be exclusively in Christ and the cross. Then the Holy Spirit, who works exclusively by and through the cross of Christ, will go to work on our behalf and do for us what only He can do. This is the key, and the only key, to more abundant life

It would do all believers a world of good if, every morning when they arise, they would state: "Lord my faith is in You and what You did for me at the cross. My faith is not in me or in any other person. My faith is not in the church, its rituals, or its ceremonies, but my faith is exclusively in You and Your finished work of Calvary."

Do you believe what I have just stated? If you do, then you are on your way to victory, and I mean victory in every respect.

WRONG DIRECTIONS

The trouble with most Christians is that they try to use, materially speaking, a handsaw for a hammer. It won't work.

Prayer, for instance, is the greatest thing that a believer can do after the cross of Christ and his faith in that capacity. But a believer cannot pray himself to victory. Now think about what I've just said because many Christians think they can. You can't!

Prayer is very important, and no Christian is going to be able to walk with the Lord as he should without a prayer life because a prayer life is absolutely essential. Still, he cannot pray himself to victory, and I'm speaking of victory over the world, the flesh, and the devil. It will help, but it cannot be done.

If a believer could pray himself to victory, fast his way to victory, or do anything else that one could name and get victory, then Jesus would not have had to come down here and die on a cross.

But He did have to come because none of those things work as it regards sin. It is the cross and the cross alone that gives one victory over sin. We must make the cross the object of our faith at all times, and that means understanding that every single thing we receive from God, and I mean everything, is by and through the cross of Christ.

THE PSYCHOLOGICAL WAY

Virtually the entirety of the church world, and I speak of denominations, have, unfortunately, opted for the psychological way. To be sure, that particular way will ultimately destroy any denomination that embraces it. And this is where most Christians presently are. They believe what their denomination tells them, and their denomination has rejected the cross and proclaimed the psychological way as the answer to man's dilemma.

Once again, if the psychological way was the answer, then Jesus did not have to come down here and die on a cross. But the very fact that He did come down here and die on a cross tells me that the psychological way is no way of victory at all.

Again, the only solution to the sin problem—and sin is the problem—is the cross of Christ.

We must make the cross of Christ the object of our faith on a continual, never-ending basis. That being done, the Holy Spirit will work mightily within our hearts and within our lives and making us what we ought to be. That is God's way, and it is the only way.

Paul said, *"But God forbid that I should glory, save in the cross of our Lord Jesus Christ, by whom the world is crucified unto me, and I unto the world"* (Gal. 6:14).

My heart was distressed 'neath Jehovah's dread frown,
And low in the pit where my sins dragged me down;
I cried to the Lord from the deep miry clay,
Who tenderly brought me out to the golden day.

He placed me upon the strong Rock by His side,
My steps were established and here I'll abide;
No danger of falling while here I remain,
But stand by His grace until the crown I gain.

He gave me a song, 'twas a new song of praise;
By day and by night it's sweet notes I will raise;
My heart's overflowing, I'm happy and free;
I'll praise my Redeemer, Who has rescued me.

I'll sing of His wonderful mercy to me,
I'll praise Him till all men His goodness shall see;
I'll sing of salvation at home and abroad,
Till many shall hear the truth and trust God.

I'll tell of the pit, with its gloom and despair,
I'll praise the dear Father Who answered my prayer;
I'll sing my new song, the glad story of love,
Then join in the chorus with the saints above.

FOOLISH

CHRISTIANS

CHAPTER 9

THE MEDIATOR

THE MEDIATOR

"NOW A MEDIATOR IS not a mediator of one, but God is one" (Gal. 3:20).

This verse is probably the most obscure verse in Galatians, if not the entire New Testament. Bible scholar Joseph Barber Lightfoot said, "The number of interpretations of this passage is said to mount up to 250 or 300."[1]

The difficulty lies in the abrupt character of the verse, and the necessity to relate to Paul's context whatever interpretation may be given of it.

The meaning is that Paul is introducing a general principle in support of the point made at the end of Galatians 3:19: *"Wherefore then serveth the law? It was added because of transgressions, till the seed should come to whom the promise was made; and it was ordained by angels in the hand of a mediator."* Mediators always act between parties. Hence, since Moses was a mediator of the law, it follows that he acted between God and the people, and that the law thereby came to man indirectly.

The last phrase in Galatians 3:20, *"but God is one,"* as we shall study, suggests that in giving the promise to Abraham (Gal. 3:15-18) God acted directly and unilaterally (one-sided, meaning it was God alone).

ONE

The phrase, *"Now a mediator is not a mediator of one,"* means that a mediator is the middle person mediating between two other persons (or more), who are at enmity with each other.
Wuest said:

> In this verse Paul shows that the promise is superior to the law, for the former was given directly from God to Abraham, whereas the latter was given to Israel by God through a mediator. We will examine the statement, 'A mediator is not of one....' Thus a mediator is one who intervenes between two, either to make or restore peace and friendship, to form a compact, or ratify a covenant. The word in the Greek text is preceded by the definite article, making the word generic in character. That is, Paul is not referring here to any particular mediator as Moses, but to the office of a mediator, and to mediators in general looked upon as a class of individuals. However, this generic statement is intended to be applied to Moses, the mediator referred to in verse 19.... That is, a mediator does not act simply in behalf of one person. The very genius of the word implies that the mediator stands 'in the midst' of two or more persons, thus acts as a go-between.[2]

A PARTICULAR MEANING

Wuest continues:

God gives the law through a mediator Moses, and man is obligated to obey it. God will bless man if he obeys and will punish man if he disobeys. But the promise of free grace is not in the nature of a contract between two parties. God acts alone and directly when He promises salvation to anyone who will receive it by the out-stretched hand of faith. There are no good works to be done by the sinner in order that he might merit that salvation. Grace is unconditional. There are no strings tied to it. God is One, that is, He acts alone without a mediator in respect to the promise of grace. Therefore, grace is superior to law. In the case of the former, God spoke directly to Abraham. In the case of the latter, He spoke to Israel through a mediator, Moses. The dignity of the law is thus seen to be inferior to that of the promise.[3]

A CONTRACT

The mention of the word *mediator* implies a contract to where there are at least two parties. Where there is a contract there must also be conditions. And if these conditions are not observed, then the whole thing falls to the ground. Such was the law.

The law was not kept, and therefore the blessings annexed to it were forfeited.

GOD IS ONE

In Galatians 3:20, the phrase, *"but God is one,"* explains this verse which seems confusing to most people.

What did Paul mean by the statement, *"but God is one"*?

The law of Moses required obedience on the part of the people if, that is, their part of the contract was upheld. If they did not keep their part, then the blessings would be forfeited, which they were, and of necessity. That is the nature of law. Moses stood as a go-between and, in a sense, represented God to the people, and represented the people to God. Sadly, the people failed in their part of the contract, and Moses failed as well, which was a given. Despite what man thought—even the best, such as Moses—man could not keep the law. But in the covenant of grace, everything is totally different.

HOW IS IT DIFFERENT?

There is a mediator in the covenant of grace exactly as there was in the covenant of law. However, whereas Moses was the mediator in that covenant, which was guaranteed of failure, Jesus is the mediator in the new covenant, which is guaranteed of victory (I Tim. 2:5).

How is it guaranteed?

As Paul said, *"God is one,"* but the manner in which this great covenant of grace was carried out, and thereby guaranteed, is that Jesus is both God and man, therefore the covenant cannot fail.

A covenant requires at least two persons. In this case, as it has always been with God, God is one, and the human race, made up of many, even billions, is the other. So, if the covenant was going to be guaranteed, it could not depend upon man, because the law proved that to be insufficient. Man simply could not live up to the covenant, irrespective as to whether it was law or grace.

So God became man—*the* Man, Christ Jesus. As man, He represents mankind, and as God, He represents deity. Consequently, He is "one," yet able to represent both, because, in reality, He is both—very man, and very God. In other words, Jesus is totally and fully man, and He is totally and fully God.

That's the reason this covenant of grace cannot fail. It is a promise (the promise of God to provide a covenant that would not fail) and not a performance.

Yet, in a manner of speaking, it is a performance, but rather the performance of Jesus Christ and not man. He performed as a man what man could not himself perform.

THE LAST SUPPER

This new covenant was made at the Last Supper (Luke 22:19-20) and was ratified (carried out) at Calvary where Jesus shed His blood, which the covenant demanded (Luke 23:44-46; John 19:30).

The words Christ uttered on the cross, *"It is finished,"* proclaim the carrying out of the covenant, and that it was now ratified.

THE PROMISES OF GOD

"Is the law then against the promises of God? God forbid: for if there had been a law given which could have given life, verily righteousness should have been by the law" (Gal. 3:21).

The Expositor's Bible Commentary said:

> The second apparent conclusion the legalizers might take from Paul's doctrine of justification is that the law becomes evil because it opposes grace as the true means of salvation. But this does not follow, Paul replies. It is an abhorrent idea, for it suggests a conflict within the nature of God, who gave both the law and the promise. True, the law increases transgressions (Ro 5:20) and it can even kill (Ro 7:7-11). Still, the law is not bad; it is good—so good that if a person could do what the law requires, that person would find life (Lev 18:5; cf. Gal 3:12).[4]

Again, if a man could do what the law requires, that would mean he is not a sinner and, in fact, has never been a sinner, i.e., "was born without sin." But of course, we know that is impossible.

THE LAW AND THE PROMISES OF GOD

Regarding Galatians 3:21, Wuest said:

> The apostle then asks the question, 'Is the law then against the promises of God?' The answer is that the law and the

promises are not in conflict because each has a distinct function. The law is a ministry of condemnation. The promises are a ministry of salvation. The law judges a person on the basis of obedience or disobedience. The promises judge man on a basis of faith. The law, whose ministry is one of condemnation, was not intended to express God's attitude towards man. God's attitude towards man is one of grace. The law is not the basis of God's judgment of man.[5]

THE REASON THAT MEN ARE ETERNALLY LOST

The law is not the basis of God's judgment of man. In fact, man cannot help the way he is or, one might say, the way he is born. He is born in original sin due to Adam's fall, which, in truth, is no fault of his own. Nevertheless, he is fallen with all of its attendant difficulties due to that first transgression.

Considering such a scenario, some may argue that God is not fair in condemning men to hell for all eternity. To stretch that thought to its limits, one might be right if that were as far as the situation went; however, that is not as far as it goes, considering what God has done in order to redeem man from this terrible predicament in which he finds himself.

Wuest goes on to say:

A sinner who rejects Christ, goes to the Lake of Fire for all eternity, not because he has broken God's laws, for his sin is paid for. He goes to a lost eternity, because he rejects God's grace in the Lord Jesus. The law is a revelation of the sinner's legal standing, and as such condemns him. It cannot therefore justify him, as the Judaizers claim. Law and grace are not in conflict, since they operate in different spheres. For instance, here is a father who has discovered that his son has disobeyed his commands. He calls the son's attention to the law which he broke, and pronounces him guilty. He uses this very sentence of guilty to bring the boy to see his misdemeanor in its true light. The son becomes repentant, and the father assures him of his forgiveness. The father is not in conflict with himself when using law to bring his son to a realization of the true nature of his disobedience, in order that he might repent and thus put himself in a position where the father can forgive him. God is not in conflict with Himself when He gives the law that man might come to see his sin as a transgression or violation of His holy will, which is the first step in his act of repentance and faith, and which latter is answered by God with the gift of eternal life.[6]

Again, sin is not a mere infraction of some type of rule or regulation, but rather a direct affront, even a declaration of war, so to speak, against God's holy Word. In other words, whether the individual understands such or not, all sin is a declaration of destruction against all that which is right, noble, holy, and true.

THE LAW AS DESIGNED

Regarding the law and the promises made to Abraham, Barnes said:

> Is the Law of Moses to be regarded as opposed to the
> promises made to Abraham? ... The object of the apostle
> in asking this question is, evidently, to take an opportu-
> nity to deny in the most positive manner that there can
> be any such clashing or contradiction. He shows, there-
> fore, what was the design of the Law, and declares that the
> object was to further the plan contemplated in the promise
> made to Abraham. It was as good as a law could be; and it
> was designed to prepare the way for the fulfillment of the
> promise made to Abraham.[7]

The truth is, the law, as designed, functioned to show man
how sinful he actually was—how helpless he was in the face of
that sin—correspondent to his need for redemption, and that
such redemption is found only in Christ.

The law was designed to bring men into the actual knowledge of themselves, which is not a pretty picture (Rom. 3). That
is the simple reasoning of the law and the promises; however,
man, in his depraved condition, automatically seeks to twist
and pervert everything that God says or does.

This only shows how lost man actually is and that his
problem is not a slight maladjustment as humanistic psychol-
ogy claims.

To be blunt, if God allowed everyone into heaven, irrespective of their spiritual condition, in a short time, heaven would
be a hell.

Therefore, God requires that man be born again, in essence
becoming a new creation in Christ Jesus.

GOD FORBID!

In Galatians 3:21, Paul's answer of *"God forbid"* presents the Apostle's customary response to "any thought of inconsistency in God's dispensations towards mankind is indignantly repelled by St Paul in the use of the formula customary with him in such cases [Rom. 9:14; I Cor. 6:15; Gal. 2:17; 6:14]."[8]

"God forbid," is a strong term. The apostle strongly resents the idea that the law is hostile to the promise.

Even though it could not supply the moral energy that men needed, which means it could not quicken toward the new higher life and, therefore, could not save anyone, still that was not its purpose to begin with.

In a sense, Paul is saying in Galatians 3:20 that it is the one God who gave both—the law and the promise—and that He did not give the one in order to destroy the other, but that He might through the law include all men under sin, and thus clear the way for bestowing upon us the promise of the Spirit on the principle of faith in Jesus Christ.

RIGHTEOUSNESS

In Galatians 3:21, the phrase, *"for if there had been a law given which could have given life, verily righteousness should have been by the law,"* means that the very nature of law militates against life and righteousness.

If men would treat instructions given in the Word of God as they treat all other instructions, then these things would be obvious. Forgetting the law of God for a moment and turning to the everyday laws made by men, we find the same order in which Paul stipulates here.

For example, a law stipulating a highway speed limit can only condemn. In no way does the law against speeding give one power not to speed; it only states what the law and penalties of speeding actually are. If a person exceeds the speed limit and is given a ticket, it's not the law nor the giver of this law—ultimately Congress—who pays the fine for him. The person who broke that law has to pay the fine himself.

The law of God is the same way. It only proclaims what the law actually is in any given situation regarding morals and the penalty thereof, which all laws have whether made by God or men.

The very nature of law in no way has a moral effect on anyone except in the region of restraint. In other words, fear. It does not give any power toward obedience, only to state the boundaries.

JUSTIFICATION

Considering what we have said, how in the world does man think that he can be justified by the law? If law could justify anyone, which of course it cannot, then the law of God, which was perfect, surely could have done so.

So, as Paul makes the point, if the law of God could not justify anyone, how in the world do we think that the puny, pitiful laws we make up on our own can bring about justification?

This is what the Galatians were attempting to do as a result of listening to these legalizers.

In other words, while they had truly been saved by grace— the only manner in which one can be saved—they were now attempting to maintain their victory over sin by law.

How were they doing that? They were attempting to do such in the same manner that all of us have tried to do in one way or another.

When a Christian sins, he has one of two choices as it regards victory over that sin:

1. He can run to Jesus with the understanding that Christ paid the price totally for his salvation and victory over sin at Calvary, place his trust in that, and claim its benefits. Then the Holy Spirit will step in with His power, which He will guarantee victory in the heart and life of that individual (Rom. 6:1-2, 6, 11; 8:1-2)

2. He can resort to law. What do we mean by that? The Galatians were trying to bring about victory over sin (after they were saved) by keeping the law of Moses. While the modern believer does not really attempt to do that, still, when he makes up laws of his own, irrespective as to how religious they might be, he is doing the same thing as the Galatians of old.

To cut to the kernel of the matter, if Christians do anything to overcome sin (irrespective of what it is or how religious it may seem) other than take their problems to the cross, which alone is the answer, then they will continue to fail, with the matter getting worse instead of better, no matter how strong their efforts.

CONDEMNATION?

That's the reason we do wrong when we condemn those who are trying very, very hard not to fail. I have heard preachers and other believers say, "They did that because they wanted to do it," referring to some type of sin. While that may be true in some cases, it is certainly not true in all or even most cases, I suspect.

The fact is, no believer wants to sin. Every believer is a new creation in Christ Jesus (II Cor. 5:17). The divine nature in that person militates against all sin (I John 3:9).

As well, the very moment the believer sins, he is instantly convicted by the Holy Spirit, which is one of the chief functions of the Holy Spirit (John 16:8-9). Conviction is a place in which no true believer can long remain, having to quickly settle the issue with the Lord (I John 1:9), which is the intended result of the Holy Spirit, at least as He works in that particular capacity. The idea that a believer desires to sin is error.

SO WHY DOES A BELIEVER SIN?

Of course, the reasons are many and varied. Some few Christians may be so deceived in some particular area that they might want to do something which is wrong. But most, I think, do not fall into that category.

Most believers sin, which means to fail God in some manner, simply because they are not properly trusting Christ, even though they may think they are. They are not depending on what Christ did at the cross, but rather in their own willpower or regimen of law of some nature.

Desiring to do no wrong, as righteous or as necessary as that may be, is not sufficient. The believer needs the power of the Holy Spirit to help him do that which is right, which is what the Holy Spirit desires to do.

Jesus plainly said, *"It is expedient for you that I go away: for if I go not away, the Comforter* (Helper) *will not come unto you"* (John 16:7). This is the only manner in which the believer can live an overcoming victorious life.

The believer must place his faith exclusively in Christ and what Christ did for him at the cross and maintain it accordingly. His faith must not be in himself, it must not be in other people, it must not even be in the church with its rituals and ceremonies, but rather altogether in Christ and the great work of Calvary. That being done, the Holy Spirit, who works exclusively within the realm of the finished work of Christ, will then and only then begin to help him, giving power as only He can do. That is God's solution! That is God's way and manner of sanctification.

THE WILL OF THE BELIEVER

The will of the believer is very important. It is absolutely necessary that the believer wills to do right. The Word plainly says, *"And whosoever will, let him take the water of life freely"* (Rev. 22:17).

Even though the will is absolutely necessary, within itself it is not enough to overcome sin or cause a believer to be what he ought to be in Christ. In truth, if the believer is not actually putting his trust and confidence in the cross, despite his will to do right, Satan can virtually override a believer's will. I realize that comes as a shock to many believers, but it's true.

Paul plainly said, *"For to will is present with me, but how to perform that which is good I find not"* (Rom. 7:18).

Many preachers pass Romans 7 off as Paul's "before conversion" experience, but that is incorrect. Romans 7 pertains to Paul's experience immediately *after* conversion. He found that even though he was truly charged with the power of God—being born again and even baptized with the Holy Spirit—he still could not live a victorious, overcoming life.

He sought the Lord as to this dilemma and the Lord gave him the great truths presented in Romans 6 and 8. Paul learned, as he outlines in Romans 6, that it is in the cross where our victory lies and the cross alone. Romans 8 details how that the Holy Spirit only functions according to the great sacrifice of Calvary.

The Holy Spirit will not increase the believer's willpower or function in any other area except on the basis of what Jesus did at Calvary and the resurrection. When the believer places his faith in that and not in his own strength— which is what willpower actually is—the Holy Spirit will then perform the needed task of overcoming power and victory.

A SHOCK?

It shouldn't have come as a shock regarding Satan overriding a person's will. In fact, he does this constantly with the entirety of mankind.

At this very moment, there are untold millions who no longer desire to drink alcohol, take drugs, or gamble. However, despite their will, they are not able to do what they desire, which is to quit sinning. In fact, that is what redemption is all about.

If man could "will" himself into victory, then Jesus did not need to come down here and die on Calvary. But the fact is, man's willpower is simply not strong enough to perform the task which is needed.

I know all Christians will agree with the previous statement, but they think because they are now believers that this situation concerning their willpower has changed. But it hasn't changed.

If they will think just a moment, there is nothing in the Word of God that says God will give us victory through our willpower. The truth is, Satan will override our will if our faith is in the wrong place.

Paul did not say, "I will glory in my willpower, strength, or faith," but rather, *"God forbid that I should glory, save in the cross of our Lord Jesus Christ, by whom the world is crucified unto me, and I unto the world"* (Gal. 6:14).

THE CROSS ALONE

The apostle is saying here that the answer is in the cross and the cross alone. This is what Jesus meant when He said, *"If any man will come after me, let him deny himself, and take up his cross daily, and follow me"* (Luke 9:23).

Also, this is what Paul again was talking about when he said, *"That I may know Him* (Jesus), *and the power of his resurrection* (which is the power of the Holy Spirit), *and the fellowship of his sufferings* (to receive the benefit of what His sufferings afforded), *being made conformable unto his death* (to realize why He died, which was to give me salvation and victory over sin)*"* (Phil. 3:10).

When many Christians come to this particular verse, they love to quote *"the power of his resurrection,"* but they draw back when it comes to *"the fellowship of His sufferings, being made conformable to His death."* Most have an erroneous concept of those statements. They think that the *"fellowship of His sufferings,"* pertain to us suffering for Him. No, that's not what the apostle is saying. While suffering for Christ may definitely happen, that's not what the apostle is speaking about in this particular statement.

He is meaning that we are to receive the benefits of that for which Jesus paid such a terrible price.

"Being made conformable unto His death," refers to conforming to that for which He died, namely as stated, victory over sin and self.

I am depending this very day on the cross for my victory. It was there that Jesus paid it all, and what He did is all that I need. I will do the same thing tomorrow, and the day after.

Faith and confidence in what Jesus did at Calvary and the resurrection, even on a daily basis, gives one victory over every sin of the flesh, irrespective as to what it might be. The believer is to understand, believe, and act upon that.

A PERSONAL EXAMPLE

A short time back, I had a preacher take exception with me over this statement: "Satan can override the will of the believer, making that believer do something that he does not want to do if, that is, the believer is merely trusting in his own willpower, and not in the great sacrifice of Calvary."

Some may argue that if a person is made to do something against his will, then he is not responsible. Of course, that is foolish. He is responsible. It goes back to the statement we previously made, that the Lord does not really condemn sinners to hell because of what they are, but rather because of their rejection of His solution—the Lord Jesus Christ.

We are responsible for our actions because we are rejecting the solution of the cross. We may be doing it ignorantly, but the results will be the same—failure and responsibility for that failure.

Regarding the preacher friend I mentioned, I happen to know him personally. I knew that he had a terrible problem with depression—a problem so severe that it was causing him great difficulties. Now some may argue that depression is not a sin. But that is not what the Bible says. Paul plainly stated, *"For whatsoever is not of faith is sin"* (Rom. 14:23).

DEPRESSION

While some depression can definitely be caused by physical problems, mostly it is brought about by a spirit of fear

(II Tim. 1:7). To give vent to that spirit brings on depression, which shows a lack of faith in God, and hence sin.

This brother, whom I love very much, and he loves the Lord, has tried to overcome this thing for years. I also know that he has tried to do this the wrong way by trusting in and using his own willpower, which cannot succeed and actually makes the matter worse.

The very thing that he said could not be—Satan overcoming the will of a believer if the believer's will is misplaced—was happening to him big time, but, strangely enough, without him recognizing the situation.

Once again, the answer for depression or any other sin or aberration is found totally and completely in the cross.

Let the reader understand that there is no other solution. The cross is it. Every other effort is doomed to failure.

Due to this problem being so severe and that every Christian must face this on a daily basis and considering that every true believer wants to be an overcomer, let's look at this situation a little more closely.

PAYDAY IS COMING

"What shall we say then? Shall we continue in sin, that grace may abound?" (Rom. 6:1).

In Romans 5, Paul had reiterated his unalterable conviction that salvation is solely by grace, thus nothing, minus nothing. He had stated that in this manner: *"Therefore, we conclude that a man is justified by faith without the deeds of the law"* (Rom. 3:28).

Paul also said, *"Therefore being justified by faith, we have peace with God through our Lord Jesus Christ"* (Rom. 5:1).

But Paul does not stop there. He goes on to show that not only we are justified for the present by faith in Jesus Christ, but it is forever and forever. We are justified once for all, never to come under condemnation again if, that is, we continue to walk after the Spirit and not *"after the flesh"* (Rom. 8:1).

This is the message of the gospel, of the death and the resurrection of the Lord Jesus Christ.

By His death, the Lord Jesus paid the penalty for our sins by bearing the curse of the law for us on the cross. By His resurrection, He proved that the penalty of death had been paid.

Had one single sin remained unatoned, Jesus would still be in the tomb in Israel, for *"the wages of sin* (even one sin, one single sin) *is death"* (Rom. 6:23). The resurrection, therefore, was the proof and the evidence that all sin—every sin—had been paid for and atoned for.

It is well to contemplate this simple and yet important fact: the resurrection is the proof that all of our sins were paid for by Him. One sin would have kept Christ in the tomb forever. Thank God there was no sin whatsoever. Jesus paid it all, and I mean all.

A PERFECT RIGHTEOUSNESS

Because of this, He has provided for us a perfect righteousness, in which we are now clothed. Consequently, we stand before God justified, as if we had never sinned. This is the reason that we are eternally secure if, that is, we continue to trust Christ.

How long ago did Jesus die for your sins? It was long before you were ever born; it was long before you had ever committed a single sin.

How many of these sins did He die for nearly two thousand years ago? For only part of them, or for all of them? It is a question to ponder.

Did Jesus die only for those sins which He knew we would commit before we were saved, or also for the sins of our whole life? If He died only for the sins which He knew we would commit before we were saved, but not for the sins after we were saved, when must Jesus die again to make atonement for these particular sins, which He did not atone for on the cross that is if we are confused about His death?

You see, all our sins were borne by Him at Calvary—past, present, and future—before we were even born. And His resurrection is our proof and assurance of this fact, for we repeat, *"the wages of sin is death,"* and one sin would have kept Christ in the tomb forever, if there had been one sin remaining for which He did not atone.

KEPT BY GRACE

Notice how this assurance of our security is stated by the apostle Paul. In Romans 5:1, he says we are justified by faith. That takes care of the past and the present for us, but what about the future?

Paul goes on: *"But God commendeth his love toward us, in that while we were yet sinners, Christ died for us. Much more then, being now justified by his blood, we shall be saved from wrath through Him. For if, when we were enemies, we were reconciled to God by the death of his Son, much more, being reconciled, we shall be saved* (kept saved) *by his life"* (Rom. 5:8-10).

We are justified by faith in His death—kept by faith in His life, i.e., resurrection.

We are pardoned according to our faith in His death—declared righteous and by faith in His resurrection.

Understanding this, we are led to believe that it makes no difference how a Christian lives after he is saved, or what he does after he has been converted. But it does make a difference, a tremendous difference. God does judge His people.

This is the reason that the subject of victory over sin in the life of the believer is so very, very important.

Sin takes a frightful toll, even in the life of a believer. And to be sure, while a believer may fail at times, and may even have a tremendous problem in some area, the truth is that no believer habitually practices sin.

John wrote and said, *"Whosoever is born of God, doth not commit* (practice) *sin; for his seed* (Jesus Christ) *remaineth in him* (the divine nature): *and he cannot* (practice) *sin, because he is born of God"* (I John 3:9).

MERCY

So, the idea that a person can practice sin, which means living a life of sin, and still, at the same time be saved, is unscriptural and wrong.

At the same time, the Lord puts no limitations on the times that He will forgive sin in the life of a believer, providing the believer rightly confesses that sin before Him (I John 1:9).

Nevertheless, despite the Lord's instant and faithful forgiveness, sin always takes a toll. So, all means have been given to the believer by the Lord to enable him to have victory over sin. Sin is not to have dominion over us (Rom. 6:14).

Let the believer understand that a person's salvation does not waiver between saved and unsaved. In other words, a Christian does not revert to a "lost condition" if he sins. Such is facetious. In fact, there is no such thing as a person being "fallen" who continues to trust Christ. While that trust may at times be flawed, or even improper, which it is in the lives of most, still, God honors faith wherever He finds it and ever how He finds it (John 3:16).

Again, any person who calls himself a believer and is, at the same time, habitually practicing sin, that person is only fooling himself. Even though millions, no doubt, fall into this category, the truth is, they were not saved to begin with or else they fell to a lost position by trying to have sin and salvation at the same time, which cannot be done.

Even though we are not studying the subject of eternal security here, we definitely do need to say that a person can quit believing and be thereby lost. But if he continues to believe, he is saved despite the difficulties, problems, and the number of times that he would sin.

Jesus plainly said to those Jews which believed on Him, "If ye continue in my word, then are you my disciples indeed" (John 8:31).

WHAT HAPPENS TO A CHRISTIAN WHO DOES NOT OVERCOME SIN?

In answer to that question, we are assuming that the believer is not practicing sin, nor looking for a way to continue in sin, but really wants to be what the Lord desires for his heart and life. Despite that, he is failing in some particular area, and failing constantly.

The greater majority of believers do not understand the truth of Calvary and the resurrection, at least as it applies to them on a daily basis. To be frank, many, if not most, fall into this category.

It is no use evading this issue. What happens to a Christian who does not overcome sin? This is a valid, important question, and it must be given a plain and definite answer. What explanation do we have that is biblical?

THE JUDGMENT SEAT OF CHRIST

The Bible clearly gives the answer, and it is probably the most completely overlooked and neglected teaching on the judgment seat of Christ.

Paul, speaking of believers, says, *"For we must all appear before the judgment seat of Christ; that every one may receive the things done in his body according to that he hath done, whether it be good or bad"* (II Cor. 5:10).

Before taking up the study of this verse, we must call your attention to one all-important fact. The judgment seat of Christ is not to be confused with the great white throne judgment of

Revelation 20. Unless we sharply distinguish between these two—the judgment seat of Christ and the judgment of the great white throne—we shall never be able to understand either one.

The judgment seat of Christ and the great white throne judgment are separated in point of time by at least a thousand years.

The judgment seat of Christ occurs *after* the rapture of the church and *before* the kingdom age.

The judgment of the great white throne occurs at the close of the kingdom age, which is clearly taught in Revelation 20.

THE JUDGMENT SEAT OF CHRIST AND THE
GREAT WHITE THRONE JUDGMENT

At the judgment seat of Christ before the millennium only believers will appear. (The kingdom age and the millennium are one and the same, just two different words for the same event.) Not a single unsaved person will be there. This is perfectly clear from every passage bearing on this important truth. It will include all the saved dead who will be resurrected at Jesus' coming together with all the saved believers who will be living when Jesus comes to raise the believing dead, i.e., the resurrection. These will be caught up together to meet the Lord in the air (I Thess. 4:13-18), and the judgment seat of Christ will then follow.

In sharp contrast to this, only unbelievers—only the lost—will appear at the judgment of the great white throne a thousand years later (Rev. 20:11-15). There will be no saved ones there at all; only those who are lost and who have rejected the Lord Jesus Christ.

At the judgment seat of Christ, before the thousand-year reign, believers will be judged on the basis of their works and given their relative position in the kingdom on the basis of this judgment. Therefore, the judgment seat of Christ has to do with rewards only and has nothing to do whatsoever with a believer's salvation, for that was settled at Calvary.

WORKS

In the very same way, at the judgment of the great white throne, the wicked will also be judged according to their works (Rev. 20:12). This has nothing to do with determining whether they are saved or lost. That was settled once for all when they died as unbelievers, and the door of opportunity was shut forever.

This judgment on the basis of works is to determine their relative suffering in hell (the degree of their punishment) based on the record of their works, their opportunities, and the light they rejected.

Both the judgment of the saved at the judgment seat of Christ before the kingdom age and the judgment of the lost at the great white throne judgment after the kingdom age, will be on the basis of their works and will determine the relative degree of rewards for believers in the kingdom, and the relative degree of suffering for the lost in hell.

Let me repeat that neither has anything to do with deciding the eternal destiny of the saved or the lost. That was settled for the believer by his acceptance of Christ, and for the unbeliever by his rejection of the Lord Jesus Christ—all before death and the resurrection—the resurrection of believers before the millennium, and the resurrection of the lost after the millennium.

SO AS TO BE NO CONFUSION

We have dealt with this at some length because our understanding of many things depends upon the proper comprehension of these basic truths.

Let me repeat, therefore, that the judgment seat of Christ occurs *before* the kingdom reign of Christ. The great white throne judgment occurs *after* the kingdom reign of Christ, which will be about a thousand years.

The judgment seat of Christ is for believers only. The great white throne judgment is for unbelievers and the lost only.

The judgment seat of Christ is to judge the believer's works, among other things. The great white throne judgment is to judge the unbeliever's works.

At the judgment seat of Christ, the believer will be assigned his proper place and reward in the kingdom, on the basis of his record. At the great white throne judgment, the unbeliever will be assigned to his proper place in hell, and the degree of his punishment will be determined by the record of his life.

Earlier we posed this question, what happens to a Christian who does not overcome sin? As it affects a believer and sin, or the failure to overcome, we might say that this will be handled at the judgment seat of Christ. But how it will be handled?

All sin was addressed and handled at Calvary and the resurrection, which pertains to the past, present, and future. No believer, irrespective of his weaknesses and failures, need ever worry about facing sin or its penalty at the judgment seat of Christ.

Consequently, no believer needs ever worry about being pronounced lost at that particular judgment.

The key is believing and continuing to believe in Christ and what He did for us at the cross.

At the judgment seat of Christ, the believer will definitely answer for wrong interpretation of the Word, failure to act upon the Word, doubt and unbelief as it respects the Word, improper motives, unforgiveness, etc.

In the answering of that—and all believers will be called to account—reward will definitely be lost in many cases, but not the salvation of the soul (I Cor. 3:15).

DENIAL OF THIS TRUTH?

There are some believers who may deny what we have said regarding believers who do not overcome particular problems within their lives, and we speak of certain sins, whatever they might be.

Let's be honest with ourselves. While some few believers truly overcome and thereby live a victorious Christian life, the truth is that many, if not most, do not.

We should not take that lightly because we miss out on so very much, incurring great problems for ourselves, when we do not properly allow the Holy Spirit to accomplish His dedicated work within our lives. Many Christians, if not most, fall into this category. They do so because they don't understand the cross of Christ and the part it plays in our everyday life and living. They don't understand that the Holy Spirit works entirely from the premise of the cross of Christ. They don't understand that it's the cross that gives the Holy Spirit the legal means to do all that He does.

So they try to live for God by their own efforts and abilities, which always fail. They don't want to fail. They try not to fail. But sadly, they do fail.

If the believer does not understand the cross of Christ relative to his sanctification, then such a believer—despite being saved, Spirit-filled, and even used by the Lord—is going to fail and fail repeatedly.

As mentioned earlier in this volume, believers are very prone to categorize sin as The Big Five—alcohol, drugs, gambling, nicotine, and pornography.

While those things are definitely wicked and evil, there are other sins such as fear, jealousy, envy, doubt, gossip, slander, and unbelief. Not to mention the terrible sins of pride and religion. The list is almost endless.

Almost all of us, in one way or another, fall into the category of having a problem in some area, which the Holy Spirit has been working on for years. Again, let's be honest about the situation.

Many of you reading these words look back with joy regarding some problem within your heart and life that you have overcome. But, if you think just a minute, there are probably one or two other things that have not yet been properly handled and still cause you problems.

It is so easy for us to condemn and judge others while we conveniently ignore or make excuses for our own problems:

- "*That Christian* has an uncontrollable temper, but I am just a little high-strung."
- "*That Christian* is eaten up with greed, but I have ambition."
- "*That Christian* is eaten up with fear, but I am just being cautious."

Need I say more?

So, all of these things are going to have to be handled at the judgment seat of Christ, at least those things which we have not yet overcome.

However, at that time, they will not be handled as a condemnation of sin, but rather of our failure to properly apply the Word, or the failure of proper faith. As stated, we will then lose reward because of that.

This song verse beautifully describes, I think, the present situation of the believer:

I can see far down the mountain,
Where I wandered weary years,
Often hindered in my journey,
By the ghosts of doubts and fears,
Broken vows and disappointments
Thickly sprinkled all the way;
But the Spirit led, unerring,
To the land I hold today.[9]

WHAT JUSTIFICATION BY FAITH REALLY IS

To those who believe in the Lord Jesus Christ, God immediately imputes a perfect righteousness, and that means they are saved from sin. That means the sin question is settled, and the believer has eternal life, which can never be lost if he continues to believe the Lord.

It is not by works, but always by faith.

In such a position and standing, the believer is now complete in the Lord Jesus Christ and stands before God as though he never sinned. This means that the vilest, lowest, and filthiest sinner—as well as the most self-righteous one—may come to the Savior and be instantly and eternally saved by faith and receive a new life, which can never die because it is the life of God Himself.

For these, hell is forever past, and heaven is their assured abode. Judgment (as far as condemnation is concerned) is past forever, for it was all placed upon the Lord Jesus Christ, and God now sees no sin on the believer, because *"the LORD hath laid on him* (Christ) *the iniquity of us all"* (Isa. 53:6).

Even as I dictate these words, I sense, so beautifully, the presence of God. Thank God, He has laid on Him all of my sins. There is no way that one can even properly understand that; he just accepts it. And when he does, there is a joy that fills his soul that is almost beyond comprehension.

Consequently, Jesus said, *"Verily, verily, I say unto you, He that heareth my word, and believeth on him* (God) *that sent me, hath everlasting life, and shall not come into condemnation; but is passed from death unto life"* (John 5:24).

Therefore, we emphasize again that this salvation is all of grace, and the moment that we accept Christ as Savior, the judgment upon our sin is forever past. God imputes to us the righteousness of His Son, Jesus Christ, and we are accepted in the beloved.

IT IS CALLED JUSTIFICATION

The judgment of our sins in the person of Jesus our substitute is called *justification*. It is the act of God declaring a sinner not guilty on the basis of that sinner's faith in Christ.

We have nothing in human experience with which to illustrate the act of justification. It has no counterpart in human law. No court on earth, no judge among men, no law which can be enacted can declare a guilty man justified.

A governor can pardon, but that cannot justify or declare guiltless. No man can die for another's sin and remove the guilt from the criminal or justify him in any sense whatsoever. We have nothing in human experience to even begin to approach the meaning of justification. Only God can justify a sinner, declare a guilty man guiltless, pronounce an unjust man just, and maintain his integrity. It defies human explanation, but that's exactly what God can do, and what He does do with any and every believing sinner.

THE CLEAR MEANING OF JUSTIFICATION

Someone long ago said, Justification is an act of God whereby a guilty sinner is declared righteous and just in God's sight by the imputation of God's righteousness to him on the basis of the satisfactory and completed work of the Lord Jesus, and that through the faith of the sinner in that completed work.

Therefore, once the believing sinner comes to Christ, he stands in the sight of God not as a pardoned sinner only, but as a justified saint, and he is in Christ before God as though he had never in all his life committed one single sin or was even born in original sin.

This justification is an act which is for all eternity. It cannot be repeated because it does not need to be repeated, but it establishes the absolute security of the believer in Christ. Of that there is no doubt.

We go back again to that tremendous truth, *"the LORD hath laid on him* (Christ) *the iniquity of us all"* (Isa. 53:6). However, that word *all* includes only those who believe (John 3:16). Again, everything is in the cross of Christ. On the cross, Jesus atoned for all sin—past, present, and future—at least for all who will believe.

Justification is made possible by the cross and the resurrection. However, we must understand that the cross of Christ was not dependent upon the resurrection, but rather the resurrection was dependent upon the cross.

If Jesus had failed to atone for even one sin, He could not have been raised from the dead because the wages of sin is death. Thank God, He was raised from the dead, proving that He atoned for all sin—past, present, and future. This means that the believing sinner can come to Christ irrespective of what sins he has committed and, by simply believing (and I speak of faith) every sin can be washed clean as snow.

Allow me to say it again, the Lord laid on Him the iniquity of us all. What a statement that is. What a miracle that is. What greatness and glory that is—that God laid on Jesus the iniquity of us all. There could be nothing greater.

Holy, holy, holy! Lord God Almighty!
Early in the morning our song shall rise to thee.
Holy, holy, holy, merciful and mighty!
God in three Persons, blessed Trinity!

Holy, holy, holy! All the saints adore thee,
Casting down their golden crowns around the glassy sea;
Cherubim and seraphim falling down before thee,
Which wert and art and evermore shalt be.

Holy, holy, holy! Though the darkness hide thee,
Though the eye of sinful man thy glory may not see,
Only thou art holy; there is none beside thee,
Perfect in pow'r, in love, and purity.

Holy, holy, holy! Lord God Almighty!
All thy works shall praise thy name, in earth, and sky and sea.
Holy, holy, holy! merciful and mighty!
God in three persons, blessed Trinity!

FOOLISH
CHRISTIANS

CHAPTER 10

SIN

SIN

"BUT THE SCRIPTURE HAS concluded all under sin, that the promise by faith of Jesus Christ might be given to them that believe" (Gal. 3:22).

This particular Scripture tells us unequivocally that the problem is sin. Some may try to believe that it isn't, but it is. As well, according to Paul's doctrine, the only solution for the sin problem—and I mean the only solution—is Jesus Christ and Him crucified (I Cor. 1:17-18, 23, 2:2; Gal. 6:14, Col. 2:10-15).

This is the problem with the modern church—it either denies that sin is the problem, or it brings in its own concoctions for the remedy. Again, there is no solution for sin except the cross, no help for sin except the cross, and no cure for sin except the cross.

If anything else would have sufficed, as it regards a cure for sin, then Jesus Christ would not have had to come down here and die on a cross. The very fact that He came proves that He had to come, and that it was the only solution for the sin problem. We need to understand that and realize the value of the cross. Without the cross, we are doomed.

Righteousness by law is impossible, but the law does fulfill its actual function by shutting all humanity up within the bounds of acknowledged sin. It condemns mankind so that man might turn from attempts to please God through legalism and instead receive the promise of God through faith in Jesus Christ.

In the first part of Galatians 3:22, Paul gives a capsule statement of the major truths of the first three chapters of Romans: the law shows that all have sinned and need a Savior—the immoral person, the ethical person, and the religious person. The second half of the verse reminds us that there is indeed a Savior, and that it had always been God's purpose to save a great company through faith in Him. Seen through this angle, even the law flowed from God's grace because it prepared men and women to receive the Lord Jesus Christ when He came, at least for those who properly believe. As we will see in the last phrase, faith—the sole means of grace—is again prominent.

The only way that we can have the rudiments of the cross—what Jesus there afforded and that for which He died—is that we do so by faith. It cannot be approached any other way, only by faith.

AND WHAT DO WE MEAN BY FAITH?

First, we have to understand that everything we receive from God comes through Jesus Christ and what He did for us at the cross. We must believe that, understand that, and function from that premise. Nothing we have was given to us except by what Jesus did at the cross. And when I say everything, I mean *everything*.

WHAT IS LAW?

Rather than go into a long, detailed discussion, I think it would suffice to say that law is anything and everything in which we place our faith other than Christ and the cross. And I mean everything.

We have many who think that they can fast their way to victory over sin. While fasting is definitely scriptural and will be a blessing if conducted correctly, it will not bring us victory over sin. Belonging to a certain church won't bring us victory over sin. Giving money will not bring us victory over sin. And the list goes on and on.

Again, we must believe that everything is in Jesus Christ and what He did for us at the cross. That being done, the Holy Spirit can then work mightily on our behalf.

THE HOLY SPIRIT

The Holy Spirit is the one we must have in order to have victory over sin. He works entirely within the domain of the cross of Christ. The cross is what gives the Holy Spirit latitude to work on our behalf and give us victory over the world, the flesh, and the devil (Rom. 8:1-19).

This thing is not complicated. Actually, it is very simple. We just have to understand that the cross of Christ has made everything possible. As well, we must understand that the Holy Spirit works exclusively by and through the cross of Christ. We must also understand that our faith must be in

Christ and the cross—that gives the Holy Spirit latitude to work, and to work mightily, on our behalf. The only victory over sin is by and through the cross of Christ. Know that, understand that, and believe that because it happens to be true (Col. 2:10-15).

THE PROMISE BY FAITH OF JESUS CHRIST

Here, in Galatians 3:22 is the word *faith*, but it must be faith in Jesus Christ and what He did for us at the cross.

In this one phrase, *"the promise by faith of Jesus Christ,"* we have the guarantee by God that if our faith is in Christ and the cross, we will receive that for which the promise has been given.

There are many of you reading this text at this very moment, and you love God, but you have been living a life of spiritual failure. Sin is dominating your life in some way. You have tried fasting, memorizing Scripture, having hands laid on you, and a host of other things—all to no avail. You are still in bondage.

But if you will place your faith exclusively in Jesus Christ and what He did for you at the cross, then you have the promise of God that the Holy Spirit will go to work bringing about the victory that you have so long sought and are now ready to receive.

TO THEM THAT BELIEVE

As we have said, it is all about faith and that which God has promised us that He would do. Do you believe God?

Again, if we could receive what we need by any way other than Jesus Christ and Him crucified, then Jesus would not have had to come down here and die on a cross. If there was any method, any other way—but the truth is, there is no way other than the cross. That being the fact, Jesus Christ had to become man for the purpose of going to the cross, which then gave the Holy Spirit latitude to work mightily in our hearts and in our lives. It is the great plan of God.

Regrettably and sadly, far too many Christians are trying to live for God by concoctions they have devised themselves.

Go to the cross! Believe what Jesus there did! This is God's way of victory over the world, the flesh, and the devil. And it is His only way because no other way is needed.

THE PROMISE BY FAITH

Let's look at this phrase in Galatians 3:22 one more time: *"that the promise by faith of Jesus Christ might be given to them that believe."* This gives us several major truths:

- *The promise.* This promise, in a sense, began in the garden of Eden, even at the fall of man (Gen. 3:15). It was given, in particular and in fullness, to Abraham, which we refer to as the Abrahamic covenant (Gen. 12:3, 15:6). Salvation has always hinged on this promise and nothing else. It is the promise of cleansing from sin and victory over sin, all through Jesus Christ and what He did for us at the cross, with the Holy Spirit given to every believer.

- *By faith.* There was no way that man could earn salvation; therefore, it had to be by faith. There was no other way. This put all men on the same level, whether rich, poor, great or small.
- *Of Jesus Christ.* The promise pointed to Jesus Christ and the price He would pay at Calvary's cross, and it was faith in Him and what He did for us at Calvary which guaranteed salvation. Faith in anything else brought a zero return, even as it continues to bring a zero return. Faith in Him brings everything.
- *Believe.* Believe in what? It is to believe in Jesus Christ and what He did for us at Calvary's cross. Everything else must be second, fourth, or tenth place. Our faith must, without fail, be in Christ and the sacrifice of Calvary. The word *believe*, as it is used here, refers to taking upon oneself all that one is and has done and, in this case, the Lord Jesus Christ. Then He becomes all in all, the satisfier of every need, the justifier of all sinners. He ceases to be a mere figure in history and becomes a living vibrant force in the heart and life of the believer, as that person sets out to follow Him, because believing also means following (Luke 9:23-26, Rom. 10:9-10, 13).

This is a simple thing to do, but it must be done God's way. In fact, there is no other way. Sadly, the church takes every avenue except the right avenue. It must be understood that what Jesus did at the cross bought our salvation, paid the ransom that we owed but could not pay, and He paid it to God. He shed His life's blood that we might be saved, that we might be victorious, and that we might have that for which He died.

BEFORE FAITH CAME

"But before faith came, we were kept under the law, shut up unto the faith which should afterwards be revealed" (Gal. 3:23).

Paul uses the word *faith* here as a compendium of the entirety of the plan of God.

The faith of which Paul speaks is faith in Christ and what He has done for us at Calvary's cross. The only thing we have to exercise in receiving all for which He died is simple faith in Christ. Please allow me to say it again:

- You must believe that every blessing comes from Jesus Christ (John 14:6).
- You must believe that the cross of Christ is the means and the only means that all of these things can be given to us (I Cor. 2:1-2).
- That being the case, that everything comes through Christ by means of the cross, then the cross, without fail, must be the object of our faith. This is critically important (Gal. 6:4).
- That being done, with the understanding that every blessing comes from Christ—all made possible by the cross—then the Holy Spirit, who works exclusively by and through the cross of Christ, will then work mightily on our behalf. Unfortunately, most Christians have precious little help from the Holy Spirit compared to what

they could have. It only remains for us exercising faith in Christ and His atoning work at Calvary and doing so constantly (Rom. 8:1-11).

WE WERE KEPT UNDER THE LAW

And yet, there was no salvation in the law. The reason being that it had to be kept perfectly, not failing in even one point for any type of salvation to be reached, which was impossible. The only one who ever kept the law was Jesus Christ. Yet the only means of reaching God was by law. If there was no salvation by the law, and there definitely wasn't, then what good did it do?

The law did many things that were wonderful and good. God was the author of all law, which means that it was beautiful and wonderful, but it was never meant to bring salvation. Understand that—the law was never meant to bring salvation.

Salvation came by simple faith in what the sacrifices represented, namely the coming Redeemer, who would be the Lord Jesus Christ. That's how salvation came, and that's the only way it came. Men were saved before the cross exactly as they are saved today, by grace.

The law showed man what he was, which was not very pleasant to see. The law presented God's standard of righteousness, which man could not keep. But until Christ came, man was shut up under the law because that's all there was at the time.

Why didn't Jesus Christ come before He did? The answer is because the world was not ready. In fact, the only people on earth at that time who knew God were the Jews. Among the

Jews there was only a few who truly knew the Lord. So, the first advent of the Savior was predicated on the number of people who truly knew the Lord, which wasn't many. When that number was reached, whatever it was, that's when Jesus came. Of course, there were many other situations involved also. But it had to do with people who truly knew Him, which were precious few.

At the time of the coming of Christ, there were only two among the ruling class of Israel (that we know of) who knew the Lord or knew something about Him. Those two were Nicodemus and Joseph of Arimathea. Now think about that. Of the several millions of people who made up Israel of that day, the ruling class only had two people who we might could say knew something about the Lord. When it came to the working class, there were many more, but to be sure Christ came at the appointed time.

SHUT UP UNTO THE FAITH WHICH SHOULD AFTERWARDS BE REVEALED

The phrase of this subheading proclaims the fact that the law pointed to Christ, always to Christ. In fact, every rudiment of the law, even as complicated as it was, portrayed Christ in His atoning work, mediatorial work, and intercessory work.

That means sinners before the cross were saved by the blood of Jesus Christ just as surely and just as eternally as believing sinners since the cross. When the faith in an historic Christ came—faith exercised in the Christ of history rather than the Christ of prophecy—then the law was obligated or fulfilled in Christ, at least for those who believe.

The idea is that the coming Redeemer was the only hope. The law condemned men and offered no hope of escape. Their only hope was in that system, which was to be revealed through the Messiah—the system that extended forgiveness on the grounds of faith in His atoning blood (Rom. 10:9-10, 13, Eph. 2:8-9).

SCHOOLMASTER

"Wherefore the law was our schoolmaster to bring us unto Christ, that we might be justified by faith" (Gal. 3:24).

It is unfortunate that the King James Version refers to the law here as a schoolmaster.

The Expositor's Bible Commentary says:

The phrase, 'put in charge' is the Greek noun paidagogos ...which means 'a child-custodian, or 'child-attendant.' The pedagogue was a slave employed by wealthy Greeks or Romans to have responsibility for one of the children of the family. He had charge of the child from about ages six to sixteen and was responsible for watching over his behavior wherever he went and for conducting him to and from school. Paul's point is that this responsibility ceased when the child entered into fullness of his position as a son, becoming an acknowledged adult by the formal rite of adoption by his father (see on 4:1-7). The reference 'to Christ' is temporal; it means, 'until we come of age at the time of the revelation of our full sonship through Christ's coming.' The final phrase of this Verse (lit., 'in order that by faith one might be justified') gives the ultimate objective of the law in its role of pedagogue. The emphasis is on justification rather than faith, for Paul has already shown that faith is the only means to salvation.[1]

WHEREFORE THE LAW
WAS OUR SCHOOLMASTER

As we have already stated, this phrase does not refer to a teacher but a guardian.

Wuest said, "By describing the law as a paidagogos [guardian] ... Paul emphasizes both the inferiority of the law of grace, and its temporary character. The law was therefore the guardian of Israel, keeping watch over those committed to its care, accompanying them with its commands and prohibitions, keeping them in a condition of dependence and restraint, and continually revealing to them sin as a positive transgression."[2]

TO BRING US UNTO CHRIST

The phrase, *"To bring us unto Christ,"* proclaims the result of the mission of the law. Barnes said:

> The ways in which the law does this may be the following:
> 1. It restrains us and rebukes us, and keeps us as the ancient pedagogue did his boys.
> 2. The whole law was designed to be introductory to Christ. The sacrifices and offerings were designed to shadow forth the Messiah, and to introduce him

to the world. [In fact, the law was not the teacher, Christ is actually the teacher.]

3. The moral law—the Law of God—shows people their sin and danger, and thus leads them to the Saviour. It condemns them, and thus prepares them to welcome the offer of pardon through a Redeemer.

4. It still does this. [Paul said, *"For Christ is the end of the law for righteousness to every one that believeth"* (Rom. 10:4). Consequently, for those who have not believed in Christ, the demands of the law are still incumbent upon them.] The whole economy of the Jews was designed to do this and under the preaching of the gospel it is still done. People see that they are condemned; they are convinced by the Law that they cannot save themselves, and thus they are led to the Redeemer. The effect of the preached gospel is to show people their sins, and thus to be preparatory to the embracing of the offer of pardon. Hence, the importance of preaching the Law still; and hence, it is needful that people should be made to feel that they are sinners, in order that they may be prepared to embrace the offers of mercy.[3]

Paul is here describing how the law puts a man under bondage like that of a minor child under the supervision of a guardian. In verses to follow, it will be seen that such supervision is no longer necessary to the man of faith—to the one who has accepted Christ.

JUSTIFIED BY FAITH

In Galatians 3:24, the phrase, *"that we might be justified by faith,"* proclaims to us that the law had no permanent function but served only until *"we might be justified by faith."*

The important observation here is that the law, shutting man up under sin—and unto faith —served the temporary function of protecting and preparing him for the coming of Christ.

Theologian Charles Ellicott said, "The work of Christ as a Teacher is not what the Apostle has in mind. It is rather a higher kind of guardianship, which is to succeed that of the Law, and to which the Law hands over its pupil. Once brought within the guardianship of Christ, and so made a member of the Messianic kingdom, the Christian is justified by faith, he receives an amnesty for his past sins, and is accounted righteous before God."[4]

To be *"justified by faith,"* which is the only way one can be justified—at least the only way that God will recognize and the only recognition that matters—simply means that one has faith in what Christ did at Calvary and the resurrection. The believing sinner accepts this. As well, he must ever understand that faith or believing also means following (Luke 9:23-26).

FAITH IS COME

"But after that faith is come, we are no longer under a schoolmaster" (Gal. 3:25).

The phrase, *"But after that faith is come,"* refers to *the* faith. Paul is speaking about the finished work of Christ on Calvary's cross, plus the resurrection. Here, faith denotes Christ and relationship with Him because faith is its distinguishing characteristic.

One can define this better perhaps by referring to Israel and the church. Under the old economy of God, which pertained to Israel, they were under law. Now that Christ has come, the church is no longer under law, but under faith. This included Israel, if they had only accepted faith, which they did not. They elected to remain under law, at least as a body politic. Consequently, they were ultimately destroyed—that is all the law can do. The law served as their guardian until Christ came, when they were supposed to accept Him by faith. Refusing that, which they did, they were left with nothing.

Looking at modern Israel in this fashion, there is no semblance of spirituality left in these people, which is sad, to say the least. They call Jesus a blasphemer and Paul a renegade. One might say that they are now without law or faith. Thankfully, they will soon be restored. But the coming restoration in no way speaks of the untold millions who have died eternally lost.

WE ARE NO LONGER
UNDER A SCHOOLMASTER

Ellicott said, "But now the Law has been exchanged for the dispensation of faith. Henceforth the old state of pupilage is at an end. We are no longer like children, but adult members of the divine family—sons of God. We have entered into this relation by faith in Christ. For to be baptised into Christ is to enter into the closest possible relation to Him. It is to be identified with Him entirely. Nor is any excluded."[5]

And please remember, when we talk about being baptized into Christ, we are not speaking of being water baptized, but rather our born-again experience. At that time, we are literally baptized into Christ (Rom. 6:3-4).

The phrase, *"we are no longer under a schoolmaster,"* should actually say, "we are no longer under the guardianship of the law." The law has been made ineffective through Christ. One might say that now we have a far greater guardian—one who can actually give power, that the things the law demanded are now fulfilled in our everyday living. Hallelujah!

The law was a regime of supervision. Before Christ, we were under jurisdiction, confined like prisoners with only one prospect of escape, the faith that was due by revelation. The law had been a kind of guardian exercising a preparatory oversight only; the ultimate purpose was that by faith we should find acceptance with God. That faith is ours now. We are done with tutors. We have reached our spiritual maturity recognized in virtue of faith as sons in God's house, in the fellowship of Christ.

THE CHILDREN OF GOD

"For ye are all the children of God by faith in Christ Jesus" (Gal. 3:26).

Wuest said:

> By the change from the first person we, with its reference to
> the Jews, to the second person ye with its reference to his
> readers, both Jew and Gentile, Paul shows that the wall of
> separation between Jew and Gentile had been broken down
> at the Cross, and that both Jew and Gentile become children
> of God in Christ Jesus. The word translated children is huios
> and is the important word here. This word signifies someone
> of full age. Under law, the individual was in his minority and
> under a guardian. Now, under grace, he has attained his major-
> ity, having outgrown the surveillance of his former guardian.[6]

To be frank, the Jews strongly resented the implication
by Paul that all were now placed on the same level. The Jew
delighted in thinking that he was the sole possessor of the ways
of God, and that therefore the Gentiles were on a much lower
status and, in fact, no status at all, at least as far as God was
concerned. By the time of Christ, they had become so sectar-
ian that they would have insulted any Gentile who would have
asked them about the law of Moses. In fact, any association with
a Gentile necessitated, at least in their thinking, the engaging
of the purification process.

The Romans probably had more problems with the Jews
than anyone else, likening them as a race of people who hated
all others, which was pretty well true. Self-righteousness puts
one in this mode, which characterized the Israel of Jesus' day
and is, in reality, what crucified Him.

BY FAITH IN CHRIST JESUS

The phrase, *"by faith in Christ Jesus,"* proclaims the ways and means by which one becomes a child of God.

Incidentally, the phrase is no longer "sons of Abraham," but "sons of God." Thus, the privilege rises high above that which was indicated previously. One might say that "sons of Abraham" refers to the time before the cross, and "sons of God" refers to the time since the cross.

Before the cross, even though there were many who were saved, they were not born again, as we think of such. They were saved by their faith in the coming Redeemer, and now we are saved by faith in the Redeemer who has already come.

The idea is that we now have many more privileges in Christ Jesus than any of the Old Testament saints ever had.

Jesus said, *"Verily I say unto you, Among them that are born of women there hath not risen a greater than John the Baptist; notwithstanding he that is least in the kingdom of heaven is greater than he"* (Mat. 11:11).

Jesus wasn't meaning greater in character as it regards modern believers, but that we now have, because of Christ and what He did at the cross, much greater privileges than any of the Old Testament saints had, even John the Baptist. That refers to the fact that we are now born again, whereas before the cross, their faith was in something that was coming. Thank God, it has now come.

Luther said, "What tongue, either of men or angels, can sufficiently extol and magnify the great mercy of God towards us, that we, which are miserable sinners, and by nature, the children of wrath, should be called to his grace and glory, to be made the children and heirs of God, fellow-heirs with the Son of God, and lords over heaven and earth, and that by the only means of our faith in Christ Jesus."[7]

Wuest adds, "The context shows that the words 'in Christ Jesus,' must be separated from the words 'by faith.' They are put at the end of the sentence so as to form a distinct proposition which Paul enlarges upon in the following verses."[8]

BAPTIZED INTO CHRIST

"For as many of you as have been baptized into Christ have put on Christ" (Gal. 3:27).

This new relationship is not something natural to men, as though all automatically were or became God's sons. The "fatherhood of God" and the "universal brotherhood of man" are not New Testament concepts. True, God has a relationship to all men as Creator. Paul can say, as he did in speaking of the Athenians, "We are His children (literally, 'begotten ones')" (Acts 17:28). But a creature is not necessarily a son. In fact, he can become a son only through union by faith with that unique Son of God, Christ Jesus, who is a Son by natural generation, and not by creation as men.

BAPTISM

The phrase, *"For as many of you as have been baptized into Christ,"* proclaims how one is united with Christ.

The reference here is not to water baptism, for that never puts a believing sinner into Christ. The baptism of which Paul speaks is the baptism into His death at Calvary, even as Paul describes in Romans 6:3: *"Know ye not, that so many of us as were baptized into Jesus Christ were baptized into His death?"*

This baptism is gained when a person puts his faith in Jesus as Savior, and the Holy Spirit then introduces or places (baptizes) that person into vital union with Christ (I Cor. 12:13).

This means that every person who is born again immediately receives the Holy Spirit. The Spirit of God, without which no one could be saved, comes into the heart and life of the believer (every born-again believer) to help that person live a holy life.

That believer is then greatly encouraged to go on and be baptized with the Holy Spirit, which is for service—to be anointed to preach, to witness, to testify, to pray, to sing, to minister—to do whatever needs to be done. We need the baptism with the Spirit.

While it is all the same Spirit (for character and then for service), it is two different situations.

A lot of Pentecostal believers are somewhat confused when they see Baptists or others who have never been baptized with the Holy Spirit with the evidence of speaking with other tongues living a more holy life than their Pentecostal counterparts.

It is because such a person—born again but not yet baptized with the Holy Spirit—has placed his faith exclusively in Christ and what Christ has done for him at the cross, which the Holy Spirit will help a believer to do.

Far too many Pentecostals, and I am Pentecostal, do not understand the twofold work of the Spirit. They think they cannot live a holy, godly life, until they speak with other tongues. And while speaking in tongues is very, very important, we must remember, it is not the place of the Holy Spirit to help us live a holy life just because we speak with other tongues, which, again, is very important.

But the moment the person is born again, at that moment when the Holy Spirit comes into the heart and life of a believer, irrespective of who he might be, the Holy Spirit is there to help that person live a holy life. And the only requirement for that believer to live a holy life is that his faith be exclusively in Christ and the cross.

Please understand, the Holy Spirit works exclusively within the parameters of the finished work of Christ. It's the cross that gives the Holy Spirit the legal means to give us victory over sin, the world, the flesh, and the devil. While the Holy Spirit is meant to help us do all things, we must remember that He works entirely within the parameters of the cross of Christ.

Paul said, *"For the law of the Spirit of life in Christ Jesus, hath made me free from the law of sin and death"* (Rom. 8:2).

Unfortunately, most Pentecostals do not understand this. They think the event of the Holy Spirit itself will give them victory over the powers of darkness. And He will—*if* our faith is in Christ and the cross. That, and that alone, is the key (I Cor. 1:17-18, 2:2; Gal. 6:14, Col. 2:10-15).

The problem is that there are millions—and that's no exaggeration—who are baptized with the Holy Spirit with the evidence of speaking with other tongues and are being used by God, but still cannot live a victorious life. They don't understand why, so too many resort to one fad after another.

If only my Pentecostal brothers and sisters would understand that the only answer for sin, and I mean the only answer, is the cross of Christ. Jesus died there to atone for all sin—past, present, and future—at least for those who will believe (John 3:16). Tragically, we seem to forget that and try to get victory over sin by machinations that we devise. They never work because they never can work.

If my Pentecostal brothers and sisters (plus all others) will place their faith exclusively in Christ and the cross and maintain it exclusively in Christ and the cross, then they will begin to see victory over sin, the world, the flesh, and the devil—victory as only the Lord can give.

Again, speaking in tongues is valuable. But remember this: you can speak in tongues every day of your life and still not be able to live a victorious life because that is not the function of the Holy Spirit. His function is to point you to the cross, that you ever make the cross the object of your faith, and then the Holy Spirit will work mightily (Rom. 8:1-11).

HAVE PUT ON CHRIST

In Galatians 3:27, the phrase, *"have put on Christ,"* means to be clothed with Him, which is typified by baptism—the believing sinner into Christ, and Christ into the believer. Jesus described this by saying, *"At that day* (after Calvary) *ye*

shall know that I am in my Father, and ye in me, and I in you"
(John 14:20).

This makes the born-again experience far more than a mere philosophy; it is an actual regeneration. In fact, man does not need reformation but rather regeneration. This union with Christ, defined as "baptism," provides that.

ALL ARE ONE IN CHRIST JESUS

"There is neither Jew nor Greek, there is neither bond nor free, there is neither male nor female: for ye are all one in Christ Jesus" (Gal. 3:28).

The Expositor's Bible Commentary says:

In what sense is this true? Clearly it does not mean that differences of nationality, status, and sex cease to exist. A Jew remains a Jew; a Gentile, a Gentile. One does not lose one's identity by becoming a Christian. Instead, having become one with God as his sons and daughters, Christians now belong to each other in such a way that distinctions that had divided them lose significance. Race is the first example. In Paul's day there was a deep division between the two, not only nationally but also religiously. Gentiles were uncircumcised and therefore not children of Abraham. They did not have the law or the ceremonies. They were not of the covenant. This barrier Paul now claims to have been broken down in Christ (cf Eph. 2:11-18). Today this principle must be extended to deny the significance of all racial barriers. In Christ there must be neither black nor white, Caucasian nor Oriental, nor any other such distinction. Social status is a second example ("slave nor free"). Again, this is not meant to deny that in actual fact there are social distinctions among people. It is merely meant to affirm that for those who are united to Christ these things do not matter. On this pattern the ideal church should be composed of members from all spectra of society: wealthy and poor, educated and uneducated, straight and long hair, management and labor, and so on. When Christians treat each other as true brothers and sisters in Christ regardless of their social standing, then the power of such distinctions is broken and a basis is laid for social change. There is also the example of sex, for Paul declares that there is neither "male nor female." It is hard to imagine how badly women were treated in antiquity, even in Judaism, and how difficult it is to find any statement about the equality of the sexes, however weak, in any ancient texts except those of Christianity.[9]

For example, Josephus wrote, "The woman, says the Law, is in all things inferior to the man. Let her accordingly be submissive."[10]

And we could add that a common morning prayer of Jewish men is, "Blessed are you, Lord, our God, ruler of the universe, who has not created me a woman."[11]

In fact, the Gentile world had similar expressions.

The Expositor's Bible Commentary notes, "But Paul reverses this. Indeed, in the statement we have one factor in the gradual elevation in honoring of women that has been known only in Christian lands."[12]

In fact, the law of Moses did not place women on a lower level at all but treated them in many ways as equals. Jesus served as the prime example in carrying out this equal treatment. However, the Pharisees placed their own interpretations on the law, in fact adding more than six hundred oral laws to the existing law of Moses. By the time of Christ, the original law of Moses had been so perverted and diluted, it was hardly recognizable.

THE UNITY IN CHRIST

Regarding the phrase in Galatians 3:28, *"There is neither Jew nor Greek, there is neither bond nor free, there is neither male nor female,"* Wuest said, "The individual differences between Jew and Greek, between slave and free, between male and female, are merged in that higher unity into which all believers are raised by the fact that they all have a common life in Christ Jesus. One heart now beats in all. The pulsating life of the Lord Jesus is the motive power. One mind guides all, the mind of Christ."[13]

The idea is that all who are baptized into Christ adopt the Christ attitude.

Barnes said:

Paul means to teach that no man has any preference or advantage in the kingdom of God because he is a rich man, or because he is of elevated rank; no one is under any disadvantage because he is poor, or because he is ignorant, or a slave. All at the foot of the cross are sinners; all at the communion table are saved by the same grace; all who enter into heaven, will enter clothed in the same robes of salvation, and arranged, not as princes and nobles, and rich men and poor men, in separate orders and ranks, but mingling together as redeemed by the same blood, and arranged in ranks according to their eminence in holiness.[14]

Barnes adds, Christianity does not admit the one to favour because he is free, or exclude the other because he is a slave. Nor, when they are admitted to favour, does it give the one a right to lord it over the other, or to feel that he is of any more value in the eye of the Redeemer, or any nearer to his heart. The essential idea is, that they are on a level, and that they are admitted to the favour of God without respect to their external condition in society.[15]

Barnes goes on to say, The slave should excite the interest, and receive the watchful care of the pastor, as well as his master.[16]

That's the way the Lord looks at the situation and treats all things. To be frank, this is peculiar to Christianity. It alone is this great leveler; it alone erases class distinction; it alone puts all on the same basis, for all must come alike, enter alike, and obtain salvation alike.

ALL ONE IN CHRIST JESUS

The phrase, *"For ye are all one in Christ Jesus,"* proclaims the destruction of one of the greatest injustices on the face of the earth, and I speak of class, status, and social distinction.

Communism claimed to address this monster, but only succeeded in making it worse. Only Christianity, and more particularly only Christ, has addressed this evil and brought it to heel.

This statement, *"For ye are all one in Christ Jesus,"* is, without a doubt, one of the greatest and most powerful statements that has ever been uttered. In this and this alone can those who are cast down find a means of salvation. In this alone can the down-trodden, the dispossessed, the broken, the ignored, the faceless masses, the unfortunate, and the disapproved find a means and way of identity that puts them on the level of everyone else. How wonderful this is, how glorious this is, what a grave injustice this erases—all in Christ.

This alone should make men desire to run to the Lord of glory. This alone should make them champion His cause. This alone should garner their allegiance because this alone is the great equalizer.

It humbles the proud and exalts the humble. And that's exactly what Jesus said He would do (Luke 18:14).

THE CONDITION

The condition for this great wonder, this glorious privilege is simply faith in Christ and what Christ did for us at the cross. Paul answered the Philippian jailer by saying, *"Believe on the Lord Jesus Christ, and thou shalt be saved"* (Acts 16:31).

If one had to do some great and noble thing to enter this great society of Christ, it would be understandable as to why most could not accomplish the task. However, money is not required, and neither is station, place, or position. Color or race do not matter. One simply has to exhibit faith and, more particularly, faith in Christ and the cross. When a person makes Him—the Lord of Glory, the gift of God—his Lord and Savior, and he does so by faith (the only manner it can be done) then he instantly becomes a member of this great family of God, this great society of righteousness. It is all *"in Christ Jesus."*

ACCORDING TO THE PROMISE

"And if ye be Christ's, then are ye Abraham's seed, and heirs according to the promise" (Gal. 3:29).

The Expositor's Bible Commentary says this regarding another result of passing from law to grace:

Through faith in Jesus Christ is that all who believe become one with those who have been saved by faith throughout the long history of salvation. Thus, by union with Christ, believers become 'Abraham's seed, and heirs according to the promise.' Here that which Paul had previously declared to be Christ's—the inheritance of the promise made to Abraham (3:16) —he now applies to the entire Christian church by virtue of its actually being Christ's body. The verse carries the thought back to the beginning of the chapter. The use of the word 'seed' without the article is of great importance, for it keeps the necessity of a union with Christ constantly before the Galatians. The prize the legalizers had been holding before the eyes of the Galatian Christians in their hope to win them to the ceremonial aspects of Judaism was the possibility of becoming part of the physical seed of Abraham. Paul now replies that what the legalizers were offering through circumcision was actually already theirs in Christ. He is the seed to whom the promises were made. Believers enter into the promises by entering into him and become spiritual seed to God as well.[17]

The last section of Galatians 3 is filled with references to Christ Jesus. He is mentioned six times, and the point of each reference is that Christians receive all that is of value spiritually by virtue of their attachment to Him.

Theologian John Stott said:

This is a three-dimensional attachment which we gain when we are in Christ—in height, breadth and length. It is an attachment in 'height' through reconciliation to the God who, although radical theologians repudiate the concept and we must be careful how we interpret it, is a God 'above' us, transcendent over the universe He has made. Next, it is an attachment in 'breadth', since in Christ we are united to all other believers throughout the world. Thirdly, it is an attachment in 'length', as we join the long, long line of believers throughout the whole course of time.[18]

It is through faith in Christ and in Christ alone that we find ourselves.

AND IF YE BE CHRIST'S

The phrase, *"And if ye be Christ's,"* refers to belonging to Him and all that implies. Wuest said:

> The Judaizers taught that by becoming subjects of the Mosaic law, the Galatian Gentiles would become the seed or progeny of Abraham. Paul asserts that this privilege comes to one by faith in Christ. In Romans 4, Paul shows that Abraham was justified by faith, and was thus constituted the spiritual father of all who put their faith in Christ, whether they are circumcised or uncircumcised. God made salvation dependent upon faith in order that it might be available to both Jew and Gentile. Since Abraham is the spiritual father of all believers, this does away with the false Jewish notion that kinship to Abraham brings one into the divine favor and gives one salvation. By belonging to Christ, believers are also Abraham's posterity, for Christ is the seed of Abraham. Since believers have entered into relationship with Christ, they must consequently have a share in the same state, and must likewise be Abraham's seed.[19]

So the phrase, *"then are ye Abraham's seed,"* presents the manner in which this is done, which is by faith in Christ and what He did for us at the cross.

HEIRS ACCORDING TO THE PROMISE

This great book of Galatians deals with both justification and sanctification, but I think it leans more toward sanctification—how we live for God on a daily basis and how we have victory over the world, the flesh, and the devil—which speaks more of a sanctified life than anything else.

Briefly, I want to tell you exactly how the believer is sanctified.

First, the believer must understand that everything he receives from God—and I mean everything—is all made possible by what Jesus Christ did for us at the cross. It is imperative that he is sure of this.

This means that everything the believer has from God—and I mean everything—is all made possible by the cross. He must understand and believe that.

The believer must anchor his faith in Christ and what Christ did for him at the cross—and then maintain his faith in Christ and what He did for him at the cross. That being done, the Holy Spirit, who is God and can do anything, will go to work on that person's behalf. The believer must understand that the Holy Spirit works exclusively within the parameters of the finished work of Christ. He will not work outside of those boundaries. It is what Jesus did at the cross that gives the Holy Spirit latitude to do all of these wonderful things. The moment a believer places his faith in Christ and the cross, at that moment, he is sanctified. At that moment, he can grow in grace and the knowledge of the Lord. At that moment, he will know victory over the world, the flesh, and the devil.

It's just that simple—faith in Christ and what He did for us at the cross and ever making the cross of Christ the object of our faith. Then the Holy Spirit, who can do all things, will mightily go to work on our behalf, and we will finally know and understand what more abundant life actually is.

———◇———

There's a Savior who stands at the door of your heart,
He is longing to enter—why let Him depart?
He has patiently called you so often before,
But you must open the door.

He has come from the Father salvation to bring,
And His name is called Jesus, Redeemer, and King!
To save you and keep you He pleads evermore,
But you must open the door.

He is loving and kind, full of infinite grace,
In your heart, in your life, will you give Him a place?
He is waiting to bless you, your soul to restore,
But you must open the door.

He will lead you at last to that blessed abode,
To the city of God, at the end of the road,
Where the night never falls, where life's journey is o'er,
But you must open the door.

REFERENCES

CHAPTER 1

[1] James Montgomery Boice, "Galatians" in *The Expositor's Bible Commentary,* Vol. 10. (Zondervan Publishing, 1976), Epub edition 2018, 3595.

[2] Ibid.

[3] Ibid.

[4] Ibid.

[5] Albert Barnes, *Notes, Explanatory And Practical, And The Epistle To The Galatians,* (London: Knight And Son, 1852), 371.

[6] Kenneth S. Wuest, *Wuest's Word Studies from the Greek New Testament: For the English Reader,* vol. 3 (Grand Rapids: Eerdmans, 1997), 84.

[7] *Pulpit Commentary* on Galatians 2:12, https://biblehub.com/commentaries/galatians/2-12.htm.

[8] Albert Barnes, *Notes, Explanatory And Practical, And The Epistle To The Galatians,* (London: Knight And Son, 1852), 372.

[9] Ibid.

[10] Ibid.

[11] Kenneth S. Wuest, *Wuest's Word Studies from the Greek New Testament: For the English Reader*, vol. 3 (Grand Rapids: Eerdmans, 1997), 84-85.

[12] Albert Barnes, *Notes, Explanatory And Practical, And The Epistle To The Galatians*, (London: Knight And Son, 1852), 372-373.

CHAPTER 2

[1] Martin Luther and Erasmus Middleton. *A Commentary On Saint Paul's Epistle to the Galatians: To Which Is Prefixed, The Life of the Author, And a Complete And Impartial History of the Times In Which He Lived.* A new ed., corrected and revised (London: B. Blake, 1838), 271.

[2] Kenneth S. Wuest, *Wuest's Word Studies from the Greek New Testament: For the English Reader,* vol. 3 (Grand Rapids: Eerdmans, 1997), 87–88.

CHAPTER 3

[1] Boice, James Montgomery, "Galatians" in *The Expositor's Bible Commentary,* Vol. 10. (Zondervan Publishing, 1976), Epub edition 2018, 3596-3597.

[2] Kenneth S. Wuest, *Wuest's Word Studies from the Greek New*

Testament: For the English Reader, vol. 3 (Grand Rapids: Eerdmans, 1997), 88-89.

[3] Ibid, 89.

[4] Ibid.

[5] Ibid, 89-90.

[6] Ibid, 90.

[7] Ibid, 90-91.

[8] Ibid, 92.

[9] Boice, James Montgomery, "Galatians" in *The Expositor's Bible Commentary*, Vol. 10. (Zondervan Publishing, 1976), Epub edition 2018, 3596-3597.

[10] Kenneth S. Wuest, *Wuest's Word Studies from the Greek New Testament: For the English Reader*, vol. 3 (Grand Rapids: Eerdmans, 1997), 92.

[11] Ibid.

[12] Ibid.

[13] Martin Luther and Erasmus Middleton. *A Commentary On Saint Paul's Epistle to the Galatians: To Which Is Prefixed, The Life of the Author, And a Complete And Impartial History of the Times In Which He Lived*. A new ed., corrected and revised (London: B. Blake, 1838),177.

CHAPTER 6

[1] Kenneth S. Wuest, *Wuest's Word Studies from the Greek New Testament: For the English Reader,* vol. 3 (Grand Rapids: Eerdmans, 1997), 96.

[2] Ibid.

[3] Ibid, 97.

[4] Ibid.

[5] Kenneth L. Barker and John L. Kohlenberger III, *The Expositors Bible, Abridged Edition, Old and New Testaments* (Zondervan, 1994), Epub edition 2018, 3599.

CHAPTER 8

[1] Kenneth S. Wuest, *Wuest's Word Studies from the Greek New Testament: For the English Reader,* vol. 3 (Grand Rapids: Eerdmans, 1997), 101–102.

[2] Albert Barnes, *Notes, Explanatory And Practical, on the Second Epistle to the Corinthians And The Epistle To The Galatians,* (London: Knight And Son, 1852), 388.

[3] Kenneth S. Wuest, *Wuest's Word Studies from the Greek New Testament: For the English Reader,* vol. 3 (Grand Rapids: Eerdmans, 1997), 102.

[4] Albert Barnes, *Notes, Explanatory And Practical, on the Second Epistle to the Corinthians And The Epistle To The Galatians,* (London: Knight And Son, 1852), 389.

[5] Kenneth S. Wuest, *Wuest's Word Studies from the Greek New Testament: For the English Reader,* vol. 3 (Grand Rapids: Eerdmans, 1997), 102–103.

[6] Albert Barnes, *Notes, Explanatory and Practical, on the Second Epistle to the Corinthians and the Epistle to the Galatians* (London: Knight and Son, 11, Clerkenwell Close, 1852), 389-390.

[7] Pulpit Commentary on Galatians 3:19, https://biblehub.com/commentaries/pulpit/galatians/3.htm

[8] Albert Barnes, *Notes, Explanatory and Practical, on the Second Epistle to the Corinthians and the Epistle to the Galatians* (London: Knight and Son, 11, Clerkenwell Close, 1852), 390.

[9] Kenneth S. Wuest, *Wuest's Word Studies from the Greek New Testament: For the English Reader,* vol. 3 (Grand Rapids: Eerdmans, 1997), 105–106.

CHAPTER 9

[1] Joseph Barber Lightfoot, ed., *St. Paul's Epistle to the Galatians. A Revised Text with Introduction, Notes, and Dissertations.,* 4th ed., *Classic Commentaries on the Greek New Testament*

(London: Macmillan and Co., 1874), 146.

2 Kenneth S. Wuest, *Wuest's Word Studies from the Greek New Testament: For the English Reader*, vol. 3 (Grand Rapids: Eerdmans, 1997), 106.

3 Ibid, 106–107.

4 Kenneth L. Barker and John L. Kohlenberger III, *The Expositors Bible, Abridged Edition, Old and New Testaments*, (Zondervan, 1994), Epub edition 2018, 3602.

5 Kenneth S. Wuest, *Wuest's Word Studies from the Greek New Testament: For the English Reader*, vol. 3 (Grand Rapids: Eerdmans, 1997), 107.

5 Ibid.

6 Ibid, 107-108.

7 Albert Barnes, *Notes on the New Testament Explanatory and Practical, Enlarged Type Edition*, Edited by Robert Frew, D.D. (Grand Rapids 6, 1950), https://ccel.org/ccel/barnes/ntnotes/ntnotes.xii.iii.xxi.html

8 The Holy Bible, According to the Authorized Version (A.D. 1611), With and Explanatory and Critical Commentary and A Revision of the Translation by Bishops and Other Clergy of the Anglican Church, Edited by F.C. Cook, M.A., Canon of Exeter, Late Preacher at Lincoln's Inn, Chaplain in Ordinary to the Queen, New Testament, Vol. III (London: 1881), pg. 518.

Is Not This the Land of Beulah? Available at: https://hymnary. org/text/i_am_dwelling_on_the_mountain_where_ the?extended=true

CHAPTER 10

[1] Kenneth L. Barker and John L. Kohlenberger III, *The Expositors Bible, Abridged Edition, Old and New Testaments* (Zondervan, 1994), Epub edition 2018, 3603.

[2] Kenneth S. Wuest, *Wuest's Word Studies from the Greek New Testament: For the English Reader,* vol. 3 (Grand Rapids: Eerdmans, 1997), 110.

[3] Albert Barnes, *Notes on the New Testament Explanatory and Practical, Enlarged Type Edition,* Edited by Robert Frew, D.D. with Numerous Additional Notes and a Series of Engravings, (Grand Rapids 6, 1950), https://ccel.org/ccel/barnes/ ntnotes/ntnotes.xii.iii.xxi.html

[4] Ellicott's Commentary for English Readers, https://biblehub. com/commentaries/ellicott/galatians/3.htm

[5] Ibid.

[6] Kenneth S. Wuest, Wuest's Word Studies from the Greek New Testament: For the English Reader, vol. 3 (Grand Rapids: Eerdmans, 1997), 111.

[7] Martin Luther and Erasmus Middleton. *A Commentary On*

Saint Paul's Epistle to the Galatians: To Which Is Prefixed, The Life of the Author, And a Complete And Impartial History of the Times In Which He Lived. A new ed., corrected and revised (London: B. Blake, 1838), 278.

[8] Kenneth S. Wuest, *Wuest's Word Studies from the Greek New Testament: For the English Reader*, vol. 3 (Grand Rapids: Eerdmans, 1997), 111.

[9] Kenneth L. Barker and John L. Kohlenberger III, *The Expositors Bible, Abridged Edition, Old and New Testaments*, (Zondervan, 1994), Epub edition 2018, 3604-3605.

[10] Gordon Fee, The New International Commentary on the New Testament, First Epistle to the Corinthians (Wm. B. Eerdmans Publishing Co., 1987), 707.

[11] My Jewish Learning, https://www.myjewishlearning.com/article/who-has-not-made-me-a-woman/

[12] Kenneth L. Barker and John L. Kohlenberger III, *The Expositors Bible, Abridged Edition, Old and New Testaments*, (Zondervan, 1994), Epub edition 2018, 3605.

[13] Kenneth S. Wuest, *Wuest's Word Studies from the Greek New Testament: For the English Reader*, vol. 3 (Grand Rapids: Eerdmans, 1997), 112.

[14] Albert Barnes, *Notes, Explanatory and Practical, on the Second Epistle to the Corinthians and the Epistle to the Galatians* (London: Knight and Son, 11, Clerkenwell Close, 1852), 400.

[15] Ibid.

[16] Ibid.

[17] Kenneth L. Barker and John L. Kohlenberger III, *The Expositors Bible, Abridged Edition, Old and New Testaments,* (Zondervan, 1994), Epub edition 2018, pg. 3604-3605.

[18] Stott, John R. W. *The Message of Galatians: Only One Way.* Inter-Varsity Press, 1992.

[19] Kenneth S. Wuest, *Wuest's Word Studies from the Greek New Testament: For the English Reader,* vol. 3 (Grand Rapids: Eerdmans, 1997), 112.

ABOUT EVANGELIST JIMMY SWAGGART

The Rev. Jimmy Swaggart is a Pentecostal evangelist whose anointed preaching and teaching has drawn multitudes to the cross of Christ since 1955.

As an author, he has written more than 60 books, commentaries, study guides, and The Expositor's Study Bible, which has sold more than 4.5 million copies.

As an award-winning musician and singer, Brother Swaggart has recorded more than 60 gospel albums and sold nearly 17 million recordings worldwide.

For more than six decades, Brother Swaggart has channeled his preaching and music ministry through multiple media venues including print, radio, television and the Internet.

In 2010, Jimmy Swaggart Ministries launched its own cable channel, SonLife Broadcasting Network, which airs 24 hours a day to a potential viewing audience of more than 2 billion people around the globe.

Brother Swaggart also pastors Family Worship Center in Baton Rouge, Louisiana, the church home and headquarters of Jimmy Swaggart Ministries.

Jimmy Swaggart Ministries materials can be found at **www.jsm.org**.

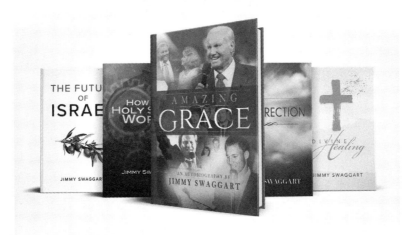

Chapter 4

Apparently Alice's CT scan was "unremarkable," which had made her feel ashamed of her mediocrity. It reminded her of her school reports with every single box ticked "Satisfactory" and comments like "A quiet student. Needs to contribute more in class." They may as well have just come right out and written across the front: "So boring, we don't actually know who she is." Elisabeth's reports had some boxes ticked "Outstanding" and others ticked "Below Standard" and comments like "Can be a little disruptive." Alice had yearned to be a little disruptive, but she couldn't work out how you got started.

"We're concerned about your memory loss, so we're going to keep you overnight for observation," said the doctor with the red plastic glasses.

"Oh, okay, thank you." Alice self-consciously smoothed her hair back, imagining a row of doctors and nurses with clipboards sitting next to her bed, watching her sleep. (She sometimes snored.)

The doctor hugged her own clipboard to her chest and looked at her brightly, as if she felt like a chat.

Oh. Gosh. Alice searched around for interesting topics of conversation and finally said, "So, did you ring my obstetrician? Dr. Chapple? Of course, you might not have had a chance . . ." She didn't want the doctor to snarl, "Sorry, I was busy saving somebody's life."

The doctor looked thoughtful. "I did, actually. It seems Sam Chapple retired three years ago." Alice couldn't believe that Dr. Chapple was no longer sitting in his big leather chair, carefully noting down answers to his courteous questions in beautiful copperplate writing on white index cards. She really needed to get this . . . this *problem* sorted out once and for all. Pronto! Quick sticks! As Frannie would say. Was Frannie still alive in 2008? Grandmothers died. It was to be expected. You weren't even allowed to be that upset about it. Please don't let Frannie have died. Please don't let anyone have died. "Nobody else in our family will die," Elisabeth had promised when she was ten and Alice was nine. "Because it wouldn't be fair." Alice had believed every single word Elisabeth had said when they were little.

Maybe Elisabeth had died? Or Nick? Or Mum? Or the baby? (*I'm sorry, but there is no heartbeat.*)

For the first time in years, Alice had that feeling she used to get when she was little, after their dad died, that someone else she loved was about to die. She longed to gather everybody she loved and stow them safely under her bed with her favorite dolls. Sometimes the stress would become so overwhelming she would forget how to breathe and Elisabeth would have to bring her a brown paper bag to breathe into.

"I might need a bag," Alice said to the doctor.

"A bag?"

Ridiculous. She wasn't a child who hyperventilated at the thought of people dying.

"I had a bag," she said to the doctor. "A red backpack with stickers on it. Do you know what happened to it?"

The doctor looked vaguely irritated by this administrative question but then she said, "Oh, yes. Over here. Would you like it?" She picked up the strange backpack from a shelf at the side of the room and Alice looked at it apprehensively.

The doctor handed it to her and said, "Well, you just rest up and someone will be along to take you up to a ward soon. I'm sorry there is so much waiting. That's hospitals for you." She gave her a motherly pat on the shoulder and quickly left the room, suddenly in a hurry, as if she'd remembered another patient who was waiting.

Alice ran her fingers over the three shiny dinosaur stickers on the flap of the backpack. They each had speech bubbles saying either "DINOSAURS RULE!" or "DINOSAURS ROCK!" She looked down at the sticker on her shirt and peeled it off. It was a definite match. She stuck it back on her shirt (she felt that she should for some reason) and waited for a feeling or a memory.

Did these belong to the Sultana? Her mind skittered away from the idea, like a frightened animal. She didn't want to know. She didn't *want* a ready-grown baby. She wanted her own little future baby back.

This could not be happening to her. *But it is, so get a grip, Alice.* She began to open the bag and her fingernails caught her attention. She held up her hands in front of her. Her nails were beautifully shaped and long and painted a very pale, beige color. Normally they were ragged and broken and rimmed with dirt from gardening or painting or whatever other renovation job they were doing at the time. The only other time they'd looked like that was for her wedding when she'd got her manicure. She'd spent the whole honeymoon flapping her hands at Nick, saying, "Look, I'm a *lady*."

Apart from that, her hands still looked like her hands. Actually, they looked quite nice.

They were bare, she noticed. No jewelry. It was a little unusual that she wasn't at least wearing her wedding ring, but perhaps she'd been in a rush when she was getting ready for her "spin class."

She held up her left hand and saw that there was a thin white indentation from her wedding ring that hadn't been there before. It gave her a disconnected feeling, like when she'd seen the feathery marks on her stomach. Her mind thought everything was still the same, but her body was telling her that time had marched on without her.

Time. She put her hands to her face. If she was supposedly sending out *"invitations to her fortieth-birthday party,"* if she was . . . *thirty-nine*—she mentally choked and gasped for air at the thought—then her face must be different. Older. There was a mirror over a basin in the front corner of the room. She could see the reflection of her feet, in their short white socks; one of the flurry of nurses had taken off the strange sneakers (chunky, rubbery things) and put them on the floor next to the bed. Alice could just hop out of the bed and walk over and look at herself.

Presumably it was against strict hospital regulations to get out of bed. She had a head injury. She might faint and hit her head again. Nobody had told her not to get out of bed, but they probably thought it was obvious.

She should look in the mirror. But she didn't want to see. She didn't want to know. She didn't want this to be real. Besides, she was *busy* at the moment. She had to look through the bag. Quickly, she undid the buckles of the backpack and shoved her hand in. She pulled out . . . a towel.

A plain, innocuous, clean blue bath towel. Alice looked at it and felt nothing but embarrassment. She was fossicking through somebody else's private stuff. Jane Turner had obviously picked up someone else's bag and insisted it was hers without really looking at it. It was just like Jane. So bossy and impatient.

Well.

Alice examined her beautifully manicured fingernails again. She put her hand in the bag again and pulled out a plastic bag, folded flat. She opened it and emptied it onto her lap.

A woman's clothes. Underwear. A red dress. A cream-colored cardigan with a single large wooden button. Knee-high beige boots. Small jewelry case.

The underwear was creamy lace-edged satin. Alice's underwear tended to be flippant and faded; jolly seahorses on her pants and purple cotton bras that clipped at the front.

She held the dress up in front of her and saw that it was beautiful. A simple design of silky fabric with tiny cream flowers. The cream of the cardigan matched the cream of the flowers on the dress exactly.

She checked the label on the dress. An S for small. It wouldn't fit her. She was a medium at best. It couldn't be hers. She folded the clothes back up and opened the jewelry case, lifting out a fine gold necklace with a big topaz stone. The stone was too big for her taste, but she dangled it over the dress and agreed that it was an excellent match. Well done, whoever you are.

The other piece of jewelry was Alice's gold Tiffany charm bracelet.

Alice said, "Fancy meeting you here." She picked up the bracelet and laid it across her wrist and felt comforted, as if Nick had finally arrived.

Nick had bought this bracelet for her the day after they found out she was pregnant with the Sultana. He shouldn't have spent that much because they were experiencing what Nick called "severe fiscal stress," due to the fact that every single thing they did to the house ended up costing more than planned, but Nick said it could go on the balance sheet under "extraordinary items" (whatever that meant) because it was extraordinary that they were having a baby.

The Sultana had been conceived on a Wednesday night, which just didn't seem exciting enough a night for such a momentous event, and the sex hadn't even been that passionate or romantic. It was just that there had been nothing much on TV and Nick had yawned and said, "We should paint the hallway," and Alice had said, "Oh, let's just have sex," and Nick had yawned again and said, "Mmmm. Okay." And then they'd discovered there weren't any condoms in the chest of drawers next to the bed, but by then the action was under way and neither of them could be bothered to get up and find one in the bathroom, and besides which it was a *Wednesday* and it was only *once* and, well, they were married. They were allowed to get pregnant, so therefore it wasn't really likely. The next day Alice discovered there actually had been a condom in the back of the drawer if she'd bothered to stretch her fingers just a bit further but by then it was too late. The Sultana had already started doing what it needed to do to become a person.

The day after they did the eight positive pregnancy tests (just in case the first seven were wrong) Nick had come home from work and handed her a small gift-wrapped box with a card that said "For the mother of my child," and inside was the bracelet.

To be honest, she loved that bracelet even more than she loved her engagement ring.

Of course, to be *really* honest, she didn't actually love her engagement ring at all. She sort of hated it.

Not a single person in the world knew this. It was her only real secret, so it was a pity it wasn't juicier. The ring was an Edwardian antique that had belonged to Nick's grandmother. Alice had never met Granny Love, but she had apparently been formidable but adorable (she sounded dreadful). Nick's four sisters, whom Nick called "the

Flakes" because of their undeniably flaky tendencies, were crazy about that ring and there had been a lot of bitter remarks when Granny Love left the ring to Nick in her will. One or another of the Flakes was always grabbing Alice's left hand and sniffing, "You just can't *get* jewelry like that anymore!"

Alice thought it was ugly. It was a big emerald set in the middle of a cluster of diamonds to look like a flower. It reminded her of a hibiscus for some reason and she'd never been a fan of the hibiscus, but what did she know, because every other girl in the world seemed to think the ring was *divine*, and apparently it was worth a small fortune.

And that was the other problem. This was the most expensive piece of jewelry Alice had ever owned, and Alice lost things. Constantly. She was always retracing her steps, emptying out garbage bins and calling up train stations, restaurants, and grocery stores to see if they had her purse or her sunglasses or her umbrella.

"Oh *no*," said Elisabeth when she heard that Alice's ring was an irreplaceable family heirloom. "You'll just have to—I don't know—get it surgically attached to your finger?"

Most of the time, except for special events or if she was seeing the Flakes, Alice just didn't wear the ring. She wore her plain gold wedding band, or nothing at all. She'd never really been a jewelry sort of person anyway.

However, she loved the gold Tiffany bracelet. Unlike the ring, it seemed to represent all the wonderful things that had happened over the last few years—Nick, the baby, the house.

Now she fastened the bracelet around her wrist, laid her head back against the white hospital pillow, and held the backpack close to her stomach. The thought crossed her mind that there were probably a million bracelets just like this one around and it could just as easily belong to somebody else. It wasn't like she recognized anything else in the bag, but she knew it was hers.

She was starting to get angry with herself. *Come on, now! Remember!* Furious, she shoved her hand back in the rucksack and pulled out a black purse. It was a long, luxurious rectangle of black leather. Alice turned it back and forth in her hands. "Gucci," it said, in tiny discreet letters. Goodness. She opened the purse and the first thing she saw was her own face staring back at her from a driver's license.

Her own face. Her own name. Her own address.

Well, here was the proof that the bag belonged to her.

The photo was typically blurry, but she could see she was wearing a white shirt and what looked like long black beads. Long beads? Had she become the sort of person who wore long beads? Her hair was cut in a bob just above her shoulders and it seemed to have been colored very blond. She'd cut her hair! Nick had once made her promise to never cut her hair. Alice had thought that exquisitely romantic, although Elisabeth had made gagging sounds when she told her and said, "You can't promise to still have a fourteen-year-old's hairstyle when you're forty."

When you're forty.

Oh.

Alice put a hand up to the back of her head. She'd been vaguely aware that her hair was pulled back in a ponytail before; she hadn't realized that it was actually more of a pigtail. She pulled out the elastic band and ran her fingers through her hair. It was even shorter than in the driver's-license photograph. She wondered if Nick liked it. In a minute, she would have to be brave and face herself in the mirror.

Of course, she was still pretty busy at the moment. No hurry.

She put the license back in the wallet and began to rifle through it. There were various credit and ATM cards with her name embossed on the front, including a gold American Express card. Wasn't a gold Amex just a status symbol for the sort of person who drives a BMW? Library card. Health Fund card.

A plain white business card for a Michael Boyle, "Registered Physiotherapist." The address was in Melbourne. She flipped it over and saw a handwritten message on the back.

Alice,

We're all settled and doing OK. I think of you often and "happier times." Call anytime.

M. xxx

She dropped the card in her lap. What did this Michael Boyle mean when he presumptuously referred to "happier times"? She didn't want to have had happier times with a physiotherapist in Melbourne. He sounded awful. She imagined a balding, paunchy type with soft hands and moist lips.

Where the bloody hell was Nick?

Perhaps Jane had forgotten to call him. She'd been acting so strangely at the gym. Alice should just phone him herself and explain that this was pretty serious and she really needed him to leave work right now. Why hadn't she thought of that before? Suddenly she was desperate to get herself a phone and hear Nick's lovely, familiar voice. She had a strange feeling as if it had been ages since she'd spoken to him.

She looked feverishly around the small room and of course—there was no phone. There was nothing in the room at all, except for the basin, the mirror, and a sign about how to wash your hands correctly.

A mobile phone! That's what she needed. She'd only recently got her first one. It was an old one belonging to Nick's father and it worked fine, except that it had to be held together with an elastic band. Something told her that she would probably have a more expensive phone by now, and when she opened the zippered pocket at the front of the bag, she saw she was right; there was a tiny, sleek, shiny, silver phone sitting right there as if she'd known it would be. (Had she? She couldn't tell.)

There was also a leather-bound day planner, which Alice opened quickly, just to confirm that it was indeed 2008, noting with sick wonder that her own handwriting filled the pages. "2008," it said in no-doubt-about-it black letters at the top of each page: 2008, 2008, 2008 . . .

She stopped flipping the pages and picked up the shiny phone, breathing shallowly, as if a huge metal bar had been plonked across her chest.

Could she even work this strange phone? She was hopeless at working out how to use new appliances, but her elegantly manicured fingers seemed to know what to do, pushing the silver buttons on either side of the phone so it snapped open. She punched in the number for Nick's direct line and held the phone up to her ear. It rang. *Please answer, please answer.* She felt like she would burst into sobs of relief at the sound of his voice.

"Hello. Sales Department!"

It was a young girl's voice, frothy with good humor. Someone in the background was roaring with laughter.

Alice said, "Is Nick there at the moment? Nick Love?"

There was a slight pause. When the girl spoke again, she sounded as though she had just been sternly reprimanded. The laughter in the background stopped abruptly. "I'm sorry, you've come through to the wrong extension, but I could put you through to Mr. Love's personal assistant if you like."

Alice paused, diverted by the fact that Nick had a "personal assistant." How posh.

The girl continued, as if Alice had argued with her: "Mr. Love is actually in Portugal this week, so his PA would be the best person to help you."

Portugal! She said, "What's he doing in Portugal?"

"Well, it's some sort of international conference, I think," said the girl uncertainly. "But if I could just put you through——"

Portugal, and a personal assistant. He must have got a promotion. They'd have to have champagne!

Alice said (cunningly!), "Um, could you remind me of Mr. Love's position with the company?"

"He's our general manager," said the girl in an everyone-in-the-world-knows-that tone.

Good grief.

Nick had the Motherfucking Megatron's job.

That was more than one promotion. That was a giant superhero leap up the corporate ladder. Alice was filled with giggly pride at the thought of *Nick* strutting about the office, telling people what to do. Wouldn't people just laugh at him?

"I'm putting you through to his PA now," said the girl firmly. The phone clicked and began to ring again.

Another female voice answered smoothly. "Mr. Love's office, this is Annabelle, how can I help you?"

"Oh," said Alice. "This is Nick's wife, ah, Mr. Love's wife. I was trying to get hold of him, but, ummm . . ."

The woman's voice turned razor sharp. "Hello, Alice. How are you today?"

"Well, actually . . ."

"As you're aware, Nick isn't back in Sydney until Sunday morning. Obviously if there is something that absolutely can't wait, I can try to get a message through to him but I'd really prefer not to disturb him. His schedule is frantic."

"Oh." Why was this woman being so mean? She obviously knew her. What could Alice have done to make her dislike her so much?

"So, can it wait or not, Alice?" She wasn't imagining it; this was real live hatred she was hearing. The pain in Alice's head got worse. She wanted to say, "Hey, lady, I'm in hospital. I came here in an *ambulance*!"

"I wish you wouldn't let people stomp all over you," Elisabeth was always telling her. Sometimes, long after Alice had forgotten the incident, Elisabeth would say, "I was up all last night thinking about what that woman in the chemist's said to you. I can't believe you just *took it*—you've got no backbone!" Alice would drop to the floor, all jelly-like, to demonstrate her lack of backbone, and Elisabeth would say, "Oh for God's sake."

The problem was, Alice needed more warning when it came to being assertive. These sorts of situations were so unexpected. She needed hours to really think things through. Were they really being nasty, or was she just being sensitive? What if they'd just found out they had a terminal disease that morning and were entitled to be in a bad mood? She was about to mumble something pleading and pathetic to Nick's PA when, against her will, her body began an unfamiliar sequence of actions. Her back straightened. Her chin lifted. Her stomach muscles clenched. She spoke and didn't recognize her own voice. It was taut and tart and decidedly snooty. "No, it can't wait," she said. "It is urgent. There has been an *accident*. Please ask Nick to call me as soon as possible."

Alice couldn't have been more surprised if she'd found herself doing a triple backflip.

The woman answered, "Fine, Alice, I'll see what I can do." Her contempt was still palpable.

"I'd appreciate it."

Alice hung up and said, with the phone still to her ear, "Cow. Bitch.

Slut." She spat the words out of the side of her mouth, like poisonous pellets.

She swallowed. Now that was even more surprising; she sounded like a tattooed girl who quite liked the occasional catfight.

The mobile rang in her hand, making her jump.

It must be Nick, she thought, awash with relief. Once again, her fingers knew what to do. She pressed the button with the green phone symbol and said, "Nick?"

A child's voice she'd never heard before said crossly, "Mum?"

Chapter 5

Frannie's Letter to Phil

Dearest Phil,

I'm a little riled up today.

You'll remember I mentioned I'd taken on the role of running the Social Committee. Well, for the last few months I've been arranging a Family Talent Night. It's next Wednesday. Children, grandchildren, and so forth will be performing a variety of acts. Should be a fun night! In all honesty it will probably be excruciating, but it will be a diversion from our arthritis if nothing else.

(I was thinking today about the musical we organized together. Oklahoma! 1972? 1973? You kissed me backstage and that sly little Frank Neary caught us. The news spread like wildfire: "Mr. Peyton and Miss Jeffrey are a couple. The school principal and the maths coordinator! Ooh, scandal!" It just made everything even more delicious, didn't it?)

Anyway, today we had a new resident turn up at the Social Committee meeting. I can't recall his name. (See? Shocking memory!) I'll call him

Mr. Mustache because that's his most defining feature: a comically large white mustache. It gives him the look of a retired used-car salesman. Or perhaps a seedy Santa Claus.

Anyway, Mr. Mustache was full of suggestions.

We're serving tea, coffee, sandwiches, pikelets, and scones on the Family Talent Night. Standard fare for a function at a retirement village. Mr. Mustache piped up and suggested we set up a cocktail bar. Said he once spent a year bartending on some Caribbean island and that he could make a cocktail "guaranteed to blow my socks off." I'm not joking, Phil. This is the way he talks.

I tried to explain about liquor licenses, but he was already on to a new topic. He said he knew a young girl who wasn't exactly a family member, but would she still be allowed to perform? Of course, I said. He said that was wonderful because she did a very entertaining "pole dancing" act. All the men slapped their knees, roaring with laughter. (You wouldn't have laughed, would you?)

Even some of the women were laughing. Rita was laughing like a loon. She has dementia, so I guess I can excuse her—but still, you'd think she'd retain a modicum of decency!

It was the strangest thing. I felt the most absurdly embarrassing desire to burst into tears. All at once, I was straight back in my very first classroom out of teacher's college. There was a very handsome boy in my class (I can still see where he sat—second row from the back) who was always cracking jokes and making everyone laugh. Did I ever tell you about him? He made me feel so humorless and stodgy. Like an old maid. (And I was twenty years old, for heaven's sake!)

You never made me feel—

Barb just phoned.

Alice has had a nasty fall during her gym class (she seems to spend half her life at that gym) and she's in hospital.

I'm in a fluster.
I'll finish this later.

"Mum?" the child spoke again, impatiently. Alice couldn't tell if it was a boy or a girl. It was just an average kid's voice. Breathy, rushed, a touch snuffly. Kind of adorable. She hardly ever spoke to children on the phone, except for an occasional stilted birthday chat with one of Nick's nephews or nieces, and she was always struck by the sweetness of their kidlike voices. They seemed so much bigger and scarier and dirtier in the flesh.

Her hand was sweaty. She took a firm grip of the phone, licked her lips, and said hoarsely, "Hello?"

"Mum! It's *me!*" The kid's voice bubbled up and out of the phone, as if he or she were yelling straight in her ear. "Why did you think it would be Dad? Is he calling you from Portugal? Oh! If you speak to him, can you please tell him that the name of the Xbox game I want is Lost Planet, Extreme Condition, okay? Got it? 'Cause I think I told him the wrong name. Okay, Mum, this is pretty important, so you might need to write this down. Do you want me to talk slowly? *Lost. Planet. Extreme. Condition.* Anyway, where are you? We've got swimming and you *know* I hate being late because then I get stuck with the stupid paddleboard. Oh, there's Uncle Ben! Is he taking us swimming today? Okay! Cool! Why didn't you tell us? HI, UNCLE BEN! Okay, gotta go, see you, Mum."

There was a scraping sound, a thud, and the sounds of children shouting in the distance. A man's voice said, "Gidday, champ," and then the line was cut off.

Alice dropped the phone in her lap and stared straight ahead at the open doorway. Had she just had a *conversation* with the Sultana?

She didn't even know the baby's name. They were still arguing over the names. Nick wanted "Tom"—a "good honest name for a man"—and Alice wanted "Ethan"—a sexy, successful name. Or if the Sultana surprised them by being a girl, Alice wanted "Madeline" and Nick wanted "Addison"—because apparently girls didn't need "good honest names."

Alice thought, I could not be mother to a child and not know his name. This is simply not possible. It is beyond the realms of possibility.

Maybe it was a wrong number! The child had mentioned an "Uncle Ben." There was no "Ben" in Alice's family. She didn't know a single Ben. She wasn't sure she'd ever even met a Ben. She searched her mind and all she could dredge up was a huge bearded neon-sign designer she'd once met while helping Nick's older sister, Dora (possibly the flakiest of the Flakes), at her "Psychic Arts" shop, and in fact his name could just as easily have been Bill or Brad.

The problem was that the kid had asked, "Why did you think it would be Dad?" when she'd said "Nick." Also, he knew Nick was in Portugal.

It was beyond the realms of possibility, yet, on the other hand, it seemed sort of conclusive. She closed her eyes briefly and opened them again, trying to visualize a ten-year-old son. How tall would he be? What color eyes? What color hair?

Part of her wanted to scream with the sheer terror of this situation, and part of her wanted to roar with laughter because it was so ridiculous. An impossible joke. A hilarious story she would be telling for years—"And *then*, I ring Nick and this woman tells me he's in Portugal! And I'm thinking, *Portugal*!?"

She picked up the phone gingerly, as if it were an explosive device, and considered calling somebody else: Elisabeth? Mum? Frannie?

No. She didn't want any more strange voices telling her things she didn't know about the people she loved.

Her body felt weak and heavy. She would do nothing. Nothing at all. Eventually something would happen; somebody would come. The doctors would fix her head and everything would be okay. She began shoving things back into the rucksack. As she picked up the leather-bound diary, a photo fell out.

It was a photo of three children in school uniforms. It was obviously a posed shot because they were sitting in a row on a step with their elbows on their knees and their chins in their hands. There were two girls and a boy.

The boy was in the middle. He had messy white-blond hair, ears that stuck out, and a turned-up nose. He had tipped his head to one side and clenched his teeth together in a grotesque grimace that Alice knew was meant to be a smile. She knew this because she must have seen at least a hundred photos of her sister pulling an identical face. "Why do I do that?" Elisabeth would say sadly when she saw the photo.

On the boy's left side was a girl who looked older. She was a chunky, stolid-looking girl with a long face and straight brown hair in a ponytail that had fallen over one shoulder. She was slumped forward in a way that clearly said, "I do not want to sit in this ridiculous position." Her mouth was compressed in a straight line and she was looking grimly off to the right of the camera. She had a nasty graze on one chunky knee, and both her shoelaces were undone. There was nothing remotely familiar about her.

To the boy's right was a little girl with blond curls bunched together in fat pigtails on either side of her head. She was smiling ecstatically with a dimple denting her cherubic cheeks. There was something stuck to both the shirt collars of her uniform; Alice held the photo up closer. They were shiny dinosaur stickers just like the one on Alice's own shirt.

Alice turned the photo over and saw there was a typewritten label stuck to the back. It said:

Children (left to right): Olivia Love (Kindergarten), Tom Love (Yr4B), Madison Love (Yr5M)

Parent: Alice Love

Number of copies ordered: 4

Alice turned the photo back over and looked again at the three children.

I have never seen you before in my life.

There was a distant buzzing sound in her ears; she could feel herself breathing short, shallow breaths, her chest rising and falling quickly as if she were at high altitude. (Oh, it was so *funny*! So, I'm looking at this photo, right, of three kids? And it's my own children! And *I don't even recognize them*! Hilarious!)

Another nurse Alice hadn't seen before came into the room, glanced briefly at Alice, and picked up the clipboard at the end of her stretcher. "I'm so sorry we're still keeping you waiting. The powers that be assure me it should only be a few more minutes and we'll have a bed free for you. How are you feeling?"

Alice put crazily trembling fingertips to her head. "The thing is, I don't actually remember the last ten years of my life." There was a quiver of hysteria in her voice.

"I think we might try and organize a nice cup of tea and sandwiches for you." The nurse looked at the photo lying in Alice's lap and said, "Your kids?"

"Apparently," said Alice, and gave a little laugh that turned into a sob, and the taste of tears in her mouth felt so familiar, and the thought came into her head, *Stop it! I'm so sick, sick, sick of crying*, but what did that mean, because she hadn't cried like this since she was little, and anyway she couldn't stop even if she wanted.

Chapter 6

Elisabeth's Homework for Dr. Hodges

In the afternoon tea break I called Ben on his mobile and he said, over a babble of noise that sounded like twenty kids, not three, that he'd picked up the children from school and he was driving them to their swimming lessons now. He said he'd been informed it was impossible to miss even one swimming lesson because Olivia had just become a crocodile or a platypus or something and I heard Olivia's gurgling laugh as she shouted, "A DOLPHIN, silly billy!" I could also hear Tom, who must have been in the front next to Ben, saying monotonously, "You are now five kilometers OVER the speed limit, you are now four kilometers OVER the speed limit, you are now two kilometers UNDER the speed limit."

Ben sounded stressed, but happy. Happier than I've heard him in weeks. Picking up the children and driving them to swimming is not something Alice would normally ask (trust) us to do and I knew that Ben was probably exhilarated by the responsibility. I imagined how people glancing over at traffic lights would see a standard dad (maybe a bit bigger and bushier than average) with his three kids.

If I think too much about this, it will hurt a great deal, so I won't.

Ben told me that Tom had just spoken on the mobile to Alice and according to Tom she didn't say anything about falling over at the gym and she sounded "just like Mum except maybe ten to fifteen percent grumpier than usual." I think he's learning percentages at school right now.

Weirdly, I'd never even thought of just ringing Alice's mobile myself. So I immediately dialed her number.

When she answered, she sounded so strange that I didn't recognize her voice and thought that a nurse must have picked up the phone. I said, "Oh, sorry, I was just trying to reach Alice Love," and then I realized it was Alice and she was sobbing, "Oh, Libby, thank God it's you!" She sounded terrible, hysterical really, babbling about a photo and dinosaur stickers and a red dress that couldn't possibly fit her but was really beautiful and being deliriously drunk in a gym and why was Nick in Portugal and she didn't know if she was pregnant or not and she thought it was 1998 but everybody else said it was 2008. It gave me a fright. I can't remember when I last saw or heard Alice cry (or call me Libby). Even though she has had so much to cry about over the past year, she doesn't cry in front of me, and there is such a horrible polite restraint in all our conversations recently, with both of us putting on these oh-so-reasonable voices.

It actually felt sort of good to hear Alice cry. It felt real.

It's been such a long time since she needed me, and that used to be such an important part of my identity, being the big sister who shielded Alice from the world. (I should save my money and analyze myself, Dr. Hodges.)

So I told her not to worry, that I was coming straight there and we would sort everything out and I went straight back onstage and said that there had been a family emergency and that I had to leave but that my very capable assistant Layla would be taking over and when I looked at Layla to see her reaction, she was pink and radiant, as if she'd just got religion. So that was OK.

Of course the hospital would have to be Royal North Shore.

I always feel as though I have swallowed something huge when I drive into that car park. It's shaped like an anchor, this thing I've swallowed, and it goes straight down my throat and stretches out on either side of my belly.

Another thing: the sky always seems so huge, like a big empty shell. Why is that? I must always look up as I'm driving in, or maybe it's something to do with me feeling tiny and useless, or maybe it's just simple geography for heaven's sake, and the road goes up before it dips down into the car park.

I'm here for Alice, I reminded myself when I got out of the car.

But everywhere I looked I could see old versions of Ben and me. We haunt the place. If you ever go there, Dr. Hodges, keep an eye out for us. There we'll be, shuffling down the pathway along the side of the hospital back toward the car park on a sunny ice-cold day, me in that unflattering hippie skirt that I keep wearing because it doesn't need ironing, and

I'm holding Ben's hand, letting him lead me, looking at the ground and chanting my mantra, "Don't think about it. Don't think about it. Don't think about it." You'll see us standing at the reception desk filling in forms and Ben is close behind me, rubbing my lower back in tiny circles and I feel like the circles are somehow keeping me breathing, in, out, in, out, like a ventilator. There we are, squashed into the back of the lift with an excited family, their arms overflowing with flowers and "It's a girl!" balloons. We both have our arms wrapped protectively around our stomachs in exactly the same way, as if we're hugging ourselves close, so all that joy can't hurt us.

You told me the other week that this doesn't define me, but it *does*, Dr. Hodges, it just does.

As I walked along the echoey corridors (clop, clop, clop, went my heels, and the *smell*, well, you probably know that horrible boiled-potato smell, Dr. Hodges, the way it floods your sinuses with memories of every other hospital visit), I ignored the badly dressed ghosts of hospital visits past and concentrated on Alice and wondered if she was still thinking it was 1998, and if so, what that would be like. The only thing I could compare it to was the one time when I was a teenager and got horribly drunk at a twenty-first party and stood up and gave a long, loving toast to the birthday boy, whom I had never met before that night. The next day, I didn't remember a thing about it, nothing, not even shadowy snippets. Apparently I used the word "paucity" in my speech, and that disturbed me, because I didn't think my sober self had ever said that word out loud before and I wasn't even entirely sure what it meant. I never got drunk like that again. I'm too much of a control freak to have other people falling about laughing while they describe my own actions to me.

If I couldn't stand losing two hours of my memory, what would it be like to lose ten years?

As I looked for Alice's ward number, I had a sudden memory of Mum and Frannie and me, giddy with excitement, just like that family in the lift, practically running through the corridors of another hospital looking for Alice's room when Madison was born. We happened to see Nick in the distance, walking along ahead of us, and we all shrieked, "Nick!" and he turned around and while he waited for us to catch up, he ran around in circles on the spot, and did a two-fisted punch in the air like Rocky, and Frannie said fondly, "He's such a card!" and I was dating that patronizing town planner at the time and I decided right then and there to break up with him, because Frannie would never call him a card.

If Alice had really lost every memory of the last ten years, I thought, then she would have no memory of that day, or of Madison as a baby. She wouldn't remember how we all shared a tin of Quality Street chocolates while the pediatrician came in to check Madison. He flipped her this way and that, and held her in one palm with casual expertise, like a basketballer spinning a ball, and Alice and Nick blurted out in unison, "Careful!" and we all laughed and the pediatrician smiled and said, "Your daughter gets ten out of ten, an A-plus." We all applauded and "whoo-hoo'd" Madison for her first-ever good mark, while he wrapped her back up in her white blanket, a neat packet of fish-and-chips, and ceremonially presented her to Alice.

I was just starting to consider the enormity of all the things that had happened to Alice over the last ten years when I found her ward number, and as I glanced through the door, I saw her in the first curtained-off cubicle, propped up against pillows, her hands resting on her lap and her eyes staring straight ahead. There was no color to her. She was wearing a white hospital gown, lying against a white pillow with a white gauze bandage wrapped around her head, and even her face was dead white. It was strange to see her so still; Alice is all about sharp, quick movement. She's texting on her mobile, jangling her car keys, grabbing one of the kids by the elbow and saying something stern in their ear. She's fingernail-tapping busy, busy, busy.

(Ten years ago she was nothing like that. She and Nick slept till noon every Sunday morning. "How will they *ever* find time to renovate that enormous house!" clucked Mum and Frannie and me, like elderly aunts.)

She didn't see me at first and as I walked up to her, her eyes flickered, and they looked so big and blue in her pale face, but more importantly, she was looking at me in a different, but familiar, way. I don't know how to describe it, except that the strange thought came into my head, "You're back."

You want to know the first thing she said to me, Dr. Hodges?

She said, "Oh, Libby, what *happened* to you?"

I told you, it defines me.

Alice had finally been moved up to a ward and given a hospital gown and a remote for the television and a white chest of drawers. A lady wheeling a trolley brought her a cup of weak tea and four tiny triangular curried-egg sandwiches. The nurse was right; the tea and sandwiches had made her feel better, except they hadn't done anything about the huge gaping crevasse in her memory.

When she'd heard Elisabeth's voice on the mobile phone, it was just like each time she'd called home on that disastrous trip around Europe when she was nineteen and trying to pretend she had a different personality—an adventurous, extroverted sort of personality; the sort of person who *loves* exploring cathedrals and ruins all day on her own and talking to drunk boys from Brisbane in youth hostels at night—when really she was homesick and lonely and often bored, and couldn't make head or tail of the train timetables. The sound of Elisabeth's voice, loud and clear in a strange phone box on the other side of the world, always made Alice's knees buckle with relief, and she'd press her forehead against the glass and think, *That's right; I am a real person.*

"My sister is coming right now," she told the nurse when she hung up, as if giving her credentials as a proper person with a family; a family she recognized.

Although, when Elisabeth first walked toward her bed, she actually didn't recognize her. She vaguely assumed that this woman in the cream suit with the glasses and the swinging shoulder-length hair must be a hospital administrator coming to do something administrative, but then something about the woman's straight-backed "I'll take you on" posture, something essentially Elisabeth, gave her away.

It was a shock, because it seemed that overnight Elisabeth had put on a lot of weight. She'd always had a strong, lithe, athletic-looking body, because of her rowing and her jogging and whatever else it was she was always so busy doing. Now she wasn't fat but definitely larger, softer, and bustier; a puffed-out version of herself, as if someone had blown her up like a plastic pool toy. She won't like that, thought Alice. Elisabeth had always been so amusingly moralistic about fattening food, refusing an offer of pavlova as if it were crack cocaine. Once, when Nick, Alice, and Elisabeth went away for a weekend together, Elisabeth spent ages at the breakfast table studying the "nutritional information" panel on the side of a container of yogurt, warning them darkly, "You have to be *really* careful with yogurt." Whenever Nick and Alice ate yogurt after that, one of them would always shout, "Careful!"

As she got closer and the bright light over Alice's bed lit up her face, Alice saw fine spidery lines etched around Elisabeth's mouth and on either side of her eyes behind the elegant spectacles. Elisabeth had large, pale blue eyes with dark lashes, like Alice, inherited from their father; eyes that attracted compliments, but now they seemed smaller and paler, as if the color had begun to wash out.

There was something bruised and wary and worn out about those washed-out eyes, as if she'd just been badly defeated in a fight she'd expected to win.

Alice felt a surge of worry; something terrible must have happened.

But when she asked, Elisabeth said, "What do you mean what happened to *me*?" so briskly and spiritedly that Alice doubted herself.

Elisabeth pulled over a plastic chair and sat down. Alice caught a glimpse of her skirt pulling unflatteringly across her stomach and quickly looked away; it made her want to cry.

Elisabeth said, "You're the one in hospital. The question is what happened to *you*?"

Alice felt herself slip into the role of irrepressible, hopeless Alice. "It's completely bizarre. It's like a dream. Apparently, I fell over at the gym. Me, at the gym! I know! According to Jane Turner I was doing something called my 'Friday spin class.'" She could be silly now, because Elisabeth was here to be sensible.

Elisabeth stared at her with such grim, frightened concentration that Alice felt her silly grin drift away.

She reached out for the photo she'd left sitting on the chest of drawers next to her bed and handed it to Elisabeth, saying in a small, polite voice, "Are these my . . ." She felt more foolish than she'd ever felt in her life. "Are these my children?"

Elisabeth took the photo, glanced at it, and something complicated crossed her face, a barely perceptible tremor, and vanished. She smiled carefully and said, "Yes, Alice."

Alice took a deep, shaky breath and closed her eyes. "I've never seen them before."

She heard Elisabeth take a deep breath herself. "It's just temporary, I'm sure. You probably just need to rest, to relax and—"

"What are they like?" Alice opened her eyes. "Those children. Are they . . . nice?"

Elisabeth said in a stronger voice, "They're wonderful, Alice."

Alice said, "Am I a good mother? Do I look after them all right? What do I feed them? They're so big!"

"Your children are your life, Alice," said Elisabeth. "You'll remember for yourself soon. It will all come back. Just—"

"I could cook them sausages, I guess," said Alice, cheering up at the thought. "Kids love sausages."

Elisabeth stared. "You would never feed them sausages."

"I thought I was pregnant," said Alice. "But they did a blood test and told me I'm definitely not. I don't feel like I am, but I can't believe I'm not. I can't believe it."

"No. Well, I don't think you would be pregnant—"

"*Three* kids!" said Alice. "We're only going to have two."

"Olivia was an accident," said Elisabeth stiffly, as if she disapproved.

"None of this seems real," said Alice. "I'm like Alice in Wonderland. Remember how much I hated that book? Because nothing made sense. You didn't like it either. We liked things to make sense."

"I can imagine it must feel *really* strange, but it's not going to last, it's all going to come back to you any minute. You must have hit your head quite . . . severely."

"Yes. Very severely." Alice picked up the photo again. "So this little girl. This little girl is the oldest, so she must be my first baby, right? So we had a girl?"

"Yes, you did."

"We thought it was a boy."

"I remember that."

"And labor! I went through labor three times? What was my labor like? I'm so nervous about it. I mean, I *was* . . ."

"I think you had a pretty easy time with Madison, but there were complications with Olivia—" Elisabeth fidgeted in her plastic seat. "Look, Alice, I think I should go and try to talk to one of your doctors. I'm finding this really hard. It's weird. It's really . . . scary."

Alice reached out for Elisabeth's arm in a panic. She couldn't stand to be alone again. "No, no, don't go. Someone will be around soon. They keep coming and checking on me. Hey, Libby, I called Nick at work and they told me he was in Portugal! Portugal! What's he doing there? I left a message with some horrible secretary. I stood up to her. You'd be proud of me! I showed backbone. My backbone was like *steel*."

"Good for you," said Elisabeth. She looked as if she'd just eaten something that disagreed with her.

"But he still hasn't called me back," sighed Alice.

Elisabeth's Homework for Dr. Hodges

It was only when she started talking about Nick being in Portugal that the obvious hit me, and it seemed even more shocking than when she asked me whether her children were "nice."

She really has forgotten everything.

Even Gina.

Chapter 7

So, you *seriously* don't remember anything, not a single thing, since 1998?" Elisabeth shifted the plastic chair in closer toward Alice's bed and leaned toward her, as if it was time to get to the bottom of this. "Nothing at all?"

"Well, I've been having some funny snippets of things come into my mind," said Alice. "But none of them make sense."

"Okay, so tell me about them," urged Elisabeth. Her face was closer now to Alice and the lines on either side of her mouth were even deeper than Alice had first thought. Goodness. Involuntarily, Alice pressed her fingertips to her own skin; she still hadn't looked at herself in a mirror.

She said, "Well, when I first woke up, I was having this dream, and I couldn't tell if it was just a dream or something that really happened. I was swimming, and it was a beautiful summer's morning, and my toenails were all painted different colors. There was somebody else with me and their toenails were painted the same way. Hey, maybe the other person was you? I bet it was you!"

Elisabeth said, "No, that doesn't mean anything to me. What else?"

Alice thought about the bouquets of pink balloons bobbing about in the gray sky, but she didn't want to tell Elisabeth about that great tidal wave of grief that kept sweeping her away, and she wasn't all that keen on finding out what it meant.

Instead she said, "I remember an American lady saying, '*I'm sorry, but there is no heartbeat.*'"

"Oh," said Elisabeth.

Elisabeth's Homework for Dr. Hodges

I admit I found it oddly touching, flattering even, that of all the billions of memories significant enough to float to the surface of Alice's mind, that was one of them.

Alice has always been good at imitating accents and she did that woman's voice perfectly. The tone and the rhythm were exactly the way I remembered, and for a moment I was back there in that gloomy room, trying to understand. I haven't thought about it in such a long time.

Imagine, Dr. Hodges, if I could travel back in time to that day and whisper in my ear, "This is only the beginning, honey." Then I'd throw back my head and laugh a demented witchy laugh.

Actually you don't really like it when I do that sort of black, bitter humor thing, do you? I've noticed that you smile politely and sort of sadly, as if I'm making a fool of myself and you know exactly why, as if I'm a teenager who isn't in control of her own embarrassing emotions.

Anyway, I didn't want to talk about the American woman

to Alice. Obviously. Especially not to *Alice*. I don't especially want to talk about it with you, either. Or think about it. Or write about it. It just happened. Like everything else.

Elisabeth smoothed the white blanket next to Alice's leg with the flat of her palm. Her face seemed to harden. She said, "Sorry, that doesn't mean anything to me, either. Not a thing."

Why did she sound angry? Alice felt as if she'd done something wrong but couldn't work out what; she felt stupidly clumsy, like a child trying to grasp something big and important that the grown-ups weren't telling her.

Elisabeth met Alice's eyes and gave her a half-smile and looked away again quickly.

A woman carrying flowers came into the ward, peered hopefully at Alice and Elisabeth, blinked dismissively, and walked past their curtained-off cubicle to the next one. They heard a disembodied voice squeal, "I was just thinking about you!"

"I should have brought you flowers," murmured Elisabeth.

Alice said suddenly, "You're married!"

"Pardon?"

Alice picked up Elisabeth's left hand. "You've got an engagement ring! It's gorgeous. That's exactly the sort of ring I would have got if we'd got to choose our own ring. Not that I don't love Granny Love's ring, of course."

Elisabeth said dryly, "You hate and despise Granny Love's ring, Alice."

"Oh. Did I tell you that? I don't remember telling you that."

"Years ago, I think you might have had too much to drink, that's why I don't understand why . . . well, anyway."

Alice said, "Well, are you going to keep me in suspense? Who did you marry? Was it that cute town planner?"

"*Dean?* No, I didn't marry Dean, and I only went out with him for five minutes. Also, he died. In a scuba diving accident. Tragic. Anyway, I married Ben. You don't remember Ben? He's looking after your children at the moment."

"Oh, that's nice of him, good," said Alice weakly, and felt sick again, because presumably a good mother would immediately have checked on who was looking after her children. The problem was that it still seemed preposterous that they existed. She pressed a hand to her flat stomach where there was no longer a baby and fought that feeling of vertigo. If she let herself think too much about this, she might start screaming and not be able to stop.

"Ben," said Alice, focusing on Elisabeth. "So you married someone called Ben." She remembered hearing that snuffly child say "Uncle Ben" on the phone. It was somehow worse when things clicked together, as if everything in the world made sense except for Alice.

She said, "It's funny, I was thinking earlier that the only Ben I knew was this huge neon-sign designer I met once at Nick's sister's shop. I always remembered that guy because he was so big and slow and silent, it was like a giant grizzly bear had been turned into a man."

Elisabeth burst out laughing, and the sound of her laugh (it was a full-throated, generous laugh that always made you want to say the funny thing again) and the way she tipped back her head made her seem like her proper self again.

"I don't get it." Alice smiled, ready to get it.

"That's the Ben I married. I met him at the opening of Dora's shop. We've been married eight years."

"Really?" Elisabeth married that huge grizzly neon-sign designer? She normally went for terribly witty, successful corporate types, who made Alice feel stupid. "But didn't he have a *beard*?"

Surely Elisabeth wouldn't have married someone with a beard.

Elisabeth shook with laughter. "Yep, he's still got it."

"And does he still design neon signs?"

"Yes, beautiful ones. My favorite is the one for Rob's Ribs and Rumps in Killara. It came in second in the annual Neon Design Awards last year."

Alice looked at her sharply, but she seemed perfectly serious.

She said, "So he's my brother-in-law. So I guess I . . . know him. I know him pretty well. Does Nick get on with him? Do we all go out together?"

Elisabeth paused and Alice couldn't read the expression on her face. Then she said, "Years ago, before Ben and I were married, when Madison was a toddler and you were just pregnant with Tom, we got a house together at Jervis Bay one Easter. It was right on Hyams Beach, you know—whitest sand in the world—and the weather was perfect, and Madison was so cute, we were all just in love with her. We played stupid card games like Cheat and one night Nick and Ben got drunk and danced to eighties music. Ben *never* dances. That might have been the only time I've seen him dance. They were being so stupid! We were just rolling around laughing so much, we woke Madison up and she got out of bed and danced with them in her pj's. Actually, that was a really special holiday. It makes me feel so nostalgic. I haven't thought about it for ages."

"I don't remember a thing about it," said Alice. It seemed so cruel that she couldn't remember a wonderful holiday, as if some other Alice had got to live her life in her place.

Elisabeth's tone changed abruptly. "It's amazing you don't remember Ben." There was something almost aggressive in her voice and she was looking sharply at Alice as if daring her to say something. "You saw him just yesterday. He came over to help you with your car. You baked him his favorite banana muffins. You had *quite* a chat."

"So," said Alice nervously. "We have a car now?"

"Mmmm. Yes you do, Alice."

"And I make banana muffins?"

Elisabeth smiled. "Low fat. High fiber. But surprisingly delicious."

Alice's mind jumped about feverishly, this way and that, until she felt dizzy, from those three strange children sitting in a row to banana muffins to a car (she didn't like cars: she liked buses, the ferry; also, she wasn't the best driver) to Elisabeth marrying a neon-sign designer called Ben.

She seized on a sudden hurtful thought. "Hey! You must have had a wedding without me!" Alice loved weddings. She would never forget a wedding.

Elisabeth said, "Alice, you were my matron of honor and Madison was flower girl. You had matching dresses the color of a Singapore orchid. You made a funny speech, and you and Nick made a spectacle of yourselves dancing to 'Come On Eileen.' You gave us a blender."

"Oh." Frustration welled up in her. "But I just can't believe I don't remember *any* of this. It doesn't even sound familiar!" She stuck her fingers through the holes in the blanket over her legs and bunched it together hard with both hands in a silly, childish movement. "There is so much . . . *stuff*!"

"Hey . . . hey, there." Elisabeth rubbed Alice's shoulder a bit too vigorously, as if she were a boxer, and looked around her feverishly for help. "You've got to let me go and find a doctor to talk about this."

She was a problem solver, Elisabeth. She always wanted to find a solution for you.

There was a burst of screechy female laughter from the cubicle next to them. "You *didn't*!" "I *did*!" Alice and Elisabeth raised their eyebrows at each other in mutual silent distaste and Alice was filled with soothing, sisterly affection.

She let go of the blanket and managed to put her hands sedately back in her lap. "Please don't go. A nurse will come along and check on me soon and you can talk to her. Just stay here and keep talking to me. I think that will cure me."

Elisabeth glanced at her watch and said, "I don't know about that," but she sat back in her chair.

Alice shifted herself against the pillows behind her back to get comfortable. She thought about asking more questions about the children in the photo (*three!*—the number was so unwieldy and impossible) but it was so surreal it was silly, like a movie that was so far-fetched you kept shifting in your seat and trying not to guffaw. It was better to ask about Elisabeth's life.

Elisabeth had her head bent, scratching at something invisible on her wrist. Alice looked again at the lines that seemed to pull her sister's mouth down into a sad sort of grimace. Was it just age? (Did her own mouth turn down like that, too? Soon she would look. Soon.) But it was more than that; there was a deep, slumping sort of sadness about her. Was she not happy being married to that grizzly-bear man? (Was it possible to love a man with a beard? Childish. Of course it was possible. Even if it was a remarkably *bushy* beard.)

As Alice watched, Elisabeth's throat moved as she swallowed convulsively.

"What are you thinking about?" asked Alice.

Elisabeth started and looked up. "I don't know, nothing." She swallowed a yawn. "Sorry. I'm just tired. I only got a couple of hours' sleep last night."

"Ah," said Alice. She didn't need an explanation. She and Elisabeth had both suffered from bouts of terrible insomnia all their lives. They had inherited it from their mother. After their dad died, Alice and Elisabeth would often stay up right through the night with their mother, sitting in their dressing gowns in a row on the couch, watching videos and drinking cocoa, and then they'd sleep the next day away, while sunlight streamed through the muffled, sleeping house.

"How has my insomnia been lately?" asked Alice.

"I don't know actually. I don't know if you still get it."

"You don't know?" Alice was baffled. They always kept each other up to date with their insomnia battles. "But don't we—don't we talk?"

"Of course we talk, but I guess you're pretty busy, with the kids and everything, so our conversations are maybe a bit rushed."

"Busy," repeated Alice. She didn't like the sound of that at all. She had always had a slight mistrust of busy people; the sort of people who described themselves as *"Flat-out! Frantic!"* What was the hurry? Why didn't they slow down? Just what exactly were they so busy doing?

"Well," she said, and felt unaccountably awkward. It felt like things weren't exactly right between herself and Elisabeth. There seemed to be a sort of stilted, friendly politeness, as if they were good friends who didn't see each other so often anymore.

She would ask Nick about it. It was one of the best things about him; he liked to talk about people, study them, and work them out. He was interested in the complexities of relationships. Also, he loved Elisabeth, and when he made fun of her, or complained about her (because she could at times be profoundly annoying), he did it in just the right brotherly way so that Alice didn't feel she had to defend her.

Alice looked at Elisabeth's beautifully cut cream suit (both their wardrobes seemed to have improved in 2008) and said, "Are you still working at the catalogue place? The Treasure Chest?"

Elisabeth had a job writing the text for a huge monthly mail-order catalogue called *The Treasure Chest*. She had to find clever, persuasive things to say about hundreds and hundreds of products, anything from banana-flavored lip gloss to an instant egg poacher to a waterproof radio you could play in the shower. She got a lot of free stuff to give away, which was nice, and every month when the catalogue came out, everyone in the family read out their favorite lines to Elisabeth. Frannie kept every issue of *The Treasure Chest* on proud display and made her friends read it when they came to visit.

"Oh, that feels like such a long time ago," said Elisabeth. She looked at Alice and shook her head slightly, as if she'd never seen anything quite like it. "You're like a time traveler. You really are."

"So I guess you don't work there anymore?" Alice felt irritable. This was going to get tiring if everyone looked at her with awe each time she asked a simple question. How much could have changed in ten years? It seemed like everything.

"*The Treasure Chest* is a website now," said Elisabeth. "And I stopped working there about six years ago. I worked for an agency for about four years, and then two years ago I started running these training seminars on how to write direct mail. Or junk mail, as most people would call it. They're quite—well, they're quite successful, actually, as strange as that may seem. Anyway, it pays the bills. I was running one today when I got the call from Jane about you."

"So it's your own business?"

"Yes."

"Wow! That's so impressive. You're a success story. I always knew you would be a success story. Can I come along and watch you?"

"Come along and watch? Watch *me*?" Elisabeth snorted.

"Oh. I guess I've already done that, have I?"

Elisabeth said, "No, Alice, you've never shown the slightest interest in coming along to one of my seminars." Her voice had that sharp edge again.

"Oh," said Alice, confused. "That seems . . . well, I wonder why not?"

Elisabeth sighed. "You're just really busy, Alice. That's all."

There was that "busy" word again.

"And also, I think you find my whole choice of career maybe a bit—tacky."

"Tacky? I said that? I said that about you? I would never say that!" Alice was horrified. Had she turned into a nasty person who judged people by their choice of a career? She'd always been proud of Elisabeth. She was the smart one, the one who was going places, while Alice stayed safely put.

Elisabeth said, "No, no, you never actually said that. You probably don't even think it. Just forget I said that."

Maybe, thought Alice fearfully, the other Alice who has been living my life for the last ten years isn't very nice.

Alice said, "Well, what about me? What do I do for a job?"

Alice had worked as an administrative assistant in the pay office at ABR. She didn't love it or hate it, it was just a job. She wasn't especially interested in a career. "You're such a domestic goddess. You're like a 1950s housewife," Elisabeth had once said to her, when Alice admitted that she'd just spent the most blissful day gardening, making new curtains for the kitchen, and baking a chocolate cake for Nick.

"You don't work." Elisabeth gave her an inscrutable look.

"Oh, well, that sounds good!" said Alice happily.

"You're very busy, though." What was it with that word? "You do a lot of stuff at the school."

"The school? What school?"

"The children's school."

Oh. Them. The three scary little strangers.

"Frannie," said Alice suddenly. "What about Frannie? She hasn't—got sick or anything, has she?" She didn't want to even say the word "died."

"She's fine," said Elisabeth. "Full of beans."

The silver mobile phone sitting on the cabinet next to Alice's bed burst into life.

"It must be Nick at last!" Alice lunged for the phone.

"Oh!" Elisabeth jumped to her feet. "Let me talk to him first!"

"No way." Alice held the phone away from her, irritated. "Why?" Without waiting for an answer, she pressed the green button and held the phone to her ear.

"Hello?"

"Yeah, hi, it's me." It was Nick; Alice felt blissful relief running straight through her bloodstream like a shot of brandy.

"What's happened?" His voice was deeper, rougher than usual, as if he had a cold. "Is it one of the kids?"

So Nick knew about "the kids," too. Everyone knew about the kids.

Elisabeth was jumping up and down, waving her arms about, gesturing for the phone. Alice poked her tongue out at her.

"No, it's me," said Alice. There was so much to tell him, she didn't know where to start. "I fell over at the, ah, gym, with Jane Turner, and hit my head. I was unconscious. They had to call an ambulance—oh, and I was sick in the lift all over this guy's shoes, so embarrassing! And wait till I tell you about this bike-riding class! So funny. Hey, you're in Portugal, I can't believe you're in Portugal, what's it like?"

There was so much to tell him, she felt like she hadn't seen him in years. When he got back from Portugal, they would have to go out for dinner at that Mexican restaurant they liked and talk, talk, talk. They would have margaritas; she could drink again, now that she wasn't pregnant anymore. Oh, she *yearned* to be in that restaurant with him right now, sitting in a dark corner booth, his thumb caressing her palm.

There was silence on the other end of the phone. He must be in shock.

"But I'm not badly hurt!" Alice reassured him. "It's not serious. I'll be fine! I feel fine!"

He said, "Then why the *fuck* did I need to call you?"

Alice felt her head snap back as if she'd been hit. Nick had never,

ever spoken to her like that before, not even when they were fighting. He was meant to fix the nightmare, not make it worse.

"Nick?" There was a tremor in her voice. She was going to be so mad with him later about this; her feelings were *extremely* hurt. "What's the matter?"

"Is there some sort of strategy to all this? Because I'm not getting it, and to be frank, I don't have time for it. You don't want to change any of the arrangements for the weekend, do you? Is that what it's about? Or, for Christ's sake, tell me it's not something to do with Christmas Day again. *Is* it?"

"Why are you talking to me like that?" said Alice. Her heart raced. This was more terrifying than anything that had happened to her today. "What did I do?"

"Oh, for God's sake, I don't have time for fucking games at the moment!"

He was shouting. He was actually shouting at her, and she was in *hospital.*

"Paprika," whispered Alice. "You have to wash your mouth out with paprika, Nick."

Elisabeth stood up. "Give it here," she ordered.

She removed the phone from Alice's trembling fingers, put the phone to her ear, and pressed a finger to her other ear. She turned her face away from Alice and dropped her chin. "Nick, it's Elisabeth. This is actually quite serious. She's had a bad head injury and she's lost her memory. She's forgotten everything since 1998. Do you understand what I'm saying? *Everything.*"

Alice let her head fall back against the pillow and breathed shallow gasps of air. What did it mean?

Elisabeth paused, listening, her forehead furrowed. "Yes, yes, I understand, but she doesn't actually remember any of that."

Another pause.

"They're with Ben. He's taken them to their swimming lesson, and I guess we'll stay over with them tonight, and then—"

Pause. "Yes, okay, and then your mum can pick them up exactly as per the arrangements, and I'm sure by Sunday night Alice should be back on her feet and everything will be back to normal." Pause. "No, I haven't talked to a doctor yet, but I will soon." Pause. "Right. Okay, well do you want me to put Alice back on?"

Alice held out her hand for the phone—surely Nick would be himself again now—but Elisabeth said, "Oh. Okay. Well, bye, Nick."

She hung up.

Alice said, "He didn't want to talk to me? He actually didn't want to talk to me?" She could feel stabbing pains all over her body, a long witchy finger poking her cruelly.

Elisabeth clicked the phone shut and put her hand on Alice's arm. She said gently, "You'll remember soon. It's okay. It's just that you and Nick aren't together anymore."

Alice felt a sensation of everything around her plummeting toward the central point of Elisabeth's moving lips. She focused on those lips. Raspberry lipstick with a darker line around the edge. Elisabeth must use lip liner. Fancy that. She must *line her lips.*

What was she saying? She could not be saying—

"What?" said Alice.

Elisabeth said again, "You're getting divorced."

Well, fancy that.

Chapter 8

Alice had one glass of champagne with her bridesmaids while they were getting their makeup done, another half a glass in the limo, three and a quarter glasses at the wedding reception (including strawberries), and another glass sitting up with Nick on the king-size bed in their hotel room that night.

So she was somewhat sozzled, but that was no problem because she was the bride and it was her wedding day, and everyone had said she looked beautiful, and so this was a beautiful, romantic drunkenness that would probably not result in a hangover.

"Do you love and adore my wedding dress?" she asked Nick for what could have been the third time, as she ran her hand across its rich, lustrous fabric. It was called Ivory Silk Duchess Satin, and touching it gave her the same sensuously satisfied feeling as when she was a little girl and she used to run her finger over the plush pink lining of her music box, except this was even better because back then she really wanted to be *in* the music box, rolling around on pink satin. "I love my wedding dress. It sort of looks like golden, magical ice cream, doesn't it? Couldn't you just *eat* it?"

"Normally I'd tuck in," said Nick. "But I'm full of cake. I had three pieces. That was outstanding cake. Everybody will be talking about the cake at our wedding for years to come. Most wedding cake is boring, but our cake! I'm so proud of our cake. I didn't make the cake, but I'm proud of it."

It seemed Nick had drunk quite a bit of champagne, too.

Alice set her glass on the bedside table and lay down on her back with a rich rustle of fabric. Nick slid down beside her. He'd taken off his tie and undone the buttons of his white dinner shirt. He had the beginnings of a five-o'clock shadow and slightly bloodshot eyes, but his hair was still perfect with a ridgelike wave at the part. Alice touched it and pulled her hand back. "It feels like straw!"

"The sisters," explained Nick. "Armed with gel."

He stroked her hair and said, "That's a nice synthetic feel you've got going there, wife."

"Hairspray. A lot of hairspray, husband."

"Is that right, wife?"

"Yes it is, husband."

"How interesting, wife."

"Are we going to talk like this forever, husband?"

"No way, wife."

They looked up at the ceiling and said nothing.

"What about Ella's speech!" said Alice.

"I think it was meant to be touching."

"Ah."

"What about your Aunt Whatsie's dress!"

"I think it was meant to be, um . . . stylish."

"Ah."

They snickered quietly.

Alice rolled onto her side and said, "Imagine," and her eyes filled with tears. She always got emotional when she drank too much champagne. "Imagine if we never met."

"It was fated," said Nick. "So we would have met the next day."

"But I don't believe in fate!" whimpered Alice, reveling in the luxurious feeling of hot, wet tears rolling down her cheeks; those triple coats of mascara would be streaked all over her face. It seemed truly frightening that it was only by sheer chance that she had met Nick. It could so easily not have happened, and then she would have had a shadowy, half-alive existence, like some sort of woodland creature who never sees sunlight, never even *knowing* how much she could love and how much she could be loved. Elisabeth once said—very definitely and severely—that the right man didn't complete you, you have to find happiness yourself, and Alice nodded agreeably, while thinking to herself, "Oh, but yes he does."

"If we'd never met," continued Alice, "then today would just be like any other day and right now we'd be watching television in separate homes, and I'd be wearing *tracksuit pants* and, and . . . we wouldn't be going on honeymoon tomorrow." The full horror of what could have been struck her. "We'd be going to work! *Work!*"

"Come here, my darling inebriated bride." Nick pulled Alice to him so that her head was resting beneath his shoulder and she breathed in the scent of his aftershave. It was much stronger than usual; he must have slapped on extra that morning, and the thought of him doing that was so unbearably sweet, it made her cry even harder. He said, "The important point here is this—wait for it, it's a very important and intelligent point—you ready?"

"Yes."

"We *did* meet."

"Yes," conceded Alice. "We did meet."

"So it all turned out okay."

"That's true," sniffed Alice. "It all turned out okay."

"It all turned out okay."

And then they had both fallen into a deep, exhausted sleep, with Alice's Ivory Silk Duchess Satin wedding dress swirled all over them, and a single red dot of confetti stuck to the side of Nick's face, which would leave a red circle that would stay there for the first three days of their honeymoon.

"We must have just had a bad argument," said Alice to Elisabeth. "We're not actually divorcing. We would never divorce."

That word—"divorce"—was so ugly; her lips pursed together like a fish on the second syllable. Dee-*vorce*. No. Not them. Never, ever them.

Nick's parents divorced when he was a child. He remembered everything about it. Whenever they heard about a couple divorcing—even a trashy, laughable celebrity couple—Nick always said, sadly, like an Irish grandma, "Ah, that's a shame." He believed in marriage. He felt that people gave up on their relationships too easily. He once said to Alice that if they were ever having troubles in their marriage, he would move heaven and earth to fix things. Alice couldn't take it seriously because heaven and earth wouldn't need to be moved; any troubles in their relationship could always be fixed with a few hours in separate rooms, a hug in the hallway, the quiet sliding of a chocolate bar under an elbow, or even just a gentle, meaningful poke in the ribs that meant "Let's stop fighting now."

Divorce was like a phobia for Nick, his only phobia! If this were true, then he would be devastated, crushed. The thing he feared most had happened. Her heart broke for him.

"Did we have a really bad argument about something?" Alice asked Elisabeth. She would get to the bottom of it, she would put a stop to it.

"I don't think it's just one argument. I guess it's probably a whole lot of little issues, but to be honest, you haven't really told me that much about it. You just rang me the day after Nick moved out and said—"

"He moved *out*? He actually moved out of the house?"

It was mind-boggling; she tried to visualize how it could actually happen, Nick throwing stuff into a suitcase, slamming the door behind him, a yellow taxicab waiting outside—it would have to be yellow, like an American cab, because this could not be real, this was a scene from a movie with a heart-wrenching soundtrack. This was not her life.

"Alice, you've been separated for six months, but you know, once you get your memory back, you'll realize it's okay, because you're fine with this. This is what you want. I asked you just last week. I said, 'Are you sure this is what you want?' and you said, 'Absolutely sure. This marriage was dead and buried a long time ago.'"

Liar, liar, pants on fire. That could not be true. That had to be a fabrication. Alice tried to keep the rage out of her voice. "You're just making that up to make me feel better, aren't you? I would never say that. 'Dead and buried!' That doesn't even sound like me! I don't talk like that. Please don't make stuff up. This is hard enough."

"Oh, *Alice*," said Elisabeth sadly. "I promise you, it's just your head injury, it's just . . . oh, hi there, hi!"

A nurse Alice hadn't seen before pulled back the curtain briskly on their cubicle and Elisabeth greeted her with obvious relief.

"How are you feeling?" The nurse pumped up the blood-pressure strap around Alice's arm once again.

"I'm fine," said Alice resignedly. She knew the drill now. Blood pressure. Pupils. Questions.

"Your blood pressure has soared from the last time I checked," commented the nurse, making a note on her chart.

My husband just yelled at me like I was his worst enemy. My lovely

Nick. My Nick. I want to tell him about it, because he'd be so angry if he ever heard somebody speak to me like that. He's the first person I want to tell when somebody upsets me; my foot pressing on the accelerator, desperate to get home from work just to tell him, the moment I tell him, the moment his face lights up with fury on my behalf, it's better, it's fixed.

Nick, you will never believe how this man spoke to me. You will want to punch him in the nose when you hear. Except it's so strange, because it was you, Nick, you were the man.

"She's had a few shocks," said Elisabeth.

"We really need you to try and stay relaxed." The nurse leaned close and did something feathery-quick with her fingers to pull back Alice's eyelids while she shone her miniature torch into each pupil. The nurse's perfume reminded Alice of something—someone?—but of course the feeling vanished as soon as the nurse moved. Was this going to be her from now on—a permanent, irritating case of déjà vu like an itchy rash?

"Now I'm just going to ask you a few boring questions again. What's your name?"

"Alice Mary Love."

"And where are you and what are you doing here?"

"I'm at Royal North Shore Hospital because I hit my head at the gym."

"And what day is it?"

"It's Friday, 2 May . . . 2008."

"Good, excellent!" The nurse turned to Elisabeth, as if expecting her to be impressed. "We're just checking that her cognitive reasoning isn't affected by her injury."

Elisabeth blinked irritably. "Yes, okay, great, but she still thinks it's 1998."

Tattletale, thought Alice.

"I do not," she said. "I know it's 2008. I just said that."

"But she still doesn't remember anything *since* 1998. Or hardly anything. She doesn't remember her children. She doesn't remember her marriage breakup."

Her marriage breakup. Her marriage was something that could be sliced up like a pizza.

Alice closed her eyes and thought of Nick's face, creased from sleep, lying on the pillow next to hers on a Sunday morning. Sometimes in the morning his hair would be all spiked up in the middle of his head. "You've got a Mohawk," said Alice the first time she observed this phenomenon. "Of course," he said. "It's Sunday. Mohawk day." Even with his eyes closed, he knew when she was awake, lying there, looking at him, thinking hopefully that he might bring her a cup of tea in bed. "No," he would say, before she'd even asked. "Don't even think about it, woman." But he always got it for her.

Alice would give anything, anything at all, to be lying in bed right now with Nick, waiting for a cup of tea. Maybe he got sick of making her cups of tea? Was that it? Had she taken him for granted? Who did she think she was, some sort of princess, lying in bed waiting for cups of tea to be delivered, without even brushing her teeth? She wasn't pretty enough to get away with that sort of behavior. She should have jumped up before he woke, done her hair and makeup and made him pancakes and strawberries, wearing a long lacy nightgown. That was how you kept a marriage alive, for God's sake, it wasn't as if there wasn't enough advice around in every women's magazine she'd ever read. It was basic knowledge! She felt as though she'd been unforgivably negligent—careless! sloppy!—with the most precious, wonderful gift she'd ever received.

Alice could hear Elisabeth murmuring urgently to the nurse, asking if she could see the doctor, wanting to know what tests had been done. "How do you know she hasn't got some sort of *clot* in her brain?"

Elisabeth's voice rose a bit hysterically, and Alice smiled to herself. Drama queen.

(Although, could there be a clot? A dark, ominous thing swooping about in her head like an evil bat? Yes, they really should look into that.)

Maybe Nick had got bored with her. Was that it? Once, when she was in high school, she overheard a girl saying, "Oh, Alice, she's okay, but she's a *nothing* sort of person."

A nothing sort of person. The girl had said it so casually, without malice, as if it were a fact, and at fourteen Alice had felt cold with the official confirmation of what she'd always believed. Yes, of course she was boring, she bored herself silly! Other people's personalities were so much more substantial. That same year, a boy at the bowling alley leaned in close with the sweet smell of Coke on his breath and said, "You've got a face like a pig." And that just confirmed something else she'd always suspected; her mother was wrong when she said her nose was as cute as a button; it wasn't a nose, it was a *snout*.

(The boy had a skinny, tiny-eyed face like a rat. She was twenty-five before it occurred to her that she could have insulted him back, but the rule of life was that the boys got to decide which girls were pretty; it didn't really matter how ugly they were themselves.)

Maybe Nick had been bringing her a cup of tea one morning and all of a sudden a veil lifted from his eyes and he thought, Hey, wait a second, how did I end up married to this lazy girl with her boring nothing personality and piglike face?

Oh Lord, were all those terrible insecurities really so fresh and close to the surface? She was grown up; she was twenty-nine! It was only recently that she'd been walking home from the hairdresser's, feeling gorgeous, and a gaggle of teenage girls walked by, and the sound of their strident giggles made her send a message back through time to her fourteen-year-old self: "Don't worry, it all works out. You get a personality, you get a job, you work out what to do with your hair, *and* you get a boy who thinks you're beautiful." She'd felt so *together*, as if all the teenage angst and the failed relationships before Nick had all been part of a perfectly acceptable plan that was leading to this moment, when she would be twenty-nine years old and everything would finally be just as it should be.

Thirty-nine. Not twenty-nine. She was thirty-nine. And that day with the teenagers must have been ten years ago.

Elisabeth came back in and sat back down next to Alice. "She's going to try and get the doctor to come around again. Apparently that's a very big deal, because you're just under observation now and the doctor is 'extremely busy,' but she's going to 'see what she can do.' So I think our chances are probably zero."

Alice said, "Please tell me it's not true. About Nick."

"Oh, Alice."

"Because I love him. I properly love him. I love him so much."

"You did love him."

"No, I *do*. Right now. I know I still do."

Elisabeth made a "tsk" sound that was full of sympathy, and lifted her hands in a hopeless sort of gesture. "When you get your memory back—"

"But we're so happy!" interrupted Alice frantically, trying to make Elisabeth see. "It's not even possible to be happier." Tears slid helplessly down the sides of her face and trickled ticklishly into her ears. "What happened? Did he fall in love with someone else? Is that it?"

Surely not. It was impossible. Nick's love for Alice was a fact. *A fact.* You were allowed to take facts for granted. Once, a friend was teasing Nick for agreeing to go with Alice to a musical (although he actually quite liked musicals). "I can see the thumbprint in between your eyes," the friend said, and Nick shrugged. "Mate, what can I do? I love her more than oxygen."

Sure, he'd been drinking a lot of beer, but he said that in a *pub*, when he was trying to be blokey. He loved her more than oxygen.

So, what—the boy didn't need oxygen anymore?

Elisabeth put the back of her hand to Alice's forehead and stroked her hair. "He didn't meet anyone else as far as I know, and you're right, you were happy together and you did have a wonderful, special relationship. I remember it. But things change. People change. It just happens. It's just life. The fact that you're getting a divorce doesn't change the fact that you had all those wonderful times. And I swear to you that once you get your memory back, you'll be fine with this."

"No." Alice shut her eyes. "No, I won't. I don't want to be fine with it."

As Elisabeth continued to stroke her forehead, Alice remembered the day from her childhood when she'd been dropped home after a birthday party still fizzing from winning the Simon Says competition. She was carrying a balloon and a basket made of shiny cardboard and filled with lollies. Elisabeth had met her at the front door and ordered, "Come with me."

Alice trotted along behind her, ready for whatever new game Elisabeth must have organized, and ready to share the lollies, but not the Freddo Frogs—she loved Freddo Frogs—and as they walked past the living room, her balloon bobbing along behind her, she noticed that it seemed to be full of strange grown-ups surrounding her mum, who was sitting on the couch with her head resting back on the couch at a strange angle (odd, but maybe she had a headache). Alice didn't call out to her because she didn't want to have to talk to all the strange grown-ups, and she followed Elisabeth down the hallway to her bedroom, where Elisabeth said, "I have to tell you something that is going to make you feel very bad, so I think you should get in your pajamas and get into bed and be ready for it so it won't hurt so much."

Alice didn't say, "What? What is it? Tell me now!" because she was six and nothing bad had ever happened to her, and besides which she always did what Elisabeth said. So she was perfectly happy to put on her pajamas while Elisabeth went to fill up a hot water bottle and put it in a pillowslip so it wouldn't burn. She also brought along a spoonful of honey, the Vicks VapoRub, and half an aspirin and a glass of water. These were all things their mother did when they were sick, and Alice loved being sick. Once Elisabeth had her tucked in bed and had rubbed the Vicks on her chest, she started stroking back the hair off Alice's forehead, just like their mum did when either of them had an especially bad stomachache, and Alice had closed her eyes and enjoyed all the good parts of being sick, without the actual sick feeling. Then Elisabeth said, "Now I have to tell you the bad thing. It's going to give you a bad, surprised feeling, so be ready for it, okay? You can suck your thumb if you want." Alice had opened her eyes and frowned, because she did not suck her thumb anymore, except for when she'd had an extremely bad day, and even then it was just the very tip, hardly the whole thumb. Then Elisabeth said, "Daddy has died."

Alice could never remember what happened next, or even how she felt on hearing the words. All she remembered was how Elisabeth had tried so hard to protect her from the "bad, surprised feeling." She was twenty-four before it occurred to her with a jolt of surprise that Elisabeth had been only a little girl herself that day. She'd phoned her to talk about it, to thank her, and the funny thing was that Elisabeth had an entirely different set of memories about when their dad died and didn't even remember putting Alice to bed.

Of course, there was also the time Elisabeth had thrown a pair of nail scissors at her, which got impaled in the back of her neck. But still . . .

Now Alice opened her eyes and said to Elisabeth, "You're such a good big sister."

Elisabeth took her hand away and said flatly, "No I'm not."

Neither of them said anything for a few seconds, and then Alice

said, "Are *you* happy, Libby? Because you seem . . ." Desperately unhappy, she wanted to say.

"I'm fine."

Elisabeth seemed to be thinking of things to say and then discard-
ing them. "Just be your proper self!" Alice wanted to scream.

Finally Elisabeth said, "I guess maybe our lives haven't turned out
quite the way we envisaged they would when we were thirty."

A voice interrupted them. "At last! I found you! I thought I'd never
find you!"

There was a woman standing at the end of the bed, her face hidden
for a moment as she ceremoniously held up a large bunch of yellow
tulips.

She lowered the tulips and revealed her face. Alice blinked and
blinked again in disbelief.

Chapter 9

M um?" said Alice.

It was Alice's mother standing at the end of her bed, but this was an extraordinarily different Barb Jones from the one Alice knew.

For a start (and there were so many possible places to start), her hair was no longer short and brown, the humble nunlike hairstyle that she'd had for as long as Alice could remember. Instead, it was a rich mahogany color and long, falling past her shoulders, with two strands pulled back on either side of her face (so her pixie ears stuck out comically) and pinned at the top with a huge, jaunty tropical silk flower. Her mother, her unassuming, fade-into-the-background mother who normally wore only an apologetic smear of the mildest pink Avon lipstick, was wearing what could only be described as theatrical makeup. Her lips were the same mahogany as her hair, her eyelids were purple, her cheeks were bright, her foundation was thick and too dark, and were those, surely not, *false eyelashes?* She was wearing a halter-neck, glittery sequined top, pulled in tight at the waist with a big black belt, and a full scarlet skirt. Alice lifted her chin and saw the outfit was completed with fishnet stockings and high, strappy shoes.

Her mother said, "Are you all right, darling? I always said those spin classes were too hard on your joints, and now look what's happened."

"Are you going to a fancy-dress party?" asked Alice with sudden inspiration. That would explain it, although even that would be amazing.

"Oh, no, silly, we were doing a demonstration at the school when Elisabeth left the message—I came straight here without stopping to change. I do get a few stares, but I'm used to that now! Anyway, enough of that, tell me what happened and what the doctors are saying. You're as white as a sheet." Her mother sat on the side of the bed and patted her leg. Sparkly bracelets slid up and down her arm. Was Mum *tanned*? Did Mum have *cleavage*?

"A demonstration of what?" asked Alice. She couldn't take her eyes off this exotic creature. It was Mum, but not Mum. Unlike Elisabeth, she didn't have any new wrinkles; in fact, that thick layer of makeup smoothed out her face so she seemed younger.

Elisabeth said, "Alice has lost a huge chunk of her memory, Mum. She doesn't remember anything since 1998."

"Oh," said Barb. "I don't like the sound of that at all. I *knew* she looked too pale. You must have concussion, I suppose. Don't fall asleep! You have to stay awake after a concussion. Whatever you do, Alice darling, you *must not fall asleep*!"

"That's a myth," said Elisabeth. "They don't advise that anymore."

"Well, I don't know about that actually, because I think I read something in the *Reader's Digest* quite recently about a little boy, a boy called Andy, and he hit his head riding one of those mini-bikes out in the bush, which is exactly what happened to Sandra's grandson, and I can tell you, I would not be letting Tom on one of those, Alice, even though I bet the little devil would love it, because they're terribly dangerous, even if you do wear a helmet, which this little boy, this Andy, was not, I think it was Andy, it could have been Arnie, although that's a funny, old-fashioned name you don't hear much these days—"

"Mum?" Alice interrupted, knowing there was no way out of the Andy/Arnie labyrinth. Her mother had always been a pathological chatterbox, although normally, when she was out in public like this, she would lower her voice in irritating deference to those around her, so you'd always be saying "Speak *up*, Mum!" If somebody she hadn't known intimately for at least twenty years turned up, her chatter would stop instantly mid-sentence, like a switched-off radio, and she would duck her head, avoid all eye contact, and smile an infuriatingly humble smile. She was so shy that when Alice and Elisabeth were at school, she became literally sick with nerves before their parent-teacher nights and would come home white and trembly with exhaustion, barely able to remember a word any of the teachers had said, as if the point of it had just been to show up, not to actually listen, which always drove Elisabeth insane, because she wanted to hear all the nice things the teachers said about her. (Alice didn't care because she knew most of her teachers probably didn't know who she was, because she suffered from the same shyness.)

Now Alice's mother was talking at a normal volume (actually, even a little louder than strictly necessary) and she wasn't darting cautious looks around to make sure any important strangers weren't about to turn up. Also, she seemed to have developed a new way of holding her head, her chin jutting and her neck strained, like a peacock. It reminded Alice of somebody, somebody she was sure she *hadn't* forgotten, somebody she knew perfectly well, although she couldn't temporarily name that person.

"But I still don't understand why you're dressed like that, Mum," said Alice. "You look . . . incredible."

Elisabeth's Homework for Dr. Hodges

I was thinking to myself, "Please don't mention Roger's name, Mum. She can't take another shock. Her brain might explode."

"Well, as I said, darling, Roger and I were doing a salsa-dancing demonstration up at the school when Elisabeth left the message. I got such a shock when I heard—"

"Did you say salsa dancing?"

"You can't possibly have forgotten our salsa dancing! I'll tell you why, because you actually described our last performance as unforgettable. It was just last Wednesday night! We had Olivia up on the floor with us, of course we couldn't convince Madison and Tom to have a go, or *you* for that matter, Roger was quite disappointed, but I tried to explain—"

"Roger?" said Alice. "Who is Roger?"

Elisabeth's Homework for Dr. Hodges

Who was I kidding? It's not like she ever goes more than five minutes without mentioning Roger's name.

"Yes, Roger, of course. Now, you can't have forgotten *Roger*. Can you?" Her mother looked frightened and said to Elisabeth, "This is quite serious, isn't it. I knew she looked too pale. She is literally bleached of color."

Alice was trying to think of other names that sounded like Roger. Rod? Robert? Her mother had a habit of getting people's names just slightly wrong, so that Jamie became Johnny, Susan became Susannah, and so on.

"The only Roger I know is Nick's dad," said Alice, with a little laugh because Nick's dad was a little laughable.

Her mother stared at her. She looked like a doll with those spiky black eyelashes. "Well, that's the Roger I'm talking about, darling. My husband, Roger."

"Your *husband*?"

"Oh, give me strength," sighed Elisabeth.

Alice turned to her. "Mum married *Roger*?"

"I'm afraid so."

"But . . . Roger? Really?"

"Yep. Really."

So here was another wedding that the other Alice had attended in her place, but this was a wedding Alice couldn't even begin to envisage.

For one thing, her mother had always refused to consider the possibility of *dating* other men. "Oh, I'm too old for all that," she'd say. "You need to be young and pretty to date! And besides, you only have one love of your life, and that was your father. How could any man ever measure up to him?" And although Elisabeth and Alice had continually tried to convince her that she was still young and attractive, and that Dad would never have expected her to mourn him forever, Alice had been secretly proud of her mother's devotion. It was sort of beautiful and moving, even though it was also annoying because it meant Alice and Elisabeth were responsible for her entire social life.

So okay, fine, she'd overcome her fear of dating (and probably that's what it had been, rather than eternal devotion), but to marry Nick's father of all people?

"But why?" said Alice helplessly. "Why would you marry Roger?"

That's right, she thought, it's *Roger* who has that peacock way of holding his head.

Barb widened her eyes and pursed her lips together coyly, with an expression that was so bizarrely unlike her that Alice had to avert her eyes as if she'd interrupted her mother doing something perverse and sexual.

She said, "I fell madly in love with him, you remember, of course you remember, it all started at Madison's christening, when Roger mentioned to me that he was thinking of taking up salsa dancing and would I be interested, and he didn't actually give me a chance to say no, he just seemed to be under the impression that I was coming along, and I didn't want to let him down, it seemed so rude, and even though I was in a state about it, and I actually thought about making an appointment to see Dr. Holden for a prescription for something to calm my nerves, and you girls got so cranky about that, as if I was going to become a *crack cocaine* addict or something, for heaven's sakes, just a little Valium was all I was thinking, which apparently just gives you a lovely floaty feeling, but I couldn't get an appointment, typical of course, that new receptionist is so snooty, I do wonder what happened to that lovely Kathy—"

"How long have you been married for?" Alice interrupted. The terror of not knowing the facts of her own life gripped her again. She was on one of those amusement park rides that slammed you left, then right, then turned the whole world upside down, giving you unfamiliar glimpses of familiar things. Alice hated amusement park rides.

"Well, it's coming up to five years. You remember the wedding, Alice, of course you do. Madison was flower girl. She looked so adorable in that yellow dress, she looks so nice in yellow, not many people do, I've bought her a yellow top for Christmas, but whether she'll wear it or not is another matter—"

"Mum," said Elisabeth tersely. "Alice doesn't even remember *Madison*. The last thing she remembers is being pregnant with her."

"She doesn't remember Madison," repeated Barbara in a hushed voice. She took a deep breath and put on a nervous, merry voice as if

to jolly Alice out of all this silliness. "Well, I can understand you wanting to forget Madison at this *particular* moment, the little grumble-
bum, although I'm sure she'll snap out of it soon, but of course, you
remember Tom and darling Olivia, don't you? Well, I can't believe I'm
asking the question. Of course you do. You can't forget your own children! That would be . . . unthinkable."

There was a tremor of fear in her voice that Alice found strangely
comforting. Yes, Mum, this is scary. Yes, this is unthinkable.

"Mum," said Elisabeth again. "Please try and get your head around
this. She doesn't remember *anything* since 1998."

"Nothing?"

"I'm sure it's just temporary."

"Oh! Of course. Temporary!"

Her mother lapsed into silence and ran a fingernail around the edge
of her thickly lipsticked mouth.

Alice tried out this new fact in her mind: *My mother married my
husband's father.*

It was as unforgettable a fact as *I have three children* and *My husband whom I adore has moved out of our house,* but somehow she'd
forgotten it.

None of it could be true. It must all be an absolutely huge, elaborate
practical joke. It must be an incredibly realistic dream. A vivid hallu-
cination. A nightmare that kept going and going.

Roger! What could have possessed her sweet, cautious mother to
"fall madly in love" (Mum never said extravagant things like "madly
in love") with someone like Roger? Roger with his overpowering aftershave, his radio-announcer voice, and his habit of saying "methinks"
and "mayhaps"? Roger, who after a few drinks at family parties would
pin Alice in a corner and treat her to a monologue all about himself
and his eternal fascination with the intricacies of his own personality.

"Am I an athletic person? Yes, definitely. Am I an intellectual? Okay, maybe not in the strictest la-di-da Ph.D. sense of the word. But put it another way, am I an *intelligent* person? The answer would have to be yes; I've got a Ph.D. from the University of Real Life, Alice. You may well ask, am I a spiritual person? Methinks the answer would have to be yes, most certainly."

Alice would be nodding helplessly, taking shallow breaths so she didn't feel sick from the scent of his aftershave, until Nick would appear, saying, "Methinks the lady needs a drink, Dad."

And what about Nick? What would he think about this development? He had such a weird, fragile relationship with his father. He imitated him mercilessly behind his back and there was something close to hatred in his voice when Nick spoke about the way his dad had treated his mother during their divorce, but at the same time Alice noticed that whenever he was in Roger's company, his voice would become deeper, his shoulders squarer, and he would often casually bring up some big deal he'd negotiated at work, or some other accomplishment that Alice didn't even know about, as if deep down he still wanted his dad's approval, even though he would have denied this vehemently, angrily even.

Alice couldn't think what his reaction would be to this news. And didn't it mean she and Nick were *related*? He was her stepbrother! Her first thought was that she and Nick would have laughed themselves silly over that, turned it into a stupid game, made lecherous remarks about incest, and pretended they were Greg and Marcia Brady. But maybe it hadn't been funny at all. He might have been angry on behalf of his mother, even though his mother seemed to treat her ex-husband like a bumbling distant uncle.

And what about Nick's sisters, the Flakes? Oh God, the Flakes. Nick's nutty sisters were now her stepsisters. There was no way they would have reacted calmly to this news; they didn't react calmly to anything—they fainted, they sobbed, they stopped talking to each other, they were offended by the most innocuous comments. There was always at least one sister in the middle of a crisis. Alice had never realized family life could be so dramatic until she met Nick's family, with all those sisters, in-laws, boyfriends, aunties, and cousins by the dozen. Her own quiet, polite, mini-sized family had seemed boring and sedate in comparison.

Alice said, "Is this why Nick and I are . . . ? Because he's upset about his dad marrying Mum?"

"Of course not!" Her mother was reenergized. "This divorce is a terrible mystery to all of us, but it's certainly got nothing to do with Roger and me! Roger would be devastated to hear you even thought about such a thing. Of course Roger does have his own theories about the divorce—"

Elisabeth cut in. "Mum and Roger got together years ago. You and Nick were a bit funny about it at the time, and the Flakes were all in hysterics of course, but it settled down and nobody thinks twice about it now. I promise you, Alice, all these things that seem so shocking aren't really that shocking. When you get your memory back, you'll be laughing at yourself."

Alice did not want to get back a self who thought there was nothing shocking about the fact that she and Nick were divorcing; she couldn't believe how casually her mother had referred to "the divorce," as if it were something solid and real, as if it were a *thing*.

"Well, I'm not getting a divorce anymore, actually," said Alice. "There is no divorce."

"Oh!" Her mother clasped her hands together rapturously, as if in prayer. "Oh, but that's wonderful—"

"Mum!" Elisabeth said. "You must promise not to say one word about that to Roger or anybody else. She doesn't know what she's saying."

"I do so," said Alice. She felt a bit drunk. "You can tell the whole world, Mum. Tell Roger. Tell the Flakes. Tell our three children. There is no divorce. Nick and I will work out whatever this thing is."

"Wonderful!" cried Barb. "I'm so happy!"

"You will not think this is wonderful when you get your memory back," said Elisabeth. "You've got legal proceedings going on. Jane Turner will have heart failure if you start doing this."

"Jane Turner?" said Alice. "What's Jane Turner got to do with the price of fish?"

"Jane is your lawyer," said Elisabeth.

"A lawyer? She's not a lawyer." A memory flitted into Alice's head of some guy losing an argument with Jane at work and saying, "You should have been a lawyer," and Jane had said, "Yes, I'm perfectly aware of that."

"She got her law degree years ago and now she specializes in divorce," said Elisabeth. "She's helping you—ah, divorce Nick."

"Oh." How ridiculous, how *stupid*, that Jane Turner was helping her "divorce Nick." "A little Jane goes a very long way," Nick once said, and Alice agreed. How could Jane Turner have anything to do with their lives?

"You and Nick are in the middle of a custody battle," said Elisabeth. "It's really serious."

Custody battle. It sounded like "custardy" battle. Alice imagined herself and Nick flinging spoonfuls of sweet yellow custard at each other, laughing and shrieking and licking it off afterward.

Presumably a custody battle wasn't as much fun as a custardy battle.

"Well, that's off, too," pronounced Alice. (Why in the world would she want "custody" of three children she'd never met! She wanted Nick.) "We don't need a custody battle because we're not getting a divorce, and that's final."

"Hooray!" said her mother. "I'm so glad you've lost your memory. This accident is going to turn out to be a blessing in disguise."

"Well, there's only one tiny problem with all that, isn't there?" said Elisabeth.

"What?"

"Nick has still got his memory."

Chapter 10

N ick?" said Alice.

"Sorry, sweetie, it's just me again," said the nurse.

They were waking her every hour to check on her and shine the light in her pupils and ask the same questions over and over. "Alice Mary Love. Royal North Shore Hospital. Hurt my head," Alice mumbled. The nurse chuckled. "Well done. Sorry about this. Go back to sleep now."

Alice slept and dreamed of nurses waking her up. "Wake up! It's time for your salsa-dancing lesson!" said a nurse with a huge hat that was actually a profiterole cake. "I dreamed we were getting a divorce," said Alice to Nick. "And we had three children, and Mum married your dad, and Elisabeth was so sad." "Why the *fuck* would I care?" said Nick. Alice gasped and sucked her thumb. Nick peeled a piece of red confetti off his neck and showed it to her. He said, "Only joking!"

"Nick?" said Alice.

"I do not love you anymore because you still suck your thumb."

"But I don't!" Alice was so embarrassed she could die.

"What's your name?" shouted a nurse, but this was another one that couldn't be real because she was floating through the air, holding on to bouquets of pink balloons. Alice ignored her.

"Me again," said a nurse.

"Nick?" said Alice. "I've got a headache. Such a bad headache."

"No, it's not Nick. It's Sarah."

"You're not a real nurse. You're another dream nurse."

"Actually, I'm a real one. Can you open your eyes and tell me your name?"

Elisabeth's Homework for Dr. Hodges

Hi, me again, Dr. Hodges. It's 3:30 a.m. and sleep feels like something impossible and stupid that only other people do. I woke up thinking of Alice and how she said to me, "You're such a good big sister."

I'm not. I'm not at all.

We still care about each other, of course we do. It's not that. We'd never forget each other's birthdays. In fact, there's a weird sort of silent competition going on to see who can give the best present each year, as if we're always jostling for the role of most generous, thoughtful sister. We see each other pretty regularly. We still have a laugh. We're just the same as a million sisters. So I don't even know exactly what I'm talking about. It's just that it isn't the same as when we were younger. But that's just life, isn't it, Dr. Hodges? Relationships don't stay the same. There isn't *time*. Ask Alice! She converted to the role of busy North Shore Mum like it was a religion.

Maybe if I'd been more vigilant? Perhaps it was my responsibility as the older sister to keep us on track.

But the only way I've been able to get through the last seven years is by wrapping myself up like a package with a tighter and tighter string. It's so tight that if I'm talking about anything (other than how to write the perfect direct-mail package), I feel as though there is something constricting my throat, as if my mouth doesn't open wide enough for proper, unthinking conversation.

The problem is the rage. It's permanently simmering, even when I'm not aware of it. If I hurt myself unexpectedly, or drop a punnet of blueberries all over the kitchen floor, it bubbles over like boiling milk. You should have heard the primeval scream of rage when I banged my forehead against an open cupboard door the other day when I was unpacking the dishwasher. I sat on the kitchen floor with my back against the fridge and sobbed for twenty minutes. It's pretty embarrassing.

Before Alice and Nick split up, I sometimes felt there were unforgivable words hovering on the tip of my tongue whenever I spoke to Alice, words like: "You think the world begins and ends with you and your perfect little family and your perfect little life and you think stress is finding the perfectly color-coordinated cushions for your new $10,000 sofa."

And I feel like scribbling those things out because they're nasty and not even true. I don't think those things at all, but I could have said them, I could still say them, and if I did, those words would have been there in both our memories forever. So it was safer to say nothing and pretend, and she knew I was pretending and she pretended too, and then we forgot how to be real with each other.

That's why when she called me to say that Nick had moved out, it was as shocking as a death. I had no idea, no inkling they were having troubles. There was the indisputable evidence that we didn't share secrets anymore. I should have known what was going on in her life. She should have been asking me for wise, sisterly advice. But she didn't. So I've let her down as much as she let me down.

And that's why, when I got the news about Gina, I couldn't think what the right thing was to do. Should I phone Alice? Should I drive straight over? Should I call and ask first? I couldn't think what Alice would want. I was worrying about the right etiquette, as if this was someone I didn't know very well. And OF COURSE I should have driven straight to her, for God's sake. What was wrong with me that I even had to think about it?

As we were walking out of the hospital, Mum said to me in a diffident, un-Mumlike voice, "I guess she doesn't remember anything about Gina, either, does she?" And I said, "I guess not." Neither of us knew what to say about that.

How do you find the thread that started it all and follow it all the way back through the tangles of phone calls and Christmases and kids' parties, right back to the beginning when we were just Alice and Libby Jones? Do you know, Dr. Hodges?

Anyway . . . maybe I should try and sleep.

No. Can't even fake a yawn.

Tomorrow I'm going to the hospital to pick up Alice and take her home. They're expecting to discharge her by 10. She just seemed to take it for granted that I would be the one to come and get her. If she were her normal self, she would be making a point of not relying on me. She only takes favors from other school mums, because they can be repaid with complicated playdate arrangements involving their children.

I wonder if she'll have her memory back by tomorrow. I wonder if she will feel embarrassed by the things she said this afternoon, especially about Nick. I wonder if that was her real self, or her old self, or just a confused, banged-on-the-head self. Deep down, is she devastated about the divorce? Was that a glimpse of what she's really feeling? I don't know. I just don't know.

The doctor I spoke to seems confident that she'll have her memory back by the morning. She was one of the nicer doctors I've met in my years of doctors. She actually looked me in the eyes and waited till I'd finished speaking before she spoke. But I could tell she was just focused on the fact that Alice's CT scan didn't show any sign of what she called "intracranial bleeding." She blinked a bit when I said Alice doesn't remember the existence of her own children, but she said people can have a wide variety of responses to concussion and that rest was the best thing. She said as her injury heals, her memory will come back. She seemed to be implying that they'd already gone above and beyond what they'd do in a normal concussion case by keeping her overnight for observation.

I felt strangely guilty leaving Alice there at the hospital. She seems so much younger. That's the thing about this I couldn't seem to get across to the doctor. It's not just Alice being confused. It's like I am *literally* talking to 29-year-old Alice. Even the way she talks is different. It's slower and softer and less careful. She's just saying whatever comes into her head.

"Did I have a thirtieth birthday party?" she asked me before we left and I couldn't for the life of me remember. But then on the way home in the car I remembered they had a BBQ. Alice had a big pregnant belly and they were right in the middle of renovations. There were ladders and paint tins and gaping holes in walls. I remember standing in the kitchen helping Alice and Nick put candles in the cake, when Alice said, "I think the baby has the hiccups." Nick pressed his hand to her stomach and then he grabbed my hand and held it over her stomach so I could feel the freaky fishy movements too. I have such a clear memory of both their faces turned to me, their eyes shiny, flushed with the excitement and wonder of it all. They both had flecks of blue paint in their eyebrows from painting the nursery. They were lovely. They were my favorite couple.

I used to secretly watch Nick listening to Alice when she told a story; that tender, proud look he got on his face, the way he laughed harder than anyone else when she said something funny or typically Alice. He got Alice, the way we did, or maybe even more so than us. He made her more confident, funnier, smarter. He brought out all the things that were there already and let her be fully herself, so she seemed to shine with this inner light. He loved her so much, he made her seem even more lovable.

(Does Ben love me like that? Yes. No. I don't know. Maybe in the beginning. All that shiny love stuff doesn't seem relevant anymore. That's for other younger, thinner, happier people, and besides which, it's not actually possible for a dried apricot to shine.)

I miss the old Nick and Alice. When I think of them

standing in that kitchen, putting candles on the cake, it's like remembering people who I once knew, who moved to another country and didn't keep in touch.

At 4:30 a.m. Alice woke with a start and the thought clear in her head: *I never asked Elisabeth how many children she has.*

How could she not know the answer to that question? But more important, how could she have forgotten to *ask* it when she didn't know? She was a selfish, self-obsessed, shallow person. No wonder Nick wanted to divorce her. No wonder Elisabeth didn't look at her in the same way anymore.

She would ring Mum in the morning and check with her and then she would pretend that of course she hadn't forgotten the existence of Elisabeth's children (just her own) and say, "Oh, by the way, how is little thingummybob?"

Except she couldn't be sure Mum still had the same phone number anymore. She didn't even know where Mum lived. Had she moved into Roger's cream-and-chrome apartment with its harbor views? Or had Roger moved into Mum's house with the doilies and knickknacks and potted plants? Either possibility seemed ludicrous.

The girl in the cubicle next to her was snoring. It was a thin, whiny sound like a mosquito. Alice turned over on her front and pushed her face hard into the pillow, as if she were trying to suffocate herself.

She thought, *This is the worst thing that has ever happened to me.*

But actually, she couldn't even be sure of that.

Elisabeth's Homework for Dr. Hodges

After we left the hospital this afternoon, Mum and I went over to Alice's place to meet Ben and the kids. We all had pizza for dinner. (Thankfully Roger had a Rotary meeting; I was not in the mood for Roger. I can't think of anyone ever being in the mood for Roger, except for Mum, presumably, and Roger, of course.) We didn't tell the children that Alice had lost her memory. We just said she'd hit her head at the gym but she was going to be fine. Olivia clasped her hands together and said, "Darling Mummy! This is an absolute tragedy!" and I could see Ben's back shaking with suppressed laughter as he stood at the cutlery drawer. Madison curled her lip and said contemptuously, "So, does Dad know about this?" and then stomped up to her bedroom as if she already knew what the answer would be. Tom waited till Olivia was busy at the kitchen table with crayons and glitter making a huge get-well card for Alice before silently taking me by the hand and leading me into the living room. He sat me down and looked me straight in the eyes and said, "Okay, tell me the truth. Has Mum really got a brain tumor?" Before I could answer, he said, "Don't lie! I'm a human lie detector! If your eyes look up to the right, that means you're lying." I had to make a superhuman effort not to look up to the right.

It was sort of a fun night. I don't know why. A fun night at poor Alice's expense.

Oh, a yawn! A precious, proper yawn! I've got to go now, Dr. Hodges. It might be sleep.

As the sky began to lighten outside the hospital Alice fell into her deepest sleep of this long, strange, fragmented night. She dreamed of Nick sitting at a long pine table she'd never seen. He shook his head, picked up a coffee mug, and said, "It's always about Gina, isn't it? Gina, Gina, Gina." He drank from the coffee mug and Alice felt pure dislike;

she turned away from him to wipe vigorously at a dried grease spot on a granite countertop.

In her sleep, Alice twitched so violently the bed moved.

She dreamed she was standing up in a small, darkened room, and Elisabeth was lying next to her, looking up at her with a frightened face, saying, "What does she mean there is no heartbeat?"

She dreamed of a giant rolling pin. She had to push it up a hill while thousands of people watched. It was important that she make it look easy.

"Good morning, sleepyhead!" said a nurse. Her bright, bubbly voice was like glass breaking.

Alice jumped and gasped for air as if she'd been holding her breath.

Chapter 11

Frannie's Letter to Phil

I'm back again, Phil.

It's six a.m. Still dark outside, and chilly. Brrrrr! I'm writing this in bed.

Barb called again last night to say that Alice is fine. They've done a CT scan apparently, whatever that is, and everything looks normal, although evidently Alice is suffering some memory loss. When she woke up, she thought she was still together with Nick!

Now Barb is celebrating because she thinks they'll get back together. She has become so irritatingly optimistic ever since she took up salsa dancing.

I think reconciliation is unlikely. Alice was here on Monday (which was lovely, although I do sometimes feel as though I'm a chore being crossed off her list, but perhaps that's unfair). I asked her about Nick and the most repellent expression crossed her face. She became quite ugly with hatred.

After she left, I was thinking about the first time Alice brought Nick around to meet me. They'd come straight from the beach, their feet sandy, their hair still wet, smelling of the sea. They were sitting on the couch chatting politely with me, not touching, or so it seemed, except that I happened to glance down and I saw that their hands were lying next to each other on the couch, and that Nick was caressing Alice's little finger with his own. I remember being shocked by a feeling of pure envy. I wanted to be Alice, young and lovely, feeling the secret caress of a handsome boy's fingertip.

Isn't it strange and sad what time can do? What became of those passionate young people?

But what do I know about marriage? It's a mystery to me. I assume it's a matter of compromise. Negotiation. Give and take.

Actually, I remember seeing Alice and Nick, after another trip to the beach, except by this time they had three children and there was certainly no fingertip caressing. Something had obviously happened (to do with Olivia, I think) and you could have cut the air with a knife. They were talking to each other in those terrible, icily polite voices I've noticed couples use in public when they're arguing.

Do you ever wonder, Phil, what sort of a marriage we would have had?

Would we have fought? For example, you always said you didn't mind that I had the more senior position, but perhaps that wasn't really true and it would eventually have become a problem for us. They say that men are defined by their work.

Do you know I've been writing to you now for over three decades? That's longer than a lot of marriages. Longer than Alice's marriage.

May I share another quibble with you about that fellow? That Mr. Mustache? Last night, I was in the dining room for dinner and he was sitting at the same table. He asked if any of my own family were performing at the Talent Night. I said that my "honorary granddaughter" would be dancing.

Mr. Mustache wanted to know what I meant by "honorary."

I briskly gave him the facts. I said that I had lived next door to a young family, and that when the father died suddenly of a heart attack the mother wasn't coping especially well and I stepped in to help out, as she had no other family. Eventually I became a sort of "pseudo" grandmother.

I didn't tell him how the shattered, white faces of those poor little girls are imprinted on my memory forever. I didn't tell him about the many days I had to drag their mother out of bed. (Once I got so frustrated, I actually pinched poor Barb, quite hard, on the arm. Isn't that dreadful! I was tough back then.)

Of course, I didn't tell him about you.

Mr. Mustache listened (I'll give him that. He really did listen.) and then he said, "I think you can drop the 'honorary.' Sounds like they really are your family."

Phil, I'm not sure why this bothered me so much. It was something about his tone. So definite. So presumptuous. I've only known the man five minutes and he's making remarks about my life. And he seemed to be implying that I was being overly pedantic.

Am I making too much of this? Am I pedantic?

I guess I've always taken secret pride in my pedantry.

Oh I can just imagine you snorting!

Must rush. I'm catching the minibus into the shops to buy a gift for Alice. I'll never get this letter finished at this rate!

Right! Time to get moving. A nice hot shower. Clothes. Hair. Makeup.

The last nurse had left and now a brisk, bossy voice in Alice's head was telling her what to do.

Too tired, replied Alice truculently. Her eyes were dry and stinging. *I've just had the worst night of my life. Also I should probably wait and ask a nurse.*

Rubbish! You'll feel more awake after your shower. You always do!

Do I?

Yes! And it's time to look in the mirror, for heaven's sake. You're only thirty-nine, not eighty-nine. How bad can it be?

What about a towel? I don't know which towel to use. There might be procedures.

You smell of sweat, Alice. From that gym class. You need a shower.

Alice sat up. She couldn't stand the thought of having any sort of body odor. It was the ultimate humiliation. She was horrified even when Nick casually mentioned she had garlicky breath the day after they'd eaten an especially garlicky dinner. She would clap a hand to her mouth and run to clean her teeth and spend the whole day chewing gum. Nick was bemused by the fuss. He couldn't care less if he smelled. After working all day on the house, he'd sniff cheerfully at his armpits like an ape and announce, "I stink!" as if it were a fine achievement.

Maybe Nick was divorcing her because she'd developed extremely bad breath.

She put a tentative hand to the tender lump on her head. The pain was still there, but it was definitely better, more like a memory of yesterday's pain.

But she didn't remember those children, and she didn't remember Nick moving out.

She slid her bare feet onto the cool floor and looked around her. The tulips her mother had given her were fat, gold bulbs against the white of the hospital room wall. She tried to imagine her mother dancing the salsa with Roger, their hips swiveling in unison. She could imagine Roger's hips swiveling all right, but Mum's? She was fascinated and repelled by the thought. She couldn't wait to talk to Nick about it.

Well.

She remembered his voice on the phone yesterday, thick with hatred. It had to be over something more than bad breath. If that had been the reason, he would have sounded compassionate and embarrassed.

Even with the memory of that phone call (the way he swore at her!), it still seemed impossible that Nick wasn't about to turn up any minute, breathless and rumpled, apologizing for the misunderstanding, hugging her to his chest. She couldn't feel properly upset about this talk of divorce because it was too stupid. This was *Nick*! Her Nick. As soon as she saw him again it would all be okay.

The rucksack with the dinosaur stickers was sitting in the cupboard next to her bed. She thought about that beautiful red dress; maybe she could squeeze into it.

She held the rucksack under one arm and prudishly clutched the hospital robe together behind her in one hand so as not to reveal her underpants, but there was no need. The curtains around the other girl's bed were pulled and she was still snoring her mosquito-whine snore.

Maybe as Alice had got older her snoring had got even worse and that's why Nick had left. She could get one of those horrible mouthguard things. That was easy to solve. Come on home, Nick.

She was so tired it felt like she was walking through wet concrete.

I think I should get back into bed.

Don't you dare get back into bed. You'll make them late for school again and you'll never hear the end of it.

Alice's chin jerked up with surprise. Where did that come from? She thought of the photo of the three children in their school uniforms. It must be Alice's responsibility to get them to school on time each day.

Maybe, just maybe, there was the tiniest, fleeting, corner-of-the-eye memory of pounding footsteps down a hallway, doors slamming, a horn tooting, a child wailing, a drilling feeling right in the center of her forehead. But as soon as she tried to grab hold of it, it vanished, as if she'd made it up.

It felt like she was facing straight ahead but just to the left and right of her were ten years' worth of memories, if only she could find a way to just turn her head to face them.

She went into the small bathroom that she and the snoring girl shared, switched on the fluorescent light, and locked the door behind her. She blinked in the all-enveloping brightness. Last night she'd managed to use the toilet and wash her hands without looking at her reflection in the mirror above the sink. There would be no more of that. Today was the day for clean, crisp action.

She undid the ties around her neck and back, let the robe fall to the floor, and stepped in front of the mirror.

She could see herself from the waist up.

Skinny, she thought, pressing her fingertips to the curve of her waist and then running them up and down her ribs. She could actually see her ribs. You're a skinny girl. Her stomach was hard and flat like that girl's at the gym. How did that happen?

Of course she'd always said that she should get fit and lose weight, without ever actually doing anything about it. It was something you were meant to say to your girlfriends at regular intervals to show you were a proper woman: "Oh God, I'm so fat!" When she was going out with Richard, the boyfriend before Nick, who would say "Heave 'em up!" when he watched her pull up her jeans over her thighs, that slight dissatisfaction with her body occasionally turned to self-hatred and she'd starve herself for a day before eating a packet of chocolate biscuits for dinner. But then she met Nick, who told her she was beautiful, and whenever he touched her, it was as if his touch were actually making her as beautiful as he seemed to believe she was. So why would she deny herself a second piece of mud cake or glass of champagne if Nick was there with the knife or the bottle poised, grinning evilly and saying "You only live once," as if every day were a celebration. Nick had a little boy's sweet tooth, and an appreciation of good food, fine wine, and beautiful weather; eating and drinking with Nick in hot sunshine was like sex. He made her feel like a well-fed, happy cat: plump, sleek, purring with sensual satisfaction.

Alice couldn't decide if she liked her flat new stomach or not. On the one hand, there was a distinct feeling of pride, like discovering a new skill. Look what I did! I've got a stomach like a supermodel! On the other hand, the feeling of hard bone under her skin gave her a slight feeling of revulsion, as if her flesh had been shaved away.

What did Nick think of this new skinny body? Perhaps he didn't care. *"So why the fuck did you ring me?"*

Her breasts were a lot smaller, she noted, and not quite as perky. Actually, they were awful, elongated and sagging like socks down toward her stomach. She held them up in her hands and let them drop again. Oh, yuck. She didn't like that at all. She missed her nice, round, cheerful, bobbing-about breasts.

Was it breast-feeding three children that had done this? And that would be perfectly fine if she had nostalgic memories of late nights sitting in a rocking chair with a downy-headed baby in her arms, except she *didn't*. She was looking forward to breast-feeding. It was meant to happen in her future, not in her past.

Okay, forget the breasts. The face. It was time for the face.

She took a step closer to the mirror and held her breath.

At first it was a relief, because it was still her own Alice face looking dopily back at her. She wasn't hideously deformed. She hadn't grown horns. In fact, she quite liked her thinner face. It seemed to have more definition and made her eyes look bigger. Her eyebrows were perfectly shaped and her eyelashes were dark. She didn't seem to have as many freckles. Her skin looked smooth and clear, although actually, there were quite a few funny, faint scratches on her face around her mouth and eyes. Maybe from when she fell over? She leaned in closer to examine them.

Oh.

They weren't scratches. They were wrinkles, just like Elisabeth's, maybe worse than Elisabeth's. There were two deep grooves in between her eyes. When she stopped frowning they didn't go away. There were little pouches of pink skin under her eyes, and Alice remembered how when she'd seen Jane yesterday she thought at first there was something wrong with her eyes. There had been nothing wrong with Jane; she was just ten years older.

She rubbed her fingertip over the fine scratchlike lines around her mouth and eyes as if she could just smear them away. They seemed wrong, as if they shouldn't be there; thank you anyway, but I don't think so, not for me, these don't belong on my face.

She gave up and stood back from the mirror so she couldn't see the wrinkles.

Her hair was still pulled back in the elastic band from the night before. She pulled it out and looked at it in the palm of her hand, amazed afresh that she didn't even recognize the black hair band and had no memory of putting it in her hair.

Her hair fell just above her shoulders. She must have had it cut, as she suspected. What brought on that decision, she wondered. The color was different, too. It was bordering on blond rather than brown; a dark ashy sort of blond. It was messy from her night of tossing and turning, but then she ran her fingers through it and saw that it was cut in an elegant shape that curved around the neck, making it seem longer. It wasn't her taste, but she had to admit it did suit her face better than any other haircut she'd had.

She'd grown up. That was it. A grown-up looked back at her. She just didn't feel that way.

Okay, then. This is you, Alice. This is who you are. A grown-up skinny mother of three in the middle of a nasty custard-throwing divorce.

She squinted her eyes and imagined her old self, her real self, staring back at her from the mirror. Long brown hair in no particular style, a rounder, softer face, perkier, bigger breasts, fatter (pretty fat) stomach, more freckles, no wrinkles to speak of—in love with Nick and pregnant with her first baby.

But that girl was gone. There was no point thinking about her.

Alice turned away from the mirror and, looking around the unfamiliar bathroom, she was overwhelmed with loneliness. She thought again of that silly solitary trip through Europe, brushing her teeth in strange bathrooms, staring at herself in speckled mirrors with a dizzy feeling of dissociation as she tried to work out who she really was without people who loved her to reflect back her personality. Now she wasn't in a strange country where people spoke a different language, but she was in a strange new world where everybody knew what was going on except for her. She was the foolish one making a goose of herself, saying the wrong thing, not knowing the rules.

She took a shaky breath.

This was only temporary. Soon she would have her memory back and life would go on as normal.

But did she *want* her memory back? Did she want to remember? What she really wanted was to hop in her time machine and go directly back to 1998.

Well. Bad luck. Deal with it, honey. Have a shower. Time for coffee and an egg-white omelette before the kids wake up.

"Before the kids wake up." The way this rather bossy, acerbic voice kept popping into her head was really freaking her out. And an "egg-white omelette"? What was that all about? Wouldn't it be entirely without flavor? She didn't fancy that at all for breakfast.

Or did she? She licked her lips experimentally. Egg-white omelette or peanut butter on toast? Both choices seemed simultaneously delicious and disgusting.

Well, it's hardly a matter of life and death, is it, Alice?

Oh shut up. No offense, but you sound like a bit of a bitch, Alice.

She went to the rucksack and pulled out the swish toiletries bag. Presumably she could rely on new Alice to have packed shampoo and conditioner. She rifled through chunky, expensive-looking jars and bottles (good Lord, wasn't this just a trip to the gym?) and found two slim, tall, dark bottles. They were brands she didn't recognize promising "salon-quality results."

As she stood under the shower and massaged the shampoo into her hair, the fragrant smell of peach filled her nostrils and it was so entirely familiar her knees buckled. *Of course, of course.* She made a sound like a strangled sob and remembered herself standing under a pounding shower, steam billowing, resting her forehead against a wall of blue tiles and howling silently while the bubbly lather from the peach-smelling shampoo slipped into her eyes. *I can't bear it. I can't ... I can't ...*

For a moment the memory was so real, it could have been happening right then, and then the next second it slithered away like the froth from her shampoo.

The smell of the shampoo remained intensely, ridiculously familiar, but she couldn't grab hold of another memory.

Oh, that feeling of hopeless grief and just wanting the pain to stop. *Am I remembering crying over Nick?*

If these were the memories that were locked away in her head—memories of a perfectly wonderful marriage disintegrating, memories of clinging to a shower wall while she cried—did she really want them back?

She turned off the shower and dried herself with the towel from the rucksack. With the towel wrapped around her, she pulled the bottles and jars out of the toiletries bag and lined them up in front of her. What did she actually do with all that stuff?

Move it, move it.

Her hand moved instinctively toward a jar with a gold lid. She opened it to reveal a thick, creamy moisturizer. With rapid, efficient movements she briskly rubbed the moisturizer all over her face. Dab, dab, dab. Without stopping to think, she picked up a glass bottle of foundation, poured some onto a sponge, and began rubbing it all over her face. A part of her mind registered all this with astonishment. Foundation? She never wore foundation. She hardly ever bothered with makeup. But her hands were moving so fast, her head tilting this way and that as if she'd done this a million times before. Next came a shiny gold-colored stick that she rubbed into her cheeks. She snapped open jars, bottles, and containers. Mascara. Eyeliner. Lipstick.

Suddenly—it must have taken less than five minutes—she was finished and stowing all the bottles away in the toiletries bag. Without stopping, she unzipped a pocket on the side of the bag and wondered what she was looking for until she pulled out a portable hair dryer and a round brush. Oh, right, fair enough. Time to blow-dry your hair. She plugged it in and once again her hands moved without waiting for her to tell them what to do. The brush moved back and forth. The hair dryer roared hot air.

Okay, so once you leave here, you've got to—

Her mind went blank.

. . . you've got to . . .

Her hair was done.

She snapped off the hair dryer, pulled the plug out of the socket, twirled the cord round and round, and shoved it back into the bag and began to rustle again for something else. Good Lord. Why was she moving so *fast*? Where was the fire?

She pulled out the flat plastic bag with the clothes, shook it open, and pulled out the matching cream underwear and dress. The underwear felt smooth and luxurious against her skin and the bra lifted her breasts back to their former perky position. Surely this beautiful dress would not fit, but she was sliding it over her head, doing up the zipper at the side without having to look for it, and there were no bulges of unsightly fat because she didn't have them anymore.

Jewelry. She found the topaz necklace and Nick's bracelet and put them on. Shoes. She slid her feet into them.

She stopped and looked at the woman in the mirror and watched her bottom lip drop in awe.

She looked, well, she had to say that she looked pretty good. She turned side to side and observed herself over one shoulder.

An attractive, elegant, slim woman. The sort of woman she never thought it was possible for her to be. She had become one of *those* women, those *other* women, who had seemed too perfectly put together to be real.

Why did Nick want to leave her if she looked this damned good?

There was still something missing.

Perfume.

She found it in the zippered section at the front of the toiletries bag. She sprayed it on both wrists and suddenly she was leaning forward, grasping both sides of the basin to stop herself from falling. The scent was vanilla, mandarin, and roses. Her whole life was right there in that scent. She was being sucked into a massive swirling vortex of grief and fury and the ring, ring, ring of the phone and the rising whiny shriek of a child and the babble of the television and Nick sitting on the end of the bed, bent right over with his hands laced tightly around the back of his head.

"Excuse me?"

There was a knock on the bathroom door.

"Excuse me? Will you be much longer? It's just that I'm dying to go!"

Alice stood slowly back up. The color had drained from her face. Was she going to be sick again, like yesterday? No.

"Sorry!" she called out. "Won't be a second."

She put her hands in the sink and used the pink soap from the soap dispenser to scrub away hard at the perfume. As the straightforward, bracing smell of strawberry bubble gum mixed with disinfectant filled her nostrils, the vortex receded.

I don't remember.

I don't remember.

I won't remember.

Elisabeth's Homework for Dr. Hodges

She was dressed and waiting for me when I went to pick her up from the hospital. She had dark circles under very red eyes, but her hair was done and her makeup perfect as always.

She looked so much like her normal self that I was sure she must have her memory back and this strange interlude in our lives was all over.

I said, "Has it all come back to you now?" and she said, "Just about," and avoided my eyes and I thought she must have felt embarrassed about what she'd said about Nick. She said she'd been checked over by the doctor, and signed all the forms, and couldn't wait to get home to her own bed.

She didn't say much as we were leaving the hospital, and I didn't either. When she finally went to speak, I thought for sure she would be talking about all the million things she had to do that weekend and the precious time she'd lost being in hospital. Instead she said, "How many children do you have?"

I said, *"Alice!"* and nearly swerved the car as I turned my head to look at her.

She said, "I'm sorry I didn't ask earlier, I think I was just in shock. I would have rung Mum to ask her but I wasn't sure whether she still had the same phone, and then I thought, What if Roger answers the phone?"

I said I thought she had her memory back, and she said, "Well, not exactly."

I started insisting that we go straight back to the hospital and asking did she lie to the doctor to get herself discharged, and she stuck her chin out (she looked just like Madison). She said if I took her back to the hospital, she would just say that she didn't know what I was talking about because her memory was perfect and then the hospital would have to decide which one was crazy and she bet they'd choose me and next thing they'd have me in a straitjacket.

I said I didn't think they used straitjackets anymore. (Do they, Dr. Hodges? Have you got an emergency one in your drawer, ready to whip out at a moment's notice?)

Alice folded her arms across her chest and writhed about as if she was in a straitjacket, saying, "Let me out! My sister is the nutter! I'm the sensible one!"

I was flabbergasted. She was being so . . . silly. So old Alice.

Next thing we were giggling like schoolkids. We laughed and laughed and I kept driving her toward her house because I didn't know what else to do. It was so strange, laughing like that with Alice. It was like tasting something delicious I hadn't eaten for years. I'd forgotten that drunken, euphoric feeling of being rocked with laughter. We both cry proper tears when we laugh hard enough. It's a family trait we inherited from our dad. How funny. I'd forgotten that too.

Eventually they stopped laughing and became quiet.

Alice wondered if Elisabeth would return to the subject of going back to the hospital, but she didn't say anything. Instead she wiped under each eye with a fingertip, sniffed, and reached over to turn on the car stereo. Alice steeled herself; Elisabeth enjoyed the sort of loud, angry, heavy metal music that normally appealed to teenage boys in hotted-up cars and made Alice's head ache. Instead, slow chords and a mellow female voice filled the car, as if they were in a smoky jazz bar. Elisabeth's taste in music had changed. Alice relaxed and looked out the window. The streets of Sydney looked pretty much as she remembered them. Had that coffee shop always been there? That block of units looked new, although it was entirely possible they'd been there for twenty years and she'd just never noticed them before.

There was an incredible lot of traffic, but all the cars looked the same. When she was little, she had assumed that by the year 2000 they'd be living in a space-age future complete with flying cars.

She glanced at Elisabeth's profile. She still had a leftover smile from their laughing fit.

Alice said, "Last night I dreamed again about that woman with the American accent, and this time I remembered you being there. Are you sure it doesn't mean anything to you?"

The leftover smile vanished from Elisabeth's face, and her cheeks, which had been puffed out and pink from laughing, seemed to collapse inward; Alice regretted saying anything.

Finally, Elisabeth said, "It was six years ago."

Elisabeth's Homework for Dr. Hodges

So I told her all about it, as if it was a story. Actually, all of a sudden I was desperate to tell her before she remembered for herself. Before she could write it off as a tiny, sad incident that had happened a long time ago.

This is what happened, Dr. Hodges. FYI.

Alice and I were both pregnant at the same time. Her baby was due exactly one week after mine.

Alice's third pregnancy was another accident of course, something complicated and typically Alice (typically old Alice; not the new and improved pedicured, manicured, peeled, waxed, and tinted Alice) to do with swapping brands of the pill.

My pregnancy was not an accident. The very idea of an "accidental pregnancy" seems so flippant and free. It makes me think of summer holidays, kissing for hours, smooth young skin, and . . . I don't know, piña bloody coladas. It feels like something that would always have been impossible for me, not just because of my stupid body, but because I don't have the right personality. I'm not whimsical enough. I don't get caught up in the moment. I want to say to people, "Why didn't you just use CONTRACEPTION?" Alice told me once that if she'd just stretched her fingertips a bit further she would have found the condom in her bedside drawer and Madison would never have been conceived. I found that immensely irritating because *how hard is it to stretch your fingertips, ALICE?*

Ben and I tried to get pregnant naturally for two years. We tried all the stuff people try. The temperature-taking, the charts, the acupuncture, the Chinese herbs, the holidays where we pretended not to think about it, the kits where you check your saliva under a microscope for the pretty fern pattern that meant you were ovulating.

The sex was still nice. It was before I became a dried apricot, you see, Dr. Hodges, and I was thin and fit. Although sometimes I would notice that Ben had the same grimly determined expression on his face as when he was trying to fix something tricky on his car with a wrench.

I was upset that we couldn't get pregnant, but I was still pretty upbeat, because I was an upbeat sort of person. I read a lot of self-help books back then. I even went along to weekend seminars and found the power within and hollered and hugged strangers. Oh yes, I was a believer. If someone gave me lemons, I made lemonade. I had inspirational quotes stuck on the noticeboards in front of my desk. This was my mountain and I was going to climb it. (I was a nerd.)

So we started IVF.

And we got pregnant on our very first cycle. That hardly ever happened! Well, we were ecstatic. We were giddy with happiness. Every time we looked at each other we laughed we were so happy. It was the proof of positive thinking! It was the miracle of modern science! We loved science. Good old science. We loved our doctor. We even loved those daily injections—they'd been no problem at all, didn't even hurt, weren't that scary! The medication hadn't really made me *that* moody and bloated. Actually, the whole process had just been interesting and fun!

I despise our old selves and at the same time I feel indulgently fond of them, because we didn't know any better (and, what, do I think everyone should lead their lives pessimistically, expecting the worst so they don't end up looking silly?). I can hardly bear to think of ourselves hugging and crying and making giggly phone calls, like we were in some inane sitcom. We actually discussed names. *Names!* I want to shout back through the years at myself, "Just because you're pregnant doesn't mean you get a baby, you idiots!"

There is a photo somewhere of Alice and me standing back-to-back with our hands pressed meaningfully to our stomachs. We look pretty. I'm not doing my stupid teeth-gritting fake smile and Alice hasn't got her eyes closed. We were thrilled when we found out our due dates were only days apart. "They could be born on the same day!" we said, pop-eyed by the coincidence. "They'll be like twins!" we cried. We were going to take photos of ourselves every month in the same position to record the progress of our bellies. It was so fucking sweet. (I'm sorry to swear, Dr. Hodges. I just wanted to sound cool and angry for a moment. A spoonful of paprika for me. That's what Mum used to give us when we swore as children, instead of washing our mouths out with soap and water, which she felt was unhygienic. I can never say "fuck" without tasting paprika. Ben laughs when-ever I swear. I don't do it right. Neither does Alice. It's some-thing to do with the paprika. I think we screw our faces up in preparation for the horrible taste.)

Alice came with me for my twelve-week ultrasound be-cause Ben was away in Canberra at a car show. Madison was at preschool, but Tom was with us, sucking on a rusk in his stroller, sitting up very straight and alert and monitoring the world. I was completely besotted with Tom's laugh when he was a baby. I used to do this thing where I would keep my face completely straight and then, without warning, puff out my cheeks and shake my head from side to side like a dog. Tom thought it was hysterical. He'd watch me closely, his eyes dancing, and when I did my head-shaking thing, he'd fall straight back in his stroller and laugh with his whole body, slapping his knee in imitation of Nick's dad, because he thought that was a rule when you laughed. He had two tiny front teeth and the sound of his laugh was as delicious as chocolate.

Alice wheeled Tom into the room with us, parked the stroller in the corner, and I took off my skirt and lay down on the chair. I wasn't taking all that much notice of the wispy-haired woman with the American accent who was rubbing cold jelly on my tummy and typing things into her computer, because I was making eye contact with Tom, ready to make him laugh again. Tom was looking straight back at me, his solid little body quivering all over with anticipation, and Alice was chatting to the wispy-haired woman about how they'd both rather the weather was cold than muggy, although not too cold of course.

The woman tapped away at the keyboard as she rubbed the plastic probe back and forth. I glanced briefly at the screen and saw my typed name in the right-hand corner over the top of the lunar landscape that apparently had something to do with my body. I was waiting for the woman to start pointing out the baby, but she was silent, tapping at her keyboard and frowning. Alice stared up at the television screen and chewed her nail. I looked back at Tom, widened my eyes, lifted my chin, and shook my head about.

Tom fell back in his stroller in an ecstasy of mirth, and the woman said, over the top of his laughter, "I'm sorry, but there is no heartbeat." She had a soft Southern accent, like Andie MacDowell.

I didn't understand what she meant, because Ben and I had already heard the heartbeat when we went for our first visit to the obstetrician; it was a strange, eerie sound like the beat of a horse's hooves underwater and it didn't seem quite real, but it seemed to please Ben and my doctor, who both grinned proudly at me as if they were responsible for it. I thought the wispy-haired woman must mean that there was a problem with her machinery; something had broken down. I was about to say politely, "That's no problem," but then I looked over at Alice, and she must have understood right away because she'd curled her hand into a fist and pressed it against her mouth and when she turned around to look at me her eyes were red and watery. The woman touched me on the arm with her fingertips and said, "I'm so sorry," and it was slowly dawning on me that maybe something quite bad had happened. I looked back at Tom gnawing on his rusk and grinning, thinking, "She's going to do that crazy thing again soon!" and I smiled involuntarily back at him, and said, "What do you mean?"

Afterward, I felt guilty because I hadn't been concentrating on my own baby. I shouldn't have been playing with Tom when my poor little baby was trying to have a heartbeat. I felt that it must somehow have known I wasn't concentrating. I should have had my eyes fixed on that screen. I should have been helping it along, thinking: Beat. Beat. Beat.

I know this is irrational, Dr. Hodges. I'm never going to give you the professional satisfaction of hearing that story so you can point out it's irrational and pat yourself on the back for a good day's work at the office.

I know it's irrational, and I know there is nothing I could have done.

But I also know that a good mother would have been concentrating on her baby's heartbeat.

I never pulled that silly face for Tom again. I wonder if some part of his baby mind missed it. Poor little Tom. Poor little lost astronaut.

"Remember?" asked Elisabeth. "The woman with the wispy hair? Tom had rusk smeared all over his face. It was a really hot, humid day and you were wearing khaki pants and a white T-shirt. On the way home you had to stop and get petrol and when you came back to the car, both Tom and I were crying. You'd bought a Twix in the service station and you handed out pieces, and a man behind you waiting for the pump tooted his horn at us, and you put your head out the window and shouted at him. I was proud of you for shouting."

Alice tried to remember. She wanted to remember this. It seemed a betrayal of Elisabeth to have forgotten. She strained her mind with all her might, like a weight lifter, heaving to lift something huge that had lodged itself in her memory.

Scenes came into her head of a baby laughing in a stroller, Elisabeth crying in the car, a man angrily tooting his horn; but she couldn't tell if they were real memories or just her imagination painting pictures as Elisabeth talked. They didn't feel like real memories; they were insubstantial and shadowy, without context.

"You remember now?" said Elisabeth.

"Maybe a bit." She didn't want to disappoint her; she looked so hopeful.

"Well. Good. I guess."

Alice said, "I'm sorry."

"What for? It's not your fault. You didn't throw yourself headfirst at the floor at the gym."

"No, I mean, I'm sorry about your baby."

Chapter 12

Alice groped for the right thing to say next. The obvious thing to ask was, "Did you try to get pregnant again?" but that would be like saying, "So! Moving right along!"

She glanced over at Elisabeth. She had put on sunglasses, so Alice couldn't see her eyes, and was steering with one hand while she used the other hand to rub compulsively at something on the side of her face.

Alice looked away and saw that they were only a block away from the house. She and Nick had gone for so many walks around this area in the twilight, stopping to look at other people's houses to steal renovation ideas for their own. Was that really ten years ago? It didn't seem possible. The memory was so clear and ordinary it could have happened yesterday. Nick always said hello first to other neighborhood walkers. "Beautiful evening!" he would call out with a cheery lack of cool, and then he'd stop and chat, as if these people were old friends, while Alice stood there, smiling tightly, thinking, "Why are we bothering with these *strangers*?" But she was so proud of Nick's uninhibited sociability, the way he could walk straight into a party full of people they didn't know and stick his hand out to a stranger and say, "I'm Nick. This is my wife, Alice." It was as though he had an amazing skill, like playing a complicated musical instrument, that Alice could never hope to master. The best part was that she could coast along safely beside him at any social event, so that parties became glittery and giggly instead of excruciating torture, so much so that she wondered if she'd ever really been that shy in the first place. Even when he wasn't right by her side, she always knew that if the person talking to her drifted off, she wouldn't be stranded in the crowd; she could go and find Nick with a purposeful expression on her face, and he'd put an arm around her shoulder and draw her smoothly into the conversation.

Did she have to go to parties on her own again now?

She remembered that raw sensation she'd felt after previous relationships had ended. For months afterward, it had felt like she'd lost a layer of skin. If she'd felt like that after those meaningless boys, what would she feel like after breaking with Nick? She'd been so cozy in the cocoon of their relationship. She assumed she got to stay there forever.

Alice looked up from her lap, where she'd been fiddling with her bracelet, and saw they were turning into Rawson Street. As she watched the long line of leafy liquid ambers and the car ahead putting on its right-hand indicator to turn into King Street, she felt a sudden sense of horror. Her heart palpitated as if she'd woken up in the middle of a nightmare; something grabbed her throat and squeezed; pure fear rammed her hard against her seat.

She went to reach out for Elisabeth, to touch her arm to let her know that she might be dying, but she couldn't move. Elisabeth braked and looked left and right to turn onto King Street. Alice was having a heart attack right next to her and Elisabeth didn't even realize.

They turned the corner and Alice's heart began to slow. She could breathe again. She made a whooshing sound of relief as air filled her lungs once more.

Elisabeth glanced over at her. "You okay?"

Alice spoke, her voice high. "I felt really, really strange for a moment there."

"Dizzy? Because I can take you straight back to the hospital right now if you like. It's no problem."

"No, no, it's gone now. It was just—nothing, really."

The fear had vanished, leaving her weak and shaky as though she'd just stepped off an amusement park ride. What did these huge tidal waves of feeling mean? First there had been that unimaginable grief. Now it was terror.

As they drove down Alice and Nick's street, she saw a For Sale sign on the house directly opposite theirs. "Oh, are the Pritchetts selling?" she asked.

Elisabeth glanced at the sign and a strange, inscrutable expression crossed her face. "Um. I think they sold years ago. The family who bought it from them is selling it now. So, anyway—" She turned into Alice and Nick's driveway and pulled on the handbrake. "Home sweet home."

Alice looked out the window at her house and pressed her hand to her mouth. She threw open the car door and jumped out, the smooth white gravel driveway crunching beneath her shoes. White gravel! "Oh," she said ecstatically. "Look what we *did*!"

They first saw the house on a gloomy July day.

"Oh dear," they both said simultaneously when they pulled up in front of it, and then as they sat there in Nick's sister's car, gazing at it for a few seconds, they both made rising "ummm?" sounds, which meant, "But maybe it's got something?"

It was a ramshackle two-story Federation house with a sagging roof, blankets hanging in the windows instead of curtains, and an overgrown junkyard lawn. It looked sad and battered, but if you squinted your eyes, you could see the stately home it had once been.

The For Sale sign out front said POTENTIAL PLUS, and everyone knew what that meant.

"Too much work," said Nick.

"Far too much," agreed Alice, and they gave each other sidelong suspicious looks.

They got out of the car and stood shivering on the street, waiting for the real estate agent to arrive. The front door of the house creaked open and a bent old lady wearing a man's jumper over a checked skirt, long socks, and sneakers came shuffling up the footpath toward the letterbox.

"Oh *God*," said Alice in agony. It was bad enough when you caught a glimpse of a harried middle-aged couple rushing out to their car to drive away before you went stomping through their house, making disparaging remarks about their choice of carpet. It broke Alice's heart when she saw the things they did to try to make their house sell—the fresh flowers, the kitchen counters with wet streaks from where they'd been vigorously wiped, the coffee plunger and cups placed just so on the living room table to make it look homey. Nick would snort cynically when people lit scented candles in the bathroom as if that's the way they always lived, but Alice was always touched by their hopefulness. "Don't go to all that effort to try and impress *me*," she wanted to tell them. And now here was this ancient, trembly old lady. Where would she go on this freezing day while they looked at her house? Had she scrubbed the floors on arthritic knees for their appointment, when they probably wouldn't even buy it?

"Hi!" called out Nick, while Alice shrank behind him, saying, "Shhh!" He pulled her out from behind him, and because she didn't want to have a full-on wrestling match in public, she had no choice but to walk along beside him toward the old lady.

"We're meeting the real estate agent here in a few moments," explained Nick.

The old lady didn't smile. "Your appointment isn't until three."

"Oh, no," said Alice. There *was* something a bit familiar about the time three o'clock and she and Nick were always getting things like that wrong. ("God help you if you two ever have children," Nick's mother had said to them once.)

"Sorry about that," said Nick. "We'll go for a drive around the neighborhood. It looks beautiful."

"You may as well come in now," said the old lady. "I can do a better job of showing it to you than that smarmy weasel."

Without waiting for an answer, she turned around and started shuffling up the path toward the house.

Nick whispered in Alice's ear, "She's going to put us in cages and fatten us up before she eats us."

"Leave a trail of crumbs," whispered back Alice.

Shaking with repressed laughter, they obediently followed her.

There were two stately sandstone lions at the top of the veranda stairs, guarding the house. Their eyes seemed to follow Nick and Alice as they walked by.

"Raaaah!" whispered Nick to Alice, lifting his hand like a claw, and Alice said, "Shhhh."

Inside, the house was better and worse than they'd expected. There were soaring ceilings, ornate cornices and ceiling roses, original marble fireplaces; Nick quietly kicked back a corner of fraying old carpet to show Alice wide mahogany floorboards. At the same time there was a nose-tickling smell of damp and neglect, gaping holes in plaster, ancient moldy bathrooms, and a kitchen with 1950s linoleum and a stove that looked like it came from a museum.

The old lady sat them down in front of a single bar heater and brought them cups of tea and a plate of Scotch Finger biscuits, waving away Alice's desperate offers to help. It was excruciating to watch her walk. She finally sat down with a dusty black old photo album.

"This is what the house looked like fifty years ago," she said.

The photos were small and black-and-white, but you could still see that the house was once beautiful and proud, not the shrunken skeleton it had become.

The old lady pointed a yellowed fingernail at a photo of a young girl standing with her arms outspread in the front garden. "That was me on the day we moved in."

"You were so pretty," said Alice.

"Yes," said the old lady. "I didn't know it, of course. Just like you don't know how pretty you are."

"No, she doesn't," agreed Nick solemnly, who was eating his third stale Scotch Finger as if he hadn't eaten for a month.

"I should be leaving this house to my children and grandchildren," said the old lady. "But my daughter died when she was thirty, and my son doesn't talk to me anymore, and so I'm putting it on the market. I want two hundred thousand for it."

Nick choked on his biscuit. The ad had listed it at over $300,000.

"The real estate agent will tell you I want a lot more, but I'm telling you if you offer that much, I'll accept. I know I can probably get more than that from an investor who will do it up quick-sticks and sell it on, but I was hoping a young couple might buy it and take their time restoring it and bring back the happy memories. We had a lot of happy memories here. Even though you probably can't feel them, they're here."

She spat out the words "happy memories" with slight disgust.

"It could be beautiful," continued the old lady as if she were reprimanding them. "It *should* be beautiful. Just a bit of a spit and polish."

Later in the car, they sat and looked at the house silently.

"Just a bit of a spit and polish," said Alice.

Nick laughed. "Yeah, gallons of spit and truckloads of polish."

"So what do you think?" asked Alice. "Should we forget it? We
should just forget it, shouldn't we?"

"You go first. What do you think?"

"No, I want you to go first."

"Ladies first."

"Okay, fine," said Alice. She took a breath and looked at the house,
imagining fresh paint, a mowed lawn, a toddler running around in
circles. It was madness, of course. It would take them years to fix it all
up. They didn't have the money. They were both working full-time.
They didn't even own a car! They had agreed they would *not* buy a
house that needed anything but superficial renovations.

She said, "I want it."

Nick said, "I want it, too."

Alice was in seventh heaven. Everywhere she looked there was something new and wonderful to see. The big square sandstone pavers leading up to the veranda (Nick's idea); the glossy white wooden window
frames with glimpses of cream-colored curtains; the pink bougainvil-
lea climbing frothily up the trellis at the side of the veranda (she could
swear she'd only just thought of that idea the other day—"We'll have
our breakfast there and pretend we're on a Greek island," she'd told
Nick); even the *front door*, for heaven's sake—at some point they must
have finally got around to stripping it back and painting it.

"We had a list," she said to Elisabeth. "Do you remember our list?" It was three foolscap pages of things we needed to do to the house. There were ninety-three things on that list. It was called "The Impossible Dream." The last thing on that list was "white stone driveway." She bent down and picked up a smooth white stone and showed it to Elisabeth in the palm of her hand. Had they crossed everything off on that list? It was nothing short of a miracle. They'd achieved the Impossible Dream.

Elisabeth smiled tiredly. "You made a beautiful home—and wait till you see inside. I assume you've got your keys in your backpack there."

Without needing to think, Alice bent down and pulled out a fat jangle of keys from a zippered pocket at the side of the backpack. The key ring was a tiny hourglass; she knew where it would be, but she had never seen it before.

She and Elisabeth walked up onto the veranda. It was beautifully cool after the heat. Alice saw a set of cane chairs with blue cushions (she loved that shade of blue) and a half-empty glass of juice sitting on a round table with a mosaic top. Automatically, she went over and picked up the glass, hefting her backpack over her one shoulder; she kicked against something with her foot and saw it was a black-and-white soccer ball. It rolled away and hit the wheel of a child's scooter lying on its side, with shiny ribbons tied around the handles.

"Oh," she said in sudden panic. "The children. Are the children in there?"

"They're with Nick's mother. It's his weekend for the kids. Nick is back from Portugal tomorrow morning. So he'll drop them back to you Sunday night, as usual."

"As usual," repeated Alice faintly.

"Apparently that's your usual procedure," said Elisabeth apologetically.

"Right," said Alice.

Elisabeth took the glass of orange juice from Alice's unresisting fingers. "Shall we go inside? You probably need to lie down for a while. You still look so pale."

Alice looked around her. Something was missing.

"Where are George and Mildred?" she said.

"I don't know who George and Mildred are," said Elisabeth in a gentle, dealing-with-crazy-person-here voice.

"That's what we called the sandstone lions." Alice gestured at the empty spot on the veranda. "The old lady left them for us. We love them."

"Oh. Yes, I think I remember them. I expect you got rid of them. Not quite the look for you, Alice."

Alice didn't understand what she meant. She and Nick would never have got rid of the lions. "Just off to the shops, George and Mildred," they'd say as they left the house. "You're in charge."

Nick would know. She would ask him. She turned around and lifted the keys to the door. The locks were new to her. There was a solid-looking gold dead bolt, but her fingers instantly found the right key, holding down the door handle and pushing with her shoulder against the door in a practiced, smooth movement. It was extraordinary the way her body knew how to do things—the mobile phone, the makeup, the lock—without her mind remembering her ever having done them before. She was about to comment on this to Elisabeth, but then she saw the hallway and she couldn't speak.

"Okay, listen to me, because I am a visionary," Nick had said standing in the musty, dark hallway in the first shell-shocked week after they'd moved into the house. (His mother had *cried* when she saw the house.) "Imagine sunlight flooding through this hallway because of the skylights we'll put here, here, and here. Imagine all this wallpaper gone and the walls painted something like a pale green. Imagine this carpet gone somewhere far, far away and the floorboards varnished and shiny in the sunlight. Imagine a hall table with flowers and letters on a silver tray, you know, as if they've been left there by the butler, and an umbrella stand and a *hat stand*. Imagine photos of our adorable children lined along the hallway—not those horrible portrait shots—but real photos of them at the beach or whatever or just picking their noses."

Alice had tried to imagine but she was suffering from a bad cold and one nostril was stinging so badly it was making her eyes water and they had two hundred and eleven dollars in the bank and twenty minutes ago they'd just discovered the house needed a new hot water system. All she could say was "We must have been out of our minds," and Nick's face had changed and he'd said, desperately, "Please don't, Alice."

And now here was the hallway exactly as he'd described it: the sunlight, the hall table, the floorboards shining liquid gold. There was even a funny old antique hat stand in the corner covered with straw hats and baseball caps and a few draped beach towels.

Alice walked slowly down the hallway, not stopping, only touching things with a vague caressing fingertip. She looked at the framed photos: a fat baby crawling on hands and knees in the grass, gazing huge-eyed up at the camera; a fair-haired toddler laughing uncontrollably next to a little girl in a Spider-Man suit with her hands on her hips; a skinny brown boy in baggy wet board shorts, caught ecstatically mid-air, bright-blue sky behind him, arms and legs flailing in every direction, droplets of water on the camera lens as he crashed down into unseen water. Every photo was another memory Alice didn't have.

The hallway led out to what had been the tiny living room where the old lady had given them tea and biscuits. Their plan had been to knock down three walls in this back area—it was Alice's idea; she'd drawn it up on the back of a Domino's Pizza napkin—so that it would create a huge open space where you could be cooking in the kitchen and see right out to the jacaranda tree in the back corner of the yard. "You're not the only visionary around here," she'd told Nick. And now here it was, almost exactly as she'd drawn it, but even better. She could see long, sleek marble countertops in the kitchen, a *huge* stainless-steel refrigerator, and complicated appliances.

Elisabeth walked into the kitchen—as if it were just an ordinary kitchen!—and poured the glass of orange juice down the sink.

Alice dropped her bag on the floor. There was no way this "divorce" talk could be serious. How could they be anything but blissfully happy living in this house?

"I can't believe it," she said to Elisabeth. "Oh look! I *knew* white shutters would be perfect on that back window. Nick wanted timber. Although, I see he won on the tiles. No, but I have to admit he was right. Oh, and we found a solution to the weird corner! Yes! Perfect! Oh, I don't know about those curtains."

"Alice," said Elisabeth. "Have you actually got *any* of your memory back?"

"Oh my God! Is that a pool out there? A swimming pool? An in-ground swimming pool? Are we rich, Libby? Is that what happened? Did we win the lottery?"

"What did you tell them at the hospital?"

"Would you *look* at the size of that television? It's like a movie screen."

She knew she was babbling, but she couldn't seem to stop.

"Alice," said Elisabeth.

Alice's legs felt wobbly. She went and sat down on the brown leather couch (expensive!) in front of the television. Something dug into her leg. She pulled out a tiny plastic toy, a figure of a murderous-looking man carrying a machine gun under one arm. She placed it carefully on the coffee table.

Elisabeth came and sat next to her. She handed her a sheet of folded paper. "Do you know who this is from?"

It was a handmade card with glitter stuck to the front and a drawing of a stick-figure woman with a turned-down mouth and a Band-Aid on her forehead. She opened it and read out loud, "Dear darling Mummy, get well soon, love from Olivia."

"It's from Olivia of course," said Alice, fingering the glitter.

"And do you remember Olivia?"

"Sort of."

She had no memory whatsoever of "Olivia," but her existence seemed indisputable.

"And what did you tell them at the hospital?"

Alice pressed her hand to the still tender spot at the back of her head. She said, "I told them that some things were a bit hazy, but I remembered most things. They gave me a referral for a neurologist and said if I kept having any significant problems to make an appointment. They said I should expect to feel totally back to normal within a week. Anyway, I think I actually do remember bits and pieces."

"Bits and pieces?"

The doorbell rang.

"Oh!" said Alice. "That's beautiful! I hated that old doorbell!"

Elisabeth lifted her eyebrows. "I'll get it." She paused. "Unless you want to get it."

Alice stared at her. Why shouldn't Elisabeth answer the door? "No, that's fine."

Elisabeth disappeared down the hallway and Alice laid her head back against the couch and closed her eyes. She tried to imagine what it would be like when Nick dropped the children off on the following night. Her natural instinct would be to throw her arms around him like she did when he'd been away. (She had a distinct feeling that she hadn't seen him in ages, as though he'd been away for weeks and weeks.) But what if he just stood there, without touching her back? Or what if he gently pushed her away? Or *shoved* her away? He would never do that. Why was she even thinking such a thing?

And "the children" would all be there. Milling about. Doing whatever kids do.

Alice whispered their names to herself.

Madison.

Tom.

Olivia.

Olivia was a pretty name.

Would she tell them? "Sorry, I know your face, I just can't quite place you." But she couldn't do that. It would be terrifying for a child to hear their mother didn't remember them. She'd have to pretend until her memory did come back, which it would, of course. Soon.

She'd have to try and talk to them in a natural voice. Not one of those jolly, fake voices people put on for children. Kids were smart. They'd see right through her. Oh heavens—what would she *say* to them? This felt worse than trying to think up appropriate conversation topics before going to one of Nick's scary work parties.

She heard voices coming down the hallway.

Elisabeth came in, followed by a man pushing a trolley piled with three cardboard boxes.

"Apparently they're glasses," said Elisabeth. "For tonight."

"Where do you want 'em?" grunted the man.

"Um," said Alice. For tonight?

"I guess just here in the kitchen," said Elisabeth. The man lifted the boxes onto the counter.

"Sign here," he said. Elisabeth signed. He ripped off a sheet of paper, handed it to her, and looked around him briefly. "Nice house," he said.

"Thank you!" Alice beamed.

There was a shout from down the hallway. "Alcohol delivery!"

"Alice," said Elisabeth. "I don't suppose you remember anything about hosting a party tonight?"

Chapter 13

Together, they flipped to the date in Alice's diary.

"Kindergarten Cocktail Party," read out Alice. "Seven p.m. What does that mean?"

"I'd say it means that it's all the parents from Olivia's class," said Elisabeth.

"And I'm hosting it?" said Alice. "Why would I host it?"

"I believe you host a lot of these sorts of things."

"You believe? Don't you know? Don't you come to all these 'things'?"

"Well, no. This is to do with the school," said Elisabeth. "It's all mothers. I'm not a mother."

Alice looked up from the diary and said, "You're not?"

Elisabeth seemed to flinch. "No, I'm not. I haven't had any luck in that regard. So, anyway"—she seemed desperate to get off of the subject—"what are you going to do about this party?"

But Alice didn't care about the party. There was no way she was going to host any "kindergarten cocktail party." She said, "So will you tell me what happened? Please? Did you try again to get pregnant after you had that miscarriage?"

Elisabeth's eyes slid away.

Frannie's Letter to Phil

So, the village minibus was pulling out of the driveway, and all of a sudden there was a commotion. It was Mr. Mustache, do you mind, running alongside the bus, rapping his knuckles on the window, shouting, "Wait for me!"

I thought there must have been some crisis, but no, he was just running late. He leapt aboard, all breathless and excited, as if we were off somewhere far more thrilling than the local shopping center. He announced to the entire bus that he'd been held up on the phone "placing a bet on the doggies." I think that means greyhound racing, Phil. Charming.

There were plenty of spare seats, but for some reason, he chose to plonk himself down next to me. It was uncomfortable. He's not a large man, but he did seem to take up a lot of room. I found I was pressing myself against the side of the bus so our thighs didn't touch. Also, he was close enough that I could smell some sort of aftershave or cologne. I'm not saying it was unpleasant. It just seemed overly personal.

I said something about the weather but he ignored that and said, "How's that honorary family of yours?"

I found myself telling him about Alice's accident and how she didn't remember anything about her marriage breakdown. I told him how worried I was about the children. He told me a rather sad story about his own son, who had gone through a divorce, and how his daughter-in-law didn't let them see their grandchildren anymore. "It broke my wife's heart,"

he said. He told me that his wife had died two years ago and that he truly
believed she would have lived longer if her grandchildren hadn't been taken
from her.

When we got to the shopping center, I naturally assumed he would go
off and do his own thing, but he cheerfully admitted he didn't have a thing
to buy and he'd be happy to keep me company. I'd had enough of him by
now but I couldn't think of a polite way to get rid of him.

So he followed me around while I bought talcum powder for Alice. I
needed some new deodorant at the chemist's, but I was too embarrassed to
buy it in front of him, as if deodorant could only be purchased in private.
Isn't that the most ridiculous thing you ever heard?

Also, we couldn't seem to synchronize our walking. We kept bumping
into each other and treading on each other's toes. It was driving me a little
batty, to be honest. (I'm sure it was his fault, not mine. I'm perfectly able
to walk alongside other people. You and I used to go on such long walks!
Never a problem!)

At one point we saw a toddler sitting in one of those toy cars. The child
was having a tantrum, screaming, "Just one more turn!" at his poor harassed
mother. Next thing, Mr. Mustache took a coin from his wallet and leaned
past the toddler and popped it in the slot to activate the ride. Of course, the
toddler shrieked with delight, while the poor mother didn't know what to do.

We were having quite a spirited argument about this (I felt that he had
rudely undermined the young mother's authority) when he suddenly got all
excited by a pink neon sign advertising free iced doughnuts with your
coffee. He insisted on buying me a cappuccino. For something to say, I told
him about Ben and how he designs rather beautiful neon signs for a living,
and that led to us talking about Elisabeth's problems.

He was very sympathetic to Elisabeth and, strangely, that made me
want to argue with him. I said that babies weren't the be-all and end-all
and that Elisabeth might do better to concentrate on her marriage and her
lovely husband.

He asked whether I'd ever had a "lovely husband" myself.

I said no.

Then I got a little snappish and said that my doughnut was stale.

That was a fib. It was actually quite delicious.

Elisabeth's Homework for Dr. Hodges

It was surreal hearing Alice ask me if I tried again, so wide-eyed and respectful. I nearly laughed. I wondered if it was an act.

It's been a long time since I've thought properly about those early "losses," as you call them with a straight-mouthed grimace, as if you're constipated. I sort of hate that face you pull, Dr. Hodges. I bet your wife does, too. It always makes me think about what else I could be doing with the $150 I spend on you. I remember in one session you wanted me to start talking through the "early losses" (grimace, grimace), and I gave a dramatic sigh and said I didn't think I could, but really I was just so irritated by that expression on your face.

Mostly now I just think of my "losses" as bullet points on my medical history. If a doctor asks me for my history I can reel off every single procedure and test and crushing disappointment without even a tremor in my voice, as if they don't mean a thing, as if they happened to somebody else.

So I can say "second first-trimester miscarriage in April 2006" without blinking, and I don't even think about what it was like, or how it felt.

I want you to know that I've missed all of *Grey's Anatomy* now. I'm really working hard on this therapy. I wish you were grading me. You should give grades to your approval-seeking patients.

I remember how happy we were when we got pregnant again, because this time, for some reason, we managed a "natural" pregnancy.

That was to be my January baby, due on 17 January (the day after Ben's birthday; imagine if it was born on the same day! But no, shhhh, don't say that out loud). We kept the pregnancy a secret this time. We thought that telling everybody about the first baby had been our beginner's mistake. I imagined announcing my second pregnancy with calm, womanly confidence after I'd passed the first trimester. It seemed a more grown-up, safer way to handle things. "Oh no, not an IVF baby this time," I'd say casually. "A *natural* pregnancy." This time we didn't talk about names, and Ben didn't pat my stomach when he kissed me goodbye each morning. We said things like "*If* I'm still pregnant at Christmas" and lowered our voices to a whisper when we used the word "baby," as if getting our hopes up had been the mistake, as if we could trick the gods into not noticing us sneakily trying to have a baby.

This time Ben was there for the first ultrasound and we both dressed up carefully as if it was for a job interview, as if our clothes would make a difference. The woman doing it was young, Australian, and a little cranky. I was worried, but on the other hand I was faking it for the cameras, if you know what I mean. I was all twitchy nerves on the surface, but deep down part of me was enjoying observing my anguish: *Ooh, look at her digging her nails into her hands as she lies down, the poor, traumatized thing, when of COURSE there is going to be a heartbeat THIS time because this sort of thing doesn't happen twice!* I could already feel the huge rush of relief that would be released. I had tears of joy banked up, just waiting for me to push "go." I was ready to send a poignant message of love to my first baby, something along the lines of "I will never forget you, I will always hold you in my heart," and then it would be time to focus on this baby: our real baby. Alice's baby would only be a few months older. We could still call them twins.

The cranky girl said, "I'm sorry . . ."

Ben clenched his jaw hard and took a step back, as if someone had just threatened to hit him in a pub brawl and he was trying not to get involved.

I've heard so many professional "I'm sorry"s now, Dr. Hodges. I'm sorry. I'm sorry. I'm sorry. Yes, your colleagues in the medical profession are all very sorry. I wonder if one day you'll be the next to say, kindly and sadly, "I'm sorry but I can't cure you. You're a nutter. It might be time to look at other options, like transplanting somebody else's personality."

I was embarrassed that it had happened twice in almost exactly the same way. I felt as if I was wasting people's time, constantly turning up for ultrasounds of dead babies. What? You thought you had a real live baby in there? Don't be ridiculous. Not you. You're not a proper woman with these half-hearted, faintly ridiculous attempts to have a baby. There are women out there with proper swollen pregnant stomachs and live kicking babies.

Afterward, I felt it had been wrong not telling the family about the baby, because then I wanted them to know about the miscarriage, so that they knew the baby had existed. But when I told people, they seemed more interested in the fact that I'd kept the pregnancy a secret. They felt they'd been tricked. They said things like "Oh, I did wonder that day when you didn't drink at the Easter BBQ but you said you just didn't feel like drinking!" In other words, LIAR.

Ben's mother was offended. We had to take her out twice for a "buy one, get one free!" meal at the Black Stump before she forgave us. The point of it seemed to be that I'd hidden the pregnancy, not that I'd lost the baby. People weren't as upset as with the first one, and how could they be, when they'd only just heard it existed in the first place. I felt this ridiculous protective feeling for my January baby, as if nobody loved her, as if she wasn't as pretty or as smart as the first baby.

I know she was a girl. This time they sent off the "fetal material" for testing and told me it was a chromosomally normal female. They said they were sorry but they couldn't find any reason why I'd lost the baby. They said there was a lot they didn't know about miscarriage, but according to the statistics I still had an excellent chance of having a healthy baby next time. Chin up. Try again.

A week after the D&C (such a chipper name for something so horrible; I never feel so desolate as I have after waking up in Recovery from a D&C) I went to visit Alice in hospital and see her new baby girl. Of course, Alice said I didn't need to go and Ben said he didn't want me to go, but I went. I don't know why but I was determined to do everything I normally would.

I went to the greeting card store and chose a card frosted with pink glitter saying "Congratulations on your darling little girl." I went to Pumpkin Patch and bought a tiny yellow dress with embroidered butterflies all over it. "It just makes you long to have a baby girl, doesn't it!" cooed the saleslady.

I wrapped up the dress in pink tissue paper and wrote on

the card and I drove to the hospital and found a parking spot and walked through the corridors with the present under one arm and some trashy celebrity magazines for Alice under the other. The whole time I floated alongside myself, impressed. "You're doing fine. Well done. It will all be over soon and you can be home watching television."

Alice was on her own in the room, breast-feeding Olivia.

My own breasts still ached and burned. It's so mean-spirited of your body, the way it keeps acting like you're pregnant, even after the baby has been scraped out of your womb.

"Oh, *look* at her!" I said to Alice, ready to begin the new-baby patter.

I'm so good at it these days. Just last week I went to visit a friend who had given birth to her third child and, even if I say so myself, my performance was flawless. "Look at his tiny hands!" "Oh, her eyes/nose/mouth is just like yours!" "Of *course* I'd love a hold!" And, breathe. And, chat. And, smile. Don't think about it, don't think about it, don't think about it. There should be Oscars for that sort of thing.

But Alice didn't let me get started on my act.

As soon as she saw me, she held out the arm that wasn't holding the baby and her face crumpled and she said, "I wish it was me visiting you."

I sat on the bed with her and let her hug me. Alice's tears dripped straight onto Olivia's soft, tiny, bald head, but she kept right on sucking Alice's nipple, as if her life depended on it. She's always loved her food, that kid.

I'd forgotten all about that day until now—how much it meant to me that Alice cried so genuinely for me. It was like she was taking on some of my grief. I thought, It's okay, I can do this, I can get through it, I'll be fine.

I just didn't realize that "this" would keep on going and
going and going.

Mmmm. I think we may have just had a mini-breakthrough
in my journal-writing therapy. Although no need to get too
big for your boots, Dr. Hodges. It wasn't like I'd *repressed*
that memory with Alice. I just hadn't thought about it for a
while, but still, bravo, maybe there is something in this, even
though I've just missed what was promised to be an "explosive" episode of *Grey's Anatomy*.

I'd toughened up by the next "loss."

Elisabeth said, "You're not just pretending you don't remember so you
can make some sort of point, are you?"

Alice felt the same punched-in-the-stomach feeling as when Nick
had yelled at her on the phone. He'd said something about her making
a point, too. Had she become a person who had points to make?

"What sort of point?"

"Forget it. I was just being paranoid." Elisabeth stood up and walked
into the kitchen. She stopped in front of the refrigerator. It was covered
with magnets, notices, photos, and children's drawings. "I wonder if
there is an invitation here for this party of yours."

Alice twisted on the couch to watch her. Her head ached.

"Libby. Please. What sort of point? I don't understand. Sometimes you talk to me like you—well, it's almost like you don't like me
anymore."

"Ha!" Elisabeth picked up something off the fridge and brought it
over to her. "Here's the invitation. There's another woman's name on
it for the RSVPs. You should ring her and ask if she can change the
party venue."

She went to hand it over, but Alice ignored it.

Elisabeth sighed. "Of course I still *like* you. Don't worry about it. There's nothing to worry about. Here—this woman's name is Kate Harper. Actually, I think I've heard you talk about her before. I think you're quite good friends with her."

She looked expectantly at Alice.

"I've never heard of her," said Alice dully.

"Okay, then," said Elisabeth. "Well, why don't I call her and you can go upstairs and lie down. You look like death warmed up."

Alice looked at Elisabeth's lined, anxious face.

Have I let you down? Have I lost you and Nick?

Chapter 14

Alice stood in the middle of her unfamiliar bedroom, looking for something—anything—that belonged to Nick. There was no sign of him. No pile of books or magazines on his bedside table. He liked bloodthirsty thrillers (they both did), war histories, and business magazines. No cylindrical piles of coins taken from the pockets of his trousers each day. No ties draped over the door handle. No giant dirty sneakers. Not even a lone crumpled T-shirt or sock.

They were both messy. Their clothes were normally tangled together on the floor in flamboyant embraces. Sometimes they purposely asked people over just to give themselves the incentive to clean up in a frantic rush before they arrived.

But the carpet (dark maroon—she had no memory of choosing it) was pristine, newly vacuumed.

She went to the wardrobe (they'd found it lying on its side outside someone's house for council pickup; it was autumn, like now; they

brushed away a layer of crackly brown leaves to reveal patterned mahogany). It was filled with spaced-out good heavy hangers containing
beautiful clothes that presumably belonged to Alice. Although it gave
her fleeting pleasure to feel the lustrous fabrics as she flipped through
the hangers, she longed to see just one of Nick's shirts. Even a boring
white business shirt. She would wrap its sleeves around her like his
arms. Bury her nose in the collar.

As she closed the cupboard door and slowly looked around the bedroom, she realized it smelled and felt essentially feminine. There was
a white lacy duvet on the bed and a row of small shiny blue cushions.
Alice thought the bed looked absolutely beautiful (actually it was her
dream bed), but Nick would have said that all that prettiness would
render him instantly impotent; so, fine, if that's what she wanted, he
was just warning her. There was a Margaret Olley print hanging above
the bed that Alice knew would have made Nick wince as if hit by a
sudden attack of nausea. The dressing table had rows of different-
colored glass bottles (*What exactly is the point?* Nick would have said)
and a crystal vase containing a big bouquet of roses.

This was the bedroom she would have created for herself if she
were living on her own. She'd always wanted to collect beautiful glass
bottles and thought it was something she would never do.

Except for the roses. She remembered how the image of exactly
those roses had popped into her mind while she was in the ambulance
yesterday. She went over to the dressing table and studied them. Who
gave her those? And why was she keeping them in her bedroom when
she hated that sort of arrangement?

There was a small square card sitting next to the vase. Nick? Nick
wanting her back and forgetting she didn't like roses? Nick *making a
point* by sending her roses he knew she would hate?

Alice picked it up and read: *"Dear Alice, I hope we can do that again
one day—next time in the sunshine? Dominick."*

Oh God. She was dating.

She plunked herself down on the end of the bed, holding the card between disbelieving fingers.

Dating was meant to be something from her past, not something from her future. She'd never enjoyed it that much anyway. The self-conscious, trapped feeling when you were sitting in the car together for the first time; the constant horrifying possibility of food caught in between your teeth; the sudden feeling of exhausted boredom when you realized it was your turn to come up with the next stilted topic of conversation. *So what do you like to do on the weekends?*

Oh, sure, yes, there was nothing better than when a date actually *worked*. She could remember the euphoria of those early dates with Nick. There was a night where they'd watched Australia Day fireworks from a bar in the Rocks. She was drinking a huge creamy cocktail, and Nick was telling a story about one of his sisters and he was so funny and so sexy and Alice's hair looked nice and her shoes weren't hurting and there were curls of shaved chocolate floating on top of her cocktail and Nick's hand massaging her lower back and she felt such an intense sensation of happiness it frightened her, because surely there was a price to pay for this sort of bliss. (And was this the price? All these years later? Nick swearing at her on the phone from the other side of the world. Had she finally been sent an exorbitant bill?)

A date with any man other than Nick would be boring and awkward and stupid. Dominick. What sort of a name was Dominick?

In a sudden rage, she took the card and tore it into tiny pieces. How could she betray Nick like that by keeping these flowers in her bedroom?

And then there was that other man—that physiotherapist from Melbourne—who had sent her the card with the mention of "happier times." Who was he? Was she already on to her *second* relationship after breaking up with Nick? Had she turned into a *hussy*? A point-making hussy who went to the gym and upset her beloved sister and hosted "Kindergarten Cocktail Parties"? She hated the person she'd become. The only good part was the clothes.

This all had to stop. She had to get Nick's coins and his socks and his sneakers back in her bedroom, and these roses gone.

She lay back on the bed. Elisabeth was downstairs phoning up that Kate Harper woman trying to get tonight's party canceled.

Alice crawled across the bed, pulled back the duvet, and got into crisp, clean sheets, still wearing her red dress.

She looked at the ceiling (plastered and painted, the water stains and cracks gone as if they'd never existed) and thought of that moment in the bathroom at the hospital when she had been going through that odd makeup routine and she had that rush of feeling after she smelled her perfume. It had seemed like she was about to fall headfirst into all her memories but then she'd deliberately resisted it, stepped back from the edge when she really should have let herself go. It would be far easier and less confusing if she could just remember what the hell was going on in her life. She sniffed at her wrist where she'd sprayed the perfume that had seemed so evocative of everything, but this time she experienced only a confused, choppy mass of half-remembered feelings; they were insubstantial and slippery, gone before she could even attempt to name them.

She woke to find Frannie sitting at the end of her bed, holding a gift.

"Hello, sleepyhead."

"Hello." Alice smiled with relief, because Frannie looked exactly as she should. She was wearing a familiar pale-pink buttoned-up blouse Alice had seen many times before, or at least one like it, and tailored gray pants. Her back was ramrod straight. She was like a little elf. She had short white hair tucked behind tiny ears, creamy white skin, and cat's-eye glasses on a gold chain.

Alice said happily, "You haven't changed a bit. You look just the same."

"You mean as I did ten years ago?" Frannie adjusted her glasses on her nose. "I guess there was no room for any more wrinkles. Here." She handed her the present. "You probably won't like it, but I wanted to get you something."

Alice sat up in bed. "Of course I'll like it." She unwrapped a bottle of talcum powder. "Lovely." She twisted the lid, poured some into her palm and sniffed. The scent was simple and flowery and reminded her of nothing. "Thank you."

"How are you feeling?" asked Frannie. "You gave us all a fright."

"Fine," said Alice. "Confused. Sometimes I feel like I'm on the verge of remembering everything, and then other times it all feels like a huge practical joke and you're all just pretending I'm thirty-nine when you know perfectly well that I'm about to turn thirty."

"I know that feeling," said Frannie reflectively. "Just the other day I woke up and felt like I was nineteen. I went into the bathroom and saw an old lady staring back at me from the mirror and it really startled me. I thought, 'Who is that dreadful old crone?'"

"You're not a crone."

Frannie waved her hand at that dismissively. "Well, anyway, I think you're probably having a nervous breakdown." Alice looked appalled. "Don't look at me like that! People do have nervous breakdowns, and you've been under so much stress lately. What with this divorce—"

"Yes, about that. *Why* are we breaking up?" interrupted Alice. She couldn't bring herself to say the word "divorce" out loud. Frannie wouldn't try to hide anything from her. She would tell her straight.

But Frannie said, "I have absolutely no idea. That's between you and Nick. All I know is that you both seem very set on the idea. There doesn't seem any chance of reconciliation. So we've all just had to button our lips and accept it."

"But you must have an opinion. You always have an opinion!"

Frannie smiled. "Yes, I generally do, don't I? But in this case, I really don't know. You haven't confided in me. It's very sad for the children. Especially this awful fighting-over-custody business. I don't approve of that at *all*, as you know."

"I don't know. I don't remember."

"Oh. Well, I've made my opinions on the matter clear. Too clear, you might say."

Alice said, "Do you think I can get him back?"

"Who back? You mean Nick? But you don't want him back," said Frannie. "Actually you talked to me on Wednesday and said you'd just received roses from some new fellow called Dominick. You seemed very excited about it."

Alice looked with dislike at the roses. She said sourly, "I thought you said I was stressed."

Frannie said, "Well, yes, you're stressed, but you were happy about the roses."

Alice sighed. "How are *you*, Frannie? You're still living next door to Mum, right?"

"No, darling." Frannie patted Alice on the leg. "I moved myself into a retirement village five years ago. Just after your mother moved in with Roger."

"Oh." Alice paused to consider this news. "Do you like the retirement village? Is it fun?"

"Fun," said Frannie reflectively. "That's what's important these days, isn't it. Everything should be *fun* and lighthearted."

"Well, not everything, obviously."

"Do you think I have a sense of humor?" asked Frannie. She gave Alice a look that was surprisingly vulnerable.

"Of course you have a sense of humor!"

Although "sense of humor" weren't exactly the first words that came to mind when you thought of Frannie.

Frannie sighed and smiled. She wasn't an especially smiley lady, so when she smiled, it was like receiving a gift. "Thank you, darling. Tell me something, would you buy deodorant in front of a man? Or would you think that was too . . . personal?"

"What man?" said Alice.

"Any man!" said Frannie irritably.

"Well, I think I probably would. There's nothing especially personal about deodorant. Unless, I guess, you had to use some really heavy-duty one that would make him think you had some sort of rare and horrible perspiration disease."

"I can assure you, Alice, I don't need a 'heavy-duty' deodorant!" said Frannie, looking affronted.

"What's this about?" asked Alice.

"Nothing. Just a very silly friend of mine asked the question."

Was *Frannie* interested in some man? Alice knew that Frannie had lost a boyfriend during the Second World War, but as far as she was aware, there had never been anyone else in her life since, although there had been that time when they were teenagers and Elisabeth had seen a half-finished letter sitting on Frannie's desk. When Elisabeth asked who she was writing to, Frannie had apparently been so flustered, she had actually (Alice thought Elisabeth must be making this part up) *blushed.* She had said she was writing to "an old friend," but Elisabeth had been convinced from her reaction that it was a "secret lover." "Probably someone else's husband," Elisabeth had said, with a knowing, cynical look. "I expect they meet at motels in the middle of the day." Alice had been deeply shocked and wasn't able to look Frannie in the eye for weeks after.

"Come on, let's go downstairs," said Frannie. "Your mother is making lunch."

As they walked out of the room and down the hallway toward the stairs, Frannie said, "Walk alongside me, Alice."

"I am," said Alice.

"No. Properly. That's it! See! We can walk side by side, without tripping all over each other, can't we?"

"We sure can," said Alice, wondering if Frannie had gone a little senile in 2008.

As they reached the top of the stairs, Alice stopped abruptly at the sound of a deep, familiar male voice. "Alice, my dear! I was just coming up to collect you!"

"How are you, Roger?" Alice peered over the banister, horrified to see him at the bottom of the stairs. He was all out of context without Nick. He was a visitor you planned for (steeled yourself for), not someone who looked comfortably up at you from the bottom of your stairs, as if he belonged in your house.

"Never better," Roger called back. "It's you we're worried about!"

Frannie's eyes met Alice's and she lifted a wry eyebrow. She wasn't senile. She was still as sharp as a tack.

"Is she up, then?" Alice's mother emerged from the kitchen and looked up at them.

Alice walked behind Frannie down the stairs, glad to see that although she was behaving oddly, she didn't seem that much frailer than Alice remembered.

Barb and Roger stood at the bottom with their palms lifted, like ministers welcoming the congregation, identical weirdly evangelical expressions on their faces.

"Did you have a good sleep, Alice?" asked Barb, trying in vain to take Frannie's elbow. "Rest is the best thing for you, I'm sure. I suppose everything has come back to you now?" She didn't wait for an answer. "Are you hungry?"

Roger took Alice by the arm and led her into the dining area, behind Barb and Frannie, his fingertips solicitously pressed to the small of her back.

"Don't *hover*, Barbara!" snapped Frannie, as Barb fussed about the best seat for her at the long pine table.

Alice sat down next to her, anxious to escape the oily feel of Roger's fingertips. She watched in fascination at the relaxed way her mother tilted her head coquettishly up at him. Thankfully, she was no longer wearing the exotic salsa-dancing outfit from the day before, but she was wearing a rather low-cut T-shirt and capri pants, and her long hair was up in a jaunty ponytail.

"Now, I've made a nice tuna salad for our lunch. I chose that specifically for you, Alice, because fish is brain food. Roger and I have been taking fish oil every day, haven't we, darl?"

Darl. Her mother just called Roger "darl."

Roger didn't seem to have changed at all in the last ten years. He was still tanned and polished and pleased with himself. Had he had plastic surgery? Alice wouldn't put it past him. He was wearing a pink polo-necked shirt, with a gold chain nestled in graying chest hair. His shorts were just a little too tight, revealing muscular brown legs.

As Barb turned to go back toward the kitchen, Roger gave her a playful, not-at-all-discreet slap on the bottom. Appalled, Alice averted her eyes. (Roger, she remembered, owned a waterbed. "The ladies love it," he'd told Alice once.)

Frannie gave a low chuckle and laid her hand over Alice's in sympathy. Alice distracted herself by examining the long pine table in front of her. She'd dreamed about this table at the hospital. Nick was sitting at it, while she was cleaning the kitchen. He'd said something that made no sense. What was it?

Elisabeth came into the room, lifting her handbag over her shoulder. "I've got to go."

"Where are you going?" asked Alice desperately. She needed support to help her cope with Roger and her mother. "Are you coming back?"

Elisabeth gave her an odd look. "I'm meeting some people for lunch. I'll come back if you like."

"Who?" asked Alice, trying to keep her there for longer. "Who are you meeting?"

"Just some friends," said Elisabeth evasively. "Anyway, make sure you listen out for the phone because I've left three messages for that Kate Harper about tonight's party but she still hasn't called back." She looked at Alice. "You still seem very pale. I think you should go back to bed after lunch."

"Oh, I agree!" said their mother as she walked in from the kitchen, carrying a glass salad bowl. "I'm packing her straight off to bed after lunch, don't worry. We need to get her completely recovered before those little terrors are back."

Alice looked at the big glass salad bowl her mother was holding and for no particular reason the name "Gina" came into her head.

It's always about Gina. Gina, Gina, Gina. That's right. That's what she'd remembered, or dreamed, Nick saying as he sat at this table.

"Who is Gina?" asked Alice.

The room became extremely still and silent.

Finally Frannie cleared her throat. Roger looked at the floor and fiddled with the chain around his neck. Barb froze at the entrance from the kitchen and hugged the salad bowl to her stomach. Elisabeth chewed hard at her lip.

"Well, who is she?" said Alice.

Elisabeth's Homework for Dr. Hodges

One thing I've been thinking about a lot is how I would feel if I lost ten years of my memory, and what things would surprise me, or please me, or upset me about how my life had turned out.

I hadn't even met Ben ten years ago. So he would be a stranger. A big scary hairy stranger sharing my bed. How could I explain to my old self that I had accidentally fallen in love with a silent mountain of a man who designs neon signs for a living and whose most passionate interest is cars? Before I met Ben, I was one of those girls who was deliberately, prettily ignorant about cars. I described them by size and color. A big white car. A small blue car. Now I know makes and models. I watch the Grand Prix. Sometimes I even flick through his car magazines.

Do you like cars, Dr. Hodges? You seem more like an art galleries and opera sort of guy. I see you have a photo of your wife and two small children on your desk. I secretly look at this photo every session when you're writing out my receipt. I bet your wife had no trouble getting pregnant at all, did she? Do you ever thank your lucky stars you didn't end up with a reproductively challenged wife like me? Do you give that photo an affectionate look as I walk out of the room and think, Thank God my wife is a good breeder? Don't worry if you do. I'm sure it's innate, it's just biology, for a man to want a woman who can give him children. I raised this with Ben once. I said he must secretly resent me and I understood that. He got so angry. The angriest I've seen him. "Never say that again," he said. But I bet that's why he got so angry, because he knew it was true.

Before I met Ben, I used to go for witty successful types. I'd never been out with a man before who owned a toolbox. A proper big dirty well-used toolbox full of, you know, screwdrivers and stuff. It's embarrassing how aroused I became when I first saw Ben selecting a chunky oily wrench from that toolbox. My dad had a toolbox. So maybe I'd been subconsciously waiting for a man with a toolbox. I bet you don't have a toolbox, do you, Dr. Hodges? No. I didn't think so.

I used to think that one of my main prerequisites for a man was that he be good at dinner parties. Like Alice's Nick. But Ben is hopeless at dinner parties. He always seems too big for his chair. He gets this trapped expression. It's like I've brought along a big tame chimp. Sometimes he's OK if he happens to find another man (or woman—he's no chauvinist) who can talk about cars, but mostly he's miserable, and he breathes out gustily when we get in the car, as if he's been let out of jail.

It's funny. I had all those years of being driven mad by Mum and Alice and their fear of social events. "Oh, *no!*" they'd say tragically, and I would think someone had died, and it would turn out they'd been invited to some party or lunch where they'd only know one person, and then there would be all the strategizing about how to get out of it, and the drama of it all and the *sympathy* they'd pour on each other. "Oh, you poor thing! That would be awful! You absolutely must not go." I couldn't stand it, and yet I ended up marrying a man who also thinks socializing is something that's meant to be endured. Not that he's shy like they were. He doesn't get butterflies in his stomach or agonize over what people think of him. Actually I don't think he has any self-consciousness whatsoever. He is a man without vanity. He's just not a talker. He has no small talk ability whatsoever. (Whereas Mum and Alice, of course, were talkers, and they were actually interested in meeting other people. In reality they were more social than me. But their shyness stopped them from being the outgoing people they actually were. They were like athletes trapped in wheelchairs.)

As it turns out, Ben and I don't really go to many dinner parties anymore. I can't stand them. I've lost my ability to chat, too. I listen to people talk about their interesting, full lives. They're training for marathons, they're learning Japanese, they're taking the kids camping and renovating the bathroom. I had a life like that once, too. I was interesting and active and informed. But now my life is three things: work, television, IVF. I no longer have anecdotes. People say, "What have you been up to, Elisabeth?" and I have to stop myself from treating them to a complete medical update. I understand now why very sick people and the elderly have such a compulsion to tell you everything about their health. My infertility fills every corner of my mind.

How things have changed. Now I'm the one groaning when I hear someone's cheerful voice on the phone asking me if I'm free next Saturday, while Alice is hosting kindergarten cocktail parties and Mum is salsa-dancing three nights a week.

Alice can't believe she's got three children. I wouldn't be able to believe I had none. I never expected to have trouble getting pregnant. Of course, no one does. It hardly makes me unique. It's just that I *did* expect so many other different medical problems. Our dad died of a heart attack, so I've always been frightened by the slightest case of heartburn. I've had two grandparents on different sides of the family die of cancer, so I've been permanently on standby, waiting for the cancer cells to strike. For a long time I was terrified I was about to be struck down by motor neuron disease for no other reason than the fact that I'd read a very moving article about a man who had it. He first noticed he had a problem when his feet started hurting on the golf course. Whenever I'd feel a twinge in my foot, I'd think, OK, here we go. I told Alice about the article and she started to worry about it, too. We'd take off our high heels and massage our sore feet and discuss how we'd cope with getting around in wheelchairs, while Nick rolled his eyes and said, "Are you two for *real*?"

Alice is the other reason I didn't expect infertility. We've always been so similar health-wise. We both get a dry, irritating cough every winter that takes exactly one month to go away. We have weak knees, bad eyesight, a slight dairy intolerance, and excellent teeth. When she had no problem getting pregnant, I thought that meant it would be the rule for me, too.

So it's Alice's fault that I never invested the appropriate time worrying about infertility. I never insured against it by worrying about it. I won't make that mistake again. Now every day I remember to worry that Ben will die in a car accident on his way to work. I make sure I worry at regular intervals about Alice's children—ticking off every terrible childhood disease: meningitis, leukemia. Before I go to sleep at night I worry that someone I love will die in the night. Every morning I worry that somebody I know will be killed in a terrorist attack that day. That means the terrorists have won, Ben tells me. He doesn't understand that I'm fighting off the terrorists by worrying about them. It's my own personal War on Terror.

That was a tiny joke, Dr. Hodges. Sometimes you don't seem to get my jokes. I don't know why I want you to laugh so badly. Ben finds me funny. He has this sudden bellow of appreciative laughter. He did, anyway—when I wasn't an obsessive bore with only one topic of conversation.

I guess it might be sensible to cover this "worrying" issue at one of our sessions because it's obviously just stupid superstition, and childish, too—as if I'm the center of the universe and what I think actually makes a difference. But I don't know, I can already guess all the sensible things you'd say, the perceptive questions you'd ask, trying to gently lead me to my own personal "Eureka!" moment. It all seems sort of pointless and dull. I'm not going to stop worrying. I like worrying. I come from a long line of worriers. It's in my blood.

I just want you to make it stop hurting, please, Dr. Hodges. That's why I'm paying you the big bucks. I just want to feel like me again.

I have wandered off from the point again. My point was that I've been imagining what it would be like if I lost memory. So, I hit my head, and I wake up and I discover it's 2008 and I've got fat and Alice has got thin and I'm married to this guy called Ben.

I wonder if I would fall in love with Ben all over again. That would be nice. I remember how it crept up so slowly on me, like that agonizingly slow old electric blanket which used to almost imperceptibly heat up my frosty sheets, second by second, until I'd think, "Hey, I haven't shivered in a while. Actually, I'm warm. I'm blissfully warm." That's how it was with Ben. I moved on from "I really shouldn't be leading this guy on when I have no interest" to "He's not that bad-looking really" to "I sort of enjoy being with him" to "Actually, I'm crazy about him."

I wonder if Ben would try to protect me from bad news, the way we've been skirting around certain subjects with Alice. He's a terrible liar. I'd say, "How many children have we got?" and he'd mumble, "Well, we haven't much luck there," and he'd scratch his chin and clear his throat and look away.

I would bossily insist on all the details, and eventually he'd just have to go ahead and say it.

Over the last seven years, you've had three IVF pregnancies and two natural pregnancies. None of those theoretical babies became real babies. The furthest you ever got was sixteen weeks and that one broke both our hearts so badly we thought we'd never recover. You've also been through eight failed IVF cycles. Yes, this has changed you. Yes, it has changed our marriage, and your relationships with your family and your friends. You are angry, bitter, and, frankly, you're often a bit strange. You are currently seeing a counselor after an embarrassing incident in a coffee shop. Yes, all this has cost a lot of money, but we really prefer not to go into the figures.

(Actually, Dr. Hodges, I've had six miscarriages. But Ben doesn't know this. I only got to five weeks, so it barely counted. Ben was away on a fishing trip with a friend, and I'd only done the pregnancy test the day before, and then the next day I started bleeding and that was that. He was so happy and dirty and sunburned when he came back from that trip, I couldn't tell him. It was just another lost little theoretical baby. Another tiny astronaut adrift in space.)

So, what would I say after Ben told me this long sorry story?

Well, this is the thing, Dr. Hodges, because I remember the old decisive, take-action, nerdy me and my first thought was that I would say something bracing along the lines of "if at first you don't succeed." After all, I was the woman who used to start each day by looking at a framed picture of a snow-capped mountain with a quote from Leonardo da

Vinci: "Obstacles cannot crush me; every obstacle yields to stern resolve."

Good one, Leonardo.

But the more I think about it, the more I think that maybe I wouldn't say anything motivational at all.

It's quite possible that I might briskly slap my hands against my knees and say, "Sounds like it's time you gave up."

Chapter 15

It was Alice's mother who finally broke the silence. She said, "Gina was a friend of yours." She placed the salad bowl on the table without meeting Alice's eyes. "Actually, I think this bowl was a gift from Gina. That's probably why you thought of her."

Alice looked at the bowl and closed her eyes. She saw crumpled yellow paper. She tasted champagne. Possibly heard a peal of feminine laughter. Then nothing.

She opened her eyes again. Everyone was looking at her.

"Well, I really have to go," Elisabeth said, looking at her watch.

There was a flurry of relieved activity. "I think I've parked you in!" Roger said happily, pulling out a huge set of keys from his pocket and jumping to his feet.

"Don't forget to listen out for that call from Kate," said Elisabeth as she hurriedly backed out of the room. "Otherwise you're hosting a party tonight."

"I'll come and wave you off," Barb said as she and Roger followed Elisabeth down the hallway, obviously wanting to speak to her privately.

When it was just Alice and Frannie left alone, Alice picked a cherry tomato out of the salad and said, "So how do I know this Gina?"

"She lived across the road," said Frannie. "I think they moved in just before Olivia was born. You don't remember anything about her?"

"No. So she doesn't live across the road anymore?"

Frannie paused. She seemed to be struggling with the right thing to say. She said, "No. The family moved to Melbourne. Not that long ago."

Suddenly Alice got it.

Something went on between this Gina and Nick. It explained everything. That's why everybody had behaved so awkwardly.

Gina. Yes. The name was definitely associated with raw pain of some kind.

Why had she thought she was exempt from infidelity? It happened all the time. It was one of those tacky soap opera events that always seemed sort of vaguely comical when it happened to someone else but was earth-shakingly horrible when it happened to you.

Alice thought of poor Hillary Clinton. Imagine having the whole world know that your husband had cheated on you in such a *messy* way. You would have thought being president of the United States should have been a pretty *distracting* sort of job. It could happen to Nick.

After all, she realized with a shock, they'd been married for over ten years by now. Maybe Nick caught a slight case of the seven-year itch (which was practically a medical phenomenon, not really his fault), and then this awful manipulative woman took advantage of him, seduced him.

The bitch.

He was probably drunk. It probably just happened once. Maybe there was a party and Nick kissed her (quickly! hardly at all!) and Alice had overreacted and Nick had apologized but Alice wouldn't budge (stupid!) and now they were getting a divorce because of it. It was all Alice's fault. And Gina's fault.

She must be very beautiful.

The thought of her beauty, and the thought of Nick finding her beautiful, hurt so sharply that she groaned out loud.

"Are you remembering?" asked Frannie anxiously.

"I think so." Alice massaged her forehead.

"Oh, darling," said Frannie, and when Alice looked up and saw the utter sympathy on her grandmother's face, she knew it had been far more than just a kiss.

How could you, Nick? She wouldn't throw her arms around him on Sunday night. She would beat closed fists against his chest. How could he make her feel so safe in their relationship, so *smug*, so comfortable— and then maliciously rip it all away? Make her look like a fool?

Still, Hillary was prepared to stand by her man while his *semen stains on another woman's dress were analyzed.* Poor old Hillary.

It occurred to Alice that the whole Monica Lewinsky affair must be ten-year-old news now. She wondered if Hillary's marriage had survived.

The phone rang.

Alice stood up automatically and went to answer it.

"Hello?"

"Alice? Kate! I've just been doing a million things at once and I've only just now picked up your sister's messages! I was so *worried* when I saw you at the gym yesterday morning, I've been telling everybody, and I meant to call you, but I'm just run off my *feet* right now, as you well know, and then Melanie said she saw you laughing in a car at the traffic lights at Roseville, so I thought, Phew, she's okay! But now, your sister says you're possibly not well enough to host the party?"

Alice recognized the terribly cultured voice. It was the sleek blond woman she'd seen at the gym before she'd been sick all over George Clooney's shoes.

"Ah," said Alice.

"Of course, normally I'd say no problem! Have it here! In an instant! But what with the renovations, and Sam's mother staying with us, it's just literally, physically *impossible*. I mean, you don't have to do a thing tonight, you really don't, if you've still got a bit of a headache. I'll take care of everything. I have to admit I haven't been feeling that well myself, but I'll be all right, just a touch of the flu. Melanie said to me, 'You're a superwoman, Kate, how do you do it?' And I said, 'Well, no, Melanie, not a superwoman, just an *exhausted* woman trying to do what she can.' Sam says I just need to learn to say no and stop putting myself out for everyone, but I can't help it, I've always been that sort of person. Anyway, as I say, if your head is aching, I promise you can just put your feet up tonight, and we'll all rush around and bring you drinks. I mean, it's not like you have to cater or anything."

A strange inertia had crept over Alice as Kate spoke. Was this woman really her *friend*? Alice couldn't imagine wanting to talk to her for more than five minutes. She'd take Jane Turner's brisk snippiness any day over this woman's prissy sweetness with its razor-sharp edges.

She said, "Oh, okay, fine."

Who cared if hundreds of strange people turned up on her doorstep tonight? Her life was a nightmare and she may as well let it continue on its nightmarish way.

"We don't need to change it, then? Well, thank *goodness*. I knew I could rely on you! I had thought to myself your sister probably had it wrong. She's the bad-tempered career woman with all the infertility problems, isn't she? I guess she just has no inkling what a mother can do when she has to! All right, I must dash, and I'll look forward to seeing you tonight. All right! Bye!"

The line went dead. Alice slammed down the phone so hard, the cradle shook. How dare that horrible woman speak about Elisabeth like that? She thought about the way Elisabeth's face had caved in when she talked about the baby's heartbeat and she wanted to punch that woman's elegant nose.

"Is everything okay?" said Frannie.

But did that mean Alice had been complaining to Kate Harper about Elisabeth? "Alice?"

There was an old-lady quaver in Frannie's voice. Alice suddenly saw her as a stranger would: tiny and frail.

She pulled herself together. She was nearly thirty—whoops, forty—years old. She couldn't go and sob in her grandmother's lap anymore.

"Everything is fine," she said. "I told Kate Harper we could still have the party here."

"You did?" Her mother had walked back into the room, followed by Roger. "Are you sure you're up to it?"

"Oh sure," said Alice. "Sure. Why not?"

"She's remembering Gina," said Frannie.

"Oh, *darling*," said Barb, while Roger's face contorted into a horrendously mournful expression which was meant presumably to convey sympathy.

Apparently Roger had affairs when he was married to Nick's mother. "I'm afraid my ex-husband was something of a philanderer," Nick's mother had once told Alice with a delicate sigh, and Alice had been impressed at the way she could make even a cheating husband sound elegant and expensive.

Was Roger cheating on her mother now?

Maybe it wasn't so surprising that Nick had turned out to be a cheat, too. Wasn't there some old proverb about the orange not falling far from the tree? She should say that to Roger, look him straight in the eye and say sneeringly, "So, Roger, I see the orange doesn't fall far from the tree." But knowing her, she'd get it wrong and nobody would understand what she was trying to say. "What do you mean, darling?" her mother would say, brightly interested, spoiling the moment.

And actually, she had a funny feeling it was meant to be an apple, not an orange. The *apple* doesn't fall far from the tree. She felt a hysterical giggle rise in her throat. She was such an idiot. "Oh, *Alice*," they would all say.

"Alice?" said her mother. "Do you want a cup of tea? Or a pain-killer?"

"Or a drink?" Roger furrowed his brow. "A brandy?"

"Oh, the last thing she needs is alcohol, Roger," snapped Frannie.

"I'm fine," said Alice.

She would think about all this later, when Roger wasn't there pulling his grotesquely sympathetic expressions.

She didn't care how much her world had changed. Apple or orange, Nick was absolutely nothing like his father.

Elisabeth's Homework for Dr. Hodges

Alice gave me such an imploring look, I almost considered canceling my lunch, but it wasn't like I was leaving her *alone* with Roger-Dodger. That's what Ben calls him. It suits him.

Anyway, I didn't want to get into a conversation about Gina. My feelings about Gina are complex. Or maybe childish is a more appropriate word.

I was having lunch with the Infertiles.

We met about five years ago when I joined this "Infertility Support Group." At first we were meeting at the community center and we had a facilitator, a professional like you, Dr. Hodges, who was there to keep us on track. The problem was that she kept trying to make us be positive. "Let's try and reframe that in a more positive light," she'd say. But we didn't want to be positive, thanks very much. We longed to say out loud all the bitter, negative, nasty things we kept in our heads. The medications, the hormones, and the relentless frustration of our lives make us bitchy, and you're not allowed to be bitchy in public or people won't like you. So we formed our own private group. Now we meet up once a month, at a swish restaurant, where we're not likely to come across Mothers' Groups and their circles of prams. We eat, we drink, and we bitch to our hearts' content—about doctors, family, friends—and most of all about the insensitivity of "Fertiles."

At first I resisted the idea of splitting the world into "Fertiles" and "Infertiles," as if we were in some science-fiction movie, but soon it became part of my new language. "What Fertiles can never understand . . ." we say to each other. Ben hates it when I say things like that. He doesn't really like the group, either, although he's never met them.

I'm making them sound awful, but they're not. Or maybe they are and I can't see it because I'm exactly the same. All I know is that sometimes it feels like lunch with those girls is the only thing that keeps me sane. And it's Mother's Day next Sunday. (As the television keeps loudly reminding me every two minutes.) That's the most painful day of the year for an Infertile. I always wake up feeling ashamed. Not sad so much. Just ashamed. Sort of stupid. It's a version of that feeling I had in high school when I was the only one in my class who didn't need to wear a bra. I'm not a proper woman. I'm not a *grown-up*.

Today we met at a restaurant in Manly right on the harbor. When I got there, they were all sitting outside in a dazzle of sun and water and blue sky, huddled over something in the middle of the table, their sunglasses pushed on top of their heads.

"Anne-Marie's pregnancy tests," said Kerry when she saw me. "We disapprove, of course, but see what you think."

Anne-Marie does this every time she does an IVF cycle. They tell you not to do a home pregnancy test after you've had an embryo transfer because the results are not conclusive. You might get a positive when you're not really pregnant because your body still has hormones left over from the "trigger injection" that mimic pregnancy, or you might get a negative just because it's too early to tell. The best thing is to wait for the blood test. I never do a pregnancy test because I like things to be conclusive and I'm a good girl, but Anne-Marie starts doing them the day after the transfer and admitted once that one day she did seven tests. We all have our own versions of this obsessive-compulsive behavior, so we don't scoff.

I squinted at Anne-Marie's tests. There were three, wrapped up in aluminum foil, as usual. They all looked negative to me, but there was no point telling her this. I said I thought I could maybe see a very faint pink line on one of them, and she said her husband had said he was sure they were all negative, and she'd yelled at him that he obviously wasn't trying. You have to want to see the second line, she'd told him, and they'd had a big fight. Anne-Marie has never had a successful IVF cycle and she's been trying for over ten years. Her doctors, her husband, her family are constantly campaigning for her to give up. She is only thirty, the youngest of us all, so she has time to ruin another decade of her life. Or maybe not, of course. That's the thing for all of us. The elusive happy ending could be just a cycle away.

Kerry (two years of IVF with donor eggs, one ectopic pregnancy that nearly killed her) said to Anne-Marie, "Elisabeth is ten days past transfer and I bet she hasn't even been tempted to do a test."

We all keep up to date with our IVF cycles by e-mail. Anne-Marie, Kerry, and I are all in the middle of cycles. The other three are in between, or just about to start.

To be honest, all the drama about Alice has meant that I haven't even been considering whether or not this cycle will work. In the early years, when I still believed in the power of the mind, I used to meditate each morning after a transfer. "Please stick around, little embryo," I'd chant. "Stick, stick, stick." I'd offer it bribes: *I'll take you to Disneyland when you're five. You'll never have to go to school if you don't feel up to it. If you would just please let me be your mother, please?*

But none of it seemed to make any difference. So now I just assume that it won't work, and that if it does work, I'll lose it anyway. This is meant to protect me, although it doesn't, because somehow the hope sneakily finds its way in. I'm never aware of the hope until it's gone, whooshed away like a rug pulled from under my feet, each time I hear another "I'm sorry."

The waiter came with our drinks and said, "Let me guess—you've left the kids with their dads and escaped for the day!"

Ah, the sweet innocence of the Fertiles. They assume any group of women of a certain age must surely be mothers.

"What's the point of looking like fucking mothers when we're fucking not," said Sarah, who is our newest recruit. She has only been through one IVF cycle, but she's already energetically bitter about infertility. She makes me realize I'm even jaded about being jaded. I admire the way she swears.

That sets us off on listing the ways we've been offended since we last met.

We had:

The boss who said, "Going through IVF is a choice, it's not like getting the flu, so, no, I can't sign your sick-leave form."

The aunt who said, "Just relax and have a massage, you're not getting pregnant because you're too tense." (Oh, there's always one of those.)

The brother who said (with screaming child in the background), "You've got such a romantic idea of having children. It's just bloody hard work."

The cousin who said sympathetically, "I know exactly what you're going through. I've been trying to finish this Ph.D. for six years."

"What about your sister?" Kerry said to me. "You said something in your last e-mail about something she'd done that had you infuriated."

"She's the supermum with three children, isn't she?" Anne-Marie's lip curled. "The one who doesn't need to work because she's got the rich husband."

They all looked at me avidly, ready to be disgusted with Alice, because, to be honest, Dr. Hodges, I've complained about her before.

But I thought about laughing with Alice on the way home from the hospital and the horrified, hurt expression on her face when she talked to Nick on the phone. I thought about how she'd said, "Don't you like me anymore?" and how when I'd left her today, her dress was all crumpled from her sleep and her hair was sticking up on one side. That was so typically old Alice, not to even look at herself in the mirror before she came downstairs. And I thought about how she'd cried at the hospital with me when Olivia was born, and how she'd said so innocently to us all today, "Who is Gina?"

I felt sick with shame, Dr. Hodges. I wanted to say to them, "Hey, that's my little sister you're talking about."

Instead I told them about how Alice had lost her memory and thought she was twenty-nine, and how it had made me think a lot about what my old self would say about this life I'm leading. I said I thought my younger self might think it was time to give up. Just to give up. Let it go. Walk away. No more injections. No more test tubes of warm blood. No more grief.

Of course they snapped to attention like good soldiers who know their duty.

"Never give up," they told me, and one by one they recounted horrendous stories of infertility and miscarriage that had all ended with healthy bouncing babies.

I listened and nodded and smiled and watched the seagulls squabbling.

I don't know, Dr. Hodges. I just don't know.

Over lunch, Roger took it upon himself to bring Alice up to date with his own interpretation of every historical event that had taken place over the last ten years, while her mother decided to simultaneously do the same thing with the personal lives of everyone she'd ever met.

"And then the U.S. invaded Iraq, because old matey, Saddam, was stockpiling weapons of mass destruction," intoned Roger.

"Except there were no weapons," interrupted Frannie.

"Well, who really knows for sure?"

"You *are* joking, Roger."

"And then Marianne Elton, oh, of course you remember her, she used to coach Elisabeth's netball team," said Barb. "Well, she married Jonathon Knox, that nice young plumber we had over that time when we had that problem with the toilets that very cold Easter, they had the wedding on some tropical island, so inconvenient for everyone, and the poor flower girl got badly sunburned, anyhow, two years ago they had a baby daughter called Madeline, which made Madeline very happy as you can imagine. I said, 'Well, I never expected my girls to name their children Barbara,' which I didn't, but Madeline is such a popular name now, anyhow, poor Madeline turned out . . ."

". . . and let me tell you, Alice, exactly what the government should have done straight after the Bali attacks . . ."

"Oh, and one of Felicity's boys was there in Bali!" said Barb, the personal world suddenly intersecting with the political. "He flew out *the day before.* Felicity thinks it means he's been chosen to do something great, but so far he doesn't seem to do anything much but visit Facebook, is that what it's called, Roger—Facebook?"

Frannie said, "Does any of this mean anything to you at all, Alice?"

Alice had only been listening with one part of her mind. She was busy thinking about the concept of forgiveness. It was such a lovely, generous idea when it wasn't linked to something awful that needed forgiving. Was she a forgiving person? She had no idea. She'd never been called upon to forgive something as big as infidelity. Anyway, did Nick *want* her forgiveness?

She said to Frannie, "I'm not exactly sure."

Some things that Roger had been saying had maybe seemed familiar, as if they were things she'd learned once at school and then forgotten. When he talked about terrorist attacks, she felt a reflexive feeling of horror, and maybe even some fleeting memories: a woman in a sun visor with a hand pressed to her mouth saying, "Oh my word, oh my word." But she couldn't remember where she was when she first heard about them, if she'd been with Nick, or alone, if she'd watched them on TV or heard about them on the radio. She also seemed to recognize some parts of her mother's stories. There was something familiar, for example, about the phrase "sunburned flower girl," like the punch line of a joke she'd heard before.

Frannie was saying, "Well, she's going to have to go back to the doctor. There's something not right here. Look at her. It's obvious."

"I doubt they can just transplant her memories back in her head," said Roger.

"Oh, I'm sorry, Roger, I didn't realize you had experience as a neurosurgeon," said Frannie.

"Who wants a nice piece of custard tart, then?" said Barb brightly.

Chapter 16

Alice was alone.

There had been a lot of intense debate about the wisdom of leaving her alone after lunch. Barb and Roger had their Saturday-afternoon advanced salsa-dancing class. They said they could *easily* miss it just this once, although, of course, it was an especially important class because they were rehearsing for the Family Talent Night at Frannie's retirement village, but really and truly, it would be no problem to miss it if Alice needed them there. Frannie had an important meeting at the retirement village—something to do with Christmas. She was chairing the meeting but she could *easily* call and ask Bev or maybe Dora to do it, although they were both nervy public speakers, and it was likely they'd be railroaded by this rather domineering new resident, but that would hardly be the end of the world; her granddaughter came first.

"I'll be fine," Alice had repeated over and over. "I'm nearly *forty* years old!" she'd added flippantly, but there must have been something strange about the way she'd said it because they'd all stared at her for a moment, and then a whole new round of offers to stay began.

"Elisabeth will be back any minute," she'd told them, shooing them out of the kitchen, down the hallway, and out the door. "Off you go! I'll be fine!"

And within minutes, they were packed into Roger's big shiny car, shadowy figures waving at her behind tinted windows, and the car was disappearing down the driveway, gravel flying.

"I'll be fine," Alice repeated quietly to herself.

She saw old Mrs. Bergen coming out of the house next door wearing a big Mexican hat and carrying a pair of gardening shears. She liked Mrs. Bergen. She was teaching her how to garden. She'd given Alice lots of advice about the problems with her lemon tree (she suggested Nick should give it the occasional "tinkle," which he had, with rather revolting enthusiasm) and was always bringing over cuttings from her own garden for Alice and gently pointing out what needed watering or pruning or weeding. Mrs. Bergen didn't like cooking much, so in return Alice took over Tupperware containers with leftover casseroles and pieces of quiche and carrot cake. Mrs. Bergen had already crocheted three sets of bootees for the baby and was starting on a matinee jacket and bonnet.

But that was all ten years ago.

So were those tiny items now faded and dusty in a cupboard somewhere?

Alice lifted her hand in affectionate greeting. Mrs. Bergen lowered her head and turned pointedly in the direction of her azaleas.

Oh.

There was no mistaking it. Mrs. Bergen had snubbed her.

Would sweet, chubby *Mrs. Bergen* yell and swear at her, as Nick had, if Alice went over to say hello? That would be like when the little girl's head spun around in *The Exorcist.*

Alice went back inside quickly and closed the door behind her, feeling an absurd desire to cry.

Maybe Mrs. Bergen was going senile and didn't recognize Alice anymore. That was a perfectly reasonable explanation. Yes, that would do. For now. Once she got back her memory, everything would fall neatly into place. "Oh," she'd say. "Of course!"

Well. What next?

She wondered exactly what she did on these weekends when "Nick had the children." Did she like the break? Was she lonely? Did she long for the children to come back?

The sensible thing to do would be to explore the house for clues about her life. That way she'd be ready for when Nick came back tomorrow night. She should have a persuasive presentation prepared: Ten reasons why we should not be getting this divorce.

Maybe she would find something about Gina. Love letters to Nick? But presumably he would have taken those with him when he moved out.

Or perhaps she should be doing something for this party tonight? But what? The party seemed strangely irrelevant.

Actually, she didn't want to be in the house at all. Her stomach felt uncomfortably full from all that custard tart she'd eaten. "You want a *second* piece?" her mother had said with pleased surprise and Alice guessed that this was unusual for her.

She would go for a walk. That would clear her mind. It was a beautiful day. Why spend it indoors?

She went upstairs and then stopped in the hallway, looking at the other three bedroom doors. That must be where the children slept now. She and Nick had left them empty, except for the one they were going to use for the baby's nursery. They'd spent a lot of time in there, sitting cross-legged on the floor, planning and imagining. They'd picked the paint color: *Ocean Azure*. It would work even if the baby surprised them by being a girl (which she had—a girl!).

Alice tentatively pushed open the nursery door.

Well. What did she expect? Of course there was no white crib or change table, no rocking chair. It wasn't a nursery anymore.

Instead there was a single unmade bed, strewn with clothes and a bookshelf crammed with books, old empty bottles of perfume, and glass jars. The walls were almost entirely plastered with moody black-and-white pictures of European cities. Alice saw a tiny square of blue in between two posters. She went over and put her finger to it. *Ocean Azure.*

There was a desk against one wall. She saw a ring binder labeled *Madison Love.* The handwriting was familiar. It looked like Alice's own writing when she was in primary school. She noticed an open recipe book face down on the desk and picked it up. A recipe for lasagne. Wasn't Madison too little to be *cooking*? And for posters of European cities? Alice was still playing with dolls at that age. Her own daughter was making her nine-year-old self feel inferior.

She carefully placed the recipe book back down and tiptoed out of the room.

The next bedroom door was closed and there was a note pinned to it. KEEP OUT. DO NOT ENTER WITHOUT PERMISSION. NO GIRLS ALLOWED. THE CONSEQUENCES WILL BE DEATH.

Goodness. Alice let go of the door handle and backed away. She was a girl, after all. This must be Tom's room. Maybe he had it booby-trapped. Little boys. How terrifying.

The next room was more welcoming. She had to push through beads hanging from the doorway. The bed was a little girl's dream: four-poster, with a purple gauze canopy. Fairy wings hung from a hook on the wall. There were tiny glass ornaments shaped like cupcakes, dozens of stuffed animals, a makeup mirror with lights around it, hair clips and ribbons, a music box, glittery bangles and long beads, a pink portable stereo, a dress-up box filled with clothes. Alice sat down and riffled through the dress-up box. She pulled out a familiar green summer dress and held it up in front of her. She'd bought it especially for her honeymoon. It was one of the most expensive dresses she'd ever owned. Dry-clean only. Now it had a brown stain on the neckline and a jagged hemline where someone had taken to it with a pair of scissors. Alice dropped the dress, her head swimming. There was a sickly-sweet scent in the room like strawberry lip gloss. Fresh air. She definitely needed air.

She went to her own bedroom and quickly found shorts and a T-shirt in the chest of drawers, and her sneakers and sunglasses still in the rucksack she'd brought back from the hospital. She hurried back downstairs and pulled off one of the baseball caps from the hat stand. It said PHILADELPHIA on the brim.

She left the house, locking the door behind her and noting with relief that Mrs. Bergen had gone back inside.

Which way? She turned to the left and took off at a brisk pace. A woman was approaching from the other direction, wheeling a stroller with a stern-faced baby who was sitting very straight-backed and solemn. As Alice got closer, the baby frowned up at her, while the woman smiled and said, "Not running today?"

"Not today." Alice smiled back and kept walking.

Running? Good heavens. She *hated* running. She remembered the way she and her friend Sophie used to shuffle around the oval in the high school, moaning and clutching their sides, while Mr. Gillespie called out, "Oh for God's sakes, you girls!"

Sophie! She would give Sophie a call when she got home. If she hadn't been confiding in Elisabeth, maybe Sophie knew more about what was going on with her and Nick.

She kept walking, seeing houses that had doubled in size, like cakes in the oven. Red-brick cottages had been transformed into smooth mushroom-colored mansions with pillars and turrets.

Actually, it was interesting, because she was walking quicker and quicker, sort of bouncing along the pavement, and the idea of running didn't seem that stupid at all. It seemed sort of . . . pleasant.

Was it a bad idea with a head injury? Probably a very bad idea. But maybe it would jar all those memories back into place.

She began to run.

Her arms and legs fell into a smooth rhythm; she began to breathe deep, slow breaths, in through the nostrils and out through the mouth. Oh, this felt good. It felt right. It felt like something she did.

At Rawson Street she turned left and picked up her pace. The fat red leaves of the liquid ambers trembled in the sunlight. A white car packed with teenagers screeched by, thudding with music. She passed a driveway where a group of kids were shrieking and brandishing water guns. Someone started up a lawn mower.

Up ahead, the white car with the teenagers pulled up at the corner.

A momentous feeling of panic exploded in her chest. It was happening again, just like in the car with Elisabeth. Her legs quivered so ridiculously she actually had to crouch down on the footpath, waiting for whatever it was to pass. A scream of horror was lodged in her throat. If she let it out, it would be very embarrassing.

She looked around, her hands on the ground to balance herself, her chest heaving, and saw that the children with the water pistols were still running back and forth, as if the world hadn't turned black and evil. She looked back at the end of the street where the white car was waiting for a break in the traffic.

It was something to do with a car pulling up at that corner.

She closed her eyes and saw the brake lights of a green four-wheel-drive. The number plate said: GINA 333.

Nothing else. She felt simultaneously hot and cold, as if she had the flu. For *God's sake*. Was she about to be sick again? All that custard tart. The children could clean it up with their water pistols.

A horn tooted. "Alice?"

Alice opened her eyes.

A car had pulled up on the other side of the road and a man was leaning out the window. He opened the car door and quickly crossed the street toward her.

"What happened?"

He stood in front of her and blocked out the sun. Alice squinted mutely up at him. She couldn't make out the features of his face. He seemed extremely tall.

He bent down beside her and touched her arm.

"Did you faint?"

She could see his face now. It was an ordinary, kind, thin, middle-aged sort of face, the unassuming face of a friendly newsagent who chatted to you about the weather.

"Come on. Up you get," he said, and lifted her by both elbows so she rose straight to her feet. "We'll get you home."

He led her across the street to the car and deposited her in the passenger seat. Alice couldn't decide what to say, so she didn't say anything. A voice from the back of the car said, "Did you fall over and hurt yourself?"

Alice turned and saw a little boy with liquid brown eyes staring at her anxiously.

She said, "I just felt a bit funny."

The man got back in the car and started the engine. "We were on our way over to your place and then Jasper spotted you. Were you going for a run?"

"Yes," said Alice. They stopped at the corner of Rawson and King. She thought of the car with the GINA number plate and felt nothing.

"I saw Neil Morris at the IGA this morning," said the man. "He said he saw you being carried out of the gym on a stretcher yesterday! I left a few messages for you, but I didn't . . ."

His voice drifted away.

"I fell over and hit my head during my 'spin class,'" said Alice. "I'm fine today, but I shouldn't have been running. It was stupid of me."

The little boy called Jasper giggled in the backseat. "You're not stupid! Sometimes my dad is stupid. Like today, he forgot three things and we had to keep stopping the car and he'd say, 'Boofhead!' It was pretty funny. Okay, first thing was his wallet. Second thing was his mobile phone. Third thing—ummm, okay, third thing—Dad, what was the third thing you forgot?"

They were pulling into Alice's driveway. They stopped the car and the little boy gave up on the third thing and threw open his car door and ran toward the veranda.

The man pulled on the handbrake and then turned to look at Alice with gentle concern. He put a hand on her shoulder. "Well, I think you'd better put your feet up while Jasper and I take care of those balloons."

Balloons. For the party, presumably.

"This is a bit awkward," began Alice.

The man smiled. He had a lovely smile. He said, "What is?"

Alice said, "I have absolutely no idea who you are."

(Although, in truth, there was something about the way he smiled and the feeling of his hand on her shoulder that was giving her an idea.)

The man's hand sprang back like an elastic band.

He said, "Alice! It's me. Dominick."

Frannie's Letter to Phil

Me again, Phil.

Barb and Roger took me for lunch at Alice's place today.

Physically she seems fine, but she is definitely not herself. She didn't remember Gina! It was disconcerting. Gina played such a big part in Alice's life. Almost too big a part.

Barb talked about it all the way home. "Sometimes I wish Alice had never met Gina," she fretted. "You can't change the past," pronounced Roger, and we were all quite overcome by his wisdom. He's a philosopher, that fellow.

It's not relevant now but I always thought that Gina did dominate Alice. (Alice does have a slight tendency toward hero worship.) I remember her making some comment about Alice's outfit at Olivia's birthday party last year. It was something along the lines of "Your such-and-such blouse looks nicer with that skirt." Alice went straight back upstairs and changed. I noticed Nick was watching the whole incident and didn't look too happy about it.

After Barb and Roger dropped me off, we had yet another Social Committee meeting. This time we were discussing plans for this year's Christmas party. Mr. Mustache suggested a "Casino Night." People loved the idea! Can you think of anything less Christmassy, Phil?

He's the most aggravating man.

I will admit, however, that he did make a point of asking me whether Alice liked the talcum powder.

Elisabeth's Homework for Dr. Hodges

A funny thing happened when I got home from lunch with the Infertiles. Not exactly ha-ha funny. Just stupid ironic funny.

Driving home after lunch, I kept thinking about "Giving Up." The idea grew stronger and stronger in my head. It suddenly seems quite obvious to me. I can't go through another miscarriage. I can't. The thought of it happening again gives me the feeling of a block of concrete dropping on my chest. I have had enough. I didn't know I'd had enough, but it turns out I have.

We used to keep setting those deadlines. No more after my fortieth birthday. No more after Christmas. But then each time we'd think, well, but what else is there to do? We'd traveled, we'd been to lots of parties, lots of movies and concerts, we'd slept in. We'd done all those things that people with children seem to miss so passionately. We didn't want those things anymore. We wanted a baby.

I remember thinking about how mothers were prepared to run into burning buildings to save their children's lives. I thought I should be able to go through a bit more suffering, a bit more inconvenience to *give* my children life. It made me feel noble. But now I realize I'm a crazy woman running into a burning house for children who don't exist. My children were never going to exist. They were always in my mind. That's what's so embarrassing about all this. Each time I sobbed for a lost baby, it was like sobbing over the end of a relationship when I'd never even gone out with the guy. My babies weren't babies. They were just microscopic clusters of cells that weren't ever going to be anything else. They were just my own desperate hopes. Dream babies.

And people have to give up on dreams. Aspiring ballet dancers have to accept that their bodies aren't right for ballet. Nobody even feels that sorry for them. Oh, well, think of another job. My body isn't right for babies. Bad luck.

At the pedestrian crossing I saw a pregnant woman, a woman pushing a pram, a woman holding a child's hand. And I actually felt nothing, Dr. Hodges. Nothing! That's a big thing for an Infertile—to see a pregnant woman and feel nothing. No knife-in-the-stomach feeling of bitterness. No ugly envy twisting my mouth.

So here's the funny thing.

I got home, and for once, Ben wasn't in the garage working on his car. He was sitting at the kitchen table with paperwork spread out all around him, and I noticed his eyes were
a bit red and puffy.

He said, "I've been thinking."

I told him so had I, but he could go first.

He said he'd been thinking about what Alice had said last
week and he'd decided she was one hundred percent right.

Oh, *Alice*.

Alice sat on the couch and watched Dominick using a helium tank to
blow up blue and silver balloons. He and Jasper had finally got sick of
breathing in the helium and talking in chipmunk voices. Jasper had
laughed so hard at his dad squeakily singing "Over the Rainbow" that
Alice had worried he might stop breathing. Now he was outside in the
backyard, using a remote control to expertly operate a miniature helicopter.

"He's very cute," said Alice, watching him. She'd gathered that Jasper was in the same class as Olivia. Her daughter. The one with the fat
blond pigtails.

"When he's not being a psychotic monster," said Dominick.

Alice laughed. Perhaps too much. She didn't really get parent
humor. Maybe he really was a psychotic monster and that wasn't funny.

"So," she said. "How long have you and I been, ummm, seeing each
other for?"

Dominick glanced quickly at her and away again. He tied the end
of the balloon and watched it float straight up to the ceiling with the
others.

Without looking at her, he said, "About a month."

Alice had told Dominick that the doctors had said her memory loss was only temporary. He looked terrified and seemed to be talking to her gently and carefully, as if she had a mild intellectual disability. Unless that was the way he always talked to her, of course.

"And it's, ah, going well?" asked Alice recklessly. It was bizarre. Had she kissed him? *Slept with him?* He was very tall. Not unattractive. Just a stranger. She felt both repelled and mildly titillated by the idea. It reminded her of gurgly, giggly teenage conversations. Oh my God, imagine having sex with *him*.

"Yup," said Dominick. He was doing something funny and nervous with his mouth. He was one of those awkward, geeky types.

He picked up another balloon and hooked it over the nozzle of the helium tank. He looked at her properly, full in the face, and said, almost sternly, "Well, *I* think so, anyway." Actually, he was not unattractive.

"Oh." Alice felt flustered and exposed. "Well, good. I guess."

She longed for Nick to be sitting next to her. His hand warm on her leg. Claiming her. So she could enjoy talking, maybe even flirting, with this perfectly nice man in an appropriate, safe way.

"You seem different," said Dominick.

"In what way?"

"I don't know how to explain it."

He didn't say anything else. Apparently he wasn't a talker, like Nick. She wondered what she saw in him. Did she even like him that much? He seemed sort of dull.

"What do you do for a living?" she asked. The standard dating question. Trying to unfairly slot him into a personality type.

"I'm an accountant," he said.

Fabulous. "Oh, right."

He grinned and said, "Just testing to see if you really had lost your memory. I'm a grocer. A fruit and veg man."

"Really?" She was imagining free mangoes and pineapples.

"Nah!"

Oh, God, this man was a nerd.

"I'm a school principal."

"No, you're not."

"I'm being serious now. I'm principal at the school."

"What school?"

"Where your kids go. That's how we met."

The school principal. *Straight to the principal's office!*

"So you'll be there tonight? At this party?"

"Yes. I'm sort of wearing two hats, because Jasper is in kindergarten, and this party is for parents of kindergarten kids. So I'll be . . ."

He had a habit of not completely finishing his sentences. His voice just drifted away, as if he thought it was so obvious how the sentence finished there was no point saying it out loud.

"And why am I hosting it?" asked Alice. It seemed extraordinary. Why would she even think of doing such a thing?

Dominick raised his eyebrows. "Well, because you and your friend Kate Harper are Class Mums."

"Like classy mothers?"

He smiled uncertainly. "The Class Mums arrange social events for all the other mothers, and communicate with the teachers, organize the reading roster, and, ah, that sort of . . ."

Oh Lord. It sounded horrendous. She'd become one of those volunteering, involved type of people. She was probably really proud and smug; she'd always known she had a tendency toward smugness. She could just imagine herself swanning about in her beautiful clothes.

"You do a lot for the school," said Dominick. "We're very lucky to have you. Speaking of which, it's the big day coming up! Wow! I hope you're going to be well enough for it!"

That man on the treadmill at the gym had mentioned a "big day," too. "What do you mean?" asked Alice with a sense of foreboding.

"You're getting us into the Guinness Book of Records."

She smiled, ready to laugh at his next joke.

"No, really. You don't remember at all? You're baking the world's biggest lemon meringue pie on Mother's Day. It's a big event. All the money raised is going to breast cancer research."

Alice remembered her dream about the giant rolling pin. Ah. The rolling pin wasn't a symbol at all. It was just a giant rolling pin. Her dreams were always so disappointingly obvious.

"I'm baking it?" she said in a panic. "This huge lemon meringue pie?"

"No, no. You've got one hundred mums baking it," said Dominick. "It's going to be amazing." He knotted the end of another balloon together. Alice looked up and saw that the ceiling was now covered with blue and silver balloons.

Tonight she was hosting a party and next weekend she was planning to break a world record. Good Lord. What had she become?

She looked back down and saw that Dominick was staring at her.

"I've worked it out," he said. "What's different about you."

He sat down beside her. Much too close. Alice tried to move unobtrusively away from him, but it was too hard on the squishy leather sofa without making a production of it. So she sat passively with her hands in her lap, schoolgirl style; surely he wasn't going to do anything, with his son just a few feet away.

He was so close, she could see tiny black whiskers on his chin and smell him: toothpaste, washing powder. (Nick smelled of coffee, aftershave, last night's garlic.)

Up close, his eyes were the same liquid chocolate as his son's. (Nick's were either hazel or green, depending on the light, the irises were rimmed with gold, and his eyelashes were so fair, they looked white in the sun.)

Dominick leaned in closer. Oh sweet heavens above, the school principal was going to kiss her, and it would be wrong to slap his face because she might have already kissed him before.

No. He pressed his thumb in between her eyebrows. What was he *doing*? Was it some sort of weird middle-aged-people ritual? Was she meant to do it back to him?

"You've lost your frown," he said. "You always have this little frown right here, as if you're concentrating, or worrying about something, even when you're happy. Now it's . . ."

He took his thumb away. Alice exhaled with relief. She said, "I don't know if you're meant to tell a woman she has a permanent frown." It came out sounding flirtatious.

"Either way, you're still gorgeous," he said, and put his hand to the back of her head and kissed her.

It was not unpleasant.

"I *saw* that!"

Jasper stood in front of them, his helicopter dangling by a rotor from one hand. His eyes were wide and delighted.

Alice put her fingers to her mouth. She'd kissed another man. She hadn't just let him kiss her; she'd kissed him back. Out of nothing more than interest really. Politeness. (Maybe the teeniest flicker of attraction.) Guilt blossomed like heartburn across her chest.

Jasper chortled. "I'm going to tell Olivia that my dad kissed her mum!" He danced on the spot, punching his fists in the air, his face screwed up in an ecstasy of pleasure and disgust. "My dad kissed her mum! My dad kissed her mum!"

Goodness. Were Alice's own children like this? Sort of . . . demented?

Dominick touched Alice gently and respectfully on her arm, and stood up. He grabbed Jasper and held him upside down by his ankles. Jasper shrieked with gasps of laughter and dropped his helicopter.

Alice watched them and felt a weird sense of dissociation. Did she really just kiss that man? That shy school principal? That jolly dad?

Maybe it was her head injury that made her do it. Yes, she had a medical reason. She was not herself.

Then she remembered there was no need to feel guilty, because of Nick's affair with that Gina girl. Right. Now they were even.

Jasper noticed that a part of his helicopter had broken off and he yelled and squirmed as though in terrible agony. Dominick said, "What? What is it, mate?" and turned him upright.

Alice's head began to ache again.

When was Elisabeth coming back? She needed Elisabeth.

Elisabeth's Homework for Dr. Hodges

As I was driving back over to Alice's place, I thought about Gina. I often think about her now. She has acquired an aura of mystery. Once upon a time I just found her irritating.

I'm not sure why I disliked her so much from the beginning. Maybe it was just because it was clear that she and Michael and Alice and Nick had formed such a cozy foursome. They used to be in and out of each other's places all the time. No need to knock. Lots of private jokes. Feeding each other's kids. Gina would walk straight over from her house in her swimming costume—no T-shirt, no towel wrapped under her armpits—just entirely unself-conscious, like a child. She had a softish, round, mocha-colored body. Beautiful jiggly breasts that dragged the men's eyes along with them. I think I remember some story about them all getting drunk and swimming naked in the pool one summer's night. So very seventies of them.

She and Alice were all bright and giggly and swilling champagne, and I was a stiff cardboard cutout. My laugh was forced. It seemed to happen so quickly that she knew my sister better than me.

Gina's kids were IVF pregnancies. She asked lots of expertly interested questions. She would sympathetically rub my hand (very touchy-feely type, soft, sweet-smelling kisses on each cheek every time you saw her; I once heard Roger say to her, "Oh, I do like the way you *European* ladies kiss hello!"). Gina said she understood *exactly* what I was going through. And quite probably she did, except that it was all behind her now. I could tell her memories were rose-colored because of the happy ending. You'd think I would have been inspired by her—she was a success story. She'd traveled across the infertility minefield and got safely to the other side. But I found her patronizing. It's easy to think the minefield wasn't that bad once you're safely watching other people get blown up. She couldn't imagine her children not existing. They were too real, filling up her mind. I felt like I couldn't complain to Alice because Gina was probably in her ear, telling her, with the benefit of experience, that it wasn't that bad and I was just whinging and being melodramatic.

One night I called Alice to tell her that we'd lost another baby.

I had terrible nausea with that pregnancy. I gagged every time I cleaned my teeth. I had to run out of a cinema because the smell of the woman's perfume sitting next to me (Opium) combined with her popcorn made me retch. I'd thought for sure it must be a sign that this one was going to be the lucky one. Ha-ha. It meant nothing.

When I rang Alice, she answered the phone laughing.

Gina was in the background, yelling out something about pineapple. They were inventing cocktails for some school function. Of course Alice stopped laughing when I told her the news and put on her sad voice, but she couldn't quite stamp out the leftover laughter. I felt like the boring sister with yet another boring miscarriage, ruining the good times for everybody with her slightly disgusting gynecological bad news. Alice must have signaled to Gina, because her laughter stopped like a switch had been turned off.

I told her not to worry, that we could talk later, and hung up fast. Then I threw the phone across the room and it smashed a beautiful vase that I'd bought in Italy when I was twenty, and I lay on the couch and screamed into a cushion. I still grieve for the vase.

Alice didn't call me the next day. And the day after that was when Madison ran through the French doors. So we were distracted and busy at the hospital worrying about her. My miscarriage got forgotten in between cocktails with Gina and Madison. Alice never even mentioned it. I wondered if she forgot.

I think that's when the coldness started between us.

Yes, I know. Petty and childish, but there you have it.

Chapter 17

Frannie's Letter to Phil

I'm tucked up in bed again, Phil. It's been a long day.

Who should be sitting next to me again in the dining room at dinner tonight? You guessed it. Mr. Mustache.

The man seems to have taken a shine to me. I don't know why because we have absolutely nothing in common and we appear to disagree on everything.

He was talking about his mustache tonight. He said that he'd always wanted a mustache but that his wife had never let him grow one because it would be "too ticklish when she kissed him." (Too much information, as the young people say!) He said that after she died, he'd "cultivated this beautiful specimen."

He asked what I thought of his mustache and I said I thought it was most unattractive.

He roared with laughter.

Then he asked how I'd managed to escape the "shackles of marriage." (Do you mind!)

You will be astonished to hear that I told him about you. Not the whole story. I just said that I was pretty much an old maid when I finally met "Mr. Right." I said that we were engaged to be married, but unfortunately the wedding never took place. It wasn't meant to be.

Mr. Mustache was uncharacteristically quiet. Then he said, "I'm sorry to hear that, Frannie," and touched my hand, and for a moment I couldn't speak.

He had an unexpectedly gentle touch.

Of course, only a few minutes after that, he was regaling the whole table with the most tasteless "dirty joke" you have ever heard.

"Nick!"

Alice sat bolt upright, her heart racing, her breath shallow. She felt about the bed with her hand for Nick, to wake him up and tell him about the nightmare, although the details were already slipping away and starting to seem silly. Something to do with a . . . tree?

A huge tree. Branches black against a stormy sky.

"Nick?"

Normally he woke up immediately when she had a nightmare, his voice gruff with sleep, automatically soothing her. "It's okay, it's just a dream, just a bad dream." Part of her mind would always think, *He's going to make such a great dad.*

She patted at the sheets. He must have gone to get a glass of water. Or had he not come to bed yet?

Nick is not here, Alice. He lives somewhere else. He flew back from Portugal this morning and you weren't there to meet him. Maybe "Gina" picked him up at the airport. Oh, and you kissed that school principal today. Remember? Remember? Can you just please REMEMBER your life, you fool!

She snapped on the bedside lamp, threw back the sheets, and got out of bed. There was no way she was going back to sleep now.

Right.

She ran her palms down her nightie. It was a sleeveless, shimmery oyster-colored silk. It must have cost a fortune. It was just so stupid that she didn't remember buying it. She'd had enough. She wanted to remember everything, right now.

She went into the bathroom and found the bottle of perfume she'd used at the hospital. She sprayed it in big lavish swoops and sniffed deeply. She was going to run and jump straight into that vortex of memory.

The perfume assaulted her nostrils, making her feel a bit sick. She waited for the images of the last ten years to fill her mind, but all she could see were the smiling strange faces from tonight's party, and Dominick's liquid brown eyes, and her mother smiling coyly at Roger, and the disappointed lines around Elisabeth's mouth.

All these recent memories were too fresh and confusing. That was the problem. There was no space for all the old memories.

She sat down on the cold bathroom tiles and hugged her knees in close. All those people tonight, trooping happily into her house, helping themselves to glasses of champagne and tiny canapés from white-aproned caterers (who had turned up at five p.m., taking over the kitchen, blandly efficient), standing around her backyard in little groups, high heels sinking into the grass. "Alice!" they said so familiarly, kissing her on both cheeks. (There was a lot of kissing of both cheeks in 2008.) "How *are* you?" Hairstyles were smoother and flatter than in 1998. It made everyone's heads seem comically smaller.

People talked about petrol prices (how could there be *anything* to say on such a boring topic?), property prices, development applications, and some political scandal. They talked about their children—"Emily," "Harry," "Isabel"—as if Alice knew them intimately. There were hilarious jokes about some school excursion she'd apparently attended where things had gone hilariously wrong. There were serious, lowered voices about some teacher everybody hated. They talked to her about jazz ballet lessons, saxophone lessons, swimming lessons, the school band, the school fête, the tuckshop, the extension class for "gifted and talented" kids. None of it made any sense. The conversations were so detailed—so many names and dates and times and acronyms—the PE-something class, the WE-something teacher. On two occasions different women hissed the unfamiliar word *"Botox"* in Alice's ear as another woman walked by. Alice couldn't be sure if it was a contemptuous insult or an envious compliment.

Dominick hovered unobtrusively close by, explaining to people that she wasn't quite herself after her accident, that she really should be in bed. "Typical Alice to soldier on!" they said. (Was it typical? How strange. Normally she loved the excuse to put herself to bed.) It didn't really seem to matter all that much that she didn't recognize a single person. Nodding and smiling seemed enough to keep the conversations flowing, while Alice kept being distracted by things in her own backyard: Was that a vegetable garden in the corner? There was a swing set creaking gently in the evening breeze—had the Sultana slid down that slippery dip into her arms?

Now Alice traced her fingertips along the grouting of the white bathroom tiles. (She and Nick had done a tiling course together in preparation for this job—number 46 on their Impossible Dream list.) She didn't remember doing it. It was possible she had lost *thousands* of memories.

Was Nick in bed with Gina right now?

Gina's name had come up at the party. It had been awkward. Alice had been talking—or, more accurately, listening—to a woman wearing distractingly large diamond earrings and a man who was obsessively interested in getting another mini-samosa and was watching the caterer's plates with an eagle eye. The topic was homework and how much of a strain it was on the parents.

"It's three a.m. and I'm sticking paddle-pop sticks together to make Erin's early settler's house, and I tell you, something inside me just snaps"—the earring woman clicked her fingers and her diamonds flashed.

"I can imagine," Alice had murmured, although she couldn't. Why hadn't this Erin kid done her own homework? Or why hadn't they done it together? Alice imagined laughing happily with a sweet daughter while they glued together paddle-pop sticks and drank hot chocolate. Also, Alice was *great* at that sort of thing. Her kid's early settler's house would be the best in the class.

"Well, they've got to learn discipline, haven't they? Isn't that the point of homework?" said the man. "Hey! Excuse me! Are they samosas you've got there? Oh, kebabs. Anyway, these days you can just Google anything."

Did he say giggle? Goggle? Alice's head ached.

"You can't Google an early settler's cottage made of paddle-pop sticks into existence! Anyway, I bet *you* don't have to help them with their homework, do you?" The woman had given Alice a womanly "Men!" look, which Alice had tried to return. (She was sure Nick would have helped.) "I'm sure Laura has it all done by the time you get home from work. I remember hearing Gina Boyle say once that she thought homework should be—"

The woman had stopped herself mid-sentence with an exaggerated wince of embarrassment. "Oh, I'm *sorry*, Alice. How insensitive of me."

The man had given Alice a brief, brotherly hug around the shoulders. "It's been so hard for you. Oh, look! Let me get you a samosa."

Alice had been horrified. Did *everyone* know that Nick had cheated on her with Gina? Was it public knowledge in this strange, cliquey circle?

Dominick had appeared from nowhere, gently extricating her. She was starting to rely on him. She even found herself looking for him in the crowd, thinking vaguely to herself, "Where's Dominick?" while at the same time imagining telling Nick the story: "So, this guy acted like my *boyfriend* for the whole night. What do you think of that?"

Elisabeth and Ben had come to the party, too, because Alice had told Elisabeth she would have a panic attack if she didn't come. Ben was even huger and grizzlier than the man Alice had remembered meeting. He looked like a woodchopper who had escaped from a fairytale picture book, and he was particularly conspicuous amongst all the other smooth-faced men with their neat button-down shirts and neat gym-toned shoulders. He seemed fond of Alice. He told her he'd been "thinking a lot about their conversation the other day" and then he said, "Oh, but of course, you probably don't even remember it," and slapped himself lightly on the side of the head. Elisabeth had folded her lips together and looked the other way. "What did we talk about?" Alice had asked. "Not now," Elisabeth had said tersely.

Elisabeth and Ben hadn't circulated much. They talked a lot to Dominick—whom they didn't appear to have met before. It was strange, seeing Elisabeth cradling one drink and sticking to Ben's side. She used to march her way from person to person at parties, as if it were her duty to talk to every single person.

Actually, the funny thing was that she thought she could have managed that party even without Elisabeth or Dominick or even Nick there to help her. Even though it had been surreal and dreamlike, meeting all those strange people who knew her name and intimate details about her health (one woman had tried to drag her into a corner to continue a conversation from a few weeks ago that appeared to be about Alice's *pelvic floor*), she hadn't ever felt that normal feeling of party panic. She seemed to know instinctively how to stand and what to do with her arms and her face. She could feel herself being gracious and vibrant, actually telling people the story of how she'd fallen over at the gym and thought she was ten years younger and pregnant with her first child. The words rolled smoothly. She made eye contact with everyone in the circle. She was *delivering an anecdote.* It appeared she had become very normal and accomplished, now that she was nearly forty.

Maybe it was because she looked so good that she'd felt so confident. She'd chosen a blue dress from her wardrobe with detailed embroidery around the neckline and hem. "Oh, you always have the most *gorgeous* clothes, Alice darling," Kate Harper, the woman from the lift, had said. Kate's rounded vowels had become even rounder the more she drank, so by midnight she sounded like the queen. Alice couldn't stand her.

The party had finished up around one a.m. Dominick had been one of the last to go, kissing her chastely on the cheek and saying he'd call tomorrow. There didn't seem to have been any question about him staying the night, so maybe their relationship hadn't progressed to that point. He was a very nice man, someone she would happily recommend as a single man to a friend, but the thought of taking her clothes off in front of him was laughable.

Then again, maybe he had just been discreet because he knew she had begged Elisabeth and Ben to stay the night. (She hadn't liked the idea of waking up in this strange new world without company.) Maybe they had quite an active sex life.

She shuddered.

Less than twenty-four hours till she saw Nick and the children and everything would finally fall into place.

The bathroom floor was becoming cold. She stood up and surveyed her tired, thin face in the mirror. *Who have you become, Alice Love?*

She walked back into the bedroom and considered trying to go back to sleep but she knew it would be impossible. Hot milk was the answer. Of course it wasn't the answer at all. It never cured her insomnia, but the ritual of it and the feeling that you were doing something that the magazines always recommended for insomnia was soothing and helped pass the time.

The door to the spare bedroom was closed as she crept down the hallway. She had been pleasantly surprised to discover a spare room (previously one of their many junk rooms) all set up with a double bed, chests of drawers and spare towels. "Was I expecting someone to stay?" she'd asked Elisabeth.

"You always keep it like this," Elisabeth had said. "You're very organized, Alice."

That hardness had come back in her voice. Alice didn't know what it meant. She was starting to feel irritated by Elisabeth.

She crept down the carpeted hallway and nearly missed her footing at the top of the stairs, grabbing for the banister. Maybe it would be convenient if she fell and banged her head again. It might bring back all her memories.

She walked down the stairs, clinging to the banister. As she got to the bottom, she saw that there was a light on in the kitchen.

"Hi," she said.

"Oh, hi."

Elisabeth was standing at the microwave.

"Hot milk," she said. "Want some?"

"Yes, please."

"Not that it ever really cures my insomnia."

"No—me neither."

Alice leaned back against the counter and watched Elisabeth pour milk into a second mug. She was wearing a huge man's T-shirt that must belong to Ben. It made Alice feel prissy in her long silk nightie.

"How are you feeling?" asked Elisabeth. "How's your—memory?"

"Nothing new," said Alice. "I still don't remember anything about the children or the divorce. Although I've worked out it's got something to do with Gina."

Elisabeth looked at her with surprise. "What do you mean?"

"It's okay, you don't need to protect me," said Alice. "I've worked out that he had an affair with her."

"*Nick* had an affair with *Gina*?"

"Well, didn't he? Everybody seems to know about it."

"It's news to me." Elisabeth looked genuinely shocked.

Alice said nonchalantly, "He's probably in bed with her now."

The microwave bell dinged but Elisabeth ignored it.

She said, "I really doubt that, Alice."

"Why?"

Elisabeth paused and then looked her in the eye. "Because she's dead," she said.

Chapter 18

Gina was dead?

"Oh," said Alice.

She paused. "I didn't kill her, did I? In a fit of jealous rage? Although I guess I'd be in jail? But maybe I got away with it!"

Elisabeth laughed in a scandalized way. "No, you didn't kill her." She frowned. "Are you saying you *remember* Nick having an affair with Gina?"

"Not exactly," admitted Alice. It had seemed so clear. She brightened. That's why everyone had seemed sympathetic when Gina's name came up—because she was dead! There had been no affair at all! Now she was filled with relief and guilty love for Nick. *Of course you didn't, darling, I never really suspected you, not for a second.*

And if there had been no affair, maybe Gina had been quite nice. So it was sort of terrible that she was dead.

Elisabeth took the mugs of milk out of the microwave and carried

them over to the coffee table, switching on a lamp. The helium balloons that Dominick had blown up were still hovering silently. Two
half-empty glasses of champagne sat on the windowsill, along with a
pile of gnawed sticks from the chicken kebabs.

Alice sat cross-legged on the leather couch, stretching her nightie
over her knees.

"How did Gina die?" she asked.

"It was an accident." Elisabeth put her finger in her milk and
stirred it around, avoiding Alice's eyes. "A car accident, I guess. About
a year ago."

"Was I upset?"

"She was your best friend. I think you were devastated." Elisabeth
took a big mouthful of her milk and put the mug down quickly. "Ow!
Too hot."

Devastated. Such a big, sweeping word. Alice took a sip of her
milk and burned her own tongue. It was so peculiar to think of being
"devastated" by this strange woman's death, yet apparently perfectly
accepting of her divorce. She had no experience with devastation.
Nothing that terrible had ever happened to her. Her dad had died
when she was six, but she mostly just remembered a feeling of confusion. Her mother had told her once that Alice had worn an old jumper
of her dad's for weeks and weeks after he died and refused to take it
off, kicking and screaming when Frannie finally pulled it off over her
head. Alice didn't remember that at all. Instead she remembered how
at the afternoon tea after the funeral she'd got told off by one of her
mum's tennis friends for sticking her fingers in the cheesecake, and
how Elisabeth had been doing it, too, even more than she was, but *she
didn't get into trouble*. Instead of remembering grief and devastation,
she remembered the terrible injustice of the cheesecake.

There had been that night before her wedding when she had found
herself crying in bed over the fact that her dad wasn't alive to walk her

down the aisle. She had been perplexed by the sudden tears and thought that maybe she was just nervous about the next day. She worried that they were fake tears because she thought she should feel that way, when in fact she couldn't even imagine what it would be like to have a father. And at the same time she'd felt pleased, because maybe it meant part of her *did* remember her dad and did still miss him, and then she'd cried harder, remembering how whenever he was shaving in the bathroom, he'd squeeze a whole lot of delicious, creamy foam into her outstretched hands so she could smear it all over her face and wasn't that *cute* and *touching* and she really hoped the hairdresser got her fringe right the next day because when she messed it up, she looked like a wombat—and there you had it, she was a horribly superficial person, actually more worried about her hair than her dead father. She had finally fallen asleep in a lather of emotion, which she didn't know whether to attribute to her father or her hair.

Now, apparently, she had experienced real grown-up grief, for a woman called Gina.

"You were there," said Elisabeth quietly.

"Pardon? I was where?"

"You saw Gina's accident. You were driving along behind her. It must have been terrible for you. I can't even imagine—"

"On the corner of Rawson and King streets?" interrupted Alice.

"Yes. Do you remember?"

"Not really. I think I just remember the feeling of it. It's happened twice now that I've got all panicky, nightmarish feelings when I see that corner."

Would those feelings stop now that she knew what they meant?

She didn't know if she wanted to remember seeing someone killed in front of her.

They drank their milk in silence for a few seconds. Alice reached up for one of the dangling strings of the balloons and pulled upon it. She watched it bob about and remembered again those pink bouquets of balloons floating angrily about in a stormy sky.

"Pink balloons," she said to Elisabeth. "I remember pink balloons and this terrible feeling of grief. Is that something to do with Gina?"

"That was at her funeral," said Elisabeth. "You and Michael—that's her husband—organized for balloons to be released at the graveyard. It was very beautiful. Very sad."

Alice tried to imagine herself talking about balloons with a bereaved man called Michael.

Michael. That was the name on that business card in her wallet. Michael Boyle—the physiotherapist from Melbourne—must be Gina's husband. That's why he'd written about "happier times" on the back of his business card. It was all very simple.

"Did Gina die before Nick and I separated?" asked Alice.

"Yes. I think about six months before. You've had a pretty hard year."

"Sounds like it."

"I'm sorry," said Elisabeth.

"Don't be." Alice looked up guiltily, worried she'd look like she was filled with self-pity. "I don't even remember Gina. Or the divorce."

"Well, you're going to have to see that neurologist," said Elisabeth, but she spoke without conviction, as if she couldn't be bothered pushing the point.

They sat in silence for a while, except for the intermittent gurgling sounds of the fish tank.

"Am I meant to be feeding those fish?" asked Alice.

"I don't know," said Elisabeth. "Actually, I think they're Tom's responsibility. I think nobody else is allowed to have anything to do with them."

Tom. The fair-haired little boy with the snuffly voice on the phone. She felt terrified at the thought of meeting him. He was in charge of fish. He had responsibilities and opinions. All three children would have opinions. They'd have opinions on Alice. They might not even like her that much. Maybe she was too strict. Or maybe she embarrassed them. Wore the wrong clothes when she picked them up from school. Maybe they preferred Nick. Maybe they blamed her for driving Nick away.

She said, "What are they like?"

"The fish?"

"No, the children."

"Oh—well, they're great."

"But tell me about them properly. Describe their personalities."

Elisabeth opened her mouth and shut it again. "I feel stupid telling you about your children. You know them so much better than me."

"But I don't even remember giving birth to them."

"I know. It's just so hard to believe. You look exactly like yourself. I feel like any second you'll get your memory back and then you'll be saying, oh please, don't tell *me* about *my* children."

"For heaven's sakes," said Alice.

"Okay, okay." Elisabeth held up her hands. "I'll have a go. So, Madison, well, Madison is—" She stopped and said, "Mum would do a much better job of this than me. She sees the children all the time. You should ask her."

"But what do you mean? You know my children, don't you? I thought, well, I thought you'd know them better than anyone. You bought me my very first present for the baby. Tiny socks."

Elisabeth had been the first person Alice had called after she and Nick had laid out all those positive pregnancy tests on the coffee table. She'd been so excited. She'd turned up with champagne ("For Nick and me, not you!"), a copy of *What to Expect When You're Expecting*, and the socks.

Elisabeth said, "Did I? I don't remember that." She put down her mug and picked up a framed photo from the table next to her. "I used to see the children all the time when they were little. I adored them. I still do adore them, of course. It's just that you're all so busy. The children have so many activities. They've all got swimming lessons. Olivia has ballet. Tom plays soccer and Madison plays hockey. And the birthday parties! They're always going to someone's birthday party. Their social lives are amazing. I remember when they were little, I always knew exactly the right thing to get them for their birthdays. They'd rip off the paper in a frenzy. Now I have to ring you, and you tell me exactly where to go and what to ask for. Or else you just buy it yourself and I give you the money. And then you make the children send me a thank-you card. *Dear Auntie Libby. Thank you so much for my blah blah.*"

"A thank-you card," repeated Alice.

"Yes. I know, I know, it's teaching them good manners and everything, but I sort of hate those thank-you cards. I always imagine the kids groaning and having to be forced into writing them. It makes me feel like an elderly aunt."

"Oh. Sorry."

"No! I can't believe I complained about thank-you cards. I've become a bitter old hag. Have you noticed?"

"It sounds more like I've become—" Alice didn't know how to describe the person it seemed she'd become. Insufferable?

"Anyway," said Elisabeth dismissively. "Your children. Well, Madison is just Madison." She smiled fondly.

Madison is just Madison. There was a whole world of memories in that sentence. If that world were lost to Alice forever, it would be unbearable.

"Mum always says, 'Where did we get her from?'" said Elisabeth.

"Okay," said Alice. This really wasn't helping much.

"Well, ever since she was a baby, she's always been so intense. She feels everything very deeply. On Christmas Eve she'd become almost feverish with excitement, but then she couldn't stand it when Christmas was over. You'd find her sobbing in a corner because she had to wait a whole year for Christmas to come again. What else? She's accident prone. She ran through those French doors last year and had to have forty-two stitches. It was very traumatic. A lot of blood. Apparently, Tom called an ambulance and Olivia fainted. I didn't know it was possible for a five-year-old to faint. But Olivia has a blood phobia. Well, she did. I don't know if she's still got it. Actually, didn't she get all excited about becoming a nurse for a while there? When Mum bought her that nurse's uniform?"

Alice just looked at her.

"I'm sorry," said Elisabeth, flustered. "I can't imagine how weird this must feel—and I keep forgetting."

Alice said, "Tell me more about the Sultana. I mean, Madison."

"Madison likes to cook," said Elisabeth. "Well, I assume she still does. I believe she's been a bit moody lately. She used to make her own recipes. They were good, too. Except the kitchen always looked like a bomb had exploded and she wasn't so good at the cleaning-up part. Also she was a bit of a prima donna about her cooking. If the recipe didn't turn out exactly the way she wanted, she'd cry. I once saw her throw this triple-layer chocolate cake she'd spent hours decorating in the bin. You went *ballistic*."

"I did?" Alice tried to readjust yet again to this new picture of herself. She never got angry. She was more of a sulker.

"Well, apparently you'd gone on some special shopping trip to find exactly the right ingredients for this cake, so I don't really blame you."

"Madison sounds like one of the Flakes," said Alice. It had never occurred to her before that Nick's sisters' genes could infiltrate her child. She had always assumed that if she had a daughter, it would be a miniature version of herself, a fresh new Alice she could improve upon, maybe with Nick's eyes thrown in for interest.

"No, she's not like the Flakes," said Elisabeth definitely. "She's just Madison."

Alice pressed her palms to her stomach and thought about how fiercely she and Nick had loved the Sultana. It had been such clean, simple, almost narcissistic love. Now the Sultana ran through glass doors and threw cakes in the bin and made Alice "ballistic." It was all so much more complex and chaotic than she'd ever imagined.

"And Tom? What's he like?"

"He's smart," said Elisabeth. "And surprisingly witty at times. He's a suspicious kid. You can't put anything over him. He goes and checks it up on the Internet. He gets obsessed with things and learns everything there is to know about them. It was dinosaurs for a while. And then roller coasters. I don't know what he's into at the moment. He does really well at school. He gets awards, and he's class captain. That sort of thing."

"That's good," said Alice.

"It was probably a relief after Madison."

"What do you mean?"

"Oh. Well, it's just that Madison has always had problems at school. 'Behavioral problems' you call them."

"Right."

"But I think you've got it all under control. I haven't heard of any dramas for a while."

Dramas. Alice had a life with "dramas."

"And then there's Olivia," said Elisabeth. "She's just one of those children everyone adores. When we took her out when she was a baby, people used to stop you in the street to compliment you. Even serious middle-aged businessmen rushing along to meetings would smile when they saw Olivia sitting in the stroller. It was like being with a celebrity, heads turning everywhere. And she's still so cute. We keep waiting for her to turn into a monster, but she doesn't. She's very loving—maybe too loving. I remember her squatting down in the kitchen saying, 'Hello, little fella,' and we all looked down and saw she was trying to pat a cockroach. Mum nearly dropped dead on the spot."

Elisabeth stopped talking and yawned enormously.

"You'd probably describe them differently," she said, and her tone was defensive. "You're their mother."

Alice was thinking about the first time she'd set eyes on Nick. She was wearing a striped apron, sitting on a high stool at a long counter, ready to learn Thai cooking. Her friend Sophie was meant to be there but she'd twisted her ankle and missed the first class. Nick came in late with a girl who Alice assumed was his girlfriend but later turned out to be the flakiest of his sisters, Ella. When they walked in, they were both laughing, and Alice, who was newly, sadly single, was immensely irritated. Typical. Here comes another happy, laughing, loving couple. Alice remembered how her eyes had met Nick's as he looked about the class for free spots (while Ella gazed reverently and weirdly at the ceiling, entranced for some reason by the ceiling fan). Nick had raised his bushy eyebrows questioningly and Alice had smiled politely, thinking yes, yes, fine, come and sit here, lovebirds, and let's make boring conversation.

There had been another free spot at the front of the class. If her eyes hadn't met his, if she'd looked down at the fish cakes recipe in front of her, or if Sophie had walked two centimeters to the left and therefore missed twisting her ankle in that pothole, or if they had decided to do the wine tasting course instead, which they very nearly did, then those three children would never have been born. Madison Love. Thomas Love. Olivia Love. Three little individuals who already had their own personalities and quirks and stories.

The moment Nick raised his hairy eyebrows in her direction, they all got their stamps of approval. Yes, yes, yes, you will exist.

Alice was filled with elation. It was amazing. Of course, a billion babies were born every second or something, so it wasn't that amazing, but still. Why weren't they just overcome with joy every time they *looked* at those kids? Why in the world were they divorcing?

She said, "So, Nick and I are fighting over custody of the children?" Such a grown-up, alien concept.

"Nick wants them with him half the time. We don't know how Nick thinks he can do it, when he works such long hours. You've always been their 'primary caregiver,' as they say. But it's all got—well, it's all turned so nasty. I guess it's just the nature of divorce."

"But does Nick think—" Alice was overwhelmed with hurt. "Does he think I'm not a good mother?" *And was she a good mother?*

Elisabeth lifted her chin and her eyes flashed like the old Elisabeth. "Well, if he thinks that, he's wrong, and we'll have a million witnesses ready to stand up in court and say otherwise. You're a *great* mother. Don't worry. He's not going to win. He hasn't got a chance. I don't know what he's trying to prove. It's just a power game for him, I think."

It was confusing because although it gave Alice pleasure to see Elisabeth angry on her behalf, at the same time she felt automatic loyalty for Nick. Elisabeth had always adored Nick. If Alice and Nick ever had an argument, Elisabeth took Nick's side. He was a "catch," she said.

Elisabeth was getting herself worked up. "I mean, it's just so *stupid*. He doesn't know the first thing about looking after them. He doesn't cook. I doubt he's ever used the washing machine. He's always traveling, anyway. He's just so—"

Alice held up her hand to make her stop. She said, "I expect it's just that he can't stand the idea of being a part-time dad like his own father. He used to hate it when Roger came to take him and his sisters out. He said Roger always tried too hard, you can just imagine, and it was awkward and strange, and the girls squabbled and took advantage of his credit card. Whenever we go out to a restaurant and Nick sees a man alone with his children, he always says, 'Divorced dad,' and shudders. I mean—that's what he did. Ten years ago."

She tried to get control of her voice. "He wanted to be there every night for his children, and hear about what they did at school, and make breakfast with them on the weekend. He talked about that a lot. It was like he was going to make up for his own childhood, and I loved it when he talked like that because it was making up for *our* childhood, too, and not having our dad around. He had such lovely, romantic ideas about how we'd be a family. Well, we both did. I can't believe—I can't *believe*—"

She couldn't talk anymore. Elisabeth came over and sat on the couch beside her. She hugged her awkwardly. "Maybe," she said tentatively. "Maybe this memory loss is sort of a good thing because it will help you see things more objectively without your mind being cluttered with everything that's happened over the last ten years. And once you get your memory back, you'll still have a different perspective and you and Nick will be able to work things out without all the fighting."

"What if it never comes back?"

"Oh, of course it will come back. You're already remembering bits and pieces," said Elisabeth.

"Maybe my old self has been sent from the past to stop the divorce," said Alice only half flippantly. "Maybe I won't get my memory back until I've done that."

"Possibly!" said Elisabeth too brightly. Then she paused and said, "Dominick seemed nice. Really nice."

Alice thought of how she'd let Dominick kiss her on this very couch and felt suffused with guilt. She said, "He is perfectly nice. He's just not Nick."

"No. He's *very* different from Nick."

Now, what exactly did that mean? Should she be offended on Nick's behalf? Anyway, she wasn't going to have a conversation comparing their pros and cons, as if they were competing boyfriends. Nick was her husband. She changed the subject instead. She said, "Well, speaking of men, I liked Ben."

"It's funny to hear you talk about him as if you've only just met him."

"What did Ben mean when he said he'd been thinking about our discussion the other day?" Alice knew there was something controversial about this topic; it was time to get to the bottom of whatever this thing was between her and Elisabeth.

"Ummm." Elisabeth yawned and stretched. "Do you want a glass of water?"

"No thanks."

"I'm really thirsty." She stood up and went into the kitchen. Alice watched her go and wondered if she was pretending not to have heard her.

She came back with the glass of water and sat back down on the single couch in front of Alice.

"It's late," she said.

"Libby."

Elisabeth sighed. "On Thursday—the day before your accident— Ben came over to help you with some problem you were having with your car. Except apparently there wasn't really a problem at all. It was a little setup."

Good grief. What had she done? Alice sat up straight. She could feel her face flushing. Surely she hadn't made a move on her sister's husband? (For one thing, the man was freakishly large.) Had breaking up with Nick sent her over the edge?

"You gave him banana muffins straight out of the oven. He loves your banana muffins."

Oh my Lord.

"With lots of butter. I never let him have butter. He's got high cholesterol, you know. I mean, you're the health-conscious one."

She'd *seduced her brother-in-law with butter.* Alice's heart pounded.

"And then you gave him your little speech."

"Little speech?" said Alice faintly.

"Yes, your little speech about why we should stop IVF and adopt. You had brochures. Application forms. Website addresses. You'd done all this research."

Alice couldn't get her head around it for a few seconds. Her mind had been filled with horrific images of herself going upstairs to "freshen up" and appearing in red lingerie.

"Adoption," she repeated confusedly.

"Yes. You think we should pop over to a Third World country like Angelina and Brad and help ourselves to a cute orphan."

"That was very presumptuous of me," said Alice sternly, weak with relief that she hadn't tried to seduce Ben. "Meddlesome. Nosy!"

Then again, she thought, wasn't adoption actually a pretty good idea?

"Well," said Elisabeth. "I was angry. When Ben came home and told me, I rang you and we got into a big argument about it. You think it's time we 'faced reality.'"

"Did I really say that?"

"Yes."

"I'm sorry."

"I guess you meant well. It's just that you made me feel as if you thought I was stupid. As if you would never have let things get so far. As if you would never be so *messy* as to keep having miscarriage after miscarriage. As if, I don't know, as if I've been overly emotional about the whole thing."

"I'm sorry," said Alice again. "I'm really sorry."

"You don't even remember it," said Elisabeth. "Once you remember it, you'll feel differently. Anyway, I said some pretty nasty things to you."

"Like what?"

"I'm not saying them again! I didn't even mean them. This lets me off the hook."

They were silent for a few seconds. Alice said, "Are Angelina and Brad friends of yours?"

Elisabeth snorted. "Brad Pitt and Angelina Jolie. You've forgotten all your celebrity gossip, too."

"I thought Brad Pitt was engaged to Gwyneth Paltrow."

"Ancient history. He's married and divorced Jennifer Aniston since then, and Gwyneth has had a baby called Apple. I'm not kidding. Apple."

"Oh." Alice felt unaccountably sad for Brad and Gwyneth. "They seemed happy in the photos."

"Everyone looks happy in photos."

"What about Bill and Hillary Clinton?" asked Alice. "Did they stay together?"

"You mean after the Lewinsky thing?" said Elisabeth. "Yes, they did. I don't think anyone even thinks about that much anymore."

Alice looked at Elisabeth. "So," she said with wild abandon, "I take it you don't want to adopt a baby?"

Elisabeth smiled a sick sort of a smile. "I would have considered it years ago, but Ben couldn't stand the idea. He's always been ideologically opposed to adoption because he's adopted himself, and his mother is—difficult. He didn't have a great childhood. My charming mother-in-law told him that his real mother couldn't afford to keep him, so Ben saved up his money. He thought once he had a hundred dollars, he could write to his real mum to tell her he could be self-supporting now, so could she please take him back. On his birthday he always ran to the letterbox, thinking that maybe this year, out of the blue, his real mum might decide to send him a card.

"He thought his baby photos were ugly—he was a funny-looking baby—and he wondered if maybe his real mother hadn't liked the look of him when he was born. He always felt that his parents wished they had chosen a smaller, smarter son. He'd spent his whole childhood keeping his room tidy, not saying much, feeling like a big clumsy visitor in his own home. It breaks my heart to think of it. When you were saying earlier that Nick wanted to be a good father to make up for his own father leaving, well, Ben was similar. He wanted his own biological child. He wanted to have someone who looked like him, who had the same eyes or whatever. And I was so looking forward to giving him that. I so badly wanted to give him that."

"Of course you did."

"So I was always very respectful of Ben's views on adoption."

"Yes. I can imagine."

Elisabeth gave a wry half-smile.

"What?"

"On Thursday you told Ben that he needed to get over it."

"Get over what?"

"Get over his problem with adoption. You said that plenty of people didn't get on with their biological parents and that it was a lottery, but that any kid who got Ben and me as parents would hit the jackpot. Thank you, by the way. That was a nice thing to say."

"That's okay." At least she'd said one thing right. "But Ben must not have appreciated me saying that."

"Well, that's the thing. Yesterday when I came home from lunch he said he'd been thinking about what you said, and he thinks you're right. We should adopt. He's all excited. He'd done all this research on the Internet. Apparently all I needed to say to him five years ago was 'Get over it.' Silly old me. All that unnecessary tiptoeing around his traumatic childhood."

Alice tried to imagine herself telling that big grizzly man to "get over it" while she fed him banana muffins. (Banana muffins. She wondered what recipe she used. Also, she must own a muffin tray.) She had never had opinions about how Elisabeth should run her life, although Elisabeth had plenty of opinions about how Alice should run hers. That was fine because she was the big sister. It was her job to be the sensible, bossy one who did her tax returns on time, got her car serviced regularly, and had a career, while Alice could be whimsical and hopeless and make fun of Elisabeth for her motivational posters of mountains and sunsets. Actually, now she thought about it, it had been *Elisabeth* who had bullied her into doing that Thai cooking course with Sophie, instead of wasting her life moping over that sneering IT consultant.

Now Alice was the one doing the bullying.

"So if Ben is considering adoption now, isn't that maybe a good thing?" she said hopefully.

"No, it's not." Elisabeth's voice became flinty. She sat up straight. Here we go, thought Alice. "It's not at all. You don't know what you're talking about, Alice."

"But—"

"It's too late now. You don't seem to realize how long adoption takes. What you have to go through. You don't just order a kid online. We're not Brad and Angelina. We've got to jump through hoops and pay thousands of dollars, which we don't have. It takes years and years, and it's stressful and things go wrong, and I don't have the energy for it. I've had enough. We'd be nearly fifty by the time we got a child. I'm too tired to start dealing with bureaucrats and trying to convince them why I'd make a good mother and how much money we earn and blah, blah, blah. I don't know why you're suddenly taking this interest in my life, but you're too late."

"I'm *suddenly* taking an interest?" Alice was wounded, desperate to defend herself, except she had no facts at her disposal. She didn't believe it. She would never have not been interested in Elisabeth's life. "Are you saying I haven't been interested before?"

Elisabeth breathed out noisily, deflating like a balloon, and sank back in her chair.

"Of course you have."

"Well, why did you say it?"

"I don't know. Sometimes I've felt it. Look, I withdraw the comment."

"We're not in court."

"I didn't even mean it. Anyway, you could probably say the same thing about me. I don't see the children as much as I did. I should have done more for you after Gina, and after Nick. But you're always so . . . I don't know. Busy. Self-sufficient." She yawned. "Just forget it."

Alice looked down at her strange wrinkled hands. "What's gone wrong between us?" she asked quietly.

There was no answer. Alice looked up and saw that Elisabeth had closed her eyes and put her head back against the couch. She looked exhausted and sad.

Finally she spoke without opening her eyes. "We really should go to bed."

Chapter 19

It was five-thirty p.m., Sunday afternoon. In half an hour Nick would be home with the children.

Alice had a sick, excited feeling in her stomach as if she were going on a first date.

She'd been wearing a pretty floral dress and makeup, her hair all fluffy and motherly, when she decided that she was trying too hard. Presumably she didn't normally dress up like a 1950s mother at a fancy-dress party. So she'd run back upstairs and scrubbed off the makeup, and pulled the dress over her head in mad panic. She'd found jeans and a white T-shirt, and flattened her hair. No jewelry except for Nick's bracelet and her wedding ring, which she'd found at the back of a drawer, together with Granny Love's engagement ring. It had been yet another fresh shock to find these symbols of her marriage carelessly tossed in with her underwear. She remembered when Nick had placed the wedding ring on her finger for the first time. Most grooms were clumsy at this point, grinning goofily, soft chuckles from the guests, but Nick had smoothly, tenderly slid it onto her finger in one go, his eyes locked on hers; she'd been proud. He was so dexterous.

With this ring I thee wed...

...until I thee divorce.

She wondered why she hadn't given the awful engagement ring back. Wasn't the ring normally torn from the finger and thrown at the man's face in a fit of rage at some point during a divorce?

She looked at herself in the bedroom mirror. This was much better, casual, unaffected—although her face looked pale and very old; she resisted an intense longing to go through that amazing dab, dab, slap, slap routine again that transformed her face. Surely she didn't normally wear makeup on a Sunday night at home.

Earlier in the day, after Elisabeth and Ben had gone home, it had suddenly occurred to Alice that it was presumably her responsibility to feed those three children. She had called her mother and asked her what she should cook for dinner, saying she wanted to cook their favorite thing. Barb had spent a full twenty minutes discussing each child's dietary idiosyncrasies throughout their lives. "Remember when Madison went through that vegetarian stage? And of course it would have to be at the same time that Tom was just refusing to eat *any* vegetable. Then Olivia couldn't decide whether she should only eat vegetables, like Madison, or refuse to eat vegetables, like Tom! Oh, you were tearing your hair out every tea time!" At last, after much changing of her mind, she'd finally settled on homemade hamburgers. "I think you found a healthy recipe in your Heart Foundation recipe book. You were saying just the other week that you were sick to death of it but the children can't get enough of it. I'm sure you remember *that*, don't you, darling? Because it was only last *week*."

Alice had found the recipe book and it had opened straight at the right food-splattered page. All the ingredients were in her amazingly well-stocked freezer and pantry. It seemed like there was enough there to feed hundreds of children. As she made the mince for the hamburgers, she realized she wasn't looking at the recipe book anymore. She seemed to know that now she grated in two carrots, one zucchini, now she added two eggs. Once it was ready, she had put the mince back in the fridge, defrosted rolls ready to be toasted, and made a green salad. Would the children eat a green salad? Who knew? She and Nick could eat it. He would stay for dinner, wouldn't he? He wouldn't just drop the children off and *leave*? But she had an awful feeling that was exactly what divorced parents did. She'd just have to ask him to please stay. Beg him, if necessary. She couldn't be left alone with the children. It wasn't safe. She didn't know the procedures. For example, did they bath themselves? Did she read them stories? Sing them songs? When was bedtime? And how was it enforced?

She went back downstairs in her jeans and looked around her gleaming, beautiful house. Two cleaners had turned up at the door at midday, laden with mops and buckets, asking how the party had gone as they plugged in vacuum cleaners. They'd scrubbed and polished while Alice had wandered vaguely about, feeling embarrassed and not sure what she was meant to be doing. Should she help? Get out of the way? Supervise? Hide the valuables? She had her purse ready to give them however much they asked for, but there had been no request for money. They told her they'd see her on Thursday at the usual time and disappeared, waving cheerily. She'd closed the door behind them, breathed in the smell of furniture polish, and thought, "I am a woman with a swimming pool, air-conditioning, and *cleaners*."

Now she looked about the kitchen and her eyes fell on a rack of wine. She should have a bottle open and breathing for Nick. She selected a bottle, went to get a corkscrew, and realized that the bottle didn't have a cork. Instead she unscrewed a normal bottle top. How funny. The smell of the wine hit her nostrils and she found she was pouring herself a glass. She buried her nose in it. Part of her mind thought, "What are you doing, you tosser?" Another part thought, "Mmmm. *Blackberries.*"

The wine slid smoothly down her throat and she wondered if she'd turned into an alcoholic. It wasn't even six o'clock. She'd never been much of a wine drinker. Yet drinking this wine felt right and familiar, even as it felt strange and wrong. Maybe that's why Nick had left her and wanted custody of the children. She'd become a drunk. Nobody knew, except for Nick and her children. It was a terrible secret. Well, but couldn't she just get help? Join AA and follow those twelve steps? Never touch a drop again? She took another sip and tapped her fingers on the countertop. Soon she would see him and then the mystery of all this would finally be solved. It wasn't logical, but she had a strong feeling that the moment she saw Nick's face her entire memory would land back in her head, fully intact.

Dominick had turned up again this afternoon. He had takeaway hot chocolates in a tray and tiny polenta cakes (she had a feeling they were her favorites and acted accordingly grateful). She'd been surprised by the pleasure she'd felt when she saw him standing at the door. Maybe it was because of his somewhat nervy demeanor. It made her feel like she was adored. Nick adored her, but she adored him back, so it was equal. Talking to Dominick made her feel as if every word she said was somehow amazing.

"How is your, ah, memory today?" he'd asked her politely, while they drank their hot chocolates and ate the cakes on the back veranda.

"Oh, maybe a bit better," she'd said. People liked to think you were making progress when it came to health matters.

Apparently Jasper was with "his mother." She realized that Dominick must be a divorced dad. How strange it all was. Wouldn't it be a lot less messy if everyone just stayed with the people they married in the first place?

That meant divorce was a shared interest. She'd had a moment of inspiration and said to him, "Have we ever talked about Nick—about why we separated?"

He gave her an odd sideways look. "Yes."

Aha!

"Would you mind giving me a quick summary of what I told you?" She said this lightly, trying not to show how desperately she needed to know the answer.

"You don't remember anything about why you and Nick split up?" he'd said slowly.

"No! I couldn't believe it! It was a total shock to me."

The words spilled out of her mouth before she realized that they might be upsetting to someone who was hoping to start a relationship with her.

He'd scratched hard at his nose. "Well. Obviously I don't know every detail, but, ah, it seemed that he—Nick—was pretty much involved with his job. He was away a lot and he worked long hours, and so I guess, I think you said, you just drifted apart. That's the way it happened. And, ummm, I guess, maybe some sexual issues. You mentioned . . ." He coughed loudly and stopped talking.

Sex? She'd talked to this man about sex? It was an unforgivable betrayal of Nick. And besides which, what *issues* could there have been relating to sex? They had a glorious, funny, tender, highly satisfying sex life.

It was so embarrassing to hear the word "sex" coming out of Dominick's mouth. He was too nice. Too grown-up and proper. Even now, when Alice was alone thinking about it, she felt her face become warm.

Dominick had seemed embarrassed, too. He'd cleared his throat so many times, Alice had offered him a glass of water, and then he'd left soon after, telling her to take care of herself. At the front door he'd suddenly wrapped his arms around her in a quick, warm hug. He'd said in her ear, "I care a lot about you," and then he was gone.

So that hadn't helped much at all. "Drifting apart because of Nick's long hours." That was such a cliché. The sort of thing that broke up other marriages. If Nick had to work long hours, they would have just made up for it in the hours they did have.

She looked at her wineglass and saw that the level had gone down considerably. What if her lips and teeth were stained purple and she opened the door to Nick and the children looking like a vampire? She rushed to the mirror in the hallway and checked her reflection. Her lips were fine. Her eyes just looked a bit wild and crazed, and she still looked extremely old.

As she walked back into the kitchen, she stopped by the Green Room, except it wasn't green anymore. It was a small room off the hallway that had originally been painted a bright lime green. Now the walls were painted a tasteful mushroom. Alice leaned against the doorway and found that she missed the green. It had made people laugh and shield their eyes whenever they saw it. Of course, it had to go—but still. The house was literally perfect now. Instead of being thrilling, that suddenly seemed depressing.

The Green Room had been turned into a study, which had always been their plan. There was a computer on a desk and bookshelves lined the walls. She walked in and sat down at the computer. Immediately, without thinking, she leaned down and pushed a round silver button on a black box sitting on the floor. The computer whirred to life and she pressed another button on the monitor. The screen turned blue. White letters ordered her "To begin, click your user name." There were four icons: Alice, Madison, Tom, and Olivia. (Did that mean the children used this computer? Weren't they too little?) She clicked on her own name and a colorful photo filled the whole screen. It was the three children. They were all rugged up in parkas and scarves, sharing a toboggan that was flying down a snowy incline. Madison was at the back, Tom was in the middle, and the little one, Olivia, was at the front. Madison had hold of the control rope. Their mouths were open as if laughing or shrieking, and their eyes were wide with fear and exhilaration.

Alice put a hand to the base of her throat. They were extraordinarily beautiful. She wanted the memory of that day back so bad. She stared at the photo and for a second she thought she heard the faint sounds of children shouting, the feeling of an icy-cold nose and fingertips . . . and as soon as she tried too hard to grab hold of it, it slipped deftly away.

Instead, she clicked on an icon that said E-mail. It asked for a password.

Naturally, she didn't know it, but as she held her hands over the keyboard, her fingers went ahead and inexplicably typed out the word OREGANO.

What in the world? But it seemed her body remembered more than her mind because the screen was obediently vanishing, to be replaced by a dancing image of an envelope and a message saying, "You have 7 new messages."

What inspired her to choose an *herb* for her password?

There was an e-mail from Jane Turner with the subject heading: "How's the head?"; another one from a Dominick Gordon (Who? Oh, of course. Him. Her *boyfriend*) with the subject heading: "Next weekend?" and five from names she didn't recognize, all with the heading: "Mega Meringue Mother's Day."

Mega Meringue Mother's Day. It made her want to snort with derision. It seemed like something Elisabeth—the old energetic Elisabeth—might have arranged. Not her.

There was also an e-mail from Nick Love, with no subject heading, dated Friday, the day of her accident. She clicked on it and read:

Well a lot of traditions are going to have to change now, aren't they? What a load of crap. XMAS Day WILL be different whatever we do. You can't reasonably expect to have them for the morning AND the night, so I only get them for five fucking minutes in the middle of the day. It makes perfect sense for them to stay at Ella's on XMAS eve. They love being with their cousins. Can't YOU think of THEM for a change? This is all about YOU. As usual.

PS. Please make sure they pack their swimming costumes for the weekend. I'm taking them to the Aquatic Center on Sunday when I get back from Portugal.

PPS. I had two sisters on the phone in tears last night about Granny Love's ring. Can you please be reasonable about this? It's not like you ever wore it that often. If you're thinking of selling it, you've really sunk to a new low. Even for you.

"Even for you." Alice struggled to catch her breath. It was like being winded. The coldness. The viciousness. The dislike.

It was impossible to believe that this was written by the same man who got tears in his eyes when she said she would marry him; who would crash-tackle her onto the bed and lift her hair and kiss the back of her neck; who told her when it was safe to look back at the television because the blood and guts had gone now; who sang all the words to "Living Next Door to Alice" to her in the shower.

And why was she refusing to give back Granny Love's dreadful ring? It was a family heirloom. Of course the Love family should get it back.

She scrolled down and saw that Nick's message was part of a whole conversation that had been going on for days.

There was one from herself dated just three days ago.

The children should wake up in their own beds on
Christmas Day this year. I'm not moving on this matter.
Obviously, I want to keep all the same traditions for
them—putting out their Santa Sacks at the end of their
beds, etc. They've had to go through enough disruption as
it is. This is just another power game for you. All you care
about is winning. I couldn't care less what points you win
over me—just don't win at the expense of the children.
By the way, I have asked you at least twice before now not
to give the children, especially Olivia, so much junk food
over the weekend. I'm sure it makes you feel like a
wonderful father to say yes to whatever they want, but
they're tired and irritable every Monday after a weekend
with you—and I'm the one who has to deal with it.

It was May! Why were they even talking about what would happen
on Christmas Day?

Some impostor had been living her life. She was stunned by her
sanctimonious, contemptuous tone.

She scrolled down further and bitter words and phrases jumped out
at her.

May I remind you . . .

You are so small-minded . . .

You are so sanctimonious . . .

You must be out of your mind if you think . . .

What is WRONG with you?

Can we just try and be rational about this?

You're the one who . . .

There was a scrunch of gravel and a flicker of headlights. A car pulled up in the driveway. Alice stood up, her heart beating like a jackhammer. She pushed a hand back through her hair as she walked down the hallway toward the front door. She was such an idiot for not doing her makeup again. She was about to see a man who hated her.

Car doors were slamming. A child was whining, "But Dad, that's not fair!"

Alice opened the front door. Her legs were shaking so badly, she thought she might collapse. Maybe that would be a good thing.

"*Mummy!*" A little girl came hurtling up the stairs and threw her arms around Alice, her head colliding hard with her stomach. She talked straight into Alice's T-shirt, her voice muffled. "Is your sore head better? Did you get my card? What was it like sleeping in the hospital?"

Alice hugged her back and couldn't speak.

I don't even remember being pregnant with you.

"Olivia?" she croaked and put her hand on top of the little girl's tangled white-blond curls. There was sand in her hair and a crooked line revealing a pink scalp. Her hair was soft and her skull was hard, and when she looked up, she was impossibly beautiful: smooth skin with a cinnamon dusting of freckles and enormous dark-lashed blue eyes.

They were her own eyes staring back at her, but much bigger and definitely much more beautiful. Alice felt dizzy.

"Oh, Mum," crooned Olivia. "Are you actually still feeling a bit sick? Poor darling Mum. *I know!* I'll listen to your heart and be your nurse! Yes!"

She was gone, slamming the screen door behind her, pounding down the hallway.

Alice looked up and saw Nick leaning over to pull out stuff from the boot of a swish silver car.

He straightened. Both his arms were filled with backpacks and soggy beach towels.

"Hi," he said.

His hair seemed to have disappeared. As he walked toward her, she saw that it was completely gray and cropped close to his head. His face had got thinner but his body was somehow thicker: his shoulders chunkier, his stomach paunchier. There were spiderwebs of lines around his eyes. He was wearing a green T-shirt and shorts she'd never seen before. Well, of course, but it was still unsettling.

He walked up the stairs toward her and stood in front of her. She looked up at him. He was different and strange but he was still essentially Nick. Alice forgot everything that she'd just read on the computer and the way he'd talked to her on the phone the other day and was filled with the pure simple pleasure of Nick coming home after a long trip away. She smiled joyously at him. "Hi yourself."

She went to step forward toward him and Nick stepped back. It seemed involuntary, as if she were an unpleasant insect. His eyes were blank, and they seemed to be fixed on her forehead.

"How are you?" he said. His tone was the frosty one he used when he was being mucked around by incompetent tradespeople.

"Mum! You should have seen the wave I caught today! It was, like, twenty feet tall. It was, like, as high as the roof there. Look. No, look, Mum, at the roof there. Yeah, there. That's how high it was. Or maybe a few centimeters less. Anyway, Dad took the best photo! Show Mum the photo on your camera, Dad. Can you show her the photo?"

So this was Tom. He was wearing long board shorts and a cap that he pulled off so he could rub the top of his head hard. His hair was the same color as Olivia's—so blond it was almost white. Nick had that color hair when he was a child. Tom's limbs were skinny and tanned and strong. He was like a miniature surfie teenager. Good Lord. He had Roger's nose. It was definitely Roger's nose. It made her want to laugh. Roger's nose in this vibrant little boy's face. She wanted to hug him, but she wasn't sure if that was appropriate.

Instead, she said, "Yeah, let me see the photo, Nick."

Nick and Tom stared at her. Her tone must have been wrong. Too flippant?

Tom said, "You sound a bit funny, Mum. Did you get stitches at the hospital for your head? I asked Auntie Libby if it was a brain tumor and she said it definitely was *not*. I did a lie-detector test on her."

"It definitely was not a brain tumor," said Alice. "I just fell over."

"I'm starved to death," sighed Tom.

"I'm making hamburgers for dinner."

"No, I mean, I'm starved right now."

"Oh."

A girl walked up onto the veranda. She dropped a wet towel on the veranda, put her hands on her hips, and said, "Did you say you're making *hamburgers* for dinner?"

"Yes," said Alice.

Madison. The Sultana. The two blue lines on all those pregnancy tests. The flashing heartbeat on the screen. The mysterious invisible presence listening to Nick's voice through the toilet roll.

Madison had very fair, almost translucent skin. There was a patch of angry red sunburn on her neck with white fingerprints as if someone had given up on putting on the sunscreen too soon. She had lank, dark brown hair that was falling in her eyes and beautiful strong white teeth. Her eyes were the same shape as Nick's but a darker, unusual color, and her eyebrows were someone's—Elisabeth's as a child! They were subtly raised at the corners, like Mr. Spock. She wasn't adorable like Olivia and Tom. Her body was chunky. Her lower lip jutted out sulkily. But one day, thought Alice, one day I think you might be striking, my darling Sultana.

"You *promised*," the Sultana said to Alice. Her eyes were murderous. She was formidable. She filled Alice with awe.

"I promised what?"

"That you would buy the ingredients so I could make lasagna tonight. I *knew* you wouldn't do it. Why do you pretend you're going to do something when you know that you're *not*." She punctuated the last sentence with rhythmic stamps of her foot.

Nick said, "Don't be so rude, Madison. Your mother had an accident. She had to spend the night at the hospital."

Alice wanted to laugh at Nick's stern dad voice. Madison lifted her chin. Her eyes blazed. She stormed into the house, slamming the screen door behind her.

"Don't slam the door!" called out Nick. "And come back and pick up your towel."

Silence. She didn't return.

Nick sucked in his lower lip and his nostrils flared. Alice had never seen him pull a face like that. He said, "Go inside, Tom. I want to speak to your mother. Will you take Madison's towel inside, too?"

Tom was standing at the front wall of the house, tracing the brickwork with his fingertips. He said, "Dad, how many bricks do you reckon there are in this whole house?"

"Tom."

Tom sighed theatrically, picked up Madison's towel, and went inside.

Alice took a deep breath. She couldn't imagine living with those three children twenty-four hours a day. She'd never imagined them actually talking. They fizzed and crackled with energy. Their personalities were right there on the surface without that protective sheen of adulthood.

"The Sultana," began Alice, but words eluded her. Madison could not be put into words.

"I beg your pardon?" said Nick.

"The Sultana. I could never have imagined her growing up to be like that. She's so . . . I don't know."

"Sultana?" He didn't know what she was talking about.

"You remember—when I was pregnant with Madison, we used to call her the Sultana."

He frowned. "I don't remember that. Anyway, I wanted to see if we could work out this thing with Christmas Day."

"Oh, that." She thought of all those nasty e-mails and got a bad taste in her mouth. "Why are we even talking about Christmas now? It's *May*!"

He stared at her as if she were crazy.

"I beg your pardon? You're the one obsessed with your precious spreadsheet. You said you wanted everything in black-and-white for the whole year ahead. Every birthday. Every concert. You said that was best for the kids."

"Did I?" Did she even know how to do a spreadsheet?

"Yes!"

"Right. Well. Whatever you want. You can have them on Christmas Day."

"Whatever I want," he repeated suspiciously, almost nervously. "Is there something I'm missing here?"

"Nope. Hey—how was Portugal?"

"It was fine, thank you," he said formally.

She had to clench her fingernails into her hands to stop herself leaning forward and laying her face against his chest. She wanted to say, "Talk in your normal voice."

"I'd better go," he said.

"What?" She nearly grabbed for him in a panic. "No. You can't go. You have to stay for dinner."

"I don't think that would be appropriate."

"Oh yes! Daddy, stay for dinner!" It was Olivia. She had a red cape tied around her shoulders and a toy stethoscope around her neck. She clung to Nick's arm. Alice was jealous she was allowed to touch him so freely.

"I think I'd better go," said Nick.

"Please stay," said Alice. "We're having hamburgers."

"Yes! See, Mummy wants you to stay." Olivia was doing a tap dance of delight back and forth across the veranda. She yelled, "Tom! Guess what? Dad's staying for dinner!"

"Jesus, Alice," said Nick under his breath, and this time he looked her properly in the eyes.

"I opened some really nice wine for us," said Alice, and smiled at him. She didn't need lipstick to get her husband back.

Chapter 20

Nick didn't seem to know what to do with himself when he came inside. He shoved his hands in the pockets of his shorts and wandered around the living room, stopping and looking at things, as if he were in somebody else's home.

"You got the pool under control?" he asked, and jutted his chin toward the backyard.

Alice stood in the kitchen, pouring them both a glass of wine. She had no idea what he was talking about. How do you get a pool under control?

"The pool has been very calm," she said. "Very serene. I think I must have it on a tight leash."

Nick turned back from the windows and looked at her sharply.

"Good," he said.

Alice walked out of the kitchen and handed him a glass of wine. She noticed that he took it from her carefully so that their hands didn't touch. "Thanks," he said. She kept standing in front of him and he backed away again as if she were contagious.

Tom was wandering around the kitchen, opening cupboard doors. He stood in front of the fridge, swinging the door back and forth.

"What can I eat, Mum?" he said.

Alice looked around vaguely for her mother.

"*Mum,*" said Tom.

Alice jumped. She was the mum.

"Well," she said, trying to sound cheery and loving. "What do you feel like? Maybe a sandwich?"

"You can wait till dinner, Tom," said Nick.

Oh, so that had been the correct response.

"Yes," she said. She put on a similar voice to Nick's. "Your father is right." Then she giggled. She couldn't help it. She gave Nick a mischievous look. Didn't he find it funny, too? The two of them being the mum and the dad?

Nick just looked back at her nervously. She saw his eyes dart involuntarily to her glass of wine. Did he think she was drunk?

The little boy slammed the fridge door so hard it rattled, and said, "I think if I don't eat soon, I might get malnourished. Look. My stomach is sticking out like a starving person. See?" He thrust out his stomach.

Alice laughed. Nick said sharply, "Stop being silly. Go and get changed out of those wet clothes." Yes, well, it probably wasn't the best idea to encourage your children to laugh at the plight of the starving.

The littlest child appeared. Olivia. She had smeared her lips with bright-red lipstick. It had got on her teeth. Was that allowed? Alice looked over at Nick for guidance, but he was standing at the back door and looking out at the pool. "The color looks a bit green to me," he said. "When was the last time you had the guy around?"

"Okay, Mummy, I'm ready now to be your nurse. Sit down and I'll take your temperature." Olivia grabbed her by the hand. Charmed by the feel of her small, warm palm, Alice let herself be led over to the sofa.

"Lie down, there's a dear," said Olivia.

Alice lay down and Olivia stuck a toy thermometer in her mouth. She stroked back Alice's hair from her forehead and said, "Now I will listen to your heart, patient." She plugged the stethoscope to her ears and pressed the other end against Alice's chest. She frowned professionally. Alice tried not to laugh. This kid was adorable.

"Okay, patient, your heart is beating," she said.

"Phew," said Alice.

Olivia removed the thermometer and looked at it. Her mouth dropped. "You have a terrible fever, patient! You're burning up!"

"Oh no! What should I do?"

"You should watch me do a cartwheel. That will cure you."

Olivia did a perfect cartwheel. Alice applauded and Olivia bowed. She went to do another one.

"Not in the house, Olivia!" snapped Nick. "You know that!"

Olivia stuck her bottom lip out. "Please, Daddy, please. Just one more."

"Should she be wearing your lipstick like that?" asked Nick.

"Oh, well," said Alice, "I'm not exactly sure."

"Let your mother get dinner started." Nick had the same exhausted, defeated look as Elisabeth had the night before. Everyone was so tired and cranky in 2008.

"Sorry, darling Daddy." Olivia threw her arms around Nick's legs.

"Go and get changed out of your swimming costume," said Nick. Olivia danced off, swirling her red cape around her.

They were alone.

"By the way, I didn't get all of Olivia's homework done," said Nick. He sounded defensive, like he was confessing something.

"You mean you do Olivia's homework for her?" asked Alice.

"Of course not! Jesus. You really do think I'm incompetent, don't you."

Alice sat up. "No I don't."

"She's only got eight questions to go. It's obviously more difficult when you're all together in a small apartment. Also we didn't quite finish Tom's reading. And we spent three hours doing Madison's science experiment today. Tom wanted to do it for her."

"Nick."

He stopped talking, took a mouthful of his wine, and looked at her. "What?"

"Why are we getting a divorce?"

"What sort of question is that?"

"I just want to know."

The longing to stand up and touch him was so strong, she had to press her hands against her thighs to stop herself from leaping up and burying her head under his chin.

"It doesn't matter why we're getting a divorce," said Nick. "I'm not having this conversation. What is the point of it? I'm not interested in playing games tonight, Alice. I'm exhausted. If you're trying to make me say something you can use against me, it's not going to work."

"Oh," said Alice.

Would her capacity for shock ever run out? She realized that ever since Elisabeth had first uttered the word "divorce" at the hospital, she'd been waiting to see Nick so that he could take it away, make it nothing to do with them.

"Maybe I should just go home," said Nick, putting his glass down on the coffee table.

"You told me once that if we were ever having trouble with our relationship, you would move heaven and earth to try and fix it," said Alice. "We were at that new Italian restaurant when you said that. We were peeling the wax off the candlestick. I remember it very, very clearly."

"Alice."

"You said we were going to get old and grumpy together and go on coach tours and play bingo. The garlic bread was cold but we were too hungry to complain."

Nick's lower lip had dropped, so he looked stupid.

"One night, we were standing in Sarah O'Brien's driveway waiting for a taxi and I asked if you thought Sarah looked even more beautiful than usual that night, and you said, 'Alice, I could never love anyone the way I love you,' and I laughed and said, 'That wasn't the question,' but it was the question, because I was feeling insecure, and that's what you said. You said that. It was cold. You were wearing that big woolly jumper that you lost at Katoomba. Don't you remember?"

She could feel her nose starting to block.

Nick was holding his palms up in a panicky fashion, as if there were a fire starting right in front of him but he couldn't see anything handy to extinguish it.

Alice sniffed noisily. "Sorry," she said, and looked at the floor because she couldn't bear to look at his familiar but strange face.

She said, "These tiles are the absolute perfect color. Where did we get them?"

"I don't know," said Nick. "It must have been ten years ago." She looked back up at him. He dropped his hands by his sides and his eyes widened as comprehension swept his face. He said, "Alice, you did get your memory back, didn't you? I just assumed—I mean, you're home from the hospital. You don't still think it's 1998, do you?"

"I know it's 2008. I believe it. It just doesn't feel like it."

"Yes, but you *remember* the last ten years, don't you? That's not why you're asking these bizarre questions, is it?"

Alice said, "Did you have an affair with that woman who lived across the road? The one who died? Gina?"

"An affair? With *Gina*? You are joking."

"Oh. Good."

He said, "You don't remember Gina?"

"No. I remember the balloons at her funeral."

"But Alice . . ." Nick leaned forward urgently. He looked around the room to make sure they were alone and lowered his voice. "You do remember the *kids*, don't you?"

Alice met his eyes and silently shook her head.

"Not at all?"

"The last thing I remember properly is being pregnant with the Sultana. I mean, Madison."

Nick slammed his palms against his knees. (He had all these new grown-up grumpy gestures.) "For God's sake, why aren't you still at the hospital?"

"Did you have an affair with someone *other* than Gina?" asked Alice.

"What? No, of course not."

"Did *I*?"

"Not that I know of. Can we get back to the point?"

"So there were no affairs at all?"

"No! Jesus. We didn't have *time* for affairs. We didn't have the energy. Well, I didn't. Maybe you did, in between your precious aerobics classes and beautician appointments, in which case, good luck to you."

Alice thought about how she'd kissed Dominick.

She said, "Do you have a girlfriend now? Oh, don't answer that. I can't bear it if you've got a girlfriend. Don't answer it." She put her hands over her ears, took them away, and said, "Do you?"

Nick said, "You must have hit your head really hard, Alice."

For a moment it seemed like the real Nick was back. He was shaking his head in comical disbelief, the way he did when he caught her crying over that margarine ad with the ducklings, or hopping around swearing because she'd hurt herself kicking the washing machine, or down on her knees frenziedly pulling everything out of the fridge in the hope of finding a forgotten bar of chocolate.

Then the look vanished as if he'd just recalled something highly irritating and he said, "Anyway, according to Olivia, you've got a boyfriend yourself. Jasper's dad. The school principal, no less. Do you remember *him*?"

Her face became warm. "I didn't remember him, but I met him yesterday."

"Right," said Nick testily. "Well, he sounds very nice. Think I remember him from the school. Tall, lanky bloke. Anyway, so glad everything is working out so well for you. The question is, are you well enough to look after the children tonight? Or should they come back with me?"

Alice said, "If neither of us had an affair, why aren't we still together? What could be bad enough to break us up?"

Nick exhaled noisily. He looked around the room in a flabbergasted way, as if looking for guidance from an equally flabbergasted audience. "It seems to me like this is a pretty serious head injury. I can't believe they let you leave the hospital."

"They did a CT scan. There's nothing physically wrong with me. Also, I sort of told them that I had my memory back."

Nick's eyes rose to the heavens. Another pompous new gesture. "Oh, great. Brilliant. Lie to the doctors. Well done, Alice."

"Why are you being so mean to me?"

"What, are we five now? I'm not being mean to you."

"You are. And you don't even sound like yourself. You've got all sarcastic and clichéd and . . . ordinary."

"Thank you. Thank you so much. Clichéd and ordinary. Yes, it's such a great mystery why our marriage has ended."

He looked around with a triumphant jeer for his invisible audience again, as if to say, "See what I have to put up with?"

"I'm sorry," said Alice. "I didn't mean . . ." She drifted off because she was remembering what it was like when you broke up with someone. Conversations became so hopelessly tangled. You had to be polite and precise. You couldn't safely criticize anymore, because you didn't have the right. You'd lost your immunity.

"Oh, Nick," she said helplessly.

She was experiencing all those familiar symptoms of a relationship breakup. The nausea. The sensation of something huge and hard lodged in the center of her chest. That trembly, teary feeling.

She wasn't supposed to ever have to feel this way again. Breakups were meant to be something from her youth. Painful memories. Actually not that painful, because it was sort of nice to look fondly back at her younger self and think, "Oh you silly thing, crying over that jerk."

This was meant to be her grown-up relationship. The one that lasted forever.

She put her wineglass on the coffee table and turned to face him. "Just tell me why we're getting a divorce. Please."

"That's an impossible question to answer. There are a million reasons. And you'd probably give a million different reasons."

"Well, just sort of . . . sum it up."

"In twenty-five words or less."

"Yes, please."

He smiled slightly and it was the real Nick again. He kept appearing and disappearing.

He said, "Well, I guess——" and then he stopped and bowed his head. "Oh, Alice." An expression of pure misery crossed his face.

It was too much for Alice. Her instinct was to comfort him, and she wanted to be comforted herself, and it was *Nick*, for heaven's sake.

She launched herself across the room and into his arms and buried her face in his chest, breathing in deeply. It was still Nick. He still smelled exactly like himself.

"Whatever went wrong, we'll fix it," she babbled. "We'll get counseling. We'll go on a nice holiday somewhere!" She was inspired. "With the *children*! They can come, too! *Our* children! How fun would that be? Or we'll just hang around here. Swim in the pool. The pool! I love the pool! How did we ever afford that? I guess with your new job. Do you like the job? I couldn't believe it! You've got your own personal assistant. She wasn't very nice to me, but that's okay, I don't mind."

"Alice."

He wasn't hugging her back. The words kept tumbling out of her mouth. She could talk her way out of this.

"I'm skinny, aren't I? I might even be too skinny. What do you think? How did I get so skinny? Did I give up chocolate? I can't find any chocolate in the whole house. My password is 'oregano.' Weird. Hey, why isn't Mrs. Bergen talking to me? Did I offend her? Elisabeth seems mad at me, too. But you still love me, don't you? You must still love me."

"Stop it." He held on to her shoulders and pushed her gently away.

"Because we have three children. And I still love you."

"No, Alice." He shook his head sternly, as if she were a toddler about to touch an electrical socket.

"What are you two fighting about this time?" Alice and Nick turned to see Madison leaning against the door frame. She must have had a shower. She was wearing a dressing gown, her face was scrubbed, and her hair was wet, pulled back from her face.

"Oh, you look so beautiful," said Alice involuntarily.

Madison's face changed, became ugly with rage.

"Why do you always say such stupid, retarded things?"

"Madison!" boomed Nick. "Do not speak to your mother like that."

"Well, she *is*! Anyway, I heard you say to Auntie Ella that Mum was a hard bitch, so why are you pretending to like her? I know you hate her."

Alice caught her breath.

"I do *not* hate your mother," said Nick. Alice could see tension pulling the skin around his mouth tight. He looked so old.

"You do so hate her," said Madison.

"He *does not* hate Mum!" It was Tom. He punched Madison in the arm. "I hate *you*."

"Tom!" snapped Nick.

"Owwww!" Madison clutched her arm, her knees collapsed beneath her, and she fell in a heap on the floor. "He *hit* me. You're not meant to hit girls. That is domestic violence. That is violence against women."

"You're not a woman," sneered Tom. "You're just a stupid girl."

Madison kicked viciously at Tom's leg. Tom threw back his head and howled. He looked at Alice, his face bright red and filled with righteous fury. "Mum, did you see how hard she kicked me? I only punched her a little bit!"

"A little bit?" Madison pulled up the sleeve of her dressing gown. "What's that? That is a mark! There will be a bruise! A huge bruise."

"Goodness," breathed Alice. She picked up her wineglass and looked around for some grown-up to take control.

"I think I should go," said Nick.

"Are you kidding?" said Alice. "You can't leave me with them!"

Madison and Tom now appeared to be trying to kill each other. They were wrestling like rabid cats on the floor. There was kicking, hair-pulling, and ear-piercing screams of rage. It was remarkable.

"Do they do this a lot?" asked Alice. She stuck her fingers in her ears. "Maybe it wouldn't be so much fun going on holidays with them."

Nick laughed, a surprised guffaw that he stopped short.

Alice said, "Did you really tell Ella I was a hard bitch?"

She paused. "Am I a hard bitch?"

Nick walked over to the children and grabbed the back of Tom's T-shirt in one hand. He wrenched him up in the air and carried him over to the couch and dropped him. Then he turned back to Madison and said, "Go to your room."

"Me? But *he* started it! He punched me first! That's not justice! *Mum?*"

Madison sat upright, her back against the wall, and looked at Alice imploringly.

At that moment Olivia came running into the room, wearing only a T-shirt and underpants dotted with pictures of strawberries. "Mummy, where are my shorts? I mean the denim ones. And don't say, 'Have I looked in the drawer?' because yes, I have looked, for ages and ages, and yes, actually, I did use my eyes." She pirouetted on the spot with her arms held gracefully above her head.

"You're very good at that," said Alice, glad of the distraction.

"Yes, I am pretty good," sighed Oliva, as if it were quite a responsibility. She lifted one skinny brown leg and admired her pointed toe. A thought struck her. "Mum, who is going to take me to the Family Talent Night concert at Frannie's retirement city? You or Daddy? Which house will I be sleeping in?"

"I'm not exactly sure," said Alice.

"We only sleep at Dad's place on weekends." Madison looked sharply at Alice. "Olivia's concert is on Wednesday night, right?"

"Well, that must be right then, Madison," said Alice.

"I'm so hungry," sighed Tom from the couch. "When is dinner? Mum? Excuse me, please, when is dinner? I think my blood sugar has dropped."

"Okay, Tom——"

"Why are you saying our names all the time?" interrupted Madison.

"Oh, sorry, I just——sorry."

Madison said, "You don't remember us, do you?"

Tom sat up straight on the couch and Olivia stopped twirling.

"She doesn't even know who we are," Madison told them.

Chapter 21

A lice pursed her lips together in the manner of a stern, distracted mother and tried not to let the panic show.

"Of course I know who you are," she said to Madison. "Don't be silly."

"How could Mum not remember us?" Olivia put her hands on her hips and stuck her stomach out. "Madison? What does that mean?"

Madison gave her a bored, superior look. "Mum fell over and hit her head at the gym. I heard Auntie Libby telling Uncle Ben she'd lost ten years of her memory. Well, guess what? We weren't born ten years ago!"

"Yes, but so—she still knows who we are! We're her *children!*" Olivia seemed both agitated and excited.

"Okay, why don't you kids watch some TV," said Nick. "Or PlayStation? And maybe it's time you stopped eavesdropping on grown-up conversations, Madison."

"I was not eavesdropping! I was just *there*! In the kitchen! Getting some juice out of the fridge. What am I meant to do? Walk around like this?" She stuck her fingers in her ears.

"Amnesia," said Tom. "That's called amnesia. Is that what you've got, Mum?"

"Your mother is perfectly fine," said Nick.

"Mum?" said Tom.

"We'll do a test," said Madison. "Ask her some questions."

"Like what?" said Olivia.

"I know!" Tom put his hand up as if he were in school. "I know! Okay, Mum, what is my favorite food?"

"French fries," said Nick. "Now that's enough."

"That's wrong!" cried Tom. "It's chicken schnitzel. Sometimes. Or otherwise sushi."

"Well, there you go, I've got amnesia, too. Now that's enough."

"My favorite food is chicken schnitzel, too," commented Olivia.

"It is not," said Tom. "Think of your own thing! You copy every single thing I do."

"What's my teacher's name, Mum?" said Madison.

"Now that's enough," repeated Nick.

"Oh! I know that one!" Alice managed to stop herself from putting her hand up. She'd seen a notice on the fridge door about a Year 5 excursion with a teacher's name on it. "Mrs. Ollaway! I mean Alloway. Ollaway? Something like that."

There was an ominous silence.

"Mrs. *Holloway* is the deputy principal," said Madison quietly, in the tone of one pointing out an incredibly foolish, potentially dangerous mistake.

"Oh, yes, of course, that's what I meant," said Alice humbly.

"You didn't," said Madison.

"When's my birthday, Mum?" asked Tom, and he pointed a warning finger at his father. "Don't you answer for her!"

"Right!" Nick clapped his hands together and made a loud hollow sound. "Your mother had an accident and she's a bit muddled about some things, that's all. She needs you all to be extra helpful and extra quiet. She doesn't need you interrogating her. So I want all three of you setting the table now."

Olivia came and stood beside Alice and slipped a hand in hers. She whispered, "You know that my birthday is twentieth June, don't you?"

"Of course I do, darling," said Alice, and suddenly she felt like a mother. "That's the day you were born. I could never ever forget that."

She looked up and saw Madison standing in the hallway, staring at her with fierce concentration.

"You're lying," she said.

Elisabeth's Homework for Dr. Hodges

Dear Doctor Hodges,

You know what? I'm going to give in and call you by your first name. I was remembering today how you made such a point of it at our first session. "Jeremy," you said firmly each time I said "Dr. Hodges." You probably don't like your name. I don't blame you. Hodges is a plump, greasy name, and you're not plump and greasy. You're actually quite good-looking, which I find distracting. Your nice looks keep reminding me that you're a real person, and I don't want you to be a real person. Real people don't have the answers. They make mistakes. They say things with great authority and they're *wrong*.

But anyway, whatever, I'm officially taking you off your pedestal.

How are you, anyway, Jeremy? What are you doing this Sunday night? Are you drinking red wine with your pretty, fertile wife while she prepares a roast dinner and you help those fair-haired kids with their homework? Is the house warm and toasty and smelling of garlic and rosemary?

There is no roast dinner in the oven here. There is no conversation. There is only the sound of the television. There is always the sound of the television. I can't stand to turn it off. I can't stand the silence. "Couldn't we just play some music?" Ben says. No. I want TV. I want gunshots and canned laughter and dog food commercials. Nothing seems too tragic when the television is blaring. (I lived for two years without a television when I was in my twenties. How did I do that? Now it's like a narcotic.)

So, what did I want to tell you? Oh yes. Ben. We're fighting.

On the way home from Alice's place today, Ben started telling me about some man he'd met at last night's party. I'd seen them talking while I was chatting with Alice's new boyfriend, who, by the by, is sweet and awkward. It made me feel a bit weird. As if I was being unfaithful to Nick. But I liked him. Anyway, I thought, oh good, Ben's found someone to talk about cars.

But no.

They were talking about infertility and adoption. Suddenly Ben is the sort of guy who reveals details of his personal life to strangers at kindergarten cocktail parties. I've had him wrong all these years. He's not the silent, strong, damaged type at all. Oh no.

This guy's sister went through eleven failed IVF cycles before adopting a baby girl from Thailand and the little girl is a talented violin player and they all lived happily ever after.

Ben got this woman's number. He's going to call her. My

husband has a zealous new look in his eyes. It's as if he's discovered religion or golf. Mr. Never Ever Adopt has become Mr. I Can't Wait to Adopt.

I asked how many years it took, but Ben didn't know.

I changed the subject.

Then, tonight, we're watching the news and they're showing the cyclone in Burma.

There was a woman wearing a red dress a bit like Alice's. She was standing in front of a pile of rubble that had once been her daughter's school. She had a photo of a solemn-faced girl. She looked about Olivia's age. The mother talked politely in good English to the reporter and explained that the local authorities were doing everything they could. She seemed fine, almost businesslike. The camera moved away. Then it came back and now the mother was writhing on the ground, wailing and biting her knuckles. The reporter explained that she'd just heard that there would be no further rescues from the school because it was too dangerous.

I was eating corn chips and watching a woman experiencing the worst moment of her life.

I have no right to be sad about anything. No right to have therapy from expensive doctors like you for losing children who never existed. There is real grief in the world. There are real mothers losing real children. I make myself sick.

And that's when Ben said, "Lots of children must have lost their parents." He said it solemnly, but also with a definite hint of cheer. As in, hey, how handy! Lots of dead parents! Lots of spare kids up for grabs! Maybe a cute little violin player is crawling out of the rubble right now. Jesus.

I said, "Yes, isn't this cyclone *great*!"

He said, "Don't be like that."

And suddenly I was screaming, "I would have adopted! I would have! I would have! But YOU SAID NO. You said you were psychologically damaged by being adopted, you said—"

And he interrupted and said, "I never EVER used the words 'psychologically damaged.'"

Which is true. But he implied it.

I said, "You did so." I mean he might as well have said it, Jeremy.

He said, "Bullshit."

I really hate that word. He knows that. And it doesn't even make sense. A bull's shit.

Then he said, and this is the kicker, Jeremy, he said, "I thought it was *you* who didn't want to adopt."

After my head stopped exploding, I said, "Why would you think that?"

He said, "Whenever people asked us about it, you'd get so angry with them. You'd say we want our own biological child."

I said, "But I was saying that because of you. Because you'd been so against it in the beginning."

He said, "I was against it, but then after we kept losing the pregnancies, it seemed the obvious thing to do, but I didn't want to bring it up because the idea seemed to upset you so much."

So there you go. How's that for great communication in a marriage?

It reminds me of that television show where they investigate airplane crashes. Sometimes a major disaster happens because of the tiniest, most stupid error.

I said, "Anyway, it's too late now."

He said, "It's not."

I said, "I'm not adopting. I'm too tired."

It's true, Jeremy. It has occurred to me recently that for the last few years I have been in a permanent state of tiredness. I'm so tired of trying and trying and trying. I don't have anything left. I'm done. I would like to go to sleep for a year or two.

I said, "We're not going to be parents. It's over."

And after a while of him munching corn chips (energetically grinding them with his teeth like a guinea pig), he said, "So are we just going to sit around and watch TV for the rest of our lives?"

And I said, "Suits me."

He got up and left the room.

Now we're not talking. I haven't seen him since. But I know when he comes back, we won't talk. Or if we do, we'll talk very, very politely and coldly—which is the same as not talking.

Right now, I feel . . . nothing.

Nothing at all.

A huge, empty, endless nothing that I am filling up with corn chips and *Australia's Funniest Home Videos*.

Chapter 22

The Love family was sitting around the dinner table. There had been an awkward moment when Alice went to sit in Olivia's place, but Nick saved her by jerking his chin at the place opposite.

The children had become wriggly and giggly, almost as if they were drunk. They seemed unable to sit still. They were sliding off their chairs, constantly knocking cutlery onto the floor, and talking in high-pitched voices over the top of one another. Alice didn't know if this was normal behavior or not. It wasn't exactly relaxing. Nick had his jaw clenched, as if this dinner were a horrible medical procedure he had to endure.

"I *knew* you wouldn't remember that you promised I could make lasagna." Madison poked disgustedly at her hamburger.

"She's got amnesia, stupid," said Tom thickly, his mouth amazingly full.

"Manners," said Alice automatically, and then caught herself. Did she just say, "Manners"? What did that even mean?

"Oh, yeah," said Madison. She turned her dark eyes on Alice. "Sorry."

"That's okay," Alice said, and dropped her eyes first. The kid could be sort of scary.

"What's for dessert, Mummy?" said Olivia. She was kicking the table leg rhythmically as she ate. "Maybe ice cream? Or I know, Chocolate Mush?"

"What's Chocolate Mush?" asked Alice.

"Oh, silly, you know that!" said Olivia.

Tom slapped his hand against his forehead. "You girls! She's got amnesia!"

"Mummy, darling," said Olivia. "Is it gone now? Your am—thing? Because maybe you could take an aspirin? I could get it for you? I could get it for you now!"

She pushed her chair back from the table.

"Eat your dinner, Olivia," said Nick.

"Daddy," groaned Olivia. "I'm trying to *help*."

"As if an aspirin is going to help," said Tom. "She probably needs an operation. Like brain surgery. By a brain surgeon. I saw a brain surgeon on television the other night." He brightened. "Hey! I would like to dissect a mouse and see its brain, as well as its intestines! With a scalpel. That would be excellent."

"Oh my *God*." Madison put down her knife and fork and put her head on the table. "That is making me sick. I am so going to be sick."

"Stop it," said Nick.

"This is a mouse's brain, Madison." Tom squished his fork into his hamburger meat. "Chop, chop, chop, mousie's brain!"

"Make him stop!" wailed Madison.

"Tom," sighed Nick.

"So!" said Alice. "How was the Aquatic Center today?"

Madison lifted her head from the table and said to Alice, "Did you remember that you and Dad were getting a divorce? After you hit your head? Did you remember that?"

Nick made a strangled, helpless sound.

Alice considered the question. "No," she said. "I didn't."

No one spoke. Olivia banged her knife against her plate. Tom twisted his arm over and frowned ferociously at something on his elbow. There were spots of crimson on Madison's cheekbones.

"So do you still love Dad?" said Madison. There was a slight tremor in her voice. She sounded much younger.

"Alice," said Nick warningly, at the same time as Alice said, "Yes, of course I do."

"Can Daddy come home, then?" Olivia looked up, elated. "And sleep in his own bed again!"

"Okay, time for a change of subject," said Nick. He avoided Alice's eyes.

"They'd fight too much," said Tom.

"What do we fight about?" asked Alice, greedy for facts.

"Oh, I don't *know*," said Tom irritably. "You said that's why you couldn't live together anymore. Because you fight too much. Even though I still have to live with my stupid sisters and we fight all the time. So it wasn't even logical."

"You fight about Gina," said Madison.

"Don't talk about Gina!" said Olivia. "It makes me sad. It's an absolute *tragedy*."

"R.I.P.," said Tom. "That's what you say when you talk about someone who has died. It means rest in peace. You have to say it whenever you hear their name."

"Why did we fight about Gina?" asked Alice.

"R.I.P.!" cried Tom, as if he were saying "snap!"

"So, the Aquatic Center was a lot of fun," said Nick. "Wasn't it, kids?"

"Well," said Madison. "I think Dad thought you liked Gina better than him."

"R.I.P.!" shouted Tom and Olivia.

"Oh shut up!" said Madison. "Someone dying is not funny!"

Alice looked at Nick. His face looked red and raw, like windburn. She couldn't tell whether it meant he was angry or embarrassed. Goodness. Had *she* had some sort of torrid lesbian affair with Gina?

"You fight about the American Expense a lot," said Tom.

"American *Express*," said Madison.

"American Expense works for me." Nick lifted his wineglass in a mocking sort of salute but he still didn't look at Alice.

"Once you had a really extremely big fight about *me*," said Olivia with satisfaction.

"Why?" asked Alice.

"Oh, you remember." Olivia looked wary. "That day. At the beach."

"For the twenty-billionth time, she doesn't remember!" said Tom.

"Olivia got lost," said Madison. "The police came. You were crying." She gave Alice a malicious look. "Like this: 'Olivia! Olivia! My daughter! Where is my *daughter*?'" She buried her face in her hands and pretended to sob dramatically.

"Did I?" Alice felt ridiculously hurt by Madison's act.

"Just in case you're wondering," said Madison, "Olivia is your favorite child."

"Your mother doesn't have favorites," said Nick.

Did she? She hoped not.

"When I was pregnant with you, Madison," said Alice, "your dad and I called you the Sultana. Did you know that? Because you were as tiny as a sultana."

"You never told me that." Madison looked doubtful.

"What did you call *me*?" asked Olivia.

"Really? I never told you that?" said Alice.

Madison turned to Nick. "Is that true? Did you call me the Sultana?"

"Your dad spoke to you through a toilet roll on my tummy," said Alice. "He said, 'Ahoy there, Sultana! It's me! Your father!'"

Madison smiled. Alice stared. It was the most exquisite smile she had ever seen. She felt a shot of love so powerful, it hurt her chest.

She looked down at her plate and a memory dropped straight into her head.

She was in a car filled with gold, filmy light. There was a smell of salt and seaweed. Her neck hurt. She turned around to check the baby. Miracle. She was asleep. Fat pink cheeks. Long lashes. Her head lolling against the side of the car seat. As Alice watched, a bar of light fell across her face. Her eyes fluttered open and she yawned and stretched sleepily. Then she caught sight of Alice and her whole face lit up with a huge, surprised grin, as if to say, "Hey! I can't believe it! You're here, too!" There was a sudden loud, rumbling snore from the driver's seat and the baby looked startled. "It's okay," said Alice. "It's just Daddy."

"The baby wouldn't sleep." Alice looked at Nick. "She wouldn't sleep unless we were driving."

Nick kept shoveling food into his mouth and looked straight ahead.

Alice stared at Madison and blinked. The angry, strange little girl at the table was the baby. The giggling baby in the car was the Sultana.

"We drove all through the night," said Alice to Madison. "Every time we stopped you screamed."

"I know," said Madison. She was sullen again. "And you drove me all the way to Manly and you stopped in the car park and you and Daddy and me all fell asleep in the car, and then you took me on the beach and I rolled over for the first time. Whatever."

"Yes!" said Alice excitedly—she remembered. "The baby rolled over on the picnic rug! We got takeaway coffees from that place with the blue awning. And toasted ham-and-cheese sandwiches."

It felt like yesterday and it felt like a million years ago.

"I slept through the night when I was eight weeks old," said Olivia. "Didn't I, Mum? I was a gold-star sleeper."

"Just—shhhh," said Alice, holding up her hand, trying to focus. She could see that morning so clearly. The baby's striped suit. Nick's unshaven face and red eyes. A seagull white and squawky against a very blue sky. They were so tired, they were light-headed. The blessed feeling of the caffeine hitting her bloodstream. They were parents. They were filled with the wonder and the horror, the bliss and the exhaustion of being parents.

"Mummy," whined Olivia.

If she remembered that day, she should be able to feel her way back to when Madison was born. And she should be able to feel her way forward to the day that Nick packed his bags and left.

"Mummy," said Olivia again. *Oh, please be QUIET.* She groped about in the dark but there was nothing else.

All she had was that morning.

"But Nick," she began.

"What?" he said grimly, irritably. He really didn't like her. It wasn't just that he didn't love her anymore. He didn't even like her.

"We were so happy."

Elisabeth's Homework for Jeremy

3 a.m.

Hi J. Ben drove off somewhere. I don't know where he is. I'm so tired.

Hey. You know how if you say a word over and over again, it starts to sound really weird?

Like, let's say the word is, oh, I don't know, INFERTILITY. Infertility. Infertility. Infertility. Infertility.

It's a twisty, curly, nasty word. Lots of syllables.

Anyway, Jeremy, my darling therapist (as Olivia would say), my point is that things become weird and pointless if you examine them for too long. I've thought about being a mother for so many years the whole concept has started to seem weird. I've wanted it, wanted it, wanted it. Now I'm not even sure if I wanted it in the first place.

Look at Alice and Nick. They were so happy before they had the children. And sure, they love their kids, but let's be honest, they're hard work. And it's not like you get to *keep* those adorable babies. Babies disappear. They grow up. They turn into children who are not necessarily that cute at all.

Madison was the most beautiful baby. We adored her. But the Madison of today doesn't seem to have anything to do with that baby. She's so furious and strange and she can make you feel like an idiot. (Yes, Jeremy, a ten-year-old can make me feel inferior. That shows a lack of emotional maturity or something, doesn't it?)

Tom used to bury his face in my neck and now he wriggles away if I try and touch him. And he tells you the plots of TV shows with a lot of unnecessary detail. It's sort of dull. Sometimes I think of other things while he's talking.

And Olivia is still gorgeous, but actually she can be manipulative. Sometimes it's like she knows she's being cute.

And the FIGHTS. You should see them fight. It's amazing.

See. I'm a terrible auntie. I'm making bitchy remarks about those three beautiful children, whom I hardly see anymore anyway. So what sort of mother would I be? A horrible one. Maybe even an abusive one. They'd probably take my children away and give them to someone else. An infertile woman could adopt them.

You know, Jeremy, once, when Olivia was a toddler, I minded her for a whole day. Alice and Gina were out at some school function. Olivia was perfectly behaved and she was so cute, she would have won an award for the cutest baby, but you know, by the end of the day, I was BORED OUT OF MY SKULL from walking around after her and saying, no don't touch that, ooooh yes, look at the bright light.

Bored. Tired. A bit irritable. I was relieved to hand her over when Alice came home. I felt as light as a feather.

How's that? All this "oh, poor me" obsession with being a mother and I was bored after one day.

I've always secretly thought that Anne-Marie, my friend from the Infertiles, would make a terrible mother. She's so impatient and brittle. But maybe they're all thinking that about me, too. Maybe we'd all make terrible mothers. Ben's mum is probably right when she says that "Nature knows best." Nature knows that I would make a terrible mother. Each time I get pregnant, Nature says, "Actually, this kid would be better off dead than having a mother like her."

After all, Ben's mum couldn't have children either and look at her, she DID make a terrible mother.

The bottom line is, we shouldn't adopt.

I don't want to be a mother anymore, Jeremy.

A mother. A mother. A mother. A mother.

Sounds like smother. It's a weird word.

I don't even know why I'm crying.

Frannie's Letter to Phil

Mr. Mustache turned up at my door this morning just as I was about to leave for Tai Chi.

I almost didn't recognize him. He'd shaved off his mustache.

I said, "I hope you didn't do that for me."

His upper lip looked so naked! He seemed like an entirely different person. Softer and gentler. Although at the same time, more sophisticated and . . . masculine.

He was wearing tracksuit pants and a T-shirt and he said he'd been thinking he might give this "Tai whatchamacallit" a go, but he said he felt "shy" about turning up on his own.

I said, "Oh, yes, because you're such a shy, retiring type."

We went along to the Tai Chi, and he was utterly hopeless. I had to keep trying not to giggle like a naughty schoolchild. Afterward he looked so endearingly rumpled, I invited him back for a cup of tea and some of Alice's banana muffins that she'd given me last week.

We had quite a chat. I told him how I'd recently become quite addicted to "Facebook" after an old student invited me to join. (Little Mattie Marks. Remember him, Phil? He's some sort of IT big shot these days.) Mr. M. was impressed. He said he used the Internet a lot but didn't know anything about Facebook. It made me feel quite hip!

He told me about his two sons and how much he misses them. (One lives in the U.K. and the other is in Perth.) He said both his boys were adopted.

"My wife and I couldn't have our own children," he explained. "That's why I felt so sorry for your granddaughter."

(He says "granddaughter" so naturally, even though he knows I'm not really related to Elisabeth. It may be to do with his own children being adopted. Perhaps it's not so presumptuous of him. Perhaps it's rather nice. I can't make up my mind.)

"It's a very lonely feeling when all your friends are having babies," he said. He told me he could still remember the expression on his wife's face while they went to her niece's baptism, even though it was over sixty years ago. "It made me want to punch a wall," he said.

I wonder if he was reprimanding me for my "babies are not the be-all and end-all" comment. I wonder if he thinks I'm being a bit harsh about poor Elisabeth.

Do you know something, Phil? I had always secretly hoped that you and I might have our own little baby. Just the one. Boy or girl. Didn't matter. I was thirty-eight, but I knew it wasn't beyond the realms of possibility. One of the sixth-form mothers at the school had a baby at forty-one. She was almost embarrassed about it. She brought the baby to the school one day and I remember holding out my finger for the baby to clutch and suddenly thinking, I'm younger than her. *I felt that sudden rush of disbelief and exhilaration you feel when your ticket number is called in a raffle.* I could still be a mother, *I thought, and I felt like dancing.*

It was two weeks before what should have been our wedding day.

One week before the phone call.

It's true I've never been pregnant, but I know what it's like to lose the possibility of a baby. So of course I sympathize with Elisabeth, Phil! Deeply. My heart breaks for her. I've cried and cried for her each time she's lost another baby.

It's just that sometimes I want to say to her, "Darling, maybe you don't get to be a mother, but you still get to be a wife."

Chapter 23

R ight. Seat belts on?" said Alice. Her hand shook slightly as she turned the key in the ignition. Did she really drive this gigantic car every day of her life? It felt like a semi-trailer. Apparently, it was called an SUV.

"Are you sure you're safe to take them to school tomorrow? Because if you think there is any risk at all to the children, I'd rather drive them myself," Nick had said the night before when he was leaving, and Alice had wanted to say, "Of course I'm not right, you idiot! I don't even know where the school is!" But there had been something about Nick's tone that made the hairs on the back of her neck stand up with a powerful, strangely familiar feeling that was close to . . . fury? He had such a sneery way of talking to her now. That snippy voice spoke up again in her head: *Sanctimonious bastard! Trying to make me look like a bad mother.* "I'll be fine," she'd said. And he'd sighed his huffy new sigh, and as she watched him walk out to his shiny car, she felt something almost like relief at the same time as she thought, "But why don't you just come up to bed with me?"

Now her three children sat in the seat behind her. They were in horrible moods. If they'd been drunk last night, now they were all suffering from terrible hangovers. They were pale and snarly, with purple shadows under their eyes. Had they slept badly because of her? She suspected she'd let them stay up way past their normal bedtimes. There had been a lot of vagueness when she asked them what time they normally went to bed.

Alice adjusted the rear-vision mirror.

"Do you remember how to drive?" asked Tom.

"Yes, of course." Alice's hand hovered nervously over the handbrake.

"We're late," said Tom. "You might have to go quite a bit over the speed limit."

It had been a strange and stressful morning. Tom had appeared at Alice's bedroom door at seven a.m. and said, "Have you got your memory back?" "Not quite," Alice had said, trying to shake her head free of a night of dreams all involving Nick yelling at her. "She hasn't got it back!" she heard Tom cry, and then the sound of the television being switched on. When she got out of bed, she found Madison and Tom lounging around in their pajamas, eating cereal in front of the television. "Do you normally watch television before school?" Alice had asked. "Sometimes," Tom had answered carefully, without removing his eyes from the TV. Twenty minutes later, he was in a frenzy, yelling that they needed to leave in five minutes' time. That's when it emerged that Olivia was still sound asleep in bed. Apparently it was Alice's job to wake her.

"I think Olivia might be sick," Alice had said, as Olivia kept collapsing back against the pillow, her head lolling to one side, saying sleepily, "No thank you, I'll just stay here, thank you, goodbye."

"Mum, she's like this every morning," Tom had said disgustedly.

Finally, after Alice had dragged a half-comatose Olivia into a school uniform and spooned cereal into her mouth, while Madison had spent half an hour with a roaring hair dryer in the bathroom, they had left the house, incredibly late, according to Tom.

Alice put her hand around the handbrake.

"Did you even brush your hair this morning, Mum?" asked Madison. "You look sort of . . . disgusting. No offense."

Alice put a hand to her hair and tried to smooth it down. She had assumed that she didn't need to dress up for dropping the kids off at school. She hadn't bothered with hair or makeup and had pulled on a pair of jeans, a T-shirt, and an old watermelon-colored jumper she'd found at the back of the drawer. The jumper was faded and frayed, and it had given Alice a start when she realized she remembered buying it brand new with Elisabeth just the other week.

Just the other week ten years ago.

"Don't be mean to darling Mummy," Olivia said to Madison.

"Don't be mean to darling Mummy!" mimicked Madison in a sugary-sweet voice.

"Stop copying me!" Alice felt the thud of Olivia's feet against her lower back as she kicked the seat.

"We're so late," moaned Tom.

"Would you three just be quiet for once in your lives!" snapped Alice, in a voice entirely unlike her own, and at the same time, she released the handbrake and reversed out of the driveway and turned left, her hands smooth and capable on the leather-clad steering wheel, as if she'd said exactly those words and done exactly that maneuver a million times before.

She drove toward the lights, her hand already on the indicator to turn right.

There was a sullen silence in the back of the car.

"So, what's happening at school today?" she said.

Madison sighed dramatically as if she'd never heard a more stupid comment.

"Volcanoes," answered Tom. "We're talking about what makes a volcano erupt. I've written down some questions for Mrs. Buckley. Some pret-ty tricky questions."

Poor Mrs. Buckley.

"We're making a Mother's Day surprise," said Olivia.

"Now it's not a surprise, is it?" said Madison.

"It is so!" said Olivia. "Mum, it is, isn't it?"

"Yes, of course it's still a surprise, I don't know what you're making," said Alice.

"We're making special candles," said Olivia.

"Ha!" said Madison.

"Well, I still don't know what color they are," said Alice.

"Pink!" said Olivia.

Alice laughed.

"Idiot," said Madison.

"Don't call her that," said Alice. Had she and Elisabeth spoken to each other in such a horrible way? Well, there was that time Elisabeth threw the nail scissors at her. For the first time, Alice felt sorry for their mother. She didn't remember her ever yelling at them when they fought, just sighing a lot, and saying plaintively, "Be nice, girls."

They were pulled up at a red light. The lights changed and Alice had no idea where to go.

"Umm," she said.

"Straight ahead. Second on the left," said Tom laconically from the back, sounding so much like his father that Alice wanted to laugh.

Alice drove. The car was huge and unfamiliar again.

She saw she was driving behind a similarly huge car with a woman at the wheel and two small heads bobbing about in the back.

Alice was a mother driving her three children to school. She did this every day. It was unbelievable. Hilarious.

"So, compared to the other mums at school," she said, "am I strict?"

"You're like a Nazi," said Madison. "You're like the Gestapo."

"You're about average," said Tom. "Like, for example, Bruno's mum won't even let him go on school excursions, that's how mean she is. But then there's Alistair's mum—she lets him stay up till nine o'clock, and they have KFC whenever they want, and they watch television when they're eating their breakfast."

"Hey!" said Alice.

"Oh, yeah." Tom gave a dry chuckle. "Sorry, Mum."

"When am I like the Gestapo?" asked Alice.

"Don't worry about it," sighed Madison. "You can't help it."

"I don't think you're strict," said Olivia. "Just—sometimes, you get a bit angry."

"What makes me angry?" asked Alice.

"Me," said Madison. "Just looking at me makes you mad."

"Running late for school normally makes you *really* mad," said Tom. "Ummm, let's see, what else. Doors slamming. You can't stand it when a door slams. You have got really delicate ears."

"Daddy makes you angry," said Olivia.

"Oh, yeah," agreed Tom. "Dad makes you the angriest."

"Why?" Alice tried not to sound too interested. "What does he do that makes me so angry?"

"You hate him," said Tom.

"I'm sure that's not true," said Alice.

"You do," said Madison wearily. "You've just forgotten that you do."

Alice looked in the rear-vision mirror at her three extraordinary children. Tom was frowning at a chunky plastic wristwatch, Olivia was staring dreamily ahead, and Madison had her forehead pressed against the car window, her eyes closed. What had she and Nick done to them? This casual talk about hatred. She was filled with shame.

"I'm sorry," she said.

"Sorry for what?" said Olivia, who seemed to be the only one listening.

"I'm sorry about your dad and me."

"Oh, that's okay," said Olivia. "Can we have hot chocolates after school?"

"That's a green arrow," said Tom tersely.

Alice pulled into a street lined with trucklike cars similar to the one she was driving. It looked like a festival. A festival of women and children. The women stood in groups of two or three, sunglasses pushed up on their foreheads, scarves slung around necks. They wore jeans and boots, beautifully cut suede jackets. Were mothers always this attractive and thin? Alice tried to remember the mothers from her own school days. Weren't they sort of chunky and plain? Sort of irrelevant and fading into the background? A few women waved when they saw Alice. She recognized someone who had got quite drunk at the kindergarten cocktail party. Oh Lord, she should have done her hair.

The children whooped and swooped about in their blue school uniforms, like flocks of tiny birds. All those innocent, smooth-skinned faces.

"We're not late," said Alice.

"We're late for *us*," muttered Tom. "I've got a meeting of my spy club. They don't know what to do without me."

They found a parking spot.

"Watch it," winced Tom as Alice backed the car into the curb with a thud.

She breathed a sigh of relief as she pulled the keys from the ignition. The children immediately unclicked seat belts and opened the heavy car doors with a clunk, sliding out of the car, backpacks slung over their shoulders.

"Hey, wait for me!" said Alice, worried about procedures and kisses goodbye.

As she got out of the car, she saw Dominick. He was wearing a tie, his shirtsleeves carefully folded up to his elbows, and he was squatting down to talk to three boys who were explaining something to him that appeared to be about a soccer ball. Dominick was nodding seriously, as if he were in a top-level business negotiation. Two mothers were standing nearby, waiting to talk to him. Dominick caught sight of Alice and winked. Alice smiled self-consciously. He was nice. There was no denying it. He was very, very . . . nice.

"Have you slept with him yet?" said a posh voice in her ear, and the heavy sweet scent of a beauty salon filled Alice's nostrils.

It was that dreadful Kate Harper woman again.

"Oh, hi." Alice reeled back. Kate was wearing a beautifully fitted trench coat, skin polished, lips shimmery. It was a bit much for this time of the morning.

Kate didn't wait for an answer. "God, I'm jealous. It's been a year for us."

"A year?"

"A year since we've done the deed. I must have cobwebs down there."

The things strangers told you.

Kate was still looking at Dominick. "The claws are out, by the way. Miriam Dane has had her eye on him for ages. Apparently, she told Felicity that she thought it was rather poor form for you to go after him only three months after you and Nick separated. I promised I wouldn't pass it on, but of course I knew you'd want to know!" She lowered her voice. Her beautiful face turned nasty. "You'll die laughing when you hear this. Apparently, after she'd had a few drinks at the party the other night, Miriam called you the S-word."

Alice looked at her without comprehension.

Kate lowered her voice and whispered, *"Slut!"* Then she raised it again and screeched, "Isn't that *hilarious*? Isn't that just so *eighties*! I thought, I must tell Alice, she'll *love* that! The woman is pea green with jealousy! And of course she hated it when Tom kicked that goal at soccer, when, you know, she's been getting all that extra training for Harry, because he's supposedly so *talented*, ha, ha, that little piglet!"

Alice felt sick. She looked around for her children, wanting an excuse to get away from Kate. Tom was sitting on a bench, lecturing two other boys, who were listening intently; one even appeared to be taking notes. Olivia was doing a cartwheel while a group of girls applauded. She couldn't see Madison.

"Well," she said, "you can tell that Miriam not to worry. Nick and I are getting back together."

Kate grabbed Alice's arm so hard, it hurt. "You're joking."

"No." She thought of Nick's cold face last night as he said goodbye. "Well, anyway, we're working on it."

"But what *happened*? I mean, the things you were saying, just last week—I mean, gosh, it just seemed completely irretrievable! You said you couldn't stand the sight of him, he made you physically *ill*! You said you could never forgive him! You said—"

"Forgive him for what?" interrupted Alice.

"This is such a surprise!" Kate pulled at a strand of gold hair that had got caught in her sticky, shimmery lips. She'd lost some of her posh accent in her excitement.

"What did I need to forgive him for?" Alice repressed an urge to put her hands around Kate Harper's perfect neck and squeeze.

"Hey there."

Someone's hand settled gently on her shoulder.

Alice looked up and saw Dominick standing next to her.

"How are you, Kate?" said Dominick. His hand was still on Alice's shoulder, invisibly caressing her. It was nice, but *Nick* did that in public. "Congratulations, you two. Saturday night was great."

He was such a strange mix of authority and shyness.

"How are *you*, Dominick?" asked Kate. Her face was shiny with sympathy and fresh new gossip.

"Fighting fit for a Monday." Dominick removed his hand from Alice's shoulder (she missed it) and shuffled his feet while doing an absurd little boxing move.

He smiled at Alice and touched her arm again. "I'll talk to you later."

She smiled back. He was looking at her the way Nick looked at her when they first started going out. It was a look that made her feel highly desirable and extremely interesting. She thought of how Nick looked at her now.

"Yes, okay," she said.

"Oh, Dominick, we need you over here!" trilled a woman.

He loped off obediently.

"So I'm assuming you haven't told him, then? About you and Nick?" asked Kate avidly.

"Oh. No. Not yet."

"But it's definite?"

"Oh, well, yes. I think so. I hope so. It's sort of a secret."

"Got it! My lips are sealed." Kate mimed the zipping up of her lips.

"What did I need to forgive Nick for?"

"Mmmm. Pardon?" Kate looked distracted. "Oh, well, you know, we were talking about Gina."

"What about Gina?" In her head she had Kate by the shoulders and was shaking her until her teeth chattered.

"You know, you were saying how he didn't even make the effort to go to the funeral. You seemed so . . . well, that's why this is so out of the blue."

So Nick didn't go to Alice's best friend's funeral. Why not? There must have been a good reason. Surely they weren't getting divorced over that.

"Can I just say one thing?" said Kate. She fiddled with a button on her jacket and looked up, her face awkward. "Just, look, don't get back together if it's just for the kids. My parents stayed together for the children." She hooked her fingers in the air to form quotation marks around "for the children." "And let me tell you, children know when their parents despise each other. It's not nice. It's not a nice way to grow up. And you know, Dominick is a catch. He really is. So, anyway, that's Kate's two cents' worth for the day, my dear! I must go! Busy, busy, busy!"

Kate clip-clopped off in her high heels, swinging her handbag over her shoulder and tightening the belt of her trench coat.

Maybe she wasn't so dreadful after all.

Elisabeth's Homework for Jeremy

I really thought about not bothering with this morning's blood test. Just not showing up. Playing truant.

But of course I was there right on eight a.m. Writing my name on the clipboard. Presenting my forearm to the nurse. Checking the spelling of my name and my date of birth on the test tube. Pressing the cotton-wool ball to the speck of blood.

"Good luck," said the nurse as I left.

She's the one who always says "Good luck." In a sort of patronizing way.

"Oh, fuck off with your good luck," I said, and punched her in the nose.

Got you, J! I never said that. Of course I didn't. I said, "Thanks!" Then I went into the office and Layla was there all bright-eyed and bushy-tailed and telling me about how well the rest of Friday's seminars went after I left, and how all the evaluations were positive and she got twelve bookings for the advanced seminar.

I said, "Are you even going to ask about the reason I had to leave early? You know, my sister? The one who was in hospital?"

And, Jeremy, her earnest face crumpled. She looked so embarrassed, I felt like I'd kicked a kitten. She was falling all over herself to apologize. She said she thought I didn't like to discuss personal stuff.

I don't! I never have! Poor woman.

This is the final confirmation that I am a horrible person.

Alice sat on her front veranda steps in the autumn sunshine, eating the leftover custard tart her mother had left behind and wondering whether she was meant to be somewhere soon. Her diary for today said: "L—10 a.m." Was "L" a person who was waiting for her somewhere? Was "L" important? She supposed she should call Elisabeth or her mother and find out, but she couldn't seem to make the effort. Maybe she would have a nap.

A nap! Are you kidding? You have got a million and one things to do.

There was that snippy voice again.

"Go away," said Alice out loud. "I can't remember what those million and one things are."

She closed her eyes and enjoyed the feeling of sun on her face. There was no sound except for the far-off roar of a motorbike. The amazing silence of the suburbs in the middle of the day. She normally only experienced this feeling if she was sick and took the day off work.

She opened her eyes again and yawned. She might as well eat the rest of the custard tart now. There was only a sliver left. From where she was sitting she could see the For Sale sign on the house opposite. So that's where Gina had lived. Alice had probably been inside that "stunning renovated character home" many times, borrowing sugar, or whatever. If Alice had thought about it at all, she would have assumed she wouldn't have made any new friends in her thirties. She had quite sufficient. Besides which, she really just wanted to hang around with Nick and Elisabeth, and she was going to become a mother. She thought that would have been enough of a distraction.

Yet it seemed as though her friendship with Gina had been a significant part of her life.

And then Gina had died and she'd been "devastated." It made Alice feel sort of silly. As if she'd made too big a fuss over something.

The sound of the motorbike got closer.

Goodness. It was coming up her driveway. Was this "L"?

Alice wiped a hand across her mouth and put the plate down on the step next to her.

A man in a black leather jacket, his face invisible behind his opaque black helmet, lifted a casual gloved hand in greeting as he pulled up in front of her. He stopped the bike and turned off the ignition.

"Hey there," he said, as he pulled off his helmet and unzipped his jacket.

"Hey," said Alice, and coughed because she'd never said "Hey" to anyone before. He was so handsome, it was like a joke. He was all broad shoulders, biceps, piercing eyes, and stubbled jaw. Alice found herself

looking around for another woman. There was no point in such a gorgeous man without a friend or sister there so you could exchange
glances.

Surely, she wasn't *dating* him as well? It wouldn't be possible. He
was way out of her league. He was a cartoon character. She felt a wave
of giggles rising in her chest.

"What are you doing eating just before a session?" asked the sex god.

"A session?" asked Alice. Her mind raced. Oh, my Lord, maybe he
was a *gigolo* and he was here to *service her*. After all, she was a middle-
aged woman with a swimming pool.

"That's not like you."

He pulled off his leather jacket and his white T-shirt rode up to reveal his stomach.

Well, it wouldn't be the end of the world.

No sirrreee. If she'd paid in *advance*, for example . . .

Alice began to giggle helplessly.

He smiled warily. "What's the joke?" He rested his helmet on the
front of his bike and walked over toward her. What could she say?
You're so good-looking, I find it hilarious.

She was giggling so hard her legs felt weak. He looked frightened.
For heaven's sake. Attractive people were still real. They had feelings.
Alice took a hold of herself.

"I had an accident," she said, looking up at him. "Last week. At the
gym. Hit my head. I'm suffering a bit of memory loss. So, I'm sorry, I
don't know who you are, or, ah, why you're here."

"You're kidding." He looked down at her suspiciously. "It's not April
Fools' Day, is it?"

"No," sighed Alice. Her giggles drifted away. She had a bit of a
headache actually. Damned head. "I don't know who you are."

"It's me," he said. "Luke."

"I'm sorry, Luke. I need more information."

He laughed a bit, and his eyes darted around nervously as if someone might be watching him make a fool of himself. "I'm your personal trainer. I come every Monday morning to give you a training session."

Oh, for heaven's sake. No wonder she was so skinny.

"So, we exercise, is that right? What do we do exactly?"

"Well, we vary it. A bit of cardio, some weights. We've been doing well with the interval training lately."

Alice had no idea what he was talking about.

"I just had three pieces of custard tart," she said, holding up the plate.

Luke sat down next to her and helped himself to the last piece of tart. "Yeah, I won't tell you how many calories you just consumed."

"Oh, thousands!" said Alice. "Thousands of divinely delicious calories."

He gave her an odd look, and said, "Well if you've got a head injury, I suppose we shouldn't be training today."

"No," said Alice. She didn't want to exercise in front of him. The very thought made her feel self-conscious. "I'll still pay, of course."

"That's okay."

"No, no, I insist."

"Well, let's just make it a hundred."

Geez. What did he normally charge?

"So, this memory thing is just temporary, I assume?" he said. "What do the doctors say?"

Alice waved him away irritably. She didn't want to talk to him about that. *One hundred dollars!* "How long have you been my personal trainer?"

Luke stretched out his long legs and leaned back on his elbows. "Oh, wow, it must be coming up to three years now. You and Gina were, like, maybe my second-ever clients. Bloody hell, she made me laugh in the beginning. Remember the fuss she made whenever we did the stairs down at the park? *Not the stairs, Luke, anything but the stairs.* She got pretty good, though. You both got so fit." He stopped talking and Alice realized with a start that he was trying not to cry.

"Sorry," he said in a muffled voice. "It's just that I never knew anyone who died before. It sort of freaks me out. Every time I come over to train you, I think of her. I mean, obviously you miss her so much more than me. Probably sounds stupid."

"I don't remember her," said Alice.

Luke looked at her, shocked. "You don't remember *Gina*?"

"No. I mean—I know she used to be my friend. And I know she's dead."

"Wow." He seemed lost for words. Finally he came up with one. "Freaky."

Alice stretched her neck from side to side. She felt a strong desire to eat or drink something quite specific, except she couldn't work out what it was. Frankly, it was making her feel quite irritable.

"Luke," she said snappishly. "Did I ever talk to you about Nick?"

If she was paying him one hundred dollars for a chat, she might as well gather some useful information.

He smiled, revealing chunky white teeth. He was a walking multivitamin advertisement. "You and Gina were always trying to get the male perspective from me on your marriage problems. I'd say, 'Hey, girls, I'm outnumbered here!'"

"Yes," said Alice. She was surprised at just how very, very irritable she was feeling. "It's just that I don't remember why Nick and I are splitting up."

"Oh," said Luke. He flipped over on his stomach and started doing push-ups on the top veranda step. "I remember once you said that in the end your divorce all came down to one thing. I went home and told my girlfriend that night. I knew she'd be interested."

He put one arm behind his back and started doing his push-ups on one hand. Was that really necessary?

"So . . ." said Alice, as he switched arms with a grunt. "What was that one thing?"

"I can't remember." He flipped back over and grinned at the expression on Alice's face. "You want me to call her?"

"Could you?"

He pulled out a mobile phone from his pocket and pushed a button.

"Hey, babe. Yeah, no, nothing's wrong. I'm just with a client. Do you remember I told you that lady said her divorce was caused by one thing? Yeah, no, I just want to know, what was that one thing?"

He listened.

"Really? You're sure? Okay. Love ya."

He hung up and looked at Alice. "Lack of sleep."

"Lack of sleep," repeated Alice. "That doesn't make much sense."

"No, that's what my girlfriend said, but I remember Gina seemed to understand."

Alice sighed and scratched the side of her face. She was sick of hearing about Gina. "I'm feeling really grumpy. I need chocolate or . . . something."

"You probably need to see your dealer," said Luke.

"My dealer?" What next? Was she a drug addict? Did she drop the kids off at school and then go home and snort a few lines of cocaine? She must be! How else did she know this drug-addict sort of terminology, like "snort a few lines"?

"The coffee shop. Your body is screaming for a flat white."

"But I don't drink coffee," said Alice.

"You're a caffeine junkie," said Luke. "I never see you without a takeaway coffee in your hand."

"I haven't had a coffee since my accident."

"Have you had a headache?"

"Well, yes, but I thought that was the injury."

"It was probably the caffeine withdrawal as well. This might be a good opportunity to give it up. I've been trying to get you to cut back for ages."

"No," said Alice, because now the desire she'd been feeling had a label. She could smell coffee beans. She could taste it. She wanted it right now. "Do you know where I get my coffee?"

"Sure. Dino's. According to you, they do the best coffee in Sydney."

Alice looked at him blankly.

"Next to the cinema. On the highway."

"Right." Alice stood up. "Well, thanks."

"Oh. We're done? Okay." Luke stood up, towering over her. He seemed to be waiting for something.

Alice realized with a start that he wanted his money. She went inside and found her purse. It was physically painful to hand over two fifty-dollar notes. He actually wasn't that good-looking at all.

Luke's huge hand closed cheerfully around the cash. "Well, I hope you're back to yourself next week, eh? We'll do a killer session to make up!"

"Great!" beamed Alice. She *paid* this man over a hundred dollars to tell her how to exercise each week?

She watched him roar out of the driveway and shook her head. Right. Coffee. She looked at the step where Luke had done his push-ups and suddenly she was down on her hands and knees, palms flat, body horizontal, stomach muscles pulled in hard, and she was bending her elbows and bringing her chest smoothly down toward the step.

One, two, three, four . . .

Good Lord, she was doing push-ups.

She counted to thirty before she collapsed, her chest burning, arms aching, and yelled, "Beat that!" as she looked around triumphantly for someone who wasn't there.

There was silence.

Alice hugged her knees to her chest and looked at the For Sale sign across the road.

She had a feeling the person she'd been looking for was Gina.

Gina.

It was very strange to miss a person she didn't even know.

Chapter 24

Elisabeth's Homework for Jeremy

Well, I don't know, you seemed a bit grumpy this morning. Is that allowed? Are therapists allowed to have feelings? I don't think so, J. Save them for your own therapy sessions. Not on my time, buddy.

I really wanted a bit more praise when I showed you how many pages I'd written for my homework. Couldn't you tell that, as a therapist? I mean, I know you're not meant to read it, but the reason I brought along my notebook was so you could say something like "Wow! I wish all my clients were as committed to this process as you!" Or you could have said what nice handwriting I had. Just a suggestion. You're the one who is meant to be good with people. Instead you just looked a bit taken aback, as if you didn't even remember asking me to do the homework. It always bugged me when teachers forgot to ask for the homework they'd set. It made the world seem undependable.

Anyway, today, you wanted to talk about the coffee shop incident.

Personally, I think you were just curious about it. You were feeling a bit bored for a Monday morning and thought it might spice things up.

You seemed quite testy when I said I preferred to talk about Ben and the adoption issue. The customer is always right, Jeremy.

This is what happened in the coffee shop, if you must know.

It was a Friday morning and I'd stopped in at Dino's on the way to work. I was having a large skim cappuccino because I wasn't pregnant or in the middle of the cycle. There was a woman at the table next to me with a baby and a toddler about two years old.

A little girl. With brown curly hair. Ben has brown curly hair. Well, actually, he doesn't because he gets it cut really close to his head like a car thief but I've seen photos from before we met. When I used to imagine our children I always gave them brown curly hair like Ben's.

So, there was that, but she wasn't particularly cute or anything. She had a dirty face and she was being sort of whiny.

The mother was talking on her mobile phone and smoking a cigarette.

Well, she wasn't smoking a cigarette at all.

But she *looked* like a smoker. That sort of thin, edgy face. She was telling someone a story on the mobile phone that was all about how she put someone in their place and she kept saying, "It was just *too* funny." How can something be too funny, Jeremy?

Anyway, she wasn't watching the little girl. It's like she forgot the child even existed.

Dino's is on the Pacific Highway. The door is always being opened and closed as people come in and out.

So I was watching the little girl. Not in a weird, obsessive infertile way. Just watching her, idly.

The door opened to let in a Mothers' Group. Prams. And mothers.

I thought, Time to go.

I stood up and the mothers came crashing through with their giant prams, sending chairs and tables skidding, and I watched the little girl slip out the door and onto the street.

The woman on the phone kept talking. I said, "Excuse me!" and nobody heard me. Two mothers had already sat down and were busy unbuttoning shirts and pulling out breasts to feed babies (this relaxed attitude to breast-feeding has got a bit too relaxed if you ask me) while they shrieked coffee orders across the room.

As I walked out of the coffee shop, the little girl was toddling straight toward the curb. Semi-trailers and four-wheel-drives were thundering down the highway. I had to run to get to her. I scooped her into the air just as she was about to step down into the gutter.

I saved the kid's life.

And I looked back to the coffee shop and the thin-faced mother was still on her mobile phone and the Mothers' Group was deep in conversation and the little girl was in my arms, smelling of sugar and maybe a touch of cigarette smoke. One fat little hand resting so trustingly on my shoulder.

And I kept walking. I just walked off with her.

I wasn't thinking. It wasn't like I was planning to dye her hair blond and drive off to the Northern Territory to live with her in a caravan by the sea, where we would both become nut brown in the sun and live on seafood and fresh fruit and I could homeschool her and . . . Kidding! I wasn't thinking any of that.

I was just walking.

The little girl was giggling as if it was a game. If she'd cried, I would have taken her straight back, but she was giggling. She liked me. Maybe she was grateful that I saved her life.

And then, pounding feet behind me, and the thin-faced woman grabbing at my shoulder, screaming, "Hey!" Her face filled with terror, her nails scratching my skin as she dragged the little girl out of my arms, and then the little girl did cry because she got a fright, and the mother was saying, "It's okay, sweetie, it's okay," and looking at me with such revulsion.

Oh God, the shame and the horror.

Some of the mothers had come out of the coffee shop and were standing silently, cupping their babies' heads and staring, as if I was a traffic accident. The owner of the coffee shop, Dino himself, I guess, had come out, too. I'd only ever seen the top half of him over the counter. He was shorter than I expected. It was a surprise: like seeing a newsreader in full length. It's the only time I've seen him serious. He's normally one of those permanent chucklers.

All those people watching me and judging. It was like I was bleeding in public. I felt something come loose in my mind. I really did. It was an actual physical sensation of going crazy. Maybe there is a word for it, Jeremy?

I collapsed to my knees on the footpath, which was so

unnecessary, and also excruciatingly painful. The grazes took weeks to heal.

That's when Alice turned up. She was wearing a new jacket I'd never seen before, hurrying into Dino's, handbag swinging, frowning. I saw the expression on her face when she recognized me. She actually recoiled, as if she'd seen a rat. She must have been mortified. I had to pick her local coffee shop for my public meltdown.

She was nice, though. I have to admit she was nice. She came and knelt down beside me and when our eyes met, it reminded me of when we were children and we'd run into each other in the school playground and I would suddenly feel as if I'd been performing on a stage all day, because only Alice knew my real self.

"What happened?" she whispered.

I was crying too hard to talk.

She fixed everything. It turned out she knew the mother of the child, as well as some of the Mothers' Group women. There was a lot of intense mother-to-mother talk while I stayed kneeling on the footpath. She made their faces soften. The crowd melted away.

She helped me up off the footpath and took me to her car and strapped me into the passenger seat.

"Do you want to talk about it?" she said.

I said I didn't.

"Where do you want to go?" she said.

I said I didn't know.

Then she did exactly the right thing and drove me to Frannie. We sat on Frannie's tiny balcony, drinking tea and eating buttered arrowroot biscuits, and we didn't talk about what had happened.

In fact, we talked about something quite interesting. I could see some new stationery on Frannie's desk, and it prompted me to ask her about the time I found her writing a mysterious letter when I was a teenager. I told her that Alice and I had been convinced that she had a secret lover.

Frannie didn't look embarrassed, just dismissive. She waved her hand impatiently as if it wasn't an important subject. She said she had once been briefly engaged when she was in her late thirties, and she still wrote occasionally to her ex-fiancé, and she probably just hadn't wanted to talk about it at the time.

"So you're still friends?" said Alice, all agog.

"I guess you could say that," Frannie had said. There was a peculiar quizzical expression on her face.

"And he writes back?" I asked.

And she said, "Well, no."

So that was odd. And it seemed like she was about to say more but then we had to rush off because Alice had to pick up the children from school, so I never got to hear more about this man, this "Phil" who never answers her letters. Did she leave him at the altar all those years ago? Why has she never mentioned him before?

I've been meaning to call Frannie to ask her about it, but I haven't even got the energy to be nosy these days. Also I've been avoiding her because I know she thinks I should stop trying to have a baby. She said it at least two years ago. She said that sometimes you had to be brave enough to "point your life in a new direction." I was a bit snappy at the time. I said a baby wasn't a "direction." Besides which, as far as I can see, *she* never pointed her life in a new direction. We just fell into her life after Dad died.

Thank goodness we did, of course. And who knows, maybe there will be a convenient death in our local area! Think positive! That father two doors down always looks like he's about to drop dead when he mows the lawn.

Anyway, the day after my psychotic episode I went to my GP and asked for a referral to see a good psychiatrist. I wonder if you pay her a spotter's fee.

So that's how I came into your life, Jeremy.

When Alice walked into Dino's Coffee Shop her senses were flooded with familiarity. The aroma of coffee and pastries. The rhythmic thud and hiss of the espresso machine.

"Alice, my love!" said a small, dark-haired man behind the counter. He was working the coffee machine with two hands, expertly and elegantly, as if it were a musical instrument. "I heard on the grapevine you had an accident! Lost your memory! But you never forget Dino, do you?"

"Well," said Alice carefully, "I think I remember your coffee."

Dino laughed as if she'd made a hilarious joke. "Of course you do, my love! Of course you do! I won't be one moment. I know you're in a hurry. Busy lady. Here you go."

Without waiting for an order, he handed her a takeaway cup. "How you feeling, anyway? You all better? You remember everything? You ready for the big day on Sunday? Mega Meringue Day at last! My daughter is so excited! All she talks about is '*Daddy, Daddy, this pie will be the biggest in the world!*'"

"Mmmm," said Alice. She was assuming that by Sunday she would have her memory back, because she really had no idea how to bake the world's biggest lemon pie.

She peeled off the lid of the cup and took a sip. Ewww. No sugar, and extremely strong. She took another sip. Actually very good. She didn't need sugar. She took another sip, and another and another. She wanted to tip back her head and pour it straight down her throat. The caffeine was zipping through her veins, clearing her head, making her heart beat faster and her vision sharpen.

"Maybe you need two today?" chortled Dino.

"Maybe I do," agreed Alice.

"How is your sister, by the way?" said Dino, still chuckling. He appeared to be a jolly fellow. He stopped and clicked his fingers. "Ah, my mind! I keep forgetting, my wife gave me something to give to her."

"My sister?" Alice ran her finger around the edge of the cup and licked the froth while she wondered how well Dino knew Elisabeth. "She's okay, I guess." She is an entirely different person. She appears to be desperately unhappy. I'm not sure how I've wronged her.

"I went home and told my wife the whole story, about how this lady walks off with a child, and then when she collapsed like that, crying, and none of us knew what to do! I was making her coffee! That's no help, is it? Even Dino's coffee! Those stupid women wanting to call the police."

Good Lord. Had Elisabeth tried to kidnap a child? Alice felt pity (Her poor darling Elisabeth, how bad must she be feeling to so publicly break a rule!), a horrified shame (How *embarrassing*! How illegal!) and guilt (How could she be worried about what people thought when her sister was obviously suffering so badly?).

Dino continued, "I said to those women, 'No harm done!' It was so lucky you showed up and made them see sense, and when you told me her story, so sad! Anyway, my wife gave me this. It's an African fertility figurine. If you have one of these dolls, you give birth to a beautiful baby. That's the legend."

He handed her a small dark wooden doll with a Post-it note stuck to it saying "Alice." The doll seemed to be an African woman in tribal dress with an oversized head.

"That's so sweet of your wife." Alice handled the doll reverently. Was his wife African perhaps and this was some sort of mystical tribal heirloom?

"She bought it off the Internet," confided Dino. "For her cousin, who couldn't get pregnant. Nine months later—baby! Although to be honest, not such a beautiful baby." He slapped his knee, his face creased with mirth. "I say to my wife, That's one ugly baby! Got a big head, like the doll!" He could hardly speak, he was laughing so hard now. "Big head, I said. Like the doll!"

Alice smiled. Dino handed her another coffee and he became serious again.

"Nick came in the other day," he said. "He didn't look too good. I said, You should get back together with your wife. I said, It's not right. I remember when I first opened the shop and you came in every week-end with little Madison. All three of you in overalls. She used to help you with the painting. You two were so proud of her. Never saw prouder parents! Remember?"

"Hmmmm," said Alice.

"I told Nick that you two should get back together, be a family again," said Dino. "I said, What went so wrong you can't fix? None of my business, right? My wife says, Dino, it's not your business! I say, I don't care, I say what I think, that's just me."

"What did Nick say?" asked Alice. She was already halfway through the next cup of coffee.

"He said, 'I would fix it if I could, mate.'"

Alice drove home chanting Nick's words in her head. He would if he could, so therefore . . . why not!

She had the takeaway cup of coffee in a handy cup holder close to the steering wheel. She found she could steer this enormous car with one hand and take sips of coffee with the other. So many useful new skills! The caffeine was making her tremble with energy. She felt like her eyes were protruding. When the light changed to green and the car in front didn't move straightaway, she shoved it along with a bossy beep of her horn.

That sharp voice was back in her head, working out everything she had to do before she picked the children up at 3:30 p.m. "You need to be on time, Mum," Tom had told her. "Monday afternoons are a pretty tight schedule."

Well, you can't spend your day lounging around eating custard tart. You won't fit into those beautiful clothes for long, will you? Speaking of which, what about laundry? You probably should do laundry when you get home. Mothers are always complaining about washing.

What else do they complain about? Groceries! When do you shop? Check pantry. Do list. You probably have a list somewhere. You seem like the sort of person who has a list. What about dinner tonight? Snacks when they come from school? Were the children used to freshly baked cookies on arrival?

Ring Sophie. She's your best friend! You must have told her something about what's going on.

Your diary says you've got a Mega Meringue meeting at 1 p.m. Presumably you've got to run it. Great! That should be a hoot. Find out where it is! How? Ring someone. Ring that Kate Harper if you must. Or your "boyfriend."

Would fix it if he could. Would fix it if he could.

Laundry.

Yes, you already said that.

Laundry!

Yes, calm down.

She shouldn't have had the two cups of coffee. Her heart was beating much too fast. She took a few deep, shaky breaths to steady herself.

She couldn't keep up with her own body. She felt as if she needed to run crazily across a huge expanse of grass, flinging her body about like a puppy let off its leash.

When she got home she ran through the house as if she were in some sort of weird competition, gathering piles of clothes from laundry hampers and the floors of the children's bedrooms and bathrooms. There was a lot. She pounded down the stairs to the laundry. No surprise to see a huge, shiny-white washing machine taking up half the room. She lifted the lid ready to toss in the clothes when she felt a rush of feelings. Embarrassed. Betrayed. Shocked.

What did it mean? The memory flipped to the front of her brain like a neat index card. Of course. Something had happened right here. Right here in this extraordinarily clean laundry. Something horrible.

That's right. It was a party.

In the summer. Still warm late in the evening. There were tubs of ice on the laundry floor. Bottles of beer and wine and champagne poking out of the melting ice cubes. She went to get a new bottle of champagne and she was laughing as she pushed open the door and when she saw them, she automatically said, "Hi!" like an idiot, before her brain caught up with what they were doing, what she was seeing. A tiny graceful woman with closely cropped red hair sitting up on the washing machine, her legs apart, and Nick standing in front of her, his hands flat on the machine on either side of her legs, his head bent. Her husband was kissing another woman in the laundry.

Alice stared down at the pile of clothes in the machine. She could see the woman's face so clearly. The delicate bones of her face. She could even hear her voice. Sugar-sweet and childlike to match her tiny body. It made her teeth ache.

She poured in a scoop of washing powder and slammed down the machine lid. How dare Nick guffaw when she asked if he'd had an affair? That kiss was worse than catching them in bed together. It was worse because it was so obviously a kiss at the beginning. Early kisses were so much more erotic than early sex. Sex at the beginning of a relationship was fumbly and silly and vaguely gynecological, like a doctor's appointment. But fully clothed kisses, before you'd slept together, were delicious and mysterious.

Nick had kissed her for the first time up against the car after they'd just seen *Lethal Weapon 3* at the movies. He tasted of popcorn, with a hint of chocolate. He was wearing a black jumper over a white T-shirt and jeans, and he was a bit stubbly under his lower lip and even as he was kissing her, she was already carefully saving it up as a memory, knowing that she'd be sitting at her computer screen the next day, reliving it. She'd pulled it out and replayed it like an old movie so many times. She had described it in minute detail to her friend Sophie, who had been in a relationship for five years and had therefore moaned with jealousy, even though Jack was the love of her life.

Sophie. Her oldest friend. Bridesmaid at her wedding.

She would ring Sophie right now. There was no way she hadn't called Sophie and told her about the horror of that kiss in the laundry. First she would have called Elisabeth. Then Sophie. She would have skewed the story for each of them. For Elisabeth she would have concentrated on her own feelings. "How could he do that to me?" she would have asked and her voice would have quivered. For Sophie she would have spun out the story for maximum shock: "So I walked into the laundry to get some champagne and you will never in a million years guess what I saw. Go on, guess." From Elisabeth she would have got sympathy and very clear instructions on what to do next. From Sophie she would have got shock and fury and an invitation to go out right now and get very drunk.

She found her address book and Sophie's mobile number. It seemed that Sophie was living in Dee Why. The northern beaches. Good for her. She'd always wanted to live by the beach, but Jack preferred to live close to the city. She must have won out in the end. They must be married with children by now, although of course Alice had to remember not to take that for granted. She hoped Sophie hadn't had fertility problems like Elisabeth. Or she and Jack could have broken up? No. Not possible.

"Sophie Drew."

Goodness. Everyone had become so professional and grown-up.

"Sophie, hi, it's me, Alice."

There was a slight pause. "Oh, hi, Alice. How are you?"

"Well, you're not going to *believe* what happened to me," said Alice, and she realized she was feeling strangely silly. Almost nervous. Why? It was only Sophie.

There was another pause. "What happened to you?"

There was something not quite right. Sophie's voice was too polite. Alice wanted to cry. Oh, for heaven's sake, I can't have lost you as well, can I? Who do I *talk* to?

She didn't bother spinning out the story. She said, "I had an accident. Hit my head. I've lost my memory."

This time there was an even longer pause. Then she heard Sophie say to someone in the background, "I won't be long. Just tell them to hold on."

Her voice came back. Louder. Maybe a touch impatient. "Sorry, Alice. So, umm, you had an accident?"

"Are we still friends?" said Alice desperately. "We are still friends, aren't we, Soph?"

"Of course we are," said Sophie immediately, warmly, except now her voice had an undercurrent of "*Something weird is going on here. Must tread carefully!*"

"It's just that my last proper memory is of being pregnant with Madison. And now I find I've got three children, and Nick and I aren't together anymore, and I can't work out why, and Elisabeth—"

"No, no, not that one! The green one!" Sophie spoke sharply. "Sorry. I'm in the middle of a shoot for the new line. It's a madhouse around here."

"Oh. What do you do?"

Another pause. "Does that look green to you? Because it sure doesn't look green to me. Alice, I'm sorry, but can I call you back?"

"Oh. Sure."

"Look. I know we keep saying it but we must catch up!"

"Okay." So they weren't friends anymore. Not proper friends. They were "must catch up" friends.

"I mean, the last time I saw you was when we had that drinks thing with that friend of yours. The neighbor? Gina. How's she?"

Gina, Gina, Gina. It occurred to Alice that she wouldn't have called Elisabeth or Sophie about the kiss in the laundry. She would have called Gina.

"She's dead."

"Sorry, she's what? Green! Green! Are you color-blind? Look, Alice, I've got to go. I'll call! Soon!"

"Just tell me one thing," said Alice, but the phone was beeping at her. Sophie had gone.

Just like everyone, it seemed.

The phone rang in her hand and Alice jumped as if it had come alive.

"Hello?"

"Oh, you sound much better." It was her mother. Alice relaxed. Barb might now be the salsa-dancing, cleavage-baring wife of Roger, but she was still her mother.

"I've just been speaking to Sophie," said Alice.

"Oh, that's nice. She's so famous these days, isn't she? After that article? I was just talking to someone about her the other day. Who was it? Oh, I know! It was the lady who comes to do Roger's feet. The chiropractor. No, no, that's not it. The podiatrist. She said her daughter wanted one of those 'Sophie Drew' handbags for her birthday. I said, well, I've known Sophie since she was eleven years old, and I was nearly going to offer to try and get a discount for her, because it has to be said, Roger has awful hairy feet, so I do feel a bit sorry for her, but then I thought, you and Sophie don't really see much of each other these days, do you? Just Christmas cards, isn't it? So I changed the subject quick smart in case she asked, because she's that sort of person, I think, who likes to try and use connections to get bargains. Gina was a bit like that, wasn't she? Not that there's anything wrong with it, I guess. It's quite a clever way to live your life really, oh dear, what an absolute tragedy, it really is, anyway, what made me think of Gina? Oh yes, ah, connections. Anyway, I've got three reasons why I rang, I've actually written them down, my memory is just shocking these days—now speaking of which, how *are* you, darling?"

"I'm fine," began Alice.

"Oh good, I'm so pleased. Frannie was making such a fuss about it. I said, 'You watch, she'll have her memory back by Monday.'"

"I'm remembering some things," began Alice. Should she ask her mother about Nick and the kiss in the laundry?

"Wonderful!" Her mother wavered and then obviously decided to take the optimistic approach. "Wonderful! Now, darling, I wondered, when you said at the hospital that you and Nick might be getting back together, is that something that I possibly shouldn't have mentioned to anyone? Because I happened to run into Jennifer Turner today at the shops."

"Jennifer Turner?" The name didn't mean anything to her.

"Yes, you know. That fierce sort of girl. The lawyer."

"Oh, you mean *Jane* Turner." Mmmm. The first face she saw when she woke up in this strange new life. Jane who was helping her divorce Nick.

"Yes, Jane. She wanted to know how you were. She said you hadn't been answering her texts."

Texts. What did that mean?

"Anyway, I said you were fine, and then I mentioned that you and Nick were getting back together. Well, she seemed quite taken aback. She said to tell you that you must not, under any circumstances, sign anything. Went on and on about it. I wondered if maybe I shouldn't have said anything? Have I messed up?"

"Of course not, Mum," said Alice automatically.

"Thank goodness, because Roger and I are just thrilled. Thrilled! We were thinking we could take the children for a weekend and you and Nick could go somewhere romantic. That was the second thing on my list. I'll just cross it off. You say the word. We'd love to have them. Roger said he'd even foot the bill for a meal at somewhere fancy-schmancy. He's so generous like that."

"That sounds great."

"Really? Oh, I'm so pleased because I mentioned it to Elisabeth and she said she thought once you got your memory back that you would be 'singing a different tune.' But you know, she takes the pessimistic approach to things these days, poor thing, and that was my third reason for calling. Have you heard from her by any chance? I'm desperate to know if she's got the results yet. I've been ringing and ringing and no answer."

"What results?"

"Today was the blood test. You know, for the last egg. Oh, wait a minute, I always get that word wrong. Embryo." Her mother's voice broke. "Oh, Alice, I've been praying and praying and sometimes I have to admit I get a bit *cross* with God. Elisabeth and Ben have tried so hard. Just one little baby isn't too much to ask for, is it?"

"No," said Alice. She looked at Dino's fertility doll sitting on the counter. Why didn't Elisabeth tell her there was a blood test today?

Her mother sighed. "I said to Roger, I'm so happy myself now, why can't my girls be happy, too?"

Elisabeth's Homework for Jeremy

A lot of people have left messages for me today.

Mum has called five times.

I just saw a missed call from Alice.

Oh, and the nurse has called twice trying to give me the results of today's blood test.

Layla has called, probably wondering where I am, because I went out at lunchtime and for some reason I just never got the energy to go back to the office. She probably thinks it's because she offended me by not asking about Alice.

Ben has called three times.

I don't seem to be able to call anyone back. I'm just sitting here behind the wheel of my car outside your office, writing to you.

Now the phone is ringing again. Ring, ring! Ring, ring! Engage with the world, Elisabeth! Go away, all of you.

Alice was hanging clothes on the line (it was taking forever) when the phone rang again. She had to run to answer it.

"Hello?" she said breathlessly.

"Oh, hi, it's me," said Nick. He paused. "Nick."

"Yes, I recognized your voice actually."

You kissed another woman in the laundry! I can't believe you did that! Should she mention the kiss? No. She should think about the right way to approach it first.

He said, "I just thought I should call and see how you, how your ah, your head, your injury, is today. Were you okay driving the children to school?"

"It's a bit late if I wasn't," said Alice tartly. Last night she'd had to *iron* all their school uniforms, do all the cleaning up, and make very specific lunches for each of them (after Tom had politely pointed out that was what she normally did on a Sunday night).

"Oh, good," said Nick. "So, I assume, you've got that memory thing all sorted out?"

"Well, I've got one memory back," burst out Alice. It appeared she was going to mention the kiss after all. It was physically impossible not to mention it. "I remember you kissing that woman in the laundry."

"Kissing a woman in the laundry?"

"Yes. At a party. I came in to get a drink."

There was silence and then Nick laughed sharply.

"Sitting on the washing machine, right?"

"Yes," said Alice, wondering how he could sound so smug, as if this point went to him, when it so clearly went to her.

"You remember *me* kissing a woman sitting on our washing machine?"

"Yes!"

"You know what? I never even looked at another woman while we were together. I never kissed another woman. I never slept with another woman."

"But I remember—"

"Yeah. I know exactly what you remember, and I find that very interesting."

Alice was baffled. "But—"

"Very interesting. Look, I've got to go, but clearly you haven't got your memory back properly yet and you need to see a doctor. If you're not capable of looking after the children, you need to let me know. You've got a responsibility to them."

Oh, but it was fine to leave her with them last night when he knew perfectly well that she didn't even recognize them, let alone know how to look after them. It wasn't logical, and yet, he was speaking in that pompous, I'm-so-rational-you're-so-irrational voice, each word stuffed with his own rightness. She could remember that voice from arguments in the past, like that morning when they didn't have milk for breakfast, and the night when they ran late for his sister's first baby's christening, and the time neither of them had enough cash for the ferry tickets, and each time he had put on that voice. That superior, crisp, businesslike voice, with a hint of a sigh. It drove her bananas.

Each time he used that voice it brought back the other occasions he'd used it before and she would think, That's right, I can't stand it when you talk like that.

"You know what?" she said. "I'm *glad* we're getting a divorce!"

As she slammed the phone down, she could hear him laughing.

Chapter 25

The Mega Meringue Committee turned up at Alice's door at 1:00 p.m. She'd forgotten all about them.

When the doorbell rang she was sitting on the living room floor surrounded by photo albums. She'd been there for hours, flipping pages, peeling photos off so she could hold them close to her and study for clues.

There were photos of picnics and bushwalks and days at the beach, birthday parties and Easters and Christmases. She'd lost so many Christmas memories! It gave her a pain in the center of her chest seeing the photos of tangle-haired children in their pajamas, their faces solemn with concentration as they unwrapped presents under a huge, gorgeously decorated tree.

Maybe she could go to the doctor and ask if she could please have all her happy memories returned, minus the sad ones.

The photos were mostly of the children and Nick. Alice would have been the one behind the camera. Nick always looked so capable when he was taking a photo, a grave, professional look on his face, but actually he was hopeless, skimming off the tops of people's heads.

Alice had discovered she could take good photos when she was a child. After their father died nobody had taken photos of them. He had been the photographer and their mother would no more think about trying to use his camera than she would have tried to change a light globe. It was Alice who picked up his camera one day and worked out how to use it. In those years when their mother disappeared into herself and "old Miss Jeffrey" next door turned into "Frannie," their honorary grandmother, Alice also taught herself how to change light globes, fix running toilets, and cook chops and veggies, while Elisabeth learned how to demand refunds, pay bills, fill in forms, and talk to strangers.

Whenever she came upon another rare photo of Nick she tried to read the expression in his eyes. Was it possible to track the decline of their marriage? No. She could track the decline of his *hair* over the years, but his smile at the person behind the camera seemed unchangingly genuine and happy.

In the ones where they were together, they always had their arms around each other, their bodies curved together. If a body-language expert were asked to objectively judge their marriage on the basis of these photo albums they would surely say, "This is a happy, loving, good-humored family and the likelihood of that couple breaking up is nil."

She didn't bother much with the photos of people she didn't recognize but one face kept appearing again and again, and it dawned on her that this must surely be Gina. She was a busty, big-toothed woman with a heap of dark curly hair. She and Alice always seemed to be photographed holding champagne or cocktail glasses up to the camera like trophies. They seemed to be very physical together, which was unusual for Alice. She had never had those sorts of lavish friendships where you threw your arms around each other, but Alice and this woman always seemed to have their heads angled together so their cheeks were touching, big wide lipsticky smiles for the camera. Alice felt embarrassed by these photos. "Oh stop it, you don't even *know* her," she said out loud at a photo of herself actually planting a big, smoochy kiss on Gina's cheek.

Alice stared at the photos of Gina for ages, waiting for the recognition—and the grief? But nothing. She looked sort of fun, she guessed, although not really the sort of woman Alice would have picked as a friend. She looked like she had the potential to be a bit overbearing. A loud, zany, tiring type.

But maybe not. Actually, Alice looked a bit loud and zany herself in some of those photos. Maybe she *was* loud and zany now that she was so slim and drank so much coffee.

There were photos of Alice and Nick together with Gina and a man who must be her husband. Mike Boyle. That physiotherapist who had moved to Melbourne. So these were the "happier times" he'd mentioned on his business card. There were a lot of BBQs and dinner parties (lots of empty wine bottles on the table in an unfamiliar room that must have been Gina and Mike's house). She worked out from the pictures that Gina and Mike had two pretty dark-haired daughters—twins, perhaps?—about the same age as Tom. There were photos of the children playing together, eating giant slices of watermelon, splashing about in the pool, curled up asleep on couches.

The two families had gone on camping trips together. It looked like they'd been back regularly to some beach house with stunning ocean views.

Friendship and holidays. A swimming pool. Champagne and sunshine and laughter. It seemed like a dream life.

But maybe every life looked wonderful if all you saw was the photo albums. People always obediently smiled and tilted their heads when a camera was put in front of them. Perhaps seconds after the shutter clicked, she and Nick sprang apart, avoiding each other's eyes, their smiles replaced by snarls.

She was just studying the photos of Elisabeth's wedding (she and Ben looked so young and unguarded, their faces rosy, Elisabeth slender and luminous) when the doorbell rang. She jumped to her feet and left the albums with all those days and days of forgotten memories on the floor.

There were two women at the door, and another three were walking up the driveway. A couple were complete strangers but she recognized the rest from the party and from dropping off the children at school that morning.

"Mega Meringue meeting?" guessed Alice as she held open the door for them. They were carrying folders and notebooks and looked terrifyingly efficient.

"Only six days to go!" said a tall, elegant, gray-haired woman, making her eyebrows pop up and down above her square-framed glasses.

"How are you?" said another one with dimples who kissed her warmly on the cheek. "I've been meaning to call all weekend. Bill said he couldn't believe it when he was on the treadmill and he saw you go past on the stretcher. He said he never expected to see Alice Love flat on her back. Oh dear, that doesn't sound quite right."

Alice remembered the red-faced man on the treadmill saying he would get "Maggie" to call.

"Maggie?" she tried.

The woman squeezed her arm. "Sorry! I'm in a silly mood today!"

Without being asked, the women all trooped into the dining room and sat themselves around the table, placing their notebooks in front of them.

"Tea, coffee?" said Alice faintly, wondering if she fed them.

"I've been hanging out for your muffins all morning," said the eyebrow popper.

"I'll come and help you bring it all in," said Maggie. Oh dear. It appeared they were used to a spread.

Alice registered Maggie's look of surprise when she saw the state of the kitchen. Last night's dinner plates and the children's breakfast dishes were still lying around. Alice had meant to clean up after she had the laundry on but the photo albums had distracted her. There were splashes of milk and hamburger mince all over the counters.

As Alice hurriedly checked through the freezer for muffins, Maggie put the kettle on and said, "I saw Kate Harper this morning. She said you and Nick were getting back together."

"*Yes!*" Alice pulled from the freezer a container labeled "Banana Muffins" and dated two weeks earlier, feeling quite fond of herself. Oh, you're a trouper, Alice.

"Well, I was a bit surprised," said Maggie.

Alice looked up at the tone of her voice. She sounded wounded.

"It's just that I know Dominick is pretty keen," continued Maggie, sounding as if she were trying to be diplomatic.

"Are you and Dominick friends?" asked Alice.

Maggie jerked her head in surprise. "I'm just saying, he's my big brother, and he's sort of vulnerable. If it's not going anywhere, maybe you should tell him?"

Oh Lord, she was his *sister*. Now that Alice looked, she could see a slight resemblance about the eyes. That Kate Harper was a real piece of work.

"And I don't know, Alice," continued Maggie. "All that stuff you were saying the other day, about how Nick never respected your opinion, and made you feel like you were stupid, and how you and Dominick had a much more equal relationship, and you loved the way he talked to you about the school, because Nick never talked to you about his work. What was that all about, then? And I don't mean to be rude, but I wondered, could this possibly be related to your head injury? I mean, I know that sounds like, 'Oh, you must be nuts not to want my brother!' But I just think that, well, you know, don't rush . . ."

Her voice drifted away, just like Dominick's did.

Nick didn't respect her opinion? But of course he did! Sometimes he thought she was a bit foolish about current affairs, but only in an adorable way.

Alice went to open her mouth, without knowing what she would say, when the doorbell rang again.

"Just a sec," she said, holding up her hand.

She ran down the hallway past the babble of female voices from her dining room and opened the door.

"So sorry I'm late," said a tiny red-haired woman with a sweet, childlike voice.

It was the woman who kissed Nick on the washing machine.

Elisabeth's Homework for Jeremy

So I called and got the blood-test results.

"Come in!" said Alice.

Her body definitely remembered this woman. The sound of her sugar-sweet voice actually made her feel slightly sick, like the way avocado always made her feel, because of that time she got violently ill after eating guacamole.

"I heard you fell over at the gym," said the woman. "Told you exercise was bad for you." Oh Lord, she was leaning in to kiss her on the cheek. This cheek-kissing thing was out of control. It was a Mega Meringue meeting! Shouldn't they keep things a bit more professional?

The woman was unraveling a scarf from her neck, casually looping it over Alice's hat stand and looking at Alice artlessly, without a shred of guilt. Could she do this if she had kissed Alice's husband in the laundry of this very house? *"I never looked at another woman. I never kissed another woman,"* Nick had said. So why did she remember it so clearly? And how did he know what she meant when she talked about it happening on the washing machine?

"You're late, Mrs. Holloway!" a voice called out from the dining room.

Holloway. Holloway. Alice mentally snapped her fingers. This was the deputy principal. She was far too tiny and pretty and sugary to be a deputy principal.

Mrs. Holloway waltzed into the dining room as if she owned the place while Alice went back into the kitchen. Dominick's sister had put Alice's muffins into the microwave and the smell of banana filled the kitchen.

"Mrs. Holloway," said Alice.

"Bleh," said Maggie, making a face without looking up from the boiling water she was pouring into a row of coffee mugs. She put down the kettle and winked at Alice. "You make sure you keep Mrs. H. in line if she tries to take over again. It's your meeting. You're in charge."

"About that," said Alice. "I can't run this meeting."

"Why not?"

"Dominick obviously didn't tell you—"

"Dominick doesn't tell me anything. You know brothers. Oh, right, you don't. Well, they're not like sisters."

Alice explained yet again about her memory loss, and how, yes, she would be seeing a doctor, and no, she didn't think she should be in bed, and no, she wasn't joking, and yes, it must have been quite a thump on the head.

Someone called out from the dining room, "What's going on in there? We can smell muffins!"

"Hold your horses!" called out Maggie. She turned back to Alice and said happily, "So *that's* why you've been talking about getting back together with Nick! You've forgotten the last ten years! Gosh. It must be the weirdest feeling. I'm trying to imagine it. What was I doing when I was twenty-six?"

Alice realized with a start that Maggie, who seemed so *middle-aged*, was actually four years younger than she was. In fact, all these grown-up women here today were probably in her age group.

Maggie chortled. "I'd say, 'Oh my God, how did you end up marrying the chubby guy who services your car!' And then I'd look down at my hips and think, 'What happened there?'"

She slapped herself on what looked to Alice like perfectly slim hips.

"It's getting boring in there." The tall, gray-haired woman with the glasses came into the kitchen and swung herself up onto the counter, swinging long, slim, blue-jeaned legs.

She lowered her voice. "You need to get in there fast, Alice, before Mrs. H. plans a coup. Don't worry, I've been subtly undermining everything she says." She lowered her voice even further. "If she thinks we'll ever let her live down the shame of the laundry incident, she's very much mistaken. The evil little troll."

"You know about the laundry incident?" Alice gripped the knife she was holding to cut the muffins.

"Alice has lost her memory," said Maggie. "She probably doesn't even know who you are. Alice, meet Nora." She paused. "Actually, you mustn't even know who I am! I'm Maggie! Did you even know that?" She had that disbelieving, self-conscious expression on her face that

Alice had seen so many times now. People couldn't quite believe you could forget *them*.

"There's a rumor going around you lost your memory," said Nora. "I didn't believe it. I heard someone in Dino's Coffee Shop talking about it, but I thought it was just the village grapevine gone haywire. Geez. What do the doctors say?"

"Did Nick kiss that Mrs. Holloway in the laundry?" asked Alice, feeling juvenile to be discussing kissing with this elegant gray-haired woman.

"Nick?" said Nora. "No, honey. It was Michael. Gina's husband. Gina walked in on them." She looked at Maggie. "She really has lost her memory."

"She doesn't remember *anything*," said Maggie, excitedly taking a huge bite of muffin. "It's like she's Rumpelstiltskin in the fairy tale."

"I think you mean Rip Van Winkle."

"Do I?"

"But I remember it so clearly," said Alice slowly. "I remember it as if it was me."

"Well, you were so upset for Gina," said Maggie. "Oh God, I just still cannot believe Gina isn't about to walk in here right this minute, carrying another bottle of champagne. Whenever I hear the pop of a champagne cork I think of her. I don't think I've accepted it yet."

"Unless, of course, the troll kissed Nick as well," said Nora thoughtfully.

"Can I take something in?" chimed a childlike voice.

"Mrs. H.!" said Nora calmly. "We were just talking about you."

"All good, I hope?"

"Of course! I'm sure our fine deputy principal doesn't have any *dirty laundry* that needs airing," said Nora.

Maggie choked on her muffin.

"Here you go," said Nora. "You can take those mugs in for Alice."

"Sure thing." Mrs. Holloway seemed unruffled. "Will we be getting started soon, Alice?" She looked at her watch. "It's just that I've got to be back at the school."

"Won't be long," said Nora briskly, her eyes hard.

Mrs. Holloway took the mugs and left.

As soon as the deputy principal walked out the door, Maggie slapped Nora on the back of her head, ruffling her smooth hair. "You're a shocker."

It was just like being with girls at school, except with wrinkles and gray hair and talk of children. Alice felt comforted by this. It seemed you still got to be silly when you grew up.

"But I don't understand," she said. "How can this Mrs. Holloway be deputy principal if she's . . ."

"Kissing dads in the laundry?" finished Nora. "We're the only ones who know about it. Gina made us promise not to tell anyone. Mrs. H. has got children herself at the school. Gina said she didn't want to be responsible for breaking up another marriage."

"You don't know how often I've had to bite my tongue whenever Dominick talks about her," said Maggie. "He thinks she's so professional. But anyway, I guess she just had too much to drink that night. We all make mistakes."

"Don't go all forgiving on us, Maggie," said Nora. "She doesn't deserve forgiveness. The bitch didn't even flinch when I said 'dirty laundry.'"

"She might have forgotten about it," said Maggie. "It's been three years."

"Were Mrs. Holloway and Mike having an affair?" asked Alice, and realized she was steeling herself for the answer. Even though she knew it hadn't been Nick, that raw, betrayed feeling remained.

"As far as we know, it was just that one drunken kiss," said Maggie.

"But it seemed to trigger all of Gina and Mike's problems. It never seemed fair. Gina and Mike break up, and meanwhile the Holloways still look like the golden couple. I saw them holding hands, do you mind, at the Trivia Night the other week and I thought, 'Someone please bring me a bucket.'"

"Maybe they've got an *arrangement*," mused Nora. "It could be an open marriage."

"Do you think?" said Maggie with wide eyes. Then she shook herself. "We'd really better go do this meeting."

"Maybe I should stay here," said Alice. "Tell them I'm sick." She had no idea how to "do a meeting."

"I'll run through the agenda," said Nora. "Just nod along. Anyway, you've had everything organized so well in advance, we all know exactly what we've got to do. You're the most efficient person I know, Alice."

"I wonder how that happened," sighed Alice. She licked her finger and pressed it against the muffin crumbs on the plate in front of her. She saw the two women were studying her, as if she were behaving oddly.

Instead of sucking her finger, she let it drop by her side and said, "Why are we making the world's biggest lemon meringue pie, anyway? Why not a cheesecake or something?"

"It was Gina's signature dish," said Maggie. "Remember? You're dedicating the day to Gina."

Of course she was. In the end, everything circled back to Gina.

Once she remembered Gina, she would remember everything.

Elisabeth's Homework for Jeremy

I feel like I could easily do one of two things.

I could drive out of Sydney. Maybe down that long winding ribbon of highway on the South Coast with the lush green hills and the flashes of turquoise sea. That would be cheerful.

And then I could find a long empty stretch of road with an appropriate telephone pole. One that's begging for a memorial cross.

And I could drive at it very fast.

Alternatively!

I could drive back to the office. And I could ask Layla to buy me a Caesar salad, yes, with anchovies, and a Diet Coke, or perhaps a banana smoothie, and I could eat my lunch while I prepare my keynote address for next month's Australian Direct Marketing Association conference.

I could do one. Or I could do the other.

The telephone pole or the office.

It seems no more important a decision than whether or not I will have the Diet Coke or the banana smoothie.

"Oh, Alice, glad I caught you, I was wondering, the weekend after this I've got that thing I was telling you about, so I was thinking, what if I picked up Tom for you from Harry's party, because I know you said you had that thing, so I could keep the boys before soccer and then you could pick them both up after the game?"

"Excuse me please, Mummy. Excuse me please, Mummy. *Excuse* me *please*, Mummy."

"Alice! Has Olivia decided what she's wearing to Amelia's fancy-dress party? Have you heard? There's a drama. *Seven* kids want to go as Hannah Montana, and apparently *Amelia* wants to go as Hannah Montana, and after all, she is the birthday girl, so apparently all other Hannahs are banned!"

"Big day coming up, Alice!"

"Mum, I *said* excuse me and you just keep ignoring me!"

"Mum, can Clara come over this afternoon? Please, please, please, please? Her mum said it was okay!"

"Mummy?"

"Mum?"

"Not long now, Alice!"

"Mrs. Love?"

"Can I talk to you, Alice?"

Alice stood in the school playground and the world of canteen duty and playdates and birthday parties whirled around her like a spinning top.

She didn't remember any of it.

Yet it all seemed oddly familiar.

Elisabeth's Homework for Jeremy

Just in case you're wondering, I decided to go to the office today.

The Caesar salad wasn't very nice. A lackluster attempt. Wilted lettuce. Stale croutons. Very disappointing. Like life.

I wasn't really serious about the telephone pole.

I would never do that. I'm far too sensible and dull.

By the way, I have canceled our next session. I do apologize for the inconvenience.

Frannie's Letter to Phil

Mr. Mustache has a name, and I guess I should use it now that he no longer has a mustache.

It's Xavier. It doesn't suit him at all, does it? What was his mother thinking? Xavier is far too elegant a name for a man who "places bets on the doggies" and loves beer and "the footie season" and tomato sauce and dreadful right-wing talkback radio.

We have nothing in common, obviously. Not like you and I! Remember the plays we saw, the books we shared, the — well.

Did we like the same books? I might be making that part up. Sometimes the details become a little hazy. I couldn't tell you, for example, whether you liked tomato sauce or not. Did you?

While I was having my shower this morning, I was thinking about how just last week Alice said to me, "Frannie, when will I stop being shocked that Gina isn't alive?"

I was full of grandmotherly wisdom about how "time heals," but I understood.

It was the same when my dear, silly Barb lost their father. She must have said it a million times: "But, Frannie, he ate a mandarin that morning. He was fine."

Because how is it possible for your husband to eat a mandarin at eight a.m. and be dead by ten a.m.?

And how is it possible to watch your best friend hop into a car and then for you to never hear her voice again? (And goodness, that Gina had a loud voice!)

And how is it possible to believe your lovely fiancé isn't still gallivanting around Queensland when a letter full of love and jokes and a pile of snapshots arrives the day after his coffin is lowered into the ground?

Your mind resists death with all its might.

Oh, Phil, it's completely foolish that I've kept writing back to you all these years. It's become one of those habits I can't seem to break. Writing to a memory.

Someone was screaming.

"Mum! Stop it! Make it stop! *Mummy!*"

Alice was catapulted up and out of her bed and was walking rapidly, blindly, down the hallway, before she woke up properly, her mouth dry, her head fuzzy with interrupted dreams.

Who was it? Olivia?

The hysterical screams were coming from Madison's room. Alice pushed open the door. In the dark, she could just make out a figure on the bed thrashing about and screaming, "Get it off! Get it off!"

Alice's eyes adjusted enough to make out the lamp on the bookshelf next to Madison's bed. She switched it on.

Madison's eyes were shut, her face screwed up tight. She was tangled up in her sheets and her pillow was on her chest. She batted it away.

"Get it off!"

Alice took away the pillow and sat down on the bed next to her.

"It's only a dream, darling," she said. "It's only a dream." She knew from her own nightmares how Madison's heart would be racing, how the words from the real world would slowly infiltrate the dream world and make it fade away.

Madison's eyes opened and she threw herself at Alice, pushing her head painfully into Alice's ribs and clutching her tightly.

"Mummy, get it off Gina! Get it off her!" she sobbed.

"It's only a dream," said Alice, stroking back sweaty strands of hair from Madison's forehead. "I promise you, it's only a bad dream."

"But Mummy, you need to get it off her! Get it off Gina."

"Get what off her?"

Madison didn't answer. Her hands loosened and her breathing began to slow. She burrowed herself more comfortably into Alice's lap.

Was she falling back asleep?

"Get what off her?" whispered Alice.

"It's only a dream," said Madison sleepily.

Chapter 26

"A untie Alice! Auntie Alice!"

A boy of about three came running into Alice's arms.

She automatically lifted his compact body up and whirled him around, while his legs gripped around her hips like a koala. She buried her nose in his dark hair and breathed in the yeasty scent. It was intensely, deliciously familiar. She breathed in again. Was she remembering this little boy? Or some other little boy? Sometimes she thought it might be easier to block her nose to stop these sudden frustrating rushes of memories that evaporated before she could pin down what exactly it was she remembered.

The little boy pressed fat palms on either side of Alice's face and babbled something incomprehensible, his eyes serious.

"He's asking if you brought Smarties," said Olivia. "You always bring him Smarties."

"Oh dear," said Alice.

"You don't know who he is, do you?" said Madison with happy contempt.

"She does so," said Olivia.

"It's our cousin Billy," said Tom. "Auntie Ella is his mum."

Nick's youngest sister had got pregnant! What a scandal! She was fifteen—still at school!

You're really not the sharpest knife in the drawer, are you, Alice? It's 2008! She's twenty-five! She's probably an entirely different person by now.

Although, actually, not that different, because here she came now, unsmilingly pushing her way past people. Ella still had a gothic look about her. White skin, brooding eyes with a lot of black eyeliner, black hair parted in the middle and cut in a sharp-edged bob. She was dressed in a long black skirt, black tights, black ballet flats, and a turtlenecked black jersey with what looked like four or five strings of pearls of varying lengths around her neck. Only Ella could pull off such a look.

"Billy! Come back here," she said sharply, trying unsuccessfully to peel her son off Alice.

"Ella," said Alice, while Billy's legs gripped harder and he buried his head in her neck. "I didn't expect to see you here." If she really *had* to pick a favorite Flake, it would have been Ella. She had been an intense, teary teenager who could dissolve into hysterical giggles, and she liked talking to Alice about clothes and showing her the vintage dresses she'd bought at secondhand shops that cost more to dry-clean than what she'd paid.

"Have you got a problem with me being here?" said Ella.

"What? No, of course not."

It was the Family Talent Night at Frannie's retirement village. They were in a wooden-floored hall with glowing red heaters mounted up high along the sides of the room, radiating an intense heat that was making all the visitors peel off cardigans and coats. There were rows of plastic chairs set up in a semicircle in front of a stage with a single microphone looking somehow pathetic in front of fraying red velvet curtains. Underneath the stage was a neat line of walkers of varying sizes, some with ribbons around them to differentiate them, like luggage at the airport.

Along the side of the hall were long trestle tables with white tablecloths laid with urns, tall stacks of Styrofoam cups, and paper plates of egg sandwiches, lamingtons, and pikelets with jam and blobs of cream melting in the heat.

The front rows of chairs were already occupied by village residents. Tiny wizened old ladies with brooches pinned to their best dresses, bent old men with hair carefully combed across spotted scalps, ties knotted beneath V-necked jumpers. The old people didn't seem to feel the heat.

Alice could see Frannie sitting right in the center row, engaged in what looked like a rather heated conversation with a grinning white-haired man who stood out because he was wearing a shiny polka-dot vest over a white shirt.

"Actually," said Ella, finally managing to wrench Billy out of Alice's arms, "it was your mother who rang and asked us to come. She said Dad had stage fright about this performance, which I find hard to believe, but still. The others all refused to come."

How strange for Barb to ring up Nick's sisters and actually ask them to do something, as if they were equals.

Alice caught herself.

Well, of *course* they were equals. What a strange thing to think.

But then, really, deep down (or maybe not even that deep down) she'd always thought of her own family as inferior to Nick's.

The Love family was from the eastern suburbs. "I rarely cross the Bridge," Nick's mother had once told Alice. She sometimes went to the opera on a Friday night, in the same way that Alice's mother might pop along to Trivia Night at the church hall on a Friday night (and maybe win a meat tray or a fruit box!). The Love family knew people. Important people, like MPs and actresses, doctors and lawyers, and people with names you felt you should know. They were Anglicans and went to church only at Christmas, languidly, as if it were a rather charming little event. Nick and his sisters went to private schools and Sydney Uni. They knew the best bars and the right restaurants. It was sort of like they owned Sydney.

Whereas Alice's family was from the stodgy northwest, home to happy clappy Christians, middle managers, CPAs, and conveyancers. Alice's mother rarely crossed the Bridge either, but that was because she didn't know her way around the city. Catching the train into town was a big event. Alice and Elisabeth went to local Catholic girls' schools, where the students were expected to become nurses and teachers, not doctors and lawyers. They went to church every Sunday, and local kids played the guitar while the congregation sang along in thin, reedy voices, following the words projected up on the wall above Father's bald head while the light from the stained-glass windows reflected off his glasses. Alice had often thought it would have been preferable to come from the proper western suburbs. That way she could have been a gritty, tough-talking westie chick. Maybe she would have had a tattoo on her ankle. Or, if only her parents could have been immigrants, with accents. Alice could have been bilingual and her mother could have made her own pasta. Instead, they were just the plain old suburban Jones family. As bland as Weet-Bix.

Until Nick came along and made her feel interesting and exotic.

"So what do you actually *confess* at confession?" he'd asked once. "Are you allowed to tell?" He'd looked at pictures of Alice in her pleated Catholic-school uniform hanging well past her knees and said into her ear, "I am crazy with lust right now." He'd sat on Alice's mother's floral couch, with a square brown coffee table next to him (the biggest one from the "nest" of coffee tables) with an embroidered doily on top, eating a thickly buttered piece of bun with bright-pink icing and drinking his tea, and said, "When was this house built?" As if their red-brick bungalow deserved such a respectful question! "Nineteen sixty-five," said Barb. "We paid twelve thousand pounds for it." Alice had never known that! Nick had given their house a *history*. He'd nodded along, making some comment about the light fittings, and he was exactly the same as when he was sitting at his mother's antique dining room table, eating fresh figs and goat cheese and drinking champagne. Alice had felt faint with adoration.

"Will we sit with Daddy when he gets here?" Olivia tugged at Alice's sleeve. "Will you two sit together? So when I'm dancing, you can say to each other, 'Oh, that's our darling daughter. How proud we are!'"

Olivia was dressed in a leotard with a frothy tulle skirt and ballet slippers, ready for her performance. Alice had done her makeup for her, although according to Olivia she hadn't applied nearly enough.

"Of course we'll sit together," said Alice.

"You are the most embarrassing person alive, Olivia," said Madison.

"No, she's not," said Ella, hugging Olivia to her, and then she pulled at the hem of Madison's long-sleeved dark red top. "That top looks gorgeous on you. I knew it would."

"It's my favorite," said Madison fiercely. "Except Mum always takes *ages* washing it."

Alice watched Ella watching Madison and saw how her face softened. It seemed that Nick's sister loved Alice's children, and judging by the way Billy was still hopefully trying to grab at Alice's bag, searching for Smarties, Alice loved her little boy. They were aunties to each other's children. Even if they hadn't become stepsisters, they were family. Alice was filled with affection for her.

"You've grown up so beautiful and elegant," said Alice to Ella.

"Is that a joke?" Ella stiffened and her jaw set.

"You might find Mum a bit weird tonight, Auntie Ella," said Tom. "She's had a traumatic head injury. I've printed some stuff out from the Internet if you want to read it. FYI. That means *for your information*. You say it when you want to tell somebody something. FYI."

"Darling Daddy!" cried Olivia.

Nick had just walked in the door of the hall and was scanning the crowd. He was dressed in an expensive-looking suit, his collar unbuttoned, and no tie. He looked like a successful, sexy, older man. A man who made important decisions, who knew his place in the world and no longer dropped toast on his shirt before a presentation.

Nick saw the children first and his face lit up. A second later he saw Alice and his face closed down. He walked toward them and Olivia threw herself into his arms.

"Oh, I've missed you three roosters," said Nick into Olivia's neck, his voice muffled, while he reached out with one hand to ruffle Tom's hair and the other to pat Madison on the shoulder.

"Hey, Dad, guess how many kilometers it was from our place to here," said Tom. "Guess. Go on guess."

"Umm, fifteen k."

"Close! Thirteen kilometers. FYI."

"Hey, kid," said Nick to Ella, using the nickname he'd always given Ella. Ella looked at him adoringly. Nothing had changed there. "And the kid's kid!" He scooped up Billy into his arms, so he was holding both Olivia and Billy. Billy chortled and repeated, "Kid's kid! Kid's kid!"

"How are you, Alice?" His eyes were on the children. He didn't look at her. Alice was last to be greeted. She was the least-favorite person. He used his polite voice for her.

"I'm well, thank you." *Do not under any circumstances cry.* She found herself longing, bizarrely, for Dominick. For someone who liked her best. How horrible it was to be despised. To feel yourself to be despicable.

A familiar quavery voice came over the microphone. "Ladies and gentlemen, girls and boys, it's my very great pleasure to welcome you all to the Tranquillity Wood Retirement Village Family Talent Night. Could I ask you all to take your seats?"

"Frannie!" said Olivia.

It was Frannie up onstage, looking rather beautiful in a royal-blue dress and speaking calmly into the microphone, although she was putting on a posh voice.

"She doesn't look nervous," said Madison. "If it was me, I would be so nervous talking to all these people, I would probably faint."

"Me too," agreed Alice.

Madison curled her lip. "No, you wouldn't."

"I would!" protested Alice.

There was some confusion as they all settled into their seats. Madison, Tom, and Olivia all wanted to sit next to their father, and Olivia needed to be at the end of the row so she could be ready to go up when her name was called, and she also wanted Nick and Alice to sit together, while Billy wanted to sit on Alice's lap, which Ella clearly did not want. She finally gave in and Alice found herself with Madison on one side and Nick on the other, and Billy's warm little body snuggled into hers. At least *he* liked her.

Where was Elisabeth? Alice twisted around in her seat to look for her. She was meant to be coming tonight, but maybe she'd changed her mind. Mum had called to say that the blood-test results had been negative and Elisabeth seemed fine, although a little peculiar. "I actually wondered if she was drunk," Barb had said. Alice still had Dino's fertility doll in her handbag to give her. Would it just upset her now? But what if she was depriving Elisabeth of its magical powers? She would ask Nick what he thought.

She glanced over at Nick's stern profile. Could she still ask his opinion on things like that? Maybe not. Maybe he didn't care.

When the crowd had settled down, Frannie tapped the microphone and said, "Our first act is Mary Barber's great-granddaughter performing 'Somewhere over the Rainbow.'"

A little girl in a glittery sequined dress, plastered with makeup ("See, Mummy?" hissed Olivia, leaning forward across Nick to look reproachfully at Alice), strode out onto the stage, shimmying her chest like an aging cabaret singer. "Jesus," said Nick under his breath. She clasped the microphone with both hands and began to sing, her voice filled with exaggerated emotion, making the audience flinch in unison each time she hit the high notes.

She was followed by tap-dancing grandchildren in top hats and canes, a great-nephew's magic show ("FYI, I know exactly how he did that," Tom whispered loudly), and a niece's gymnastic routine. Ella's little boy got bored and started a game where he clambered from lap to lap, touching each person on the nose, saying, "Chin," or touching them on the chin and saying, "Nose," and then falling about laughing at his own wit.

Finally Frannie said, "Next up, Olivia Love, my own great-granddaughter, performing a routine she choreographed herself called 'The Butterfly.'"

Alice was terrified. Choreographed it *herself*? She'd assumed Olivia would be performing something she'd learned at ballet school. Good Lord, it would probably be dreadful. Her hands were sweaty. It was as if she were going up there herself.

"Hmmmm," said Olivia without moving.

"Olivia," said Tom. "It's your *turn*."

"I actually feel a bit sick," said Olivia.

Nick said, "All the best performers feel sick, sweetie. It's a sign. It means you're going to be great."

"You don't have to—" began Alice.

Nick put a hand on her arm and Alice stopped.

"As soon as you start, the sick feeling will go away," he said to Olivia.

"Promise?" Olivia looked up at him trustingly.

"Cross my heart and hope to be killed by a rabid dog."

Olivia rolled her eyes. "You're so silly, Dad." She slid down from the chair and marched down the aisle toward the stage, her tulle skirt bobbing. Alice's heart twisted. She was so *little*. So alone.

"Have you seen this routine?" whispered Nick, as he adjusted the focus on a tiny silver camera.

"No. Have you?"

"No." They watched as Olivia climbed the stairs of the stage. Nick said, "I actually feel a bit sick myself."

"Me too," said Alice.

Oliva stood in the center of the stage with her head bowed and her arms wrapped around herself, her eyes closed.

Alice massaged her stomach. She could feel the tension emanating from Nick.

The music started. Olivia slowly opened one eye, then the other. She yawned enormously, wriggled and squirmed. She was a caterpillar sleepily emerging from its cocoon. She looked over her shoulder, pretended to catch sight of a wing and her mouth dropped comically.

The audience laughed.

They *laughed.*

Alice's daughter was funny! Publicly funny!

Olivia looked over her other shoulder and staggered with delight. She was a butterfly! She fluttered this way and that, trying out her new wings, falling over at first and then finally getting the hang of it.

It was true that she probably wasn't quite in time with the music, and some of her dance moves were, well, unusual, but her facial expressions were priceless. In Alice's opinion, and she felt she was being quite objective, there had never been a funnier, cuter performance of a butterfly.

By the time the music had stopped Alice was suffused with pride, her face aching from smiling so much. She looked about at the audience and saw that people were smiling and clapping, clearly charmed, although they were perhaps holding themselves back so as not to make the other performers feel bad (why not a standing ovation, for example?), and she was shocked to see a woman in the middle of checking her mobile phone. How could she have dragged her eyes away from the stage?

"She's a comic genius," she whispered to Nick.

Nick lowered the camera, and his face, when he turned to look at her, was filled with identical awe and pleasure.

"Mum. I helped her a bit," said Madison tentatively.

"Did you?" Alice put her arm around Madison's shoulder and pulled her close. She lowered her voice. "I bet you helped her a lot. You're a great big sister. Just like your Auntie Libby was to me."

Madison looked amazed for a second, and then she smiled that exquisite smile that transformed her face.

"How did I get such talented children?" said Alice, and her voice shook. Why had Madison looked so surprised?

"Comes from their father," said Nick.

Olivia came dancing back down the aisle and sat up on the chair next to Nick, grinning self-consciously. "Was I good? Was I excellent?"

"You were the best!" said Nick. "Everybody is saying we may as well just pack up our bags and go, now that Olivia Love has performed."

"Silly," giggled Olivia.

They sat through another four acts, including a comedy act by someone's middle-aged daughter that was so incredibly unfunny it was sort of funny, and a little boy who lost his nerve and got stage fright halfway through reciting a Banjo Paterson poem until his grandfather came unsteadily up onstage and held his hand, and they read it together, which made Alice cry.

Frannie walked up to the microphone again. "Ladies and gentlemen, boys and girls, this has been such a special night and in a moment you can enjoy supper, but we have just one final act for you and I hope you'll forgive me, but it's another one of my own family members. Please put your hands together for Barb and Roger performing the salsa!"

The stage went dark. A single spotlight revealed Alice's mother and Nick's father in full Latin costumes, standing completely still. Roger had one knee thrust between Barb's legs, his arm around her waist. Barb was leaning back, exposing her neck. Roger's head was bowed toward hers, his face dramatic, frowning tremendously.

Nick made a sound like something was stuck in his throat. Ella made a sympathetic choking sound back.

"Grandma and Grandpa look like people on TV," said Tom happily. "They look *famous*."

"They do not," said Madison.

"They do so."

"Shhhh," said Alice and Nick together.

The music started and their parents began to move. They were good in a horrendous sort of way. Swiveling their hips proficiently. Moving in and out of each other's arms. It was just so mortifyingly *sexual*— and in front of all these *old* people!

After five agonizing minutes of dancing, Roger stopped at the microphone while Barb danced around him, flicking up the sides of her skirt and stamping her feet provocatively. Alice could feel an attack of giggles about to sweep over her. What on earth are you *doing*, Mum?

"Folks!" said Roger in his best plummy radio-announcer voice. The spotlight lit up the beads of sweat on his yellow-tanned forehead. "You may have heard that my lovely wife and I will be offering salsa-dance lessons every second Tuesday. It's great exercise, and a lot of fun to boot! Now, anybody can do the salsa, and to prove it, I want to invite two people out of the audience who have never salsa-danced before up onto the stage. Let's see now . . ."

The spotlight began bouncing around the audience. Alice watched the light, hoping Roger had the sense to choose a couple who could actually walk.

The spotlight stopped on Alice and Nick and they both held up their hands to shield their eyes.

"Yes, those two blinking like rabbits in the headlights look like the perfect victims, don't you think, Barb?" said Roger.

Olivia, Tom, and Madison jumped from their seats like lottery winners. They began pulling at their parents' arms, shrieking, "Yes, yes! Mum and Dad dance! Come on!"

"No, no! Pick somebody else!" Alice swatted away their hands in a panic. She never, ever volunteered for this sort of thing.

"I think they'd be perfect, Roger," said Barb from the stage, with a big game-show-hostess smile.

"I'm going to kill them," said Nick quietly. Then he yelled, "Sorry! Bad back!"

The old people weren't buying that. They were the ones with arthritis.

"Bad back, my foot!" cried out an old lady.

"Have a go, you mug!"

"Don't be party poopers!"

"Don't worry, the sick feeling will go away, Daddy," said Olivia sweetly.

"Dance, dance, dance!" shouted the old people, stamping their feet with surprising energy.

Nick sighed and stood up. He looked down at Alice. "Let's just get it over with."

They walked up onto the stage, Alice pulling self-consciously at her skirt, worried it was riding up at the back. Frannie shrugged from her place in the front row and held up her hands in a "nothing to do with me" gesture.

"Facing each other, please," said Roger.

Roger stood behind Nick and Barb stood behind Alice. Their parents maneuvered them so that Alice's hand was on Nick's shoulder, his around her waist.

"Closer now," boomed Roger. "Don't be shy. Now look into each other's eyes."

Alice looked miserably up at Nick. His face was blankly polite, as if they were two strangers who had been pulled out of the audience. This was excruciating.

"Come on now, are you a man or a mouse?" Roger clapped his son on the shoulder. "The man has got to take charge! You're the leader. She's the follower!"

Nick's nostril twitched, which meant he was highly irritated.

In a sudden movement, he put his hand on Alice's lower back and pulled her close to him, frowning masterfully in an over-the-top imitation of his father.

The audience erupted.

"I think we've got a natural here, folks!" said Roger. His eyes met Alice's and seemed to be sending her some sort of kindly message. He was a pompous old twit, but he meant well.

"Okay, light on your toes!" said Barb, demonstrating to Nick. "And forward on your *right* foot, back with your *left* foot, rock back onto your *right* foot, step back with your *left* foot. Shift your weight to your *left* foot, step back with your *right* foot. That's it! That's it!"

"And let's get those hips moving!" cried Roger.

Alice and Nick didn't dance much in public. Alice was always too self-conscious, and Nick wasn't fussed either way, but sometimes at home, if they'd had wine with dinner and they had the right sort of CD on while they were packing the dishwasher, they danced in the

kitchen. A silly, hamming-it-up dance. It was always Alice who initi-
ated it, because actually, she quite liked to dance, and actually, she
wasn't bad.

She began to move her hips in imitation of her mother, while trying
to keep the top half of her body still. The crowd roared its approval and
she heard a child, probably Olivia, shout, "Go, *Mummy*!" Nick laughed.
He was stepping on her toes. Barb and Roger were grinning like
Cheshire cats. She could hear their children shouting out from the
audience.

There was still chemistry. She could feel it in their hands. She could
see it in his eyes. Even if it was just a memory of chemistry. There was
still something. Alice's head was dizzy with hope.

The music stopped. "See! Anyone can learn to salsa!" cried Roger as
Nick dropped his hands from her waist and turned away.

Elisabeth's Homework for Jeremy

We were driving to the Family Talent Night when I had a
sudden craving for television.

House was on. I needed to see Dr. House being nasty and
sarcastic while he diagnosed impossible medical conditions.
What would Dr. House say about me? I wish you were more
like Dr. House, Jeremy. You're so nice and polite. It's annoying. Niceness doesn't cure anyone. Why don't you just bring
me face-to-face with a few home truths?

"You're infertile. Get over it," House would sneer, brandishing his cane, and I'd be shocked and invigorated.

"Can we turn around?" I told Ben.

He didn't try to change my mind. He is being very gentle
and careful at the moment. The adoption application forms
have disappeared from the kitchen counter. He's put them

away. Temporarily. I can see the idea still shining in his eyes. He still has hope. Which is exactly the problem. I cannot afford any more hope.

I rang him after I got the blood-test results and when I went to speak, I found no words came out of my mouth, and when he didn't say anything, I knew he was trying not to cry. You can always tell when he's trying not to cry. Like he's fighting off something invisible trying to take over his head.

"We'll be okay," he finally said.

No we won't, I thought. "Yes," I said.

I almost told him the truth.

Actually, no I didn't. Not even close.

After *House* I watched *Medium*, and then *Boston Legal* and then *Cheaters*! That's the show where they spy on real people cheating on their spouses and then confront them with television cameras. It's seedy and gray and trashy. We sure do live in a seedy, gray, trashy world, Jeremy.

It's possible my mental health is poorly at the moment.

The show was over and the adults were standing around, drinking tea and coffee from paper cups and balancing pikelets on serviettes in the palms of their hands.

A huge gang of grandchildren and great-grandchildren were whooping with joy, racing on wheelchairs down the front of the hall.

"Should they be playing on those?" Alice asked Frannie, trying to be a responsible grown-up, as she saw Madison pushing a chair with Olivia and Tom squished in side by side, their legs stuck straight out in front of them.

"Of course not," sighed Frannie. "But I think it might be one of our residents running the race." She pointed to the white-haired man she'd been arguing with earlier who was wearing the shiny polka-dot waist-coat. He was racing along in a wheelchair, spinning the wheels with his hands, yelling, "You can't catch me!"

Frannie's lips twitched. "He's eighty-five going on five." She paused. "Actually, I might just take some photos for the newsletter." She hurried off. Nick, Alice, and Ella were left together.

"Well, that was quite a performance." Ella was carrying Billy, who had his thumb in his mouth, his head draped over her shoulder. She squinted over his head at Nick and Alice as if they were scientific specimens. "That was the last thing I expected to see."

"Just wanted to show Dad up," said Nick. He picked up a scone and put the whole thing in his mouth.

"Are you hungry?" asked Alice. She scanned the tables. "Do you want a sandwich? They've got curried egg." Nick liked curried egg sandwiches.

He cleared his throat uncomfortably and glanced at Ella. "No, that's okay, thanks."

Ella was now openly staring.

"So how come you're the only one of the sisters here tonight, Ella?" asked Alice. Normally the Flakes traveled in a pack.

"Well, to be frank, Alice," said Ella, "they sort of refuse to be in the same room as you."

Alice flinched. "Goodness." She wasn't used to provoking such violent reactions in people, although, then again, she didn't mind the idea of having such power over the Flakes. It was sort of delicious.

"Ella," remonstrated Nick.

"I'm just saying it like it is," said Ella. "I'm trying to stay neutral. Of course, it would help if you gave back Granny Love's ring, Alice."

"Oh! That reminds me." Alice unzipped her handbag, pulled out a jewelry box. "I brought it to give to you tonight. Here it is."

Nick took the ring slowly. "Thank you." He held the jewelry case in his palm as if he didn't know what to do with it and finally stuffed it into the pocket of his suit jacket.

"Well, if it's that easy," said Ella, "maybe I should bring up another few issues, like, I don't know, the financial situation."

"Ella, this is really none of your business," said Nick.

"And why are you being such a *cow* over the custody?"

"Ella, this is not acceptable," said Nick.

"Moo," said Alice.

Ella and Nick stared.

Alice recited, "Who says 'moo'? A *cow* says 'moo'!" She smiled. "Sorry. It just came into my head when you said 'cow.'"

Billy lifted his head from Ella's shoulder, removed his thumb from his mouth, and said, "Moo!" He grinned appreciatively at Alice before replacing his thumb and putting his head back down on Ella's shoulder again. Ella and Nick seemed lost for words.

"I guess it must come from a book we used to read the children," said Alice.

It had been happening a lot. Strange words and phrases and lines from songs kept appearing in her head. It seemed that those ten years' worth of memories had been stuffed in a too-small cupboard at the back of her mind, and every now and then a fragment of nonsense would escape.

Any second now that cupboard door was going to burst open and her head was going to overflow with memories of grief and joy and who knew what else. She didn't know if she was looking forward to that moment or not.

"I dropped something the other day," said Alice, "and I said, 'Oh my dosh.' And it just sounded so familiar. Oh my dosh."

"Olivia used to say it when she was little," said Nick. He smiled. "We all said it for a while. Oh my dosh. I'd forgotten that. Oh my dosh."

"Am I missing something here?" said Ella.

"Maybe it's time you got Billy home to bed," said Nick.

"Right," said Ella. "Fine. I'll see you on Sunday." She kissed Nick on the cheek.

"Sunday?"

"Mother's Day? Lunch with Mum? She said you were coming."

"Oh, right. Yes, of course."

How did Nick handle his social life without Alice? That was *her* job, telling Nick what he was meant to be doing on the weekend. He must be missing things all over the place.

"Bye, Alice," said Ella, without making a move to kiss her. The only person in 2008 who didn't seem intent on plastering her with kisses. She paused. "Thanks for giving back the ring. It means a lot to our family."

In other words, *You are not our family any longer.*

"No problem," said Alice. *You're perfectly welcome to that horrendous ring.*

When Ella had gone, Nick looked at Alice and said, "Still haven't got your memory back, then?"

"Not quite. Any minute now."

"How are you coping with the children?"

"Fine," said Alice. No need to mention her daily failures with lost permission notes, unwashed school uniforms, and forgotten homework, or how she didn't know what to do when they fought with each other over the computer or the PlayStation. "They're lovely. We made lovely children."

"I know we did," said Nick, and his face seemed to collapse. "I know we did." He paused, as if not sure whether he should speak, and then said, "That's why the thought of only seeing them on weekends kills me."

"Oh, that," said Alice. "Well, if we don't get back together, then of course we should do the fifty-fifty thing. One week for you. One week for me. Why not?"

"You don't mean that," said Nick.

"Of course I do," said Alice. "I'll sign something!"

"Fine," said Nick. "I'll get my lawyer to draft something. I'll have it couriered over to you tomorrow."

"No problem."

"Once you get your memory back, you're going to change your mind," said Nick. He laughed harshly. "And you're not going to want to get back together, I'd put money on that."

"Twenty bucks," said Alice, holding out her hand.

Nick shook her hand. "Done."

She still loved the feel of his hand holding hers. Wouldn't her body tell her if she hated him?

"I found out it was Gina's husband who kissed the woman in the laundry," said Alice. "Not you."

"Oh yes, the infamous laundry incident." Nick smiled at an old lady with a walking stick in one hand attempting to hand around a sagging plate of sandwiches. "Oh, all right, you twisted my arm!" He took a sandwich. Alice noted it was curried egg.

"What did you mean when you said you found it interesting that I thought that was you?" asked Alice, taking a sandwich herself to save it from sliding onto the floor.

"Because I was always saying to you, 'I'm not Mike Boyle,'" said Nick. Even with his mouth full of sandwich, she could hear the left-over anger in his voice. "You identified so strongly with Gina, it was as if it was happening to you. I said to you, 'But it wasn't me.' You got so caught up in that 'all men are bastards' thing."

"I'm sorry," said Alice. Her sandwich was ham and mustard, and the taste of mustard was reminding her of something. This constant feeling of fleeting memories was like having a mosquito buzzing in your ear when you're asleep, and you know that when you turn out the light, it will have vanished, until you lie back down, close your eyes, and then . . . *bzzzzzzz.*

Nick wiped his serviette across his mouth. "You don't need to be sorry. It's all water under the bridge now." He paused and his eyes went blank, looking back on a shared past that Alice couldn't see.

He said, "I often think the four of us were too close. We got all tangled up in Mike and Gina's marriage problems. We caught their divorce. Like a virus."

"Well, let's just get better from it," said Alice. How dare this stupid Mike and Gina come into their lives, spreading their germy marriage problems?

Nick smiled and shook his head. "You sound so . . ." He couldn't find the right word. Finally he said, "Young."

After a pause, he continued: "Anyway, it wasn't *just* Mike and Gina. That's too simplistic. Maybe we were too young when we got together. Mmmm. Do you think fame might have gone to Olivia's head?"

Alice followed his gaze to see Olivia back onstage. She had the microphone held close to her mouth and was doing a grandiose performance of some song they couldn't hear because the sound was turned off. Tom was on his hands and knees next to her, following the microphone lead back to the power plug. Madison was sitting in the front row of the empty chairs in the audience, next to the white-haired wheelchair-race organizer. They were deep in conversation.

"Tell me a happy memory from the last ten years," said Alice.

"Alice."

"Come on. What's the first thing that comes into your head?"

"Ummm. God. I don't know. I suppose when the children were born. Is that too obvious an answer? Although not the actual births. I didn't like the actual births."

"Didn't you?" said Alice, disappointed. She'd imagined herself and

Nick sobbing and laughing and holding each other while a movie soundtrack played in the background. "Why not?"

"I guess I was in a crazy panic the whole time, and I couldn't control anything, and I couldn't help you. I kept doing the wrong thing."

"I'm sure you didn't."

Nick glanced at Alice, then looked away again quickly.

"And all the blood, and you screaming your head off, and that incompetent obstetrician who didn't turn up until it was all over with Madison, I was going to knock him out. If it wasn't for that midwife—she was great, the one we said could have been Melanie Barker's twin sister."

He looked distractedly down at his hands. Alice wondered if he knew he was twisting the skin beneath the knuckle on his finger where his wedding ring should have been. It had become a habit of his, fiddling with his ring when he was thinking. Now he was still doing it, even though he wasn't wearing the ring.

"And when they had to do the emergency cesarean with Olivia"—Nick shoved his hands in his pockets—"I genuinely thought I was having a heart attack."

"How horrible for you," said Alice. Although she guessed maybe it hadn't been a barrel of laughs for her either.

Nick smiled and shook his head in wonder. "I remember, I didn't want to distract them from you and the baby, you know, like some man in a movie who faints. I thought, I'll just die discreetly in this corner. I thought you were going to die, too, and the children were going to be orphans. Have I ever told you that before? I must have."

"I thought we were talking happy memories." Alice was appalled. Without those memories, it felt like all that blood and screaming were still ahead of her, still to be endured.

"The happy part was when it was all over and quiet, and they left us alone, with the baby all wrapped up, and we could talk about which doctors and nurses we hated, and have a cup of tea, and just look at the baby for the first time. Count their tiny fingers. That new little person. That was—special." He cleared his throat.

"What's your saddest memory of the last ten years?" said Alice.

"Oh, I've got lots of contenders." Nick smiled strangely. She couldn't tell if it was a nasty smile or a sad one. "Take your pick. The day we told the children we were separating. The day I moved out. The night Madison rang me up, sobbing her heart out and begging me to come home."

All around them people talked and laughed and drank their cups of tea. Alice could feel the warmth from the heaters beating down upon her head. She felt as though the top of her head were melting, softening like chocolate. She imagined Madison on the phone, crying for her dad to come home.

He should have put down the phone and come right home that second, and they should have watched a family video together, snuggled on the couch, eating fish-and-chips. It should have been *easy* to be happy. There were poor Elisabeth and Ben, desperately trying to have a family, while Nick and Alice had just let theirs fall apart.

She stepped closer to Nick.

"Don't you think we should try again? For them? For the children? Actually, not just for them. For us. For the old us."

"Excuse me!" It was another old lady, with a blue-gray perm and a wrinkled, happy face. "You're Nick and Alice, aren't you!" She leaned toward them confidentially. "I recognize you from Frannie's Facebook page. She mentioned that you were separated now, and I just want you to know that I think you two belong together. I could tell it was true love by the way you danced just then!"

"Frannie has *photos* of us on the Internet?" said Nick.

The old lady turned to Alice. "Have you got your memory back yet, love? You know, a similar thing happened to a friend of mine in 1954.

We could not convince her that the war was over. Of course, she ended up forgetting her own name, which I'm sure won't happen to you."

"No," said Alice. "It's Alice. Alice, Alice."

"Tell me she doesn't post photos of the children on the Internet," said Nick.

"Oh, your children are just beautiful," said the old lady.

"Great. An open invitation to murderers and pedophiles," said Nick.

"I'm sure she doesn't actually *invite* people to murder the children," said Alice. " 'Murderers, check out our delicious little victims here!' "

"This is serious. Why do you always think bad things can't happen to us? It's just like that time you let Olivia go missing at the beach. You're so blasé."

"Am I?" said Alice, bemused. Had she really let Olivia go missing?

"We're not immune from tragedy."

"I'll keep that in mind," said Alice, and Nick's face gave an actual spasm of irritation, as if he'd just been bitten by a mosquito.

"What?" said Alice. "What did I say?"

"Is your sister here?" said the old lady to Alice. "I wanted to tell her that I think she should adopt a baby. There must be lots of lovely babies up for adoption after that cyclone in Burma. Of course, in my day a lot more babies were left on church doorsteps, but that doesn't seem to happen so much anymore, which is a pity. Oh, there's your mother!" The old lady spotted Barb, still in her outfit and makeup, holding a clipboard and surrounded by eager old ladies. "I'm going to sign up for salsa! You two have inspired me!"

She tottered off.

"Will you please tell Frannie that I don't appreciate her putting photos of my children on the Net," said Nick. That detached, pompous voice was back.

"Tell her yourself!" said Alice. Nick adored Frannie. The old Nick would have been off to accost Frannie for a spirited debate. At family functions they argued about politics and played cards together.

Nick sighed heavily. He massaged his cheeks as if he had a toothache, pushing the flesh up around his eyes, causing them to crease oddly, so that his face looked like a gargoyle.

"Don't do that," said Alice, pulling on his arm.

"What?" said Nick. "Jesus, what?"

"Oh my goodness," said Alice. "How did our relationship get so *prickly*?"

"I should go," said Nick.

"What happened to George and Mildred?" said Alice.

Nick just looked at her blankly.

"The sandstone lions," Alice reminded him.

"I have no idea," said Nick.

Chapter 27

O h, *Alice*," said Alice to herself.

It was the morning after the Family Talent Night. The children had been safely delivered to school and she was sitting at the desk in the study, searching for things to help jog her memory. She'd just stumbled upon the reason why Mrs. Bergen wasn't speaking to her.

She sat back in her chair, put her feet up on the desk, and leaned right back on the chair so she was staring up at the ceiling. "What were you *thinking*?"

It seemed that Alice was an active member of a residents' committee lobbying the local council to have their street rezoned to allow the building of five-story apartment blocks. Mrs. Bergen was heading up the committee of residents fighting the rezoning proposal.

She took her feet off the desk and pulled out the next piece of paper in the file, biting into a Twix bar to fortify herself. (She had stocked the pantry with essential chocolate. The children were delirious about this, even while they pretended this was nothing out of the ordinary.)

It was a clipping from the local paper with the headline KING STREET RESIDENTS CLASH, showing pictures of Mrs. Bergen and Alice. They had photographed Mrs. Bergen in her front garden, next to her rosebushes, wearing her gardening hat, holding a mug and looking sad and sweet.

> "This proposal is an outrage. It will ruin the character and heritage of this beautiful street," said Mrs. Beryl Bergen, who has lived in her King Street home for the past forty years and raised five children there.

"Of course it will," said Alice out loud.

The photo of Alice showed her sitting in the very chair she was sitting in now, looking grim and officious and definitely forty.

She groaned out loud as she read her own words.

> "It's inevitable," said Mrs. Alice Love, who moved into the area ten years ago. "Sydney needs high-density housing close to public transport. When we purchased this home, we were told the rezoning would happen in the next five years. We took that into account as part of the property's investment potential. The council can't go back on its word and leave people out of pocket."

What? What was she talking about? They had no idea that rezoning was a possibility. They had talked about growing old in this house. They had not talked about selling it to a developer to knock it down and build some horrendous modern apartment block.

She read on, and somehow she wasn't surprised when she came to the final paragraph.

Alice Love has taken over as president of the Residents for Rezoning Committee following the tragic death of its founder, Gina Boyle.

Of course. Gina. Bloody Gina.

She stood up decisively and went into the kitchen, where a tray of freshly baked chocolate brownies was cooling.

"Have I ever made these for you?" she had asked the children the night before, showing them the photo in the recipe book. "I asked you once," said Olivia, "but you said they were full of sugar." "Well, yes, but so what?" Alice had asked, while Olivia giggled and Tom and Madison shot each other worried, grown-up glances.

She got a Tupperware container, filled it with chocolate brownies, and, without stopping to think about it, marched next door and rang the doorbell.

Mrs. Bergen's welcoming smile vanished when she saw Alice and she dropped the hand that was about to open the screen door by her side.

"Mrs. Bergen," said Alice. She pressed her hand to the screen door as if she were visiting her in jail. "I am so, so sorry. I've made a terrible mistake."

Elisabeth's Homework for Jeremy

I was delivering a one-day seminar today called "Using Direct Mail to Beef Up Your Sales!" to the Retail Butchers Association.

No, I'm not kidding. Any businessperson or professional

can use direct mail to their advantage. Even you could, Jeremy.

Feel like driving your car into the nearest telephone pole?
Therapist Jeremy Hodges can steer you in a better direction.
FREE bottle of antidepressants for the first 10 appointments.

Or something like that. I'm a bit off my game.

Anyway, the butchers were a friendly, interested lot. There was much industry banter going across the room, and some surprisingly astute questions. (I thought the butchers were going to be sort of simple, red-faced, and jolly, but I think that's an act they put on to sell more sausages.) The seminar was going well. It is impossible to feel suicidal when you're explaining how to inject personality into a letter about lamb cutlets.

Then I saw someone sitting in the audience with a very un-butcherlike appearance.

It was Alice. She looks different these days. Less makeup, I think. Her hair is messier. She's wearing the same clothes but in a different way, and she's pulled out old things I haven't seen in years. Today she was wearing a long skirt, a faded cream jersey pulled in at the waist with a big belt, and a glittery tasseled scarf that I recognized from Olivia's dress-up box. She looked lovely, Jeremy, and for once I didn't resent her for having the time and the money to always keep her body in such perfect shape and for not having to stick needles in her stomach every night. When I saw her, she smiled and waved and held a palm in front of her face meaning, pretend I'm not here.

For some reason, the sight of her made me feel strangely

emotional. My voice quivered as I went to answer a question about postage costs from Bill of Ryde Fresh Meats.

She came up to me in the morning tea break and said breathlessly, "I feel nervous, like I'm talking to a celebrity!" I don't think she was being sarcastic. It was sort of nice.

She said, "Why didn't you come to Frannie's thing last night?"

And I really did nearly tell her the truth. It was dancing away on the tip of my tongue, ready to jump off. Except that it didn't answer her question, and, anyway, I knew she'd react exactly the wrong way.

Which isn't her fault. Anyone would.

But seeing her reaction would push me right over the abyss into crazy-land, and I'm only just managing to stay on this side of sanity.

I guess I could tell you, Jeremy, at our next appointment.

But no. I'm not saying it out loud. I'm just going to . . . wait it out, I guess.

Pretend it's not happening and wait for the inevitable, and not let it touch me.

Frannie's Letter to Phil

The Family Talent Night was a triumph, if I do say so myself.

Olivia did the most beautiful silly funny dance. I nearly burst with pride. And Barb and Roger performed one of their salsa dances, which wasn't unbearable. In point of fact, it was probably the most popular act of the night. All the ladies are desperately in love with Roger. There is no accounting for taste.

Alice and Nick even got up to dance, and for a moment there, I thought I might have seen a spark of something between them.

However, at the end of the night I saw Nick stomping out to the car park, obviously in a terrible mood. They take their lives so seriously, these young people. "Just appreciate the fact that you can stomp so energetically," I wanted to say to him. I'd pay a million dollars to be Alice and Elisabeth's age again for just one day. I'd dance like Olivia's butterfly and bite into crisp green apples and run across hot sand into the surf, and I'd walk, as far as I wanted, wherever I wanted, in big loping, leaping strides, with my head held high and my lungs filling with air.

And I'd probably have sex!

Wasn't sex nice, Phil?

It was extremely nice.

For some reason I've been thinking about it lately, and the nights we spent in your cramped little flat in Neutral Bay with the lights winking on the harbor.

I'd pay two million for just one more night with you in that flat.

Not that I have two million. Or even a million. I'd have to take out a loan.

My apologies, Phil. I'm in a peculiarly flippant mood. Goodness, I'm going to have to make sure I don't leave this letter lying around for anyone to read. (Actually I might have to destroy it. What if I should drop dead in the middle of the night? What if Barb should find it and show it to the girls. Or far worse, Roger?)

Elisabeth didn't turn up at the Family Talent Night. I've been trying to call her, but without success.

Mr. M. (I can't seem to call him Xavier) spent a long time talking with Madison. He said, "She's a very complex, intelligent little girl with a lot on her mind," and I was filled with affection for him. (I wonder what's on Madison's mind?)

I do believe I might have found a new friend, which is a fine and wonderful thing at my age.

He's asked me out to dinner at the local Chinese restaurant.

I automatically went to decline, and then I thought, For heaven's
sake, Frannie, why not?

"Look, Tom, police car!" cried Alice, as a police car with its siren flashing blue streaked by. "Nee nar, nee nar!"

She turned her head, ready to see an excited little face in the backseat, then realized she was alone in the car, and that Tom was too old
to be excited by police cars anyway, and also, she actually didn't remember him as a baby.

These involuntary flashes of memory, or whatever they were, were
happening almost every few minutes now. It was like a weird nervous
tic. Just then, at the morning tea break at Elisabeth's seminar, she'd
seen one of the butchers taking two chocolate biscuits at once and she
only just managed to stop herself from grabbing his hairy wrist and
saying, "One is plenty!"

She constantly found herself heading purposefully somewhere, into
the study, the kitchen, or the laundry, and then realizing she didn't
know why she was heading there. Once, she was all the way across the
road, walking up the driveway of Gina's old house, when she stopped
and said out loud, "Oh." She picked up the phone and dialed numbers,
before quickly dropping the phone with no idea who she was calling.
One time, while waiting outside the school for the children, she caught
herself rocking her handbag, patting it, and humming a song she didn't
recognize. "Yummy, yummy, yummy in your tummy, tummy!" she'd
said at dinner the other night, zooming a spoonful of food toward
Olivia's mouth. "I think you might be going a bit crazy, darling
Mummy," Oliva had said, with wide eyes.

Her memory was coming back any moment now. She could feel
it creeping up on her, like the fuzzy head and ticklish throat that

heralded a cold. She just couldn't decide if she should resist it or encourage it.

Now she was on her way from Elisabeth's seminar to "help in the library" at the school. This was something she apparently did every third Thursday, which seemed excessively generous of her.

As she drove, she thought about Elisabeth, and how smooth she'd been up onstage, talking to all those butchers, making them laugh, telling them what to do. She'd seemed so natural talking into the microphone. So herself. The same way celebrities casually chatted away in interviews to journalists, as if there weren't cameras right in front of them. But then when Elisabeth had talked to her in the break, she had the strangest feeling that Elisabeth wasn't really there, that she was just pretending to be Elisabeth. That she was more herself up onstage than right now.

Alice still hadn't even got to talk to her yet about the unsuccessful IVF cycle. She'd called the night before when she got home from the Family Talent Night, but Ben had said Elisabeth was watching a favorite TV show and could she call back once it was over? She never called back, and of course she could hardly talk to her about it when she was working. It was ridiculous that she had no idea what was going on in her own sister's mind. She couldn't even take an educated guess as to how Elisabeth was feeling right now. Angry? Devastated? Sick of the whole thing?

She would try to call her again tonight, but it was weirdly hard to find time once she'd driven the children to all their activities, helped with homework (so much homework! It gave Alice a headache. She'd actually groaned when she saw the number of worksheets Tom had pulled out from his bag the other night, which wasn't very parental of her), cooked their dinner, cleaned up, made their lunches, tried to convince them to stop fighting over the computer and the television. By the end of it, she was exhausted.

There just wasn't enough time in 2008. It had become a limited re-
source. Back in 1998, the days were so much more spacious. When she
woke up in the morning, the day rolled out in front of her like a long
hallway for her to meander down, free to linger over the best parts.
Days were so stingy now. Mean slivers of time. They flew by like
speeding cars. *Whoosh!* When she was pulling back the blankets to hop
into bed each night, it felt as if only seconds ago she'd been throwing
them off to get up.

Maybe it was just because she wasn't used to this life. This life as a
separated mother of three children.

She was doing things differently, trying to slow down time. She had
a feeling the new Alice, the one with that snippy voice, wouldn't approve of some of the changes.

When she'd picked the children up from school yesterday, Olivia
had whined, "I don't want to go to violin," and Alice, who had no idea
that she was meant to be "going to violin," had said, "Okay, fine," and
taken the three children to Dino's, where they'd done their homework
sitting at a round table, drinking hot chocolates, and Dino had been
quite helpful with Tom's maths homework.

There had been a very cranky call from someone about the violin
lesson who had told Alice that she would still have to pay, seeing as
twenty-four hours' notice hadn't been given. "Oh, well," Alice had
said, and was met by a shocked silence.

After they had got home from the Family Talent Night, she'd let
Madison stay up past eleven baking an enormous Black Forest cake for
a "Food from Different Cultures Day" they were having at the school.

"I don't want your help," Madison had insisted before Alice even
offered to help. "I want to do it myself."

"That's fine," said Alice.

"You always say that," Madison said. "And then you end up
helping."

"I bet you a thousand dollars that I will not lift a finger to help," Alice had said, and held out her hand.

Madison stared, before giving her that sudden beautiful smile and shaking her hand.

"*I* want to bet you something for a thousand dollars," Tom said. "Bet me something!"

"*Me too!*" shouted Olivia. "Bet me something, Mum!"

"No, I'm doing the next bet," said Tom. "Mum, I bet you . . . ummm, I bet you, ummm, just hold on, while I think of something really good."

"I bet you I can do a handstand for five minutes!" cried Olivia. "No, two! No, let's maybe just make it one minute."

"I bet you a thousand dollars I can't count to one million!" said Tom. "I mean that I *can*! The way it works is that you give me a thousand dollars if I *can*."

"Nobody can count to one million," said Olivia solemnly. "That would take, like, a week."

"No it wouldn't," said Tom. "Okay, so let's say that it takes you sixty seconds to count to sixty. Or, wait. Okay, maybe you could count, like, to ninety in sixty seconds. So, ummm, where's the calculator? Mum? Do you know where the calculator is? Mum, are you listening?"

"Are you children always this *tiring*?" Alice had asked. Sometimes it felt like they sucked every thought out of her brain.

"Pretty much," said Tom.

Elisabeth's Homework for Jeremy

While the butchers were in groups brainstorming ideas on butcher paper (ha ha), I sat and thought about the transfer of the last embryo two weeks ago.

It had been frozen for a year.

A tiny, ice-encrusted potential person.

When we first started IVF, I would stand at the freezer door and take a sparkly fragment of ice on the tip of my finger and think about my frozen potential children. All those possible people. We had seven frozen at one time. Such a treasure trove of possibility. This one could be a swimmer. This one could be musical. This one could be tall. This one could be short. This one could be sweet and shy. This one could be funny. This one could be like Ben. This one could be like me.

Ben and I talked about it all the time. We sent them telepathic messages of support. "Hang in there," we said. "Hope you're not too chilly."

But as the years went by, we stopped talking like that. We became detached from the process. It was just science. It was just unpleasant medical procedures. We weren't even amazed by the science anymore. Yeah, yeah, they make babies in test tubes. Incredible. But it just doesn't work out for us.

This last time, we'd run late, and we got a ticket for doing an illegal right-hand turn. It was my idea to do the illegal turn to get there faster, and Ben was so cranky with himself for listening to me, because as a result we were even later. "How could you not see that sign?" the policeman had said, and Ben's mouth twisted with everything he probably wanted to say. "It was *her*!" The policeman took an incredible amount of time writing out the ticket, as if he knew we were running late and this was part of our punishment.

"Let's just go home," I'd said to Ben. "It's not going to work anyway. This is a sign. Let's not waste our money on the parking."

I wanted him to say something positive and comforting, but he was in a bad mood by now. He said, "That's a great attitude. Really great." He's not normally sarcastic.

Anyway, I know now that he didn't think it was going to work either. A week later he was eating Alice's banana muffins and getting all excited about adoption, before we even knew if this one had worked or not.

The embryologist was a young girl who didn't look all that much older than Madison. She tripped on something when we were walking into the treatment room, which I didn't think was a very good sign. Oops. There goes your embryo!

When I was in the chair, with my legs elegantly spread, waiting for the gigantic needle, she muttered something and none of us heard her.

"There's your embryo," she said again, embarrassed. Maybe it was her first time. We looked, and there, projected on the lit-up screen, was our potential baby.

It looked just like its non-brothers and non-sisters. A froth of bubbles. A magnified drop of water.

I didn't bother to marvel. I didn't bother to say anything like, "Oh, isn't it amazing." I didn't bother to keep the memory in my head, in case I one day had to describe it to my child. "I saw you when you were just a pretty little blastocyst, sweetie."

I didn't know the doctor who was doing the transfer. My lovely doctor is away in Paris at the moment because her daughter is getting married to a French lawyer. This doctor was a man, with a long somber face, and he reminded me of our tax accountant. An especially ominous sign. (We never get refunds.) My doctor normally chats away about whatever comes into her head, but this man didn't say anything until it was done. Then he showed us the embryo on the ultrasound.

"Good. It's in the right spot," he said blandly, as if my uterus was a piece of industrial equipment.

It looked like the others did on the ultrasound. A tremulously blinking star.

I knew it wouldn't blink for long.

I looked away from the ultrasound screen to Ben, and he was studying his hands.

Bad signs all around.

Breathe in. Breathe out. Breathe in. Breathe out.

After the butchers had finished their brainstorming I went up onstage and told them that my assistant Layla would be taking the remainder of the day, as if that was always the plan.

The butchers clapped her amiably when she stood up, a confused look on her face.

I walked out. I just couldn't get that blinking star out of my damned head.

Alice was walking toward the library at the school (her body seemed to know that it was through that double red door at the corner of the schoolyard) when Dominick appeared. He looked ruffled, his face creased with worry.

"Alice," he said. "I saw you through my office window. I've been trying to phone you."

"Sorry," said Alice. "I keep forgetting to charge my phone. Memory!"

He didn't smile. "I called Nick, too," he said. "He's on his way."

"You called Nick? Why?" Was he going to fight him for her hand?

Challenge him to a duel? (Except Nick didn't want her hand anymore. So, you know, maybe not much of a fight. *Sure, mate, have her.*)

"We've got a problem," said Dominick. "A serious problem with Madison."

Elisabeth's Homework for Jeremy

After I left the seminar I got a phone call from Ben. His voice sounded like sandpaper.

"Why didn't you tell me?" he said.

I hung up.

I didn't like his tone.

Chapter 28

Is she all right?" Terror flooded Alice's bloodstream, making her legs wobble so badly she had to hold on to Dominick's arm to steady herself.

"Oh, yes, sorry." Dominick smiled distractedly and patted Alice on the arm. "Physically, she's fine. It's just that we've had another incident, and I don't think we can ignore this one."

"Another incident?"

"Another bullying incident."

"Someone is bullying Madison?" She would throttle the kid. She would demand to see the parents. She was light-headed with rage. Someone had hurt the Sultana and she was going to have the brat for breakfast.

"Alice," said Dominick. He looked a little stern. School-principal stern. "It's Madison who is the bully."

"Madison wouldn't bully anyone." She knew her daughter. She'd only known her for five days, but she knew her.

And sure, maybe she could be moody and a little, well, *aggressive*, toward her brother and sister when she was riled, but that was just normal sibling rivalry (she hoped). Her heart was in the right place. Look at the way she helped Olivia choreograph her butterfly dance. Look at the way she helped Tom with his geography homework the other day. Okay, Tom said she was being annoying, and it had ended up with Madison stomping off in floods of tears and Tom slapping his hand to his forehead and rolling his eyes like a miniature version of his father, but, well . . . Alice's daughter would not, could not, be a bully.

"Are you still—not yourself?" asked Dominick carefully.

"Not quite," said Alice.

"Well, this isn't the first time we've had problems with Madison. A little boy had to have stitches a few weeks ago after an altercation with Madison."

Ah, thought Alice. That was the "little incident" that Kate Harper had mentioned at the gym.

"I know she's having problems, after Gina's death, and with the divorce," continued Dominick, his forehead puckered with school principal-ish concern. "Alice, I'm so sorry, but this is really—oh." His voice changed as he saw someone over Alice's shoulder. "Here's your, ah—your . . ."

Alice turned around and saw Nick coming toward them. He was wearing his suit and tie and talking into his mobile phone. His aura of business and decisions and important mustn't-be-disturbed meetings looked alien in the sunlit playground, with the sounds of children chanting something from the open window of a nearby classroom.

Dominick caught her eye. "Hope this isn't too awkward."

"Yes," said Alice awkwardly.

As he got closer, they heard him say, "Well, let's say two mil. Does that sound okay? Excellent. Bye." He snapped the phone shut with one hand and Alice wanted to say, *Oh, Nick, honey, stop being such a wanker.*

"Dominick, isn't it?" said Nick, holding out his hand, as if Dominick were there to sell them something.

"Yes, hi. How are you?" said Dominick. He was about a head taller than Nick and looked like a gangly schoolboy next to him. Alice wanted to hug him, but she wanted to hug Nick, too. They seemed like boys dressed up in grown-up bodies.

"This must be pretty important for you to call us both down," said Nick, an edge to his voice.

"Yes," said Dominick, and there was an answering edge in his voice. "Madison threatened to stab Chloe Harper with a pair of scissors. She also cut off a huge chunk of her hair and pushed her face into a cake. I'm going to have to suspend her at least until the school holidays. I think she needs to see a counselor."

"I see," said Nick, and he seemed to deflate and sag. All the power had gone to Dominick.

"There must be more to the story," said Alice. "She must have had a reason."

"It doesn't matter about her reason," said Dominick (a bit snootily, Alice thought, for someone who was trying to be her boyfriend). "It's unacceptable. And you can imagine how Kate Harper is going to react to this. She's on her way to the school, too."

So Chloe was the horrendous Kate Harper's little girl. Well, there you go. That explained everything.

"We'll have to—I don't know—offer some sort of compensation," sighed Nick.

"I don't think money is the answer in this particular case," said Dominick. *Ke-pow.*

"I didn't mean—"

"Anyway, I've got both girls waiting for us in my office," interrupted Dominick.

Alice and Nick followed behind him like naughty children. Alice made an "Isn't this appalling" face at Nick, and he grimaced.

In Dominick's office, Madison and another little girl were sitting on chairs in front of his desk. The little girl was sobbing in an outraged "I *so* deserve to cry" way, cradling something in her arms, and Alice saw with sick horror that it was a long, blond plait. She had bits of chocolate cake and cream and cherries smeared all over her face and school uniform and the shocking, hacked-off line of her blond hair stuck up over the back collar of her uniform.

"Oh, Madison," said Alice involuntarily. "How *could* you?"

Madison's face was dead white, her eyes shining with fury. She was sitting very still and straight with her hands in fists on her lap, the image of a little psychopathic killer brought into the police station for questioning.

"You've got some explaining to do, young lady," said Nick, and Alice nearly laughed. He sounded like a man playing the angry dad in a bad amateur play.

Madison didn't say anything.

"Do you want to tell your parents what happened?" said Dominick, sounding much more authentic.

Madison shook her head passionately, as if she were refusing to reveal state secrets to her torturers.

"She hasn't said a word," said Dominick to Alice.

The little girl dangled the blond plait in front of her, tears continuing to roll down her face. "Look at my *hair*. My mum is going to *kill* you, Madison Love. My hair is *beautiful*. It will take me years and years and years to grow it back. I will be, like, forty. You just did it because you're *jealous*, and you haven't even said . . ." Her voice quavered, as if she were overcome with the horror of it. "You haven't even said *sorry*."

"Okay, Chloe," said Dominick. "Let's calm down."

"Madison, apologize to Chloe," said Alice, in a grim, forbidding voice she didn't recognize. "Right now."

"Sorry," muttered Madison.

"She *isn't!*" wailed Chloe, looking up at Alice and Nick. "She's just saying that! Just wait till my mum gets here!"

"Actually," said Dominick. "I don't think we will wait. I think Mr. and Mrs. Love can take Madison with them now."

He squatted down in front of Madison so they were face-to-face.

"Madison, I'm suspending you from school as of now," he said. "You can't be a part of this school and behave like that, do you understand? This is very, very serious."

Madison nodded. Her face had now gone from white to flaming red.

"Right then." Dominick stood up. "Go and get your bag and meet your parents at the gate."

Madison shot from the room, and Chloe burst into a fresh flood of tears.

"Okay, Chloe," said Dominick wearily. "Your mum will be here soon. Just wait here."

He ushered Nick and Alice out of the room, closing the door behind him.

"There's probably not much point you having to see Kate now, while everyone is in such a state," he said. "I think you should take Madison home and try and talk to her and get an idea of what's going on in her head. I would seriously recommend counseling. I can give you some names." There was a sound of hurriedly clicking heels in the distance. "I bet that's Kate. Go." He waved them away, as if he were saving them from the secret police. "Disappear!"

Nick and Alice fled through the playground. They stopped at the school gates. Nick was panting. Alice wasn't. She was much fitter than he was.

"That was awful," said Alice. "I feel like I cut off that child's hair myself. And the cake! She spent so long making that cake. Poor little thing."

"Chloe?" said Nick.

"No, Madison," said Alice. "Who cares about Chloe?"

"Alice, our child threatened to stab her with a pair of scissors."

"Well, I know that," said Alice.

Nick pulled out his mobile phone from his pocket, flipped it open. "I don't see how suspending her helps anything," he said, while frowning at something on the screen of his phone. "It's like they're putting their hands in the air and saying, 'We don't know what to do with her.' Absolving themselves of responsibility." He looked up at Alice. "Not to criticize your boyfriend or anything."

"I guess it's school policy," said Alice, feeling both defensive of Dominick and betrayed by him. Didn't kissing the school principal give you a free pass when it came to suspending your daughter?

"Anyway"—Nick looked at his watch—"I'll get back to the office. I guess we'd better talk about this later. I don't know what sort of punishment you're thinking, but obviously it has to be severe—"

"What do you mean?" said Alice. "I think we should talk to her now. Right now. Both of us."

Nick seemed startled. "Now? You want me to be there, too?"

"Of course I do," said Alice. "I think we should take her for a drive. And we're not going to jump in and start *punishing* her. I hate that word. Punishment."

"Oh, sorry. I guess we should reward her. Say 'Well done, honey, maybe you should consider a career in hairdressing.'"

Alice giggled. Nick smiled. The sunlight was shining directly onto his face. He shielded his eyes with one hand and said, "I'll know when you get your memory back."

"How?"

"The way you look at me. As soon as you remember, I'll see it in your eyes."

"Will they shoot death rays at you?" said Alice.

Nick smiled sadly. "Something like that." He looked again at his watch. "I've got a meeting at midday. I guess I could move it." He seemed uncertain. "So you mean both of us take her for a drive somewhere?"

Alice said, "Is this really so unusual?"

"Normally you'd take charge and make it clear that my assistance was not required."

"There's a new Alice in town," said Alice.

"You're not wrong about that." Nick seemed about to say something. He stopped and looked over her shoulder. "Here comes our little thug."

Madison was walking toward them, her school backpack held loosely in one hand so it was almost dragging along the ground, her head hanging.

"Who am I going with?" she said when she got to them, not meeting their eyes.

"Both of us," said Alice.

"Both of you?" Madison looked up and frowned. She seemed frightened.

"Come here," said Alice.

Madison stomped over to her, still staring at the ground, and Alice pulled her close and hugged her.

"We're going to work this out," said Alice quietly into her hair. "You, your dad, and me are going to sit on the beach, eat ice creams, and work out whatever the problem is."

Madison gave a tiny gasp of surprise and burst into tears.

Elisabeth's Homework for Jeremy

He keeps saying, "Turn the television off."

And I keep saying, "Not yet."

He turned it off himself a while ago, and as soon as he did, I screamed over and over, as if he was hurting me.

A tiny bit dramatic. I will feel embarrassed later.

But it did hurt me. That loud buzzing silence after the TV was switched off was actually painful to my eardrums.

He was probably worried the neighbors would call the police. After all, he looks exactly like the sort of man you expect to see dragged away in handcuffs for domestic violence. So he shrugged and turned it back on.

I am watching Oprah now. She's talking about an exciting new diet. The audience is excited. I'm excited, J. I might try it. I'm taking notes.

They sat on the harbor-side beach at Manly, near the ferry stop, in the same spot where they'd had coffee that early morning after they drove Madison through the night when she was a baby.

They even had the same blue-and-white-checked picnic rug. It was in the boot of Nick's car. The blue wasn't as bright as it was in Alice's memory, but her palms remembered its nubbly feel.

"Where did we get this rug?" asked Alice as they sat down.

"I don't know," said Nick. He sounded defensive. "You can have it if you want. I didn't realize it was in my car."

Oh, for heaven's sake. She hadn't meant she wanted it. It was yet another glimpse of how stupid their lives had become. Would she really have wanted to make a point about who got the picnic rug?

Madison plonked herself down and sat with her arms wrapped around her knees, chin down, lank hair falling down on either side of her face. (Alice itched to snip it off. She would look so much prettier with short hair. Actually that could be the perfect "punishment"! *You cut her hair, kid, so I'm going to cut yours.*)

After her tears in the schoolyard, Madison hadn't said a word. Nick had driven in his shiny car, and he'd spent a lot of time talking on his hands-free mobile. He laughed. He listened. He gave short, sharp instructions. He said, "Let me think about it." He said, "Well, that's a disaster," while glancing over his shoulder to switch lanes. He said, "Well done. That's great news." He was such a boss.

"Do you enjoy work at the moment?" Alice asked him at one point in between calls.

Nick glanced over at her. "Yes," he said, after a few seconds. "I love it."

"That's great," said Alice, happy for him.

Nick raised an eyebrow. "You really think so?"

"Of course," said Alice. "Why wouldn't I?"

"Nothing," said Nick, and Alice could sense Madison listening carefully from the backseat.

Nick had turned his phone off now and had left his jacket and tie in the car. Now he was taking off his shoes and socks. Alice looked at his bare feet digging into the sand. His feet were as familiar as her own. How could she not be with someone forever when even their *feet*—his huge, not especially attractive feet, with their long hairy toes—felt like home?

"Beautiful," said Nick, gesturing at the smooth, hard, yellow sand, the huge turquoise sky, the ferry chugging its way across the harbor to the city. *"Beautiful."* He said it in the same satisfied tone that he would use to describe a good meal at a restaurant, as if the weather and the beach had been prepared especially for him, and presented on a plate, and yes, thank you, it was all up to his high standards and there would be a generous tip as a result. It was so typical Nick. He held up his face to the sun and closed his eyes.

Alice took off her own boots (beautiful—her taste was impeccable, if she did say so herself) and pulled off her socks.

"They're Tom's soccer socks," said Madison, looking up from her knees.

"I was in a rush," said Alice.

Madison gave her a look. "And that scarf you're wearing is from Olivia's *dress-up box*."

"I know, but it's so beautiful." Alice lifted up the gauzy material.

Madison gave her an inscrutable look and lowered her chin again.

Nick opened his eyes. "Well, Madison—"

"You *promised* ice creams," said Madison, glaring at Alice, as if this was to be yet another in a long line of broken promises.

"That's right, I did," said Alice.

Nick sighed. "I'll go." He put his shoes back on and looked down at Madison. "Don't you be telling your brother and sister that you got ice cream on the beach, will you? Or next thing, we'll have all the Love children suspended from school."

Madison giggled. "Okay."

As Nick walked off, Madison said, "I don't want to say what happened in front of Daddy."

It must be girl stuff. "All right. Just tell me."

Madison dropped her chin back to her knees and said in a muffled voice, "Chloe said that you and Mr. Gordon had—"

Alice didn't catch the last word.

"Pardon?" she said.

"*Sex!*" Madison choked out. "She said that you and Mr. Gordon probably did sex in his office. Like, a hundred times."

Mr. Gordon. Oh. *Dominick*.

"Darling," began Alice, wondering where to start. For one thing she wasn't sure if it was true. Surely they wouldn't have had sex in his office? Would they?

"I nearly threw up. I had to take sort of deep breaths and put my hand over my mouth. You *didn't*, did you? You never took off your clothes in front of Mr. Gordon, did you?"

Well, if she had, surely Chloe wasn't privy to the information. Presumably Dominick hadn't made an announcement about it at school assembly.

"Chloe Harper is a horrible liar," said Alice decisively.

"I *know*," said Madison with relief. "That's what I said!" She looked out at the water and pushed her hair back behind her ears. "Then she said that I was the ugliest girl in the whole school, but that part wasn't a lie, that part was true."

Alice's heart broke for her. "It certainly was not true."

"I got this feeling," said Madison. "A feeling like my head was going to explode. She was standing in front of me and I got out my scissors for art and I cut off her plait. I just went, snip! And it fell straight to the ground. And then when she turned around, I threw my cake at her. It wrecked the cake. Nobody even got to taste it. It was the best cake I ever made."

"Did you threaten to stab her with the scissors?"

"No! She just made that bit up so I would get into more trouble."

"Is that the truth?"

"Yes," said Madison.

"Okay," said Alice. Well, that was something.

Alice said, "You know, Madison, people are going to say mean things to you all through your life, and if you keep reacting like that, you're going to end up in jail."

Madison seemed to consider that. Alice wondered whether her wise, tough-love words were sinking in.

"Actually, I'm too young for jail," said Madison.

"Well, *now* you are, but when you're grown up——"

"When I'm a grown-up it won't matter."

"You mean, you won't care if you go to jail? I think you will."

Madison rolled her eyes. "No. I won't care if people say mean things to me, because I'll be grown up. I can just say, 'Who cares? I'm going to France.'"

Ah. Of course. Alice could remember thinking something similar when she was a child. Once you were a grown-up nobody could hurt your feelings because how could your feelings possibly be hurt when you could *drive a car wherever you wanted.*

Before she could think of a way to answer without disillusioning her (what was there to look forward to otherwise?), a shadow fell over them.

"Ice cream delivery." Nick was standing above them, holding three ice cream cones.

"I assume you still like rum and raisin," he said to Alice.

"Of course." Fancy having to ask her that.

They sat and ate their ice creams, looking out at the water.

"Madison has just told me what Chloe said to her," said Alice. "And it was something nasty and untrue."

"Okay," said Nick carefully. He licked his ice cream and looked at them both.

"So, I guess we need to help Madison find some better ways to react when she feels angry."

"I always take ten deep breaths before I say anything when I'm angry," said Nick.

"No you don't," said Madison. "You just yell straightaway. So does Mum. And what about that time Mum threw that pizza box at you?"

Oh my, they'd been setting fine examples for their children.

Alice cleared her throat. "Well, the thing is——"

"Are you going to come home, please, Dad?" said Madison. "I think you should come home now and be Mum's husband again. I'm pretty sure then I would stop being angry. Then I would never do another bad thing in my whole entire life. I could write that in a *contract* for you. So that means you could, like, *sue* me if I was ever bad, which I would not ever be."

She looked at her father with desperate entreaty.

"Sweetheart," began Nick, his face screwed tight as if he had a toothache. Then he stopped, distracted by some sort of disturbance on the beach. There were shouts and people running. Alice could see a small crowd of people forming up on the cliff above the aquarium, pointing at something in the water.

"Humpback whales in the harbor!" a man cried at them, running along with a camera bouncing on his chest.

Nick immediately leapt to his feet, still holding his ice cream. Madison and Alice looked up at him.

"What are you waiting for?" he said, and next thing the three of them were running breathlessly along the beach, up onto the foreshore, and running around the walkway, their ice creams held precariously in front of them.

They had to run a steep set of concrete steps and Alice drew ahead, one hand holding her ice cream, the other holding up her skirt as she effortlessly leapt up the steps, two at a time.

As she reached the top, she was in time to see a massive plume of water shoot up from the water below them.

"It's a mother and her calf," said a woman to Alice. "Watch. Just there. You'll see them again."

Nick and Madison pounded up the stairs behind her. Nick was breathing heavily. (How did he get so unfit?)

"Where? Where?" said Madison. Her face was pink and anxious.

"Just watch," said Alice.

For a few seconds there was nothing but silence. The surface of the harbor rippled in the breeze and a seagull squawked plaintively.

"They've gone," said Madison. "We've missed them. Typical."

Nick looked at his watch.

Come on, whale, thought Alice. *Give us a break.*

The water erupted as a massive creature shot straight into the air. It was like something prehistoric had crashed through an invisible barrier into ordinary life. Alice caught a glimpse of a barnacle-encrusted white front. It seemed to hover in the air before slamming back into the water, with a flurry of icy, salty raindrops against their faces.

Madison grabbed hold of Alice's arm. Her face was radiant with joy, speckled with droplets of water. "Look, Mum! Look!"

The whale rolled luxuriously about, revealing huge curves of velvety black skin, its tail slapping the water, as if enjoying a hot bath.

"Madison, Alice, over there—it's the baby!" shouted Nick, and he sounded like a sixteen-year-old boy.

The calf was splashing about in miniature imitation of its mother. Alice could almost imagine it gurgling with laughter.

"Ha!" said Nick idiotically. "Ha!"

All around them were faces full of joy and wonder. The sea air was cool on their faces, the sun warm on their backs.

"Do it again!" said Madison. "Jump up again, mother whale!"

"Yeah!" agreed the man with the camera. "One more time."

And right on cue, she did.

Elisabeth's Homework for Jeremy

Ben is threatening to ring you up. He thinks I'm behaving like a crazy person.

Frannie's Letter to Phil

Something quite extraordinary has happened, Phil.

As they walked back to the picnic rug, Madison danced around them. She was euphoric. Skipping. Jumping. Swinging on Nick's hand, then Alice's, then both. People walking by smiled at her.

"That was the best thing I've ever seen!" she kept saying. "I'm going to blow that photo up into a poster and put it over my bed!"

The man with the camera had taken Nick's e-mail address and was going to send him the photo he'd taken.

"Let's hope he didn't miss it," said Nick.

"No, he got it," said Madison. "He definitely got it. Can I go paddle? Just to feel the water?"

She looked at Alice, and Alice looked at Nick. He shrugged.

"Sure," said Alice. "Why not?"

They watched her run down toward the water.

"Do you think she needs counseling?" said Alice.

"She's been through a lot," said Nick. "Gina's accident. You and me. And she always feels things so deeply."

"What do you mean, Gina's accident?" Alice thought about Madison's nightmare. *Get it off her.*

"Madison was with you," said Nick. "She saw it happen. You don't remember it, do you?"

"No," said Alice. "Just the feeling of it." Although that feeling of sick horror seemed impossible here today, with the sun and sea, ice creams and whales.

"There was a storm," said Nick. "A tree fell on Gina's car. You and Madison were driving behind."

A tree. So that horrible image of a black leafless tree swaying against a stormy sky was real.

"It must have been horrendous for both of you," said Nick quietly. He lifted a handful of sand and let the grains fall through his fingers. "And I didn't—I wasn't—"

"What?"

"I wasn't as supportive as I should have been," said Nick.

"Why weren't you?" asked Alice curiously.

"Honestly, I don't know," said Nick. "I just felt detached. I felt like you wouldn't want my sympathy. I felt like—I felt that if you'd had the choice, you would have preferred that I'd died rather than Gina. I remember I tried to hug you and you pushed me away as if I made you sick. I should have tried harder. I'm sorry."

"But why would you think I'd prefer you to die?" asked Alice. It seemed such a silly, childish, wrong thing to think.

"We weren't getting on that well at the time. And you two were such good friends," said Nick. "I mean—that was great—that was fine—but . . ." His lips did something funny. "You told Gina that you were pregnant with Olivia before you told me."

"Really?" Why would she have done that? "I'm sorry."

"Oh, well, it was only a small thing." He stopped. "Also, once I overheard you saying something about our sex life. Or lack thereof. I mean, I know women always talk about sex together. It was just the tone in your voice. It was such *contempt* for me. And then, when she and Mike broke up, and you were going out to bars with her, trying to help her pick up men, I got the feeling that you were jealous. You wanted to be a single woman with her. I was in the way. Cramping your style."

"I'm so sorry," said Alice. She felt like some other woman had been horrible to Nick. As if he were describing an awful ex-girlfriend who had broken his heart.

"And then Gina died. And that was it. You froze up. That's how it felt. You were like ice."

"I don't understand why I did that," said Alice. If *Sophie* had died, she would have cried for hours in the safe, comforting circle of Nick's arms.

"Is that why you didn't come to the funeral?" she asked.

Nick shrugged.

"I had to be in New York. It was a huge meeting. Something we'd been planning for months, but I told you a million bloody times I was happy to cancel. I kept asking if you wanted me at the funeral, and you said, 'Do what you want.' So, I thought, maybe you'd actually prefer it if I *wasn't* there. I wanted to go. She was my friend, too, once upon a time. You always seem to forget that. She drove me crazy the way she bossed you around, but I still cared about her. It just got so confusing after she and Mike split up. I wanted to stay friends with him, too, and you saw that as a betrayal of Gina. So did she. She was so mad with me. Each time I saw Gina, she'd say, 'Seen Mike lately?' and you'd both be shooting me evil looks as if I was the villain. I didn't see why I had to dump a good mate just because of one drunken—anyway, we've been over it a million times. I'm just trying to say that I felt so, I don't know, *awkward*, when she died. I didn't know how I was meant to act. I just wanted you to say, 'Of course you should cancel the trip. Of course you should come to the funeral.' I felt like I needed your permission."

"So all our problems were because of Gina and Mike," said Alice. These two *strangers* had destroyed their marriage.

"I don't think we can blame them for everything," said Nick. "We argued. We argued over the most trivial things."

"Like what?"

"Like, I don't know, cherries. One day we were going over to Mum's place for dinner and I ate some cherries we were meant to be taking. It was the crime of the century. You would not let it go. You were talking about those cherries for months."

"Cherries," pondered Alice.

"I'd be at work, where people respected my opinions," said Nick.

"And then I'd come home and it was like I was the village idiot. I'd pack the dishwasher the wrong way. I'd pick the wrong clothes for the children. I stopped offering to help. It wasn't worth the criticism."

They didn't say anything for a few moments. Next to them, a family with a toddler and a baby laid out a rug. The toddler picked up a handful of sand with a determined expression on his face and went to drop it all over his baby sister's face. They heard the mother say, "Watch him!" and the father pulled him away just in time. The mother rolled her eyes, and the father muttered something they didn't catch.

"I'm not saying I was perfect," said Nick, his eyes on the father. "I was too caught up in work. You'd say I was obsessed with it. You always talk about the year I was working on the Goodman project. I was traveling a lot. You had to cope on your own with three children. You said once that I 'deserted you.' I always think that year made my career, but maybe . . ." He stopped and squinted out at the harbor. "Maybe that was the year that broke our marriage."

The Goodman project. The words put a bad taste in her mouth. *The bloody Goodman project.* The word "bloody" seemed to belong naturally before "Goodman."

Alice leaned back and pushed the heels of her boots deep into the sand. It all seemed so complicated. Her mistakes. Nick's mistakes. For the first time it occurred to her that maybe their marriage couldn't be put back together.

She looked over at the family with the two small children. Now the father was spinning the little boy around and the mother was laughing, taking photos of them with a digital camera.

Madison walked up from the water toward them, carrying something in her cupped-together hands, her face radiant.

Nick's hand was next to Alice's on the picnic rug.

She felt the tip of his finger lightly touch hers.

"Maybe we should try again," he said.

Chapter 29

George and Mildred turned up on Friday.

Alice found them at the back of the garage. George was lying on his side, as if he'd been kicked over. His once dignified lion's face was now stained a moldy green, which made him look ashamed, as if he were an old man with food all over his face. Mildred was sitting in the middle of a pile of old pots. There was a huge chip out of one paw, and she looked sad and resigned. They were both filthy.

Alice had dragged them both onto the back veranda and was scrubbing them with a mixture of bleach and water, as recommended by Mrs. Bergen next door, who was thrilled that Alice had swapped sides on the development issue, and who was once again waving and smiling when she saw her and asking Alice to send the children over to play on her piano anytime they wanted. "We're not *five* anymore," said Tom wearily. "Doesn't she know we have a PlayStation?"

Barb had offered to take Madison for a shopping trip on the first day of her suspension. "Don't worry, I won't spoil her," she'd told Alice. "No new clothes or anything. Unless she sees something really *special*, of course, in which case I'll put it away for her next birthday."

As Alice scrubbed, she wondered if George and Mildred would ever look the same again. Was it too late? Were they too scarred by the years of neglect?

And would it be the same for her and Nick? Had each argument, each betrayal and nasty word built up into an ugly rock-hard layer covering what was once so tender and true?

Well, if it had, they would just chip away at it until it was gone. It would be fine. Good as new! She scrubbed so vigorously at Mildred's mane that her teeth chattered.

The phone rang and Alice put down the scrubbing brush with relief.

It was Ben. His voice on the phone was deep and slow and very Australian, as if someone from the outback were calling. He said that Elisabeth had been sitting in bed watching television for the last forty-eight hours and screaming if he tried to turn it off, and he wasn't sure how long he should let this go on for.

"It must be because she's so upset about the last IVF cycle failing," said Alice, looking at her fridge with the photos of the children and the school newsletters, and wishing she could somehow share this life with her sister.

There was a slight pause and then Ben said, "Yeah, well, that's the other thing. I found out that it didn't fail. I got a call from the clinic about her first ultrasound. She's pregnant."

Elisabeth's Homework for Jeremy

I can hear him in the next room calling Alice. I made him promise not to tell anyone I was pregnant.

I knew he would. Liar.

You have no idea of the fury I feel. Against him. His mother. My mother. Alice. You, Jeremy. I hate you all. For no particular reason.

I guess it's for the sympathy, the pity and understanding, but most of all, for the hope. For the comments I'm about to hear. "This one could be the one!" "I have a good feeling about this one!"

Waves of red-hot fury keep rising up inside me. I'm trying to ride them like I imagine you might do with labor pains. I feel sick, and my breasts ache, and there is a funny taste in my mouth, and we've been here so many times before, and I can't go through it again, I can't.

And the thing that infuriates me the most, Jeremy, is that even though I'm saying it and I'm believing it and I know with all my heart that I'm going to lose this baby like all the others, I also know that underneath it all, that inanely positive, pathetic voice is still chirping, "But maybe . . . ?"

Alice drove over to Elisabeth's place.

She had to get directions from Ben, and none of the streets or the area seemed remotely familiar. Perhaps she didn't visit Elisabeth much? Because she was so busy. Busy, busy, busy.

They lived in a red-brick cottage with a neatly mowed front lawn. It was a family neighborhood. There was a children's swing set in the front yard of the house next door, and a woman across the road was leaning into her car and unstrapping her baby from a car seat. It reminded Alice of her own street ten years ago.

She could hear the clamor of the television as soon as Ben opened the door. "She wants it up really loud," said Ben. "Be ready. If you try and turn it off, she sounds like a trapped animal. It's freaking me out.

I had to go sleep in the spare room last night. I don't know if she even slept at all."

"So, what do you think is going on?" asked Alice.

Ben shrugged his massive bear shoulders. "I guess she's scared she's going to lose it again. So am I. I mean, in a way, I was almost relieved when I thought the blood-test results were negative."

Alice followed Ben through the house (very clean, neat, and bare; no clutter) into the bedroom, where Elisabeth was sitting up in bed with the remote in one hand and an exercise book and pen resting on her lap.

She was still wearing the same outfit she wore at the seminar for the butchers on Wednesday, except her hair was a tangled mess and her mascara had smudged so she had thick black shadows under her eyes.

Alice didn't say anything. She just kicked off her shoes and hopped into bed beside Elisabeth, pulling the covers up and putting a pillow behind her back.

Ben hovered uncertainly at the door. "Okay," he said, "I'll be working on the car."

"Okay." Alice smiled at him.

Alice glanced at Elisabeth's profile. Her face was set, her eyes fixed on the television.

Alice stayed silent. She couldn't think of the right thing to say. Maybe just being there would be enough.

An old episode of *M*A*S*H* was on the television. The familiar characters and the sudden bursts of canned laughter took Alice straight back to 1975. She and Elisabeth sitting on that old beige couch after school, waiting for their mother to come home from work, eating ham-and-tomato-sauce sandwiches on white bread.

Alice's mind drifted. She thought about this strange little period of time in her life that began when she woke up in the gym last Friday morning. It was like this past week had been a holiday in an exotic destination that required the learning of unusual new skills. So many things had happened. Meeting the children. Seeing Mum and Roger together. The Family Talent Night.

Finally, she felt Elisabeth stir next to her. Alice held her breath.

Elisabeth said irritably, "Don't you have things to do?"

"Nothing more important than this."

Elisabeth grimaced and pulled at the blanket so it came away from Alice's legs. Alice pulled it back over her.

*M*A*S*H* finished and Elisabeth changed the channel. Audrey Hepburn's delicate features filled the screen. Elisabeth switched it again to a cooking show.

Alice felt like coffee. She wondered if it would break the moment, whatever this moment was, if she went into the kitchen and made herself a cup to bring back to bed. Oh, for a Dino's large double-shot skim latte.

Dino.

She dived for her handbag, which she'd left on the floor next to the bed and rummaged through it. She pulled out the fertility doll and carefully placed it on the sheets between herself and Elisabeth. It looked back at them with inscrutable boggle-eyes. Alice angled it so it was facing Elisabeth.

More time passed and Elisabeth said, "Okay, what is that thing?"

"It's a fertility doll," said Alice. "Dino from the coffee shop gave it to me to give to you."

Elisabeth picked it up and examined it. "I guess he's trying to insure against me kidnapping more of his customers' children."

"Probably," agreed Alice.

"What am I meant to do with it?"

"I don't know," said Alice. "You could bring it sacrificial offerings?" Elisabeth rolled her eyes. There was a glimmer of a smile.

Elisabeth put the doll on the bedside table next to her.

"It would be due in January," she said. "If it . . ."

"Well, that seems like a good time to have a baby," said Alice. "It wouldn't be too cold when you got up in the night to feed."

"There won't be any *baby*," said Elisabeth viciously.

"We could ask Dad to put in a good word for you," said Alice. "He must be able to pull some strings up there."

"Do you think I didn't ask Dad with the other pregnancies?" said Elisabeth. "I prayed to the lot of them. Jesus. Mary. Saint Gerard. He's meant to be the patron saint of fertility. None of them listened. They're ignoring me."

"Dad wouldn't be ignoring you," said Alice, and her father's face was suddenly clear in her mind. So often she could only remember the face that appeared in photos, not the face from her own memory. "Maybe he's got to deal with a lot of bureaucrats in Heaven."

"I don't think I believe in life after death anyway," said Elisabeth. "I used to have all these romantic ideas about Dad taking care of my lost babies, but then it got out of hand. He'd be running a whole bloody day care center."

"At least it would take his mind off the sight of Mum and Roger salsa-dancing," said Alice.

This time Elisabeth definitely smiled.

She said, "Mum remembers all my due dates. She calls first thing in the morning and chats, doesn't say anything about the date, just chats away."

"She seems good with the children," said Alice. "They adore her."

"She's a good grandma," sighed Elisabeth.

"I guess we've forgiven her," said Alice.

Elisabeth turned to look at her sharply, but she didn't say "Forgiven her for what?"

It was something they'd never really talked about (well, as far as Alice knew they'd never talked about it); the way Barb had stopped being a mother after their dad died. She'd just given up. It had been shocking. Overnight, she became a mother who couldn't care less if they left the house without warm clothes, or if they cleaned their teeth, or if they ate vegetables—and did that mean she'd only been *pretending* to care before? Even months afterward, she just wanted to drift around all day, holding their hands while she cried over photo albums. That's when Frannie had stepped in and given their lives structure and rules again.

Alice and Elisabeth had stopped thinking of Barb as their mother and more as a slightly simple older sister. Even when she eventually recovered and started trying to exert her authority, they didn't really let her be the mother again. It was a subtle but definite form of revenge.

"Yes," said Elisabeth after a while. "I guess we did eventually forgive her. I don't know when exactly, but we did."

"It's strange how things work out."

"Yes."

They watched an ad for a carpet sale, and Elisabeth spoke again. "I feel really angry. I can't tell you how angry I feel."

"Okay," said Alice.

More silence.

"We've wasted the last seven years trying to create a life for ourselves, just a standard suburban life with two-point-one kids. That's all we've been doing—we haven't been actually *living*—and now this will put everything on hold for a few months longer until I lose it, and then I'll have to get over that, and then Ben will be at me to fill in the adoption papers, and everybody will be all enthusiastic and supportive. 'Oh, yes, adoption, how lovely, how *multicultural*!' And they'll expect me to forget this baby."

"You might not lose it," said Alice. "You might actually have this baby."

"Of course I'm going to lose it."

The cooking show host drizzled honey into a pan. "You must use non-salt butter. That's the secret."

Elisabeth said, "All I need to do is pretend I'm not pregnant, so that if I lose it, it won't hurt so much, but I can't seem to do that. And then I think, Okay, just be hopeful! Assume it will work. But then every moment I'm scared. Every time I go to the bathroom I'm scared of seeing the blood. Every time I go for an ultrasound I'm scared of seeing their faces change. You're not meant to worry, because stress is bad for the baby, but how can I not worry?"

"Maybe you could delegate the worrying to me," said Alice. "I could worry all day long for you! I'm an excellent worrier, you know that."

Elisabeth smiled and looked back at the television. The cooking show host pulled something out of the oven and sniffed rapturously. "Voilà!"

Elisabeth said, "I should have driven over straightaway when Gina died, and I didn't. I'm sorry."

How strange, thought Alice. Everyone had to apologize for something to do with Gina's death.

"Why didn't you?"

"I didn't know if you'd want me there," said Elisabeth. "I felt as if I'd say the wrong thing. You and Gina were such a pair, and you and I, we've . . . drifted."

Alice moved closer to Elisabeth so their thighs were touching. "Well, let's drift back."

The credits were rolling on the cooking show.

"I'm going to lose this baby," said Elisabeth.

Alice put a hand over onto Elisabeth's stomach.

"I'm going to lose this baby," said Elisabeth again.

Alice put her face down close. She said, "Come on, little niece or nephew. Why don't you just stick around this time? Your mum has been through so much for you."

Elisabeth picked up the remote, turned off the television, and began to cry.

Frannie's Letter to Phil

He kissed me. Mr. Mustache, I mean. Xavier. In the backseat of a cab.

And I kissed him back.

You could knock me down with a feather, Phil.

"I like the lions," said Dominick.

It was nine o'clock at night and he was standing at the front door, holding a packet of chocolate biscuits, a bottle of liqueur, and a bunch of tulips. He was wearing jeans and a faded checked shirt, and he needed a shave.

Alice looked at George and Mildred, back in their old places, guarding the house. It had been an exhausting effort, cleaning them up, and then she'd had to use a wheelbarrow to get them out to the front of the house. Now she couldn't decide if they looked quirky and fun, or grubby and tacky. "I just thought I'd drop by on the off chance you felt like some company," he said. "If you're too busy planning for tomorrow . . ."

Alice hadn't been doing anything, except lying on the couch, staring at the ceiling, and thinking vague thoughts about Elisabeth's baby, and Nick: "trying again." Nick seemed to think they should start out with a "date." "Maybe a movie," he'd said, and Alice had wondered how hard they would have to "try" as they sat in the movie. Would they have to eat their popcorn really enthusiastically? Have an especially animated conversation afterward? Score each other on how many times they'd been funny, their levels of affection? Would they have to *try* to kiss as romantically as possible? No, she didn't want any of this "trying." She just wanted Nick to move back home and for everything to be the way it should be. She was tired of all this nonsense.

It had been an exhausting day. All the children had sports, one after the other. Olivia played netball (lots of histrionic leaping about but not much actual contact with the ball), Tom played soccer (excellently—scored two goals!), and Madison played hockey (abysmally, miserably). "Do you enjoy it?" Alice had asked her as she came off the field. "You know I hate it," Madison had answered. "So why do you play it?" "Because *you* say I have to play a team sport," she'd answered. Alice had gone straight up to the coach and pulled Madison from the team. Both the coach and Madison were thrilled.

Alice had various duties at each game that she had somehow fulfilled smoothly, almost as if she wasn't an impostor in her own life. She'd kept score at Madison's hockey game. She'd helped cook the sausage sizzle at Tom's soccer game. Incredibly, she'd even *umpired* Olivia's netball. Someone had handed her a whistle, and even as Alice was saying, "No, no, I couldn't possibly," the cool shape of the whistle felt right in her hand. Next thing she was striding up and down the sideline, blowing sharply on the whistle, while strange words and phrases flew from her mouth. "Step!" "Held ball!" "Goal attack, you were off side." The children obeyed without question.

Nick had been there at all the games. There had been no time to talk. He had duties, too. He had to be the referee for Tom's soccer game. We're such *parents*, Alice had thought with a mixture of pride and fear—because, was that the problem? Was that why they would have to "try"? Because she was a "mum" and he was a "dad," and mums and dads were generic, boring, and not very sexy. (That's why kissing still went on in laundries at parties? To remind them that they were once randy teenagers?)

Tomorrow was Mother's Day. Mega Meringue Day. The "big day." Probably Alice should have been preparing things—finishing off paperwork, making last-minute phone calls to check people had done what they were meant to do, but she wasn't especially interested in Mega Meringue Day. Anyway, the committee had seemed to have things under control the other day.

"Come in," she said to Dominick, her eyes on the chocolate biscuits.

"The children asleep?" he asked.

"Yes, although——" She was about to say something lighthearted about Tom probably still playing with his Nintendo under the covers, but the hair-cutting experience with Madison made her stop. It would be like ratting on her son to the school principal.

"How was Kate about Chloe's hair?" she asked.

"Predictably hysterical," said Dominick.

"I left a message apologizing," said Alice. "She never called back."

"You understand that I didn't have any choice but to suspend Madison?" said Dominick, as Alice took the flowers out of his hands. "I didn't want . . ."

"Oh, yes, of course, don't worry about it. These are beautiful, by the way. Thank you."

Dominick put down the biscuits on the counter and twisted the bottle of liqueur around and around in his hands.

He said, "I'll know when you get your memory back."

"How?" said Alice.

"By the way you look at me. Now you have this friendly, polite way of looking at me, as if you don't really know me, as if we never even . . ."

Oh God, little Chloe Harper was right. They had "done sex."

He put down the bottle of liqueur and moved closer to her.

No, no, no. Not another kiss. That would be wrong. That would not be within the spirit of "trying."

"Dominick," she said.

The doorbell rang.

"Excuse me," said Alice.

It was Nick at the front door.

He was holding a bottle of wine, cheese, biscuits, and a bunch of tulips identical to the ones Dominick had brought over. They must be on special at some local shop.

"You've fixed the lions," said Nick, delighted. He bent down and patted George on the head. "Gidday, old mate."

"I should be going." Dominick had come to the front door. Alice saw his gaze take in the flowers and wine.

"Oh, hi." Nick straightened, his smile disappearing. "I didn't realize, I won't stop—"

"No, no. I was just going," said Dominick firmly. "I'll see you tomorrow." He touched Alice on the arm and ran lightly down the steps.

"Was I interrupting something?" Nick followed her down the hallway and saw Dominick's bunch of tulips. "Oh. Everyone is bringing offerings tonight."

Alice yawned. She longed for her life to be normal again. A Saturday night at home. She wanted to say, "I'm tired. I think I'll go to bed," and for Nick to say, without turning his head from the television, "Okay, I'll just finish watching this movie and I'll be up." And then she wanted them to read their books together and switch off the lamps and fall asleep. Who would have thought that a Saturday night at home would ever seem so impossibly exotic?

Instead, she opened Dominick's chocolate biscuits and ate one and watched Nick standing awkwardly in his own kitchen.

"Shall I open this?" he said.

"Sure."

He opened the wine and poured them both glasses. Alice put the cheese on a plate and they sat down on opposite sides of the long table.

"Are you coming tomorrow?" asked Alice, eating another chocolate biscuit. "To Mega Meringue Day?"

"Oh, no, I wasn't. Do you want me to go?"

"Of course!"

Nick laughed, in that slightly flabbergasted way. "All right, then."

"I think it will all be over by lunchtime," said Alice. "So you'll be able to make it to your mother's place."

Nick looked blankly at her.

"For the Mother's Day lunch," said Alice. "Remember? You told Ella you were going at the Family Talent Night."

"Oh. Yeah. Right."

"How do you cope without me?" said Alice lightly.

Nick's face closed up. "I cope fine. I'm not totally useless."

Alice flinched at his tone. "I never said you were." She took a piece of cheese. "Or have I said that?"

"You don't believe I'm capable of looking after the children for half the time. According to you, I wouldn't remember all their after-school activities, sign their permission notes, or whatever. I'd forget to read the all-important school newsletter. Not sure how I manage to run a company."

Well, you have a secretary to handle all the pesky details.

She wasn't sure which Alice said that: Snippy Alice from the future or real Alice. Nick had always been a big-picture man.

He refilled their wineglasses. "I can't stand only seeing them on weekends. I can't be natural with them. Sometimes I hear my father's voice come out of my mouth when I see them. Fake jolly. I'm driving over to pick them up and I find myself preparing jokes for them. And I think—how did I end up here?"

"Did you spend a lot of time with them during the week?"

"Yeah, I know the point you're trying to make. Yes, I work long hours, but you never seem to remember the times I *did* come home early. I went bike riding with Madison that time, and Friday nights in summer I played cricket for hours with Tom—well, you always say it was just one Friday night, but I know it happened at least twice, and I—"

"I wasn't trying to make a point."

Nick twirled the stem of his wineglass and looked up at Alice with an "I'm going to come clean" expression. "I haven't been very good at achieving a life-work balance. I need to work on that. If we work things out, I'll get better at that. I'm committed to that."

"Okay," said Alice. She wanted to make fun of him for saying "I'm committed to that," but Nick was acting as though it was some sort of breakthrough moment. It just didn't seem that big a deal to her. So he had to work long hours sometimes. If that's what he had to do for his career, then fair enough.

"I guess my competition doesn't work such long hours," said Nick.

"Competition?" The wine was going to Alice's head. Her mind was filled with hazy half-thoughts, glimpses of people's faces she didn't know, and vague memories of intense feelings she couldn't describe.

"Dominick."

"Oh, him. He's nice, but the thing is, I'm married to you."

"We're separated."

"Yes, but we're *trying*." Alice giggled. "Sorry. I don't know why I find it funny. It's not funny. It's not at all funny. I might actually need a glass of water."

She stood up, and as she walked by Nick, she suddenly plonked herself down on his lap like a flirty girl at a party.

"Are you going to *try*, Nick?" she gurgled into his neck. "Are you going to try really, really hard?"

"You're tipsy," he said, and then he kissed her, and at last everything was as it should be. Her body melted against his with exquisite relief. It was like sinking into a hot bath after being caught in the rain, like sliding under crisp cotton sheets after an exhausting day.

"Daddy?" said a voice from behind them. "What are you doing here?"

Nick's legs jerked up so that Alice was catapulted onto her feet.

Olivia stood in the kitchen in her pajamas, rubbing her eyes with her knuckles, her cheeks flushed with sleep. She yawned hugely, stretching her arms above her head. She frowned, perplexed, and then an expression of pure delight crossed her face.

"Do you love Mummy again?"

Frannie's Letter to Phil

Kissing! At my age! Is it allowed? Is it unseemly? I feel as though I've broken a rule. I've gone full circle and I'm fourteen again.

We had a lovely night at the Chinese restaurant. It's been so long since I've eaten Chinese. (I used to take Elisabeth and Alice when they were little for a special treat. They adored it. Of course now they would be horrified at the thought. Too many calories. Or "carbs" or something.)

We shared a nice bottle of white wine and the steamed dim sums were fabulous. Mr. M. was his ridiculous self. After we paid the bill, he asked the waitress if we could go to the kitchen and "pay our compliments to the chef"!

The little girl looked alarmed. (She probably thought we were undercover health inspectors.) I was saying to her, "Just ignore him, darling," but next thing, Mr. M. marched out to the kitchen and dragged out three young Chinese men dressed in white. There he was, clapping them on the shoulders, loudly telling them a long story about a meal he'd eaten at a fancy hotel in Hong Kong in 1954, and how this was even better than that meal, while all the other diners put down their chopsticks and stared.

I got such an attack of the giggles watching those poor young chefs with

*their polite, bemused smiles, nervously bobbing their heads up and down,
obviously thinking this man was quite deranged. In the end, Mr. M.
convinced the whole restaurant to give them a round of applause.
(The food wasn't that good!)*

*I giggled in the cab the whole way home until finally Mr. M. said, "I
think there's only one way to shut you up," and next thing he was
kissing me.*

I'm very sorry, Phil.

Do you mind?

*Well, bad luck if you do. It's your fault anyway! Why did you need a
camping trip "with the fellows" just before our wedding? You were forty
years old! You shouldn't have had any wild oats left to sow. And then you
happily, idiotically, dive headfirst into a river without checking the depth
first. You silly fool.*

*Tonight a handsome man (I may not have referred to his handsomeness
previously) kissed me and it was heavenly.*

Do you hear that, Phil? HEAVENLY.

*Am going to bed, my dear. May have drunk a little too much sauvignon
blanc at dinner.*

Chapter 30

It was the "big day." Alice felt like a small piece of clothing, a sock perhaps, in a large load of washing, on the spin cycle. People pulled her this way and that. At one point she literally had a person on each arm (neither of whom she recognized), trying to pull her in different directions. Worried faces, excited faces, smiley "ooh, this is it!" faces floated by and vanished. People gathered around her in worried clumps, firing questions, telling her about problems, about things that should have been delivered by now. "Where are the eggs meant to go?" "Where are the pastry ladies meant to be standing?" "The news crew wants to confirm they'll be here by twelve. They want to interview you at twelve-thirty. Is that still okay? Are we on schedule?"

News crew? Interviewing her?

Cameras flashed like strobe lights. She should have listened more at the Mega Meringue meeting. She hadn't fully grasped the immense scale of this production. It was . . . mega.

They were in a giant colorful marquee that had been erected on the school oval with a banner proclaiming: "Mega Meringue Day: Watch 100 Mums Bake the World's Biggest Lemon Meringue Pie! $10 Entry. (Children Free.) All Proceeds to Breast Cancer Research."

Inside, the marquee had been set up auditorium style, with raised benches around the sides where people could sit and watch. All around the sides of the tent were placards with the names of companies that were "proud to sponsor Mega Meringue Day." Alice saw one for Dino's Coffee Shop. In the middle was all the equipment for making the pie. It looked like a construction site. There was huge industrial equipment: a forklift, a concrete mixer, a *crane*, and a specially created pie dish and oven where the pie would be baked. A large round conference table had been set up with mixing bowls placed at intervals. Next to each mixing bowl was a neat selection of ingredients: eggs, flour, butter, lemons, and sugar. Maggie's husband, the red-faced man on the treadmill, who appeared to run some sort of manufacturing company, was in charge of the equipment and was ordering around bemused workmen.

"Now, let me get this straight, we bake the pastry *without* the filling first, is that right?" he said to Alice.

Well, at least she knew the answer to that question. "Yes," she said, and then more firmly: "Yes. That's right."

"Righto, boss," he said, and hurried off.

People were filing into the tent, handing over their cash to two women from the Mega Meringue Committee sitting at the entryway. The benches were filling up fast. A group of children with brass instruments struck up a tune.

A corner of the tent had been devoted to activities for the children. All the activities had a "mega" theme. They could blow giant soap bubbles, toss around a giant foam ball, and paint on a massive canvas with oversized paintbrushes. Alice had left Madison, Tom, and Olivia to enjoy themselves.

"All coming together?" said someone.

It was Dominick. Jasper was with him, swinging on his father's hand. Alice looked up, met Dominick's eyes, and looked away guiltily. She felt like she'd cheated on him, which . . . well, maybe she had.

"I'm sorry about last night," she said.

"Don't even think about that today," he answered. "Oh—but, ah, I wondered if you'd remember about tonight? *Phantom of the Opera*?"

Nick had taken Olivia back up to bed the night before and then left. They had agreed that their first "date" would be the following night. They were going back to their old favorite Italian restaurant. Nick had sent a text message saying he'd got the reservations.

"Um, well, I had actually forgotten," began Alice. She really needed to break up with this kind, but essentially irrelevant, man. "The thing is, Dominick—"

"Alice, my *dear*!" It was Kate Harper, looking especially glossy in the morning sunlight streaming through the tent. An unhappy-faced man trailed behind her, along with a sullen Chloe. Chloe's shorn hair had been cut into a stylish bob, but, it had to be said, she wasn't nearly as pretty without her flowing locks.

"That's all right, we'll talk later," said Dominick. "Let me know if you need me for anything. I'm right here for you."

"I'm right here for you too, Alice!" piped up Jasper.

"I was surprised to see Madison here," said Kate, her voice steely. "I thought you might have kept her at home, in light of . . . the incident."

"Yes, well . . ." began Alice. It really would have been more comfortable if she'd been in the right in this situation, instead of the indisputable, shameful wrong.

"Madison is being very severely punished," she said. Well, she would be, eventually, once Alice got around to thinking of something appropriate. She glanced over and saw Madison looking entranced as she had a turn blowing the giant soap bubbles. It was just that Madison was in such a lovely mood these days. It seemed a pity to spoil it.

"I hope so," said Kate. She lowered her voice. "Because Chloe is *traumatized*. She's not eating or sleeping properly. This will be something that will mark her for life."

"Kate, give the poor woman a break," said Kate's husband. "She's got her hands full at the moment."

Kate's nostrils flared, as if it had been Alice asking for the break for herself. "I realize you're busy, but I'm not sure you fully appreciate the seriousness of this. Your phone message sounded almost flippant. What Madison did was outrageous."

"Sorry! I'm afraid we need to steal Alice away from you."

It was Maggie and Nora, her friends from the Mega Meringue Committee, scooping up Alice by the elbows and smoothly dragging her away.

"You're not one of our Mega Meringue Mums, are you, Kate?" said Nora. "You might want to take a seat."

As Alice looked back over her shoulder, she saw Kate talking furiously into her husband's ear, her hand like a claw on his arm.

"I don't know what I'm meant to be doing," she admitted to Nora and Maggie. "I'm just nodding when people ask me questions." This wasn't like the netball umpiring, when her mind had somehow switched to autopilot.

"It's all right," said Maggie. "Everything is running like clockwork thanks to you."

She waved a sheet of paper in Alice's face with a running sheet for the day and notations in her own handwriting that she didn't remember writing. She could see she'd written, "STICK TO SCHEDULE!!" in full capitals and underlined it twice.

A disgusted expression crossed Maggie's face. "Oh dear, your *ex* is here. What's he doing here? Trying to look like an involved father, I suppose."

Ex. At the word "ex" Alice immediately visualized her most recent ex-boyfriend before Nick. Peter Bourke. The patronizing one who broke her heart. But when she turned around, it was Nick coming through the marquee entrance, looking gorgeous in a blue shirt. She'd told him once he should always wear blue.

"I invited him," she said to Maggie.

Maggie studied her. "Oh. Well, all right."

"By the way, we're assuming one of us should take over as MC?" said Nora. "We could say you haven't been well. Of course, our resident troll, Mrs. H., would love to get her hands on the microphone and take credit for the whole event if we don't stop her."

"Microphone?" said Alice, confused.

Nora gestured toward a microphone on a stand in the center of the marquee.

Good lord. The idea had been for *Alice* to get up in front of all those people.

"Oh, no, absolutely not, I mean absolutely *yes*, one of you can do it," she said.

"No problem," said Nora. Her face became neutral as Nick reached them. "Hi, Nick."

"Hi, Nora, Maggie. How are you both?" Nick nodded uncomfortably at the two women. It made Alice feel protective of him to see poor Nick in the unpopular ex-husband role. Just like she'd been the "cow" of an ex-wife with his sister at the Family Talent Night.

"Happy Mother's Day," said Nick, as Nora and Maggie disappeared into the crowd. "Did you get breakfast in bed?"

Alice nodded. "Pancakes. I think they started cooking them at five a.m. There were bangs and crashes and yells. You should see the kitchen now. But I have to say, the pancakes were outstanding. I think Madison is going to be a chef one day. A really messy, bossy, noisy one."

"Sorry I wasn't there to supervise," said Nick. "Your first Mother's Day without me."

"Hopefully my last," said Alice.

"Definitely," said Nick. His eyes held hers. "I think definitely."

"Well, well, well, what have we here, Barb? Methinks it's our fine young salsa students!" Nick's father and Alice's mother were upon them. Roger clapped them on the shoulders car-salesman style, the familiar scent of his aftershave drifting across their faces like a filmy scarf, while Barb stood to the side, shiny with pride, as if Roger were once again performing a rather tricky feat.

"How are you, darling?" said Barb to Alice. "You look lovely, of course, but you're so pale. And shadows under your eyes. There must be something going around at the moment, because Elisabeth is pea *green*."

"Is Libby here?" said Alice with surprise.

"She's there with Frannie," said Barb, pointing up to one of the bench seats, where Elisabeth was sitting with Ben. She did look quite ill. Nausea. That must be a good sign. At least she wasn't watching television.

Sitting next to Ben was Frannie, and next to her the white-haired man from the Family Talent Night who had organized the wheel-chair races. Frannie was sitting very upright, glancing around self-consciously, but as Alice looked at her, the man said something in her ear and she clapped her hands together and burst out laughing.

"That's Frannie's *gentleman friend*," said Barb. "Xavier. Isn't it lovely! After all these years of holding a candle for her silly dead fiancé!"

"Her what?" said Alice. She pressed a fingertip to her forehead. She didn't think her head could handle any fresh new surprises today.

"Her fiancé died just two weeks before their wedding. It wasn't all that long before your father died," said Barb calmly, as if this weren't a huge revelation. "He went away with some mates on a camping trip and he broke his neck diving into a river. That's why I was always telling you girls to never, ever dive *anywhere* without checking the depth."

"Are you saying you knew about this all these years?" said Alice. She looked up at Frannie smiling at Xavier and tried to incorporate this sad new information about her grandmother. "And *you* kept it a secret?"

"No need to look so surprised," said Barb crisply. "I can keep secrets. Frannie didn't like to talk about it. She's so private! She admitted to me once that she had kept on writing to him all these years, as if he was still away on holiday. She said she felt silly about it, because she knew perfectly well that he'd died, but that it was nice to keep writing to him. She'd seal the letters up and put them in a drawer. She told me she'd address them but she didn't go so far as to waste her money putting stamps on them. So we agreed that proved she wasn't completely deluded! It was just a funny little quirk of hers."

"And you never said a word," marveled Alice. The fact that her mother had kept a secret was more surprising than the secret itself.

"Although she has let the cat out of the bag now," chortled Roger.

"Only because Frannie told me she intended to tell the girls now!" retorted Barb. "Apparently she started to tell you and Elisabeth the whole story just a few weeks ago, but then you had to go pick up the children."

"I don't remember," said Alice. Her catchcry.

"Anyway, she's finally found love again!" Barb sighed and shook her head regretfully. "If only it hadn't taken so *long*!"

"She's probably just fussy," said Roger. "Needed to find the right fellow. Like you."

"Oh, you!" said Barb flirtatiously, and she gleamed with happiness. "I was lucky to find you!"

"Dad was lucky to find you," said Nick, suddenly serious. Alice's mother looked up at him with surprise, her cheeks pink with pleasure. "Well, that's a lovely thing to say, Nick."

Maggie appeared again wearing a long apron that said *Mega Meringue Day* on the front, with a picture of a huge lemon meringue pie. Underneath it said, *Mother's Day, Sydney, 2008*. She was holding another one for Alice.

"The aprons turned out beautifully, Alice!" she said as she slid the apron over Alice's neck and tied it at her waist.

Alice looked around and saw rows of pink-aproned women lining up around the big table with the mixing bowls.

"It looks like we're about ready to start," said Maggie. "Is that okay with you?"

"Sure thing," said Alice recklessly.

"You're over here," said Maggie. "Next to me."

"Good luck, darling," said Barb. "I do hope they're careful with that oven. It's very easy to burn the meringue on a lemon meringue pie. I remember once I was making one when your father's boss was coming for dinner. I was terribly upset, I remember looking in the oven and thinking—"

"Come on, Barbie," said Roger, pulling on her arm. "You can tell me the rest of the story while we're sitting down."

He winked at Alice as he guided her still-chattering mother into the audience, and Alice was filled with affection for him. He loved Barb—in his own self-satisfied way, he loved her.

"I'll get the kids to come and sit down," said Nick, and he headed off to the children's area.

Alice went to stand beside Maggie behind the tables.

"What an event," said the woman standing next to Alice. She had a birthmark like a burn across the bottom half of her face. "You're a bloody marvel, Alice."

I'm a bloody marvel, thought Alice. Her head was feeling fuzzy.

Nora stood at the microphone. "Can everybody take their seats, please? The baking is about to commence!"

Alice found Nick in the audience. He had Olivia on his lap. The fairy wings she'd insisted on wearing that day were brushing against his face. Tom was on Nick's left, taking photos with a digital camera, and Madison was on his right, seemingly intensely interested in the proceedings. Nick said something and pointed at Alice, and all three children beamed and waved in her direction.

Alice waved back, and as she did, Dominick and Jasper caught her eye. They were sitting just two rows behind Nick and the children, and waving enthusiastically, as if they'd thought Alice had been waving at them.

Oh dear. Now she could see Libby and Ben waving at her, along with Frannie, Xavier, Barb, and Roger.

Alice tried to make her smile and wave seem all encompassing and personal to each of them.

Nora was speaking again.

"I'm stepping in on behalf of Alice Love to be your host today. As many of you know, Alice had an accident at the gym last week and still isn't feeling a hundred percent. You know, I can still remember the day Alice said to me that she wanted to get one hundred mums together to bake the world's largest lemon meringue pie. I thought she was nuts!"

The audience chuckled.

"But you all know Alice. She's like a bull terrier when she gets an idea in her head." There was appreciative laughter. *A bull terrier?* How had she changed so much in just ten years? She was more like a Labrador. Anxious to please and overexcited.

"But just a few months later, no surprise, here we are! Let's put our hands together for *Alice*!"

There was a burst of enthusiastic applause. Alice nodded and smiled fraudulently.

"We're dedicating this day to a very dear friend and member of the school community who we tragically lost last year," said Nora. "We're using her lemon meringue pie recipe and we're sure she's with us in spirit today. I'm referring, of course, to Gina Boyle. We miss you, Gina. A minute's silence, please, for Gina."

Alice watched as people reverently bowed their heads and remembered the woman who had apparently been such a significant part of Alice's life. Her own mind was blank. This morning's pancakes sat uncomfortably in her stomach. After what seemed much longer than a minute, Nora lifted her head.

"Ladies," she said. "Pick up your whisks."

Chapter 31

The women picked up their whisks solemnly as if they were musicians in an orchestra.

"Whisk the eggs, cream, sugar, lemon rind, and juice until combined," read out Nora.

There was a pause and then everyone put their whisks back down and began to select ingredients.

Alice cracked her eggs one after the other into her bowl. All around her, women were doing the same thing. There were nervous giggles and whispers.

"Don't get any eggshell in there!" called out someone from the audience, to much hilarity.

After a few minutes, the sound of brisk whisking filled the marquee.

Under Nora's instructions, once they were all finished, they stood in line to pour their mixture into a huge yellow industrial vat.

This is going to be an absolute disaster, thought Alice.

"Place the flour, almond meal, icing sugar, and butter into a food processor and process until it resembles fine bread crumbs," read out Nora. "Instead of using a food processor, we're going to use a concrete mixer. Don't worry, it's clean! So could each mum please place her combined ingredients into the mixer."

"I can't believe we're doing this," whispered Alice to Maggie, as the mothers lined up with their bowls of ingredients. "It's madness."

Maggie laughed. "It's all your doing, Alice!"

One of the bemused workmen operated the concrete mixer while the mothers separated yolks from whites.

"Add the egg yolk and process," ordered Nora.

Once again the women lined up to add their egg yolks. A few minutes later a massive glob of yellow dough was upended from the concrete mixer and onto the floury surface of the center table.

"Knead until smooth."

The women gathered around the table, kneading and pulling at the dough. *This pastry is going to be inedible,* thought Alice, watching inexpert hands pushing and pulling. Cameras flashed.

"Now we really should be putting the pastry into the fridge for half an hour, but today is all about quantity, rather than quality," said Nora. "So we're going to go straight to rolling out the pastry."

The workmen carried over the giant rolling pin.

Alice stood back and watched as three women stood on each side of the rolling pin, took a firm grip of the handles, and began to push forward, as if they were pushing along a broken-down car.

There was giggling and shrieking and yelled suggestions from the audience as the women went off in different directions, but, incredibly, after a few minutes, the dough began to flatten. It was working. It was actually working. A huge sheet of pastry, the size of a king-size bed, was emerging.

"Now, the hard bit," said Nora. "Line the pie dish."

We'll never do it, thought Alice, as the women gathered around the sheet of pastry and lifted it into the air, with their palms flat, as though they were carrying some sort of precious canvas. Every woman had the exact same expression of terrified concentration on her face.

"Shit, shit, shit, shit," said the woman with the birthmark, as the pastry began to sag in the middle. Another woman rushed to try and save it. They were treading on each other's toes, calling out sharp orders like "Be careful there!" and "Watch that part there!"

No one smiled or laughed until the delicate sheet of pastry was safely placed in the massive pie dish. They'd done it. No serious tears or cracks. It was a miracle.

"Hooray!" cried the crowd, and the women shared ecstatic grins as they used their thumbs to push the pastry against the sides of the dish. Next they covered it with sheet after sheet of baking paper and weighted it down with rice, and the workmen lifted the dish and placed it into the oven.

"We'll bake that for ten minutes," said Nora smoothly, as if it weren't at all surprising that they had got this far. "And in the meantime our clever mums will make the meringue."

The ladies went back to their tables and began to whisk egg whites, gradually adding the sugar as they did so.

The tent filled with heat from the giant oven. Alice could feel her face flushing and beads of perspiration forming at her hairline. The fragrance of cooking pastry filled the air. Her head ached. She wondered if she was coming down with the flu.

The smell of the pastry was making her want to remember something. Except it was somehow too large to remember. It was like the huge sheet of pastry. Too big for one person. She couldn't find an edge to grasp so she could pull it in front of her. But there was definitely something there.

"Are you okay?" Maggie's face loomed in front of Alice.

"Fine. I'm fine."

The pastry shell was pulled from the oven to a round of applause. It was golden brown. The baking paper and rice were removed and the vat of lemon-colored filling was poured into the pastry. Next came the meringue. The women seemed tipsy with relief. They danced around the pie like schoolgirls, pouring their frothy white meringue mixtures over the filling and using wooden spoons to create snowy peaks.

More cameras flashed.

"Alice?" said Nora into the microphone. "Do we have your approval?"

Alice felt like the world had been wrapped in some sort of gauzy material. Her vision was slightly blurred, her mouth felt full of cotton wool. It was as though she'd just woken up and was trying to clear her head of the previous night's dreams. She blinked and considered the pie. "Can someone just smooth the meringue over in that corner?" she said, and was surprised that her voice came out sounding quite normal. A woman rushed to obey her.

Alice nodded at Nora.

"And now, ladies and gentlemen, we *bake*," said Nora.

Maggie's husband gave the thumbs-up signal to the forklift driver. Everyone's eyes were fixed on the magnificent pie as it was lifted by the forklift and slid into the oven. There was a round of applause.

"Year 4 has kindly offered to keep us entertained while the lemon meringue pie is baking," said Nora. "As many of you will remember, our dear friend Gina loved Elvis. Whenever she was cooking, she always had Elvis playing. You couldn't get her to play anything else. So Year 4 is going to perform a medley of Elvis hits for us. Gina, honey, this is for you."

There was a burst of laughter and cheers as thirty miniature Elvises swaggered into the center of the marquee. They were wearing dark glasses and white satin jumpsuits complete with sparkly rhinestones. A teacher pressed a button on a stereo and the children began to dance, Elvis style, to "Hound Dog."

There was nowhere for the Mega Meringue mums to sit, so they all leaned back against the long tables. Some of them took off their pink aprons. Alice's legs ached. Actually, everything ached.

Oh, this song is so . . . familiar.

Yes, that's because it's Elvis. Elvis is familiar to everyone.

The song switched to "Love Me Tender."

The sweet lemony smell of the baking pie was overpowering. It was impossible to think of anything else but lemon . . . meringue . . . pie . . .

That smell is so . . . familiar.

Yes, that's because it's a lemon meringue pie. You know what a lemon meringue pie smells like.

But there was something more than that. It meant something.

Alice's face had been feeling flushed and hot. Now she felt cold, as if she'd stepped into an icy wind.

Oh dear, she wasn't well. She really wasn't well.

She looked desperately into the audience for someone to help.

She saw Nick suddenly lift Olivia off his lap and stand up.

She saw Dominick bounce to his feet, frowning with concern.

Both men were making their way past people's knees, trying to get to her.

Now the song was "Jailhouse Rock."

The scent of lemon meringue was becoming stronger and stronger. It was going straight up her nostrils and trickling into her brain, filling it with memory.

Oh, God, of course, of course, of course.

Alice's legs buckled.

Elisabeth's Homework for Jeremy

I missed seeing Alice collapse because I'd gone outside to the toilet.

They had a row of those blue plastic Port-a-loos.

I was bleeding.

I thought, How fitting. That I should be losing my last baby in a Port-a-loo.

Trashy and slightly laughable. Like my life.

Chapter 32

"Hi!"

The woman who opened the door was smiling delightedly, wiping her hands on a floury apron, as if Alice were a very dear friend.

Alice hadn't wanted to come. She hadn't been at all thrilled when this "Gina" had moved into the house across the road and turned up the very next day, knocking on their door to invite Alice for "high tea." For one thing, shouldn't Alice have been the one doing the asking—seeing as she was the one already living there? That made her feel guilty, as if this woman already had some sort of etiquette point over her. And she could tell just by looking at Gina that she wasn't her sort of person. Too loud. Too many teeth. Too much makeup for the middle of the day. Too much perfume. Too much everything. She was one of those women who drained Alice of her personality. And "high tea"? What was wrong with just ordinary old afternoon tea?

This was going to be awful.

"HELLO there, sweetie!" Gina bent down to say hello to Madison.

Madison clung to Alice's leg in an agony of shyness, burying her face in Alice's crotch. Alice hated it when she did that. She always worried people might think the kid had inherited her poor social skills from her mother.

"I'm terrible with children," said Gina. "Terrible. That's probably why I'm having so much trouble getting pregnant."

Alice followed Gina through the house, trying to dislodge Madison, who was still clinging to her leg. There were boxes everywhere waiting to be unpacked.

"I should have invited you to my place," said Alice.

"It's okay, I'm the one desperate to make friends," said Gina. "I'm going to try and seduce you with my lemon meringue pie." *She turned around quickly and then walked into a box.* "Not literally seduce you."

"Oh, that's a pity," said Alice. *And then she said quickly, idiotically,* "That was a joke."

Gina laughed and led her into the kitchen. It was warm and filled with the sweet smell of lemon meringue pie. Elvis was playing on the stereo.

"I thought I'd say 'high tea' instead of 'afternoon tea,'" said Gina, "so we could have champagne. Would you like champagne?"

"Oh, sure," said Alice, *although she normally wouldn't drink in the day.*

Gina danced a jig on the spot. "Thank God! If you'd said no, I wouldn't have been able to drink on my own, and you know, it just makes it a bit easier when you're talking to new people." *She popped the cork and produced two glasses she had waiting.* "Mike and I are from Melbourne. I don't know a soul here in Sydney. That's why I'm on the prowl for friends. And Mike is working such long hours at the moment, I get lonely during the week."

Alice held out her glass to be filled.

"Nick has started working pretty long hours, too."

"Alice?"

"Alice."

Nick was supporting one side of her and Dominick was supporting the other. Her legs had turned to jelly.

"Back," said Alice.

"You've hurt your back?" said Dominick.

No, I meant it's all coming back. My memory is coming back.

It was as if a dam wall had burst in her brain, releasing a raging torrent of memories.

"Get her some water," said someone.

Alice had needed a new friend. When Madison was about one, Sophie had broken up with Jack (such a shock) and she found a new circle of single, glossy, stiletto-heeled friends who shrieked a lot and started their nights at nine p.m., catching taxis into elegant bars in the city. She and Alice grew apart.

And Elisabeth was distracted, sad, never really listening.

So Alice's friendship with Gina grew fast. It was like falling in love. And Nick and Mike got on, too! Camping trips. Impromptu dinners that went on late into the night, while the kids slept on sofas. It was wonderful.

Gina's twin girls, Eloise and Rose, were born a few months before Olivia. Big brown eyes and snub freckled noses and Gina's bouncing hair. They all played so well together.

One year, the two families hired houseboats together on the Hawkesbury River. They moored their boats next to each other. Rowed the dinghies across in the moonlight for BBQs on the top deck. Olivia and the twins painted Alice's and Gina's toenails different colors. Gina and Alice went for a swim after breakfast, floating on their backs, admiring their toenails, while Nick and Mike and the kids played Marco Polo. They all agreed, it was the best holiday they'd ever had.

Of course she'd told Gina she was pregnant with Olivia before she told Nick.

Nick was in the UK for two weeks. He only called twice.

Twice in two weeks.

He was too busy, he said. He was distracted.

But they won the account! He got the bonus! We can afford a swimming pool!

"There," she said to Nick.

"What did you say?"

She was trying to say, *You were never there.*

The year of the Goodman project Nick was never there. Never there. When he came home, he smelled of the office. Corporate sweat. Even when he was talking to her, he was still thinking about the office.

Olivia had three ear infections in three months.

Tom was throwing terrifying tantrums.

Overnight, Madison became so nervous about school she was vomiting every morning. That's not normal, Nick. We've got to do something about it. I can't sleep I'm so worried about it.

Nick said, It's just a stage. I can't talk about it now. I've got an early flight tomorrow morning.

Gina said, I've found a child psychologist who might be able to help. Should you talk to the school principal about it? What does her teacher say? Could I look after the kids for you while you have some special time with her? What a worry for you.

———————

Gina was the sort who got involved with things at the school. Volunteered for everything. Alice became that sort of person, too. She liked it. She was good at it.

Mike and Gina were having problems. Gina told Alice every cruel remark, every thoughtless gesture. Mike told Nick he wasn't happy with his life. Alice and Nick had a Christmas party one hot December night. Mike got drunk and kissed that horrendous Jackie Holloway in the laundry. Gina went in to get champagne and found them.

Nick and Alice were in bed one night talking in the darkness.

Mike is my friend.

Are you saying you approve of him kissing another woman in our laundry?

Of course not, but there are two sides to every story. Let's just stay out of it.

There are not two sides! It's not excusable. He shouldn't have kissed her.

Well, maybe if Gina stopped trying to turn him into something he's not.

She is not! What do you mean? Because she's encouraging him to get a different job? But that's because he's not happy there!

Look. Is there any point in us playing out another version of their fights? You playing Gina and me playing Mike?

They turned away from each other, carefully not touching.

It was not "cherries." It was half a fruit platter. A beautifully presented fruit platter she'd spent the morning making to take to his mother's place. She was rushing around trying to get the children dressed and instead of helping, he was reading the paper and happily eating his way through the fruit platter, as if Alice were the hired help.

After Mike moved out, Gina wanted to lose weight. So Alice and Gina decided to get a personal trainer. They joined a gym. They started doing spin classes. The weight fell off them. They got fitter and fitter. Alice loved it. She dropped two dress sizes. She had no idea exercise could be so exhilarating.

Gina went on a date with a guy she'd met on the Internet. Alice minded the kids. Nick was working late.

When Gina came home, she was all glittery and flushed. Alice, lying on the couch in her tracksuit pants, felt envious. First dates. How wonderful to experience a first date again.

When Nick came home that night he said, You're getting too thin.

When Nick heard that his dad was dating Alice's mother, he laughed out loud.

She's not his type. He goes for eastern suburbs women with fake boobs and big divorce settlements. Women who read all the right books and see all the right plays.

Are you saying my mother isn't cultured enough for your father?

I hate the sort of woman my father normally dates!

So your dad's slumming it, then? With my poor simple Hills District mother?

It is impossible to talk to you. It's like you want me to say the wrong thing. Fine. Dad is slumming it. Is that what you want me to say? Satisfied?

Elisabeth had disappeared. Her sister turned into this bitter, angry person, with a hard, sarcastic laugh. Nothing as bad had ever happened to anyone else as was happening to Elisabeth. Alice couldn't say the right thing to her. Once she asked if she'd had another embryo implanted and Elisabeth's lip curled contemptuously. The embryo is "transferred," she sneered, it's not implanted. If only it were that easy. How the hell was Alice meant to know all the right terminology? If she invited her to one of the kids' birthday parties, Elisabeth sighed, in a way that meant it would be excruciating for her, but she would still come, and she'd look like a martyr the whole time. Didn't offer to help, just stood there with her lips folded together. Don't do me any favors, Alice wanted to say. After the fourth miscarriage, she tried to talk to Elisabeth. She offered to donate her eggs. Your eggs are too old, Elisabeth had said. You really don't know what you're talking about.

When Roger proposed to Alice's mother, Nick was angry.

Well that's just fabulous. Wonderful. How is that going to make my mother feel?

As if it were somehow Alice's fault. As if her mother had somehow trapped Roger into marrying her.

They stopped having sex. It just stopped. They didn't even talk about it.

"Let's get her outside into the fresh air."

She was dimly aware that she was being half carried, half dragged out of the marquee. People were staring, but she couldn't focus on anything but the memories rushing through her brain.

When she felt her first labor pain with Madison, she thought to herself, They must be joking. They can't expect me to put up with this. But it seemed they did. Seven hours later, when the baby was born, neither she nor Nick could believe it was a girl. They'd both been so ridiculously convinced it was a boy. It's a girl, they kept saying to each other. The surprise made them euphoric. She was extraordinary. As if a baby girl had never been born before.

———

Tom was in the posterior position. She kept screaming at that midwife with the soft, worn face—it's my back, the pain is in my back. And the whole time she was promising herself, I will never, ever go through this again.

Olivia was the worst. Your baby is in distress. We need to do an emergency cesarean, they told her, and suddenly the room filled with people, and she was being wheeled down a long corridor, watching the ceiling lights flash rhythmically by, and wondering what she'd done to distress her poor baby before it was even born. When she woke up from the anesthetic, a nurse said, You have the most beautiful baby girl.

Madison got her first tooth when she was eight months old. She kept touching it with her finger and frowning.

Tom refused point blank to ever sit in the high chair. Never ever sat in it.

Olivia didn't walk until she was eighteen months old.

Madison's little red hooded jacket with the white flowers.

Tom's filthy blue elephant that had to come everywhere with him. Where's Elephant? Have you seen his damned elephant?

Olivia ran into the schoolyard on her first day of school shrieking with joy. Madison had to be dragged out of Alice's arms.

Alice walked into the kitchen one day and found Tom carefully stuffing his nose with frozen peas. I wanted to see if the peas would come out of my eyeballs, he told the doctor.

———

They lost Olivia at Newport Beach. The panic made Alice hyperventilate. You were meant to be watching her, Nick kept saying. As if that were the point. That Alice had made a mistake. Not that Olivia was missing, but that it was Alice's fault.

"Alice? Take big deep breaths."

She ignored their voices. She was busy remembering.

It was a really cold August day. She and Gina were driving in separate cars home from the gym. Normally, they would have driven together, but Alice had taken Madison to the dentist beforehand. The dentist said there was nothing wrong with Madison's teeth. He didn't know what was causing that ache in her jaw. He'd sent Madison to the waiting room and asked Alice quietly, Could it be stress?

Alice had looked at her watch impatiently, desperate to get to the gym. She didn't want to miss the beginning of the spin class. She'd already missed a class yesterday because Olivia had some school presentation. Stress? What did Madison have to be stressed about? She was just impossible. She probably just wanted to get out of school.

As they were driving home Madison was whining about having to stay in the gym day-care while Alice and Gina did their class.

I am too old for the crèche. It is just stupid crying babies.

Well, you should have gone to school today instead of making up stories about toothaches.

I didn't make it up.

It was a black stormy day. Lightning cracked across the sky. It started to rain. Heavy drops splattering on the windscreen like pebbles.

Mum. I didn't make it up.

Be quiet. I'm trying to concentrate on the road.

Alice hated driving in the rain.

The wind was howling. The trees were swaying about as if they were performing some sort of ghostly dance.

They pulled into Rawson Street. Alice saw Gina's brake lights turn red.

Gina was driving her wildly impractical fortieth-birthday present to herself. A little red Mini with white stripes along the side and personalized number plates. Not a family car. It makes me feel young and crazy, said Gina. She drove it with the sunroof open and Elvis on full blast.

Alice watched the Mini in the rain and knew that Gina would be singing along lustily to Elvis.

That tree looks like it's going to fall right over, said Madison.

Alice looked up.

It was the liquid amber on the corner. Beautiful in the autumn. It was rocking back and forth, making a horrible creaking sound.

It won't fall.

It fell.

It was so fast and violent and unexpected. Like a dear friend suddenly punching you in the face. Like some cruel god had done it on purpose. To be nasty. Picked up the tree and slammed it across the Mini in a fit of temper. The sound was tremendous. An explosion of terrifying sound. Alice's foot jammed on the brake. Her arm flew sideways protectively across Madison's chest, as if to save her from the tree. Madison screamed—Mummy! Mummy! Mummy!

And then silence, except for the sound of the rain. The beeps for the one-o'clock news came on the radio.

There was a massive tree trunk lying on the road in front of them. Gina's little red Mini looked like a squashed tin can.

A woman came running out from her house. She stopped when she saw the tree, her hands pressed to her mouth.

Alice pulled over to the side of the road. She put the hazard lights on. Stay here, she said to Madison. She opened the car door and ran. She was still wearing her shorts and T-shirt from the gym. She slipped and fell,

hard on one knee, stood up and kept running, her arms flailed uselessly
at the air, trying to pull back time to just two minutes ago.

"Get her a blanket. She's shivering."

Nick didn't come to the funeral. He didn't come to the funeral.
   He didn't come to the funeral.

The school principal was at the funeral. Mr. Gordon. Dominick. He said,
I'm so sorry, Alice. I know you were such close friends. And he hugged
her. She cried into his shirt. He stood close by her while they released pink
balloons into the gray sky.

She didn't know how to live her life without Gina. She was part of her
daily routine. Gym. Coffee. Taking the kids to swimming lessons. Per-
sonal training. Minding each other's kids. Movie nights. Laughing at
stupid things. Sure she knew lots and lots of other mums at the school, but
not like Gina. She was her one true friend now that Nick was too busy
with work.
   All the joy had gone.
   Everything seemed pointless. Each morning in the shower she cried,
her forehead against the bathroom tiles, the shampoo sliding into her
eyes.
   She fought with Nick. Sometimes she deliberately picked fights be-
cause it was a good distraction from the grief. She had to stop herself
from hitting him. She wanted to scratch and bite and hurt him.

Nick said one day, I think I should move out. She said, I think you should,
too. And she thought, As soon as he goes, I'll phone Gina. Gina will
help me.

———

The nastiness seemed to begin so quickly and easily, as if they'd always hated each other, and here at last was their opportunity to stop pretending and let each other know how they really felt. Nick wanted the children to be with him fifty percent of the time. It was a joke. How could he possibly take care of them on his own with the hours he worked? It would be so disruptive for them. He didn't even really want them. He just wanted to reduce the amount of maintenance he would have to pay. Luckily, she remembered that her old work friend Jane had become a family lawyer. Jane was going to take him on.

Four months after Nick moved out, Dominick asked her out on a date. They went for a bushwalk in the National Park and got caught in the rain. He was easy and kind and unaffected. He didn't know the right restaurants. He liked unpretentious cafés. They talked a lot about the school. He respected her opinions. He seemed so much more real than Nick.

They had made love for the first time just the other night at his place. The children were with her mother.

(The night before she hit her head.)

It was beautiful.

Well, okay, it was awkward. (For example, he seemed to think he should lick her toes. Where had he got such an idea? It tickled unbearably, and she accidentally kicked him in the nose.)

But still, it had been so, so lovely to have a man appreciating her body again. Right down to her toes.

Dominick was the right sort of man for her. Nick had been a mistake. How can you pick the right man when you're in your twenties and stupid?

The grief started to ease a little. It was still there, but it wasn't an impossible weight crushing her chest. She kept herself very busy.

———

She stopped by at Dino's one afternoon for a coffee and found a small crowd of solemn-faced people surrounding a woman having some sort of attack on the footpath. Even Dino was out there. Alice went to avert her eyes—it seemed like the poor woman might be mentally ill—when she saw to her horror that it was her sister. It was Elisabeth, and when Dino told her what had happened, her first feeling was shame. How could she not have seen that it had got so bad? As she was explaining to Dino what Elisabeth had been going through, she felt a growing anger at herself. It was like she'd just come to accept Elisabeth's miscarriages as part of life. She'd led Elisabeth to her car and left her sitting in the passenger seat, staring straight ahead, and then she'd gone back and managed to soothe the mother of the child Elisabeth had apparently tried to kidnap. (It was Judy Clarke. Judy had a son in Madison's class.) On the way home Elisabeth said, "Thanks," and nothing else.

Well, enough was enough. This endless cycle of miscarriages had to stop. They were just beating their heads against a brick wall, and Elisabeth was losing her mind. Alice had lost her best friend and her marriage had fallen apart but she was still getting on with things. Someone needed to talk sense to Elisabeth. As soon as she got home, Alice got on the Internet to research adoption. Last Thursday she made a fresh batch of banana muffins and then she rang up Ben and told him she was having trouble with her car. He said he'd be right over.

"I wonder if we should call a doctor?"

"No," said Alice out loud, her eyes shut. "I'm all right. Just give me a minute."

Now she was remembering the past week. It was as if she'd been permanently drunk. She was mortified.

She hadn't had time for breakfast the morning of the spin class with Jane, and actually, now she thought about it, she hadn't even had any water, which was stupid, no wonder she'd fainted. Her last memory was pedaling hard, sweat dripping, listing off in her head everything she had to do for Mega Meringue Day, only half listening to Narelle (the annoying instructor: Spin Crazy Girl) going on about "the finish line" and "the semi-trailer holding you up." Instead, she was watching the television screen playing soundlessly above Narelle's head. There was a commercial on that always irked Alice, featuring a woman looking flirtatiously at the camera while licking a glob of cream cheese off the tip of her finger (she looked a bit like Jackie Holloway) and Alice was feeling sick at the very thought of eating cream cheese.

That's why her mixed-up brain had been thinking about cream cheese when she regained consciousness.

Being carried out of the spin class like that. How completely bizarre that she didn't recognize the gym, or Maggie's husband on the treadmill, or Kate Harper coming out of the lift.

The shock of finding she and Nick were divorcing.

Talking to Nick's PA on the phone. That awful woman had never liked her (Alice suspected a crush) and since the separation she'd become quite breathtakingly rude.

Dancing the salsa at the Family Talent Night. That "chemistry" she imagined she felt. Good Lord, she'd given back Granny Love's ring. She'd been determined to keep that ring for Madison. Now it might go to Nick's new wife if he ever remarried. It was part of Madison's heritage.

He'd bet her twenty dollars that she wouldn't want to get back together when she got her memory back. He must have been laughing at her the whole time.

She had kissed Nick. It made her sick to the stomach. He was using her

*memory loss to get her to agree to the fifty-percent care arrangement.
Thank God she'd never signed anything.*

*For heaven's sake, they'd taken Madison for ice creams and whale
watching after she'd cut off Chloe's hair. Talk about the right way to
bring up a delinquent.*

*She'd told Mrs. Bergen that she'd switched sides on the development
issue. Well, she'd just have to tell her that she'd switched right back. She
didn't want to stay living in the house. Too many memories. The developers could knock it to the ground and put up the tackiest, most sterile high-
rise apartment block for all she cared.*

*Tom was meant to have been one of the Elvis dancers today! She had
his suit already. He'd deliberately not reminded her.*

Nora hadn't mentioned the sponsors in her speech!

*She needed to check all the paperwork for the Guinness Book of Re-
cords. Everything had to be done properly or it wouldn't be an official
record. Maggie and Nora meant well but they didn't really know what
they were doing.*

*The mum standing next to her with the birthmark was Anne Russell,
mother of little Kerrie, in Tom's class. They helped together at the library on the same day. How could she have forgotten Anne Russell?*

How could she have forgotten any of it?

Alice opened her eyes.

She was sitting on the grass of the school oval.

Nick and Dominick were both squatting down uncomfortably in
front of her.

"Are you all right?" said Nick.

Alice looked at him. He flinched, as if she'd hit him.

"You've got your memory back," he said. It wasn't a question. He
stood up. It was as if he were folding up his face, making it bland and

cold. "I'll go let the kids know you're okay." He started to turn away and then looked back at her and said, "You owe me twenty bucks."

Alice turned to Dominick.

He smiled, hugged her to him, and said, "Everything is all right now, darling."

Chapter 33

Alice was running with her mobile in her hand so she wouldn't miss the call when it came.

She was running the route that Luke used to take her and Gina on. She'd let Luke go. She couldn't justify spending one hundred and fifty dollars on a personal-training session. Not when she and Nick were still trying to work out the money settlement. She'd also dropped the gym membership. These days she just liked to run and remember.

Since she'd lost her memory and got it back again, she was obsessed with remembering her life. She kept a daily journal, and whenever she went running she let memories drift through her head. When she got home she would write them down. It was hard to know whether she'd fully recovered her memory of the ten years she'd lost, or if there were still gaps. She understood that even before the accident she wouldn't have had perfect recall of the previous decade, but she kept scouring her mind, searching for any missing pieces.

Today she was remembering a night when Tom was a baby. Everyone had told her that her second child would be a wonderful sleeper after her problems with Madison. Everyone was wrong. Tom was a "cluster feeder." He didn't like having a proper feed every three to four hours, thanks anyway. He much preferred a snack every hour. Every *single hour*. That meant Alice slept for only forty minutes at a time before she was wrenched awake again by the sound of his cry through the baby monitor. And Madison was a toddler but she *still* had never slept through a single night in her life.

It was a time in her life when Alice was obsessed with sleep. She lusted for it. She saw television ads for sleeping pills or beds with people sleeping and they made her want to spit with envy. After feeding Tom, she would half stumble, half run back to the bedroom and dive into the bed. Her sleep would be full of dreams about the baby: she'd fallen asleep on the baby and suffocated him; she'd left him on the change table halfway through changing his nappy and he'd rolled onto the floor. And then, just at the moment she was sleeping the deepest, most exquisite sleep, the sound of the monitor would wake her again. It was like being desperately thirsty and having somebody hand you a tall glass of ice water and then tear it away from your mouth just as you took a sip. Better not to have any water at all.

On this particular night, Nick was leaving early the following morning for an important business trip. She'd just got back into bed after convincing Madison to go back to sleep (*Why* can't I play outside now? *Why* is it the middle of the night?) when Tom began wailing. Her head swam as she bent over the crib to pick him up. She felt a wave of pure rage at this person who refused to let her sleep. *Just what do you expect of me?* Her arms tightened around the baby. *You ... need ... to ... be ... quiet.*

She laid him back down with elaborate care. Tom was enraged, and screamed as though she'd just put him down on a bed of knives. Alice went back to the bedroom, switched on the light, and said to Nick, "You need to lock me up. I wanted to hurt the baby."

Nick sat up in bed, his eyes bleary and confused. "You hurt the baby?"

Alice was trembling all over. "No. I *wanted* to. I wanted to squeeze him until he stopped crying."

"Right, then," said Nick calmly, as if she'd just reported something perfectly normal. He got up and led her by the hand back to bed. "You need sleep."

"But I need to feed him."

"I'll give him the expressed milk you've got in the freezer. Just go to sleep. I'm canceling tomorrow. Sleep."

"But——"

"Sleep. Just sleep."

It was the most erotic thing he'd ever said to her. He pulled the covers up under her chin, unplugged the monitor, and left, switching off the light and closing the door behind him. The room became divinely silent and dark.

She slept.

When she woke, her breasts rock hard and leaking, the room was filled with sunlight, and the house was quiet. She looked at the clock and saw that it was nine o'clock. He'd done it. He actually canceled his trip. She'd slept for six straight glorious hours. Her vision was brighter, her brain sharper. She went downstairs and found Nick giving Madison her breakfast, while Tom cooed and kicked in his bouncer.

"Thank you," said Alice, almost delirious with gratitude and relief.

"No problem." Nick smiled.

She could still see the pride on his face, because he'd saved her. He'd fixed things. He'd always loved to fix things for her.

So it wasn't strictly true that he was never there, or that he always put work first.

Maybe if she'd just asked him for help more? If she'd fallen apart more often so he could be the knight in shining armor (but how sexist and wrong was that?); if she hadn't made herself the expert on everything to do with the children; if she hadn't been so condescending when he dressed the children in weirdly inappropriate combinations. He couldn't stand being made to feel stupid, so then he just stopped offering to dress them. His stupid pride.

Her stupid pride about being the best, most professional mother. *I might not have made it in your world, Nick, like Elisabeth, and all those career women in suits, but I've made it in my world.*

She'd come to the steepest part of the route, the part that always made Gina use terrible language. Her calf muscles tightened.

It was good to remember that for every horrible memory from her marriage, there was also a happy one. She wanted to see it clearly, to understand that it wasn't all black, or all white. It was a million colors. And yes, ultimately it hadn't worked out, but that was okay. Just because a marriage ended didn't mean that it hadn't been happy at times.

She thought about that strange period of time straight after she'd got her memory back. At first, images, words, emotions crashed over her in violent waves. She could hardly breathe for the chaos. Then, after a few days, her mind had calmed, the memories had fallen into their correct places, and she felt a kind of beautiful relief. Without her memory, she'd been swimming through cloudy water, half blind: now she had clarity of vision again. And what she saw was this: her marriage was over and she was in love with Dominick. That was that. With Dominick she felt the sweet, soothing comfort of being with a man who was besotted by her, fascinated by her, and wanted to find out who she was. With Nick, all she felt was bitterness, fury, and hurt. He was a man who had already decided who she was, who could list all her flaws, annoying tendencies, and mistakes. She could hardly stand to be in the same room with him. The idea that she'd planned to get back together with him was terrifying and shocking. As if someone had drugged her, hypnotized her, duped and deceived her.

It wasn't just that her memories of the last ten years were back. It was that her true self, *as formed by those ten years,* was back. As seductive as it might have been to erase the grief and pain of the last ten years, it was also a lie. Young Alice was a fool. A sweet, innocent fool. Young Alice hadn't experienced ten years of living.

But even as she tried to reason with her, scolded her, and grieved for her, young Alice stubbornly refused to go away.

Over the months that followed she kept popping up. She'd be paying for petrol at the service station and find her hand reaching out for a bar of heavenly Lindt chocolate. She'd be talking seriously to Nick about complicated logistical arrangements with the children and she'd find herself asking him something flippant and entirely unrelated to the conversation, like what he'd had for breakfast that morning. She'd be rushing to the beautician and find herself calling Elisabeth to suggest they meet for a coffee instead. She'd be hurrying between appointments and a voice would whisper in her head: *Relax.*

Finally she stopped resisting and called a truce. Young Alice was allowed to stay as long as she didn't eat too much chocolate.

Now it seemed like she could twist the lens on her life and see it from two entirely different perspectives. The perspective of her younger self. Her younger, sillier, innocent self. And her older, wiser, more cynical and sensible self.

And maybe sometimes Young Alice had a point.

Like with Madison, for example. Before she'd lost her memory, Alice had been going through a bad stage with Madison. She'd been so tough on her, so frustrated by her behavior, and in the deepest, most shamefully childish part of her mind, she had blamed Madison for Gina's accident. If she hadn't had to take her to the dentist that morning, Gina wouldn't have been pulling up at the corner at that time. They would have stopped to have coffee instead.

And of course Madison would have been smart enough to pick up on Alice's resentment. She was already a child who felt everything far too deeply. She'd seen her mother's friend killed in an accident and then her parents separated.

No wonder she'd been playing up. Elisabeth recommended a psychiatrist she'd heard about. A Dr. Jeremy Hodges. Madison had been going to see him twice a week, and it seemed to be helping. At least she hadn't assaulted anyone lately at school; and Kate Harper's husband had been transferred to somewhere in Europe, so the Harper family was now thankfully out of their lives.

There was a friendly toot of a horn and Alice looked up to see Mrs. Bergen driving by in her little blue Honda. It was strange, but after she got her memory back Alice found she'd lost interest in the development issue. The idea of selling up for a nice profit and moving to a fresh, new house without memories no longer seemed that important. She knew the bad memories would come with her anyway, and she didn't want to leave the good ones behind.

On the other hand, if the developers won—well, that was life. Things changed. Oh, things sure did change.

She came to the corner where Gina had died and remembered yet again the terror and disbelief of that moment. Her grief had changed since she lost and regained her memory. It was simpler, calmer, sadder. Before, she had somehow channeled her grief into a whole lot of different directions: fury toward Nick (*He should have taken Gina's side when she was splitting up with Mike*), coldness toward Elisabeth (*She never really liked Gina all that much*), and irritation toward Madison (*Gina would still be alive if they'd driven in the same car*). Hearing the facts of her life—"Your friend died"—without the memories, had untangled her feelings. Now she just missed her.

The phone rang in her hand. She stopped to answer it without looking at the name on the screen.

"Heard anything yet?" It was Dominick.

"No!" she said. "Stop taking up the phone line."

"Sorry." He laughed. "I'll see you tonight. I'm bringing a chicken, right?"

"Yes, yes! Go away!"

He liked to check things. And double-check. And triple-check. Just to be sure. It could potentially become an annoying habit, but then, everyone had annoying habits. And she wouldn't have even considered asking Nick to do something so menial as buy a barbecue chicken on a weeknight! Nick was too busy and important. When Dominick came over after a day's work, he was totally present. Not like Nick, who would sometimes act as if Alice and the children weren't quite real, as if his real life was at the office. It wasn't as if Dominick didn't have a stressful job, too. Nick might run a company but Dominick ran a school. And which one was contributing more to the community?

She just wished she would stop comparing Dominick to Nick, as if all the reasons she loved Dominick were simply because he was so different from Nick. It sometimes seemed as if the whole *point* of her relationship with Dominick was how it compared to her relationship with Nick.

The other day she and Dominick had been at Tom's soccer game and Nick was there, too. She'd been so aware of his eyes on them from the other side of the field as she laughed extra hard at Dominick's jokes. She'd made herself a bit sick, to be honest.

The awful thing was that even when Nick *wasn't* there, she was always imagining him watching. *Look at us snuggled up on the couch together watching TV, Nick. He's rubbing my feet. You never did that. Look at us walking hand in hand into this café. No fuss about finding the "perfect" table—we just sit down! Look, Nick, look!*

So did that make her relationship with Dominick nothing more than a performance?

She slowed down to a brisk walk, panting hard, and remembered how she'd sat in the kitchen drinking wine with Nick and the blissful relief she'd felt kissing him.

Stupid. So mortifying. He'd kissed her back, though. He'd been willing to "try again."

She had absolutely no desire to try again. None whatsoever. Been there, done that. Time to move on with her life. She had made the right decision. The children loved Dominick. He'd probably spent more time with them than they'd ever spent with their father.

And she and Nick were so civil and grown-up nowadays! They had finally worked out a "shared parenting arrangement" that suited them both. Nick wasn't having them fifty percent of the time, but he was seeing them a lot more than just on weekends. He was actually taking Friday afternoons off from work so he could pick them up from school.

Recently, she had found she was actually looking forward to seeing him when he dropped off the children. It was going to be one of those "amicable" divorces.

Yes, a good marriage (if you averaged it all out) followed by a good divorce. According to the children, Nick had a girlfriend. Megan.

Alice wasn't exactly sure how she felt about *Megan*.

The phone rang again.

At last. It was him. She sat down on somebody's red-brick garden wall.

"Tell me," she said. "Hurry up and tell me!"

At first she couldn't understand him. He seemed to be in the middle of blowing his nose.

"What? What did you say?"

"A little girl," said Ben, loud and clear. "A beautiful little baby girl."

Chapter 34

Elisabeth's Homework for Jeremy

I never believed I was going to have a baby until I heard her cry.

Sorry to admit that, Jeremy, because I know you worked your heart out trying to stop me from being a basket case.

But I never believed it. That day in the Port-a-loo, while the world's largest lemon meringue pie baked, I was convinced I was having my last miscarriage.

But then the bleeding stopped. It was just "spotting," as the medical world cheerily calls it. A spot of rain. A spot of bother.

But even when the spotting finally stopped, I didn't believe I was having a baby. Even when every ultrasound was normal. Even when I could feel the baby kicking and rolling, even when I was going to prenatal classes, choosing a crib, washing the baby clothes, and even when they were telling me, Okay, you can push now, I still didn't believe I was having a baby. Not an actual baby.

Until she cried. And I thought, *That sounds like a real newborn baby.*

And now she's here. Little Francesca Rose.

Through all those horrible years I hardly ever saw Ben cry. Now he can't stop crying. It seems like he had gigantic drums of tears stockpiled that he can finally release. I look over at him holding her asleep in his arms, and he has tears running silently down his face. We'll be bathing her together and I'll ask him to pass me a towel, and I'll discover he's crying again. I say, Ben, *please.* Darling.

I don't cry as much. I'm concentrating too hard on doing it all right. Ringing Alice up to ask questions about breast-feeding. How do you know if she's getting enough? Worrying about her crying. What is it this time? Wind? Worrying about her weight. Her skin. (It seems a bit dry.)

But sometimes, in the middle of the night, when it's a good breast-feed and she's attached properly and sucking well, suddenly the reality of her, the actuality of her, the aliveness of her, the exquisiteness of her, hits me so hard, wham, and the happiness is so huge, so amazing, it explodes like fireworks through my brain. I don't know how to describe it. Maybe it's like your first hit of heroin.

(How will I get her to just say no to drugs? Could I put her in some sort of early preventative therapy? What do you think, J? So much to worry about.)

Anyway, I wanted to tell you that we did finally have a ceremony for the lost babies, like you suggested. We took a bunch of roses to the beach one calm sunny winter's day, and we walked around the rocks and dropped one in the water for each lost little astronaut. I'm glad we did that. I didn't cry. But as I watched each rose float off, I felt something loosen, as if I'd been wearing something too tight around my chest for a very long time. As we walked back to the car, I found myself taking very deep breaths of air, and the air felt good.

(We were going to read a poem as well, but I thought the baby's ears might have been cold. She hasn't had a cold yet. She was a bit sniffly the other day, but it seemed to go away, so that was a relief. I'm thinking about giving her a multivitamin. Alice says it's not necessary but—anyway, I digress.)

I also wanted to apologize for thinking that you were a smug dad with a perfect life. When you told me at our last session that you and your wife were actually going through fertility treatments too, and that photo on your desk wasn't your children, but your nephews, I was ashamed of all my self-centered thoughts.

So, here is my homework, Jeremy. I know you never wanted to read it, but I thought I'd submit it anyway. Maybe it will help you with other patients. Or maybe it will help you when your wife is acting crazy, as she will sometimes do.

The Infertiles came to visit yesterday, laden with expensive gifts. It was sort of horrible. I knew exactly how they were feeling. I knew how they would be trying to hold it together, promising themselves they would only stay for twenty minutes and they could cry in the car, keeping their voices light and bright, their poor, tired, bloated bodies aching with need when they each dutifully held the baby. I complained about the lack of sleep (we'd had a really bad night) and I knew I was overdoing it, even though I *knew* there is nothing more patronizing to an Infertile than to hear a new mother complaining, as if that will make you feel better for not having your own baby. It's like telling a blind person, "Oh, sure, you get to see mountains and sunsets, but there are also rubbish dumps and pollution! Terrible!" I don't know why I did it, except that I understand now that desperate, clumsy desire to make people feel better—even when you know perfectly well that nothing will. The Infertiles will probably bitch about me at the next lunch. I won't see them again—the distance between us is just too great—unless, I guess, one of them gets to join me here on the other side.

I don't know if this is presumptuous of me, Jeremy, but I was wondering if you and your wife might be struggling with the problem of when is the right time to give up.

And if so, I want to say something that will make no sense.

We should have given up years ago. It's so clear now. We should have "explored other options." We should have adopted. We gave up years of our lives and we very nearly destroyed our marriage. Our happy ending could have and should have arrived so much sooner. And even though I adore the fact that Francesca has Ben's eyes, I also see now that her biological connection to us is irrelevant. She is her own little person. She is Francesca. If we weren't her "natural" parents, we would still have loved her just as much. I mean, for heaven's sake, I named Francesca after her great-grandmother, who has no genetic connection to us at all and wasn't even part of our lives until I was eight years old. I couldn't love Frannie any more than I do.

So there's that.

But now, to be completely honest, I have to contradict myself.

Because if your wife were to ask me if I would go through it all again, then this is how I would answer.

Yes. Absolutely. Of course I would. No question. I would go through it all again, every needle, every loss, every raging hormone, every heartbreaking second, to be here right now, with my beautiful daughter sleeping beside me.

PS. I'm enclosing a strange, rather ugly doll. It might just do the trick. Good luck, Jeremy. I think you'll make a wonderful dad. However long it takes and whichever way you choose to get there.

Chapter 35

Frannie's Letter to Phil

Hello again, Phil.

I've had this unfinished letter in my desk for months now.

My days are so full at the moment, I don't seem to have time to write to you. (Or to your memory, or your ghost, or to myself, or to whoever it was I've been writing all these years!)

I've just returned home from seeing Madison compete in an oratory competition and I'm still on cloud nine.

SHE WON FIRST PLACE!

It was a competition against the best children from other primary schools, so it was quite a big deal. She gave an extremely informative and entertaining speech about world records. (Did you know that the world record for the most live rattlesnakes held in the mouth at the same time is . . . eight!)

We were all so nervous beforehand. Xavier was pale and perspiring, and Alice was snapping at everyone. When they announced Madison's name, we went quite crazy. Olivia danced in the aisle. Roger leapt to his feet, knocking his elbow into some poor woman's eye. (Somewhat embarrassing.) Barb burst into tears. I could hear Xavier telling the man next to him, "That's my great-granddaughter you just heard. Gets all her talent from me!" He has appropriated my family in typical Xavier fashion. They don't seem to mind.

Elisabeth and Ben were there with the baby. You know what I love? Secretly watching Barb when she's secretly watching Elisabeth. The bliss on Elisabeth's face every time she looks at her baby is mirrored on Barb's face — and maybe it's mirrored on mine, too.

(Sometimes Barb comes across as a bit of a silly thing, but there's more to her than people think. That Roger knows he's on to a good thing. And I'm not just saying that because she's my daughter. A daughter I wouldn't swap for the world.)

Of course, little Francesca gets prettier every day. Tom kept her amused by rattling Ben's keys. He's good with babies. He finds them scientifically interesting.

Alice and Dominick seemed quite happy together. Alice is so much more relaxed since her accident. She's lost that tense, gaunt look. Perhaps we all need a good thump on the head from time to time? There is talk of them moving in together.

I hear Nick has a new girlfriend too, although she wasn't there, thankfully. Nick was kept busy with his sisters and his mother. I believe the modern term for these women is "high maintenance."

Everyone keeps telling me there is no chance of reconciliation between Alice and Nick. "No chance at all," they tell me, as if I'm a deluded old woman. And yet . . .

Xavier and I happened to be sitting next to Nick, directly behind Alice and Dominick. When they announced Madison was the winner, Alice didn't even look at Dominick. She turned straight around to look for Nick.

She reached out her hand to him almost involuntarily. He took it. Just her fingertips. Just for a fleeting second. I saw the expressions on their faces. That's all I'm saying.

Well, I think perhaps it's time I signed off, Phil, and I hope you don't mind, but I think this may be my last letter.

Xavier is waiting for me to come to bed.

Love,

and goodbye,

Frannie

Epilogue

She was floating, arms outspread, water lapping her body, breathing in a summery fragrance of salt and coconut. There was a pleasantly satisfied breakfast taste in her mouth of bacon and coffee and possibly croissants. She lifted her chin and the morning sun shone so brightly on the water, she had to squint through spangles of light to see her feet in front of her. Her toenails were each painted a different color. Red. Gold. Purple. Funny. The nail polish hadn't been applied very well. Blobby and messy. Someone else was floating in the water right next to her. Someone she liked a lot, who made her laugh, with toenails painted the same way. The other person waggled multicolored toes at her companionably, and she was filled with sleepy contentment. Somewhere in the distance, a man's voice shouted, "Marco?" and a chorus of children's voices cried back, "Polo!" The man called out again, "Marco, Marco, Marco?" and the voices answered, "Polo, Polo,

Polo!" A child laughed; a long, gurgling giggle, like a stream of soap bubbles.

We're on the Hawkesbury River. This is our magical houseboat holiday.

Alice lifted her head from the water and looked at Gina. She had her eyes shut; her long curly hair was floating out from her head like seaweed.

"Gina! You're not dead, are you?"

Gina opened one eye and said, "Do I look dead?"

Alice was filled with exquisite relief. "Let's have champagne to celebrate!"

"Oh, definitely," said Gina sleepily. "Definitely."

There was someone swimming toward them. Bobbing up and down in a clumsy breaststroke. Brown shoulders rising in and out of the water. It was Dominick. His hair plastered close to his head. Drops of water sparkling on his eyelashes.

"Hi, girls," he said, treading water next to them.

Gina kept quiet.

Alice felt embarrassed in front of Gina. For some reason it was wrong. It wasn't right that Dominick was here.

Gina rolled over onto her stomach and swam away.

"No, no, come back!" shouted Alice.

"She's gone," said Dominick sadly.

"You shouldn't be here," said Alice to Dominick. She splashed him and he looked hurt. "This isn't your holiday."

The radio alarm went off. An eighties song, loud and jarring in the morning silence.

There was a flurry of movement and the quilt slid off her shoulders. "Sorry." The radio was switched off again.

She turned over and pulled the quilt back up again.

A Gina dream. She hadn't dreamed of her for so long. She loved those dreams that felt so real, it was almost like she was seeing her again, spending another day with her. Except Dominick shouldn't have popped up like that. It felt like a betrayal of Nick to let Dominick into her houseboat holiday memory. Nick had loved that holiday. She could see him standing on the top deck of the boat, loping about, pretending to be a pirate. "Arg! Arg!" He would grab Tom around the waist and say, "Time to walk the plank, my boy!" and throw him high, so high in the air. She could see Tom's exhilarated face so clearly, his little brown boy's body suspended forever against a bright blue sky.

Tom.

She opened her eyes.

Had Tom come home last night?

He'd promised to be home by midnight and they'd gone to bed early. She'd meant to get up and check on him, but for some reason she'd fallen asleep so soundly.

Was that a memory of his key in the door? The car scraping in the driveway, music hastily switched off, the explosive sounds of teenage boys trying to be quiet. Huge feet thumping up the stairs.

Or was that another night?

Maybe she'd better go and check, but it was so early, and she was sleepy, and it was Sunday. Her one sleep-in day. She would get up, push open his bedroom door, and he'd be there, sprawled out fully dressed on top of his bed. The room dank and musty with the smell of after-shave and unwashed socks. Then she'd be wide awake with no chance of getting back to sleep. She'd have to spend the next two hours sitting in the kitchen, waiting for someone to wake up.

And it was Mother's Day! They were meant to bring her breakfast and presents in bed. If they remembered. Last year they forgot entirely. They were teenagers, full of the tragedies and the ecstasies of their own lives.

But what if Tom hadn't come home? And she didn't report him missing until ten a.m.? "I was asleep," she'd have to explain to the police officers when they asked why it had taken her so long to report that her eighteen-year-old son was missing. The police officers would exchange glances. Bad, lazy mother. Bad, lazy mother who deserves to have her son killed on Mother's Day.

She pushed back the covers.

"Tom came home," said a sleepy voice beside her. "I checked earlier."

She pulled the covers back up.

Tom would always come home. He was reliable. Did what he said he would. He didn't like being asked too many questions about his life (no more than three in a row was his rule), but he was a good kid. Studying hard for his exams, playing his soccer, and going out with his friends, bringing home pretty, eager-faced girls, who all seemed to think that if they just sold themselves to Alice they'd be in with a chance. (How wrong they were! If Alice showed too much interest in a girl, she was never seen again.)

It would be Olivia who wouldn't come home one night.

Alice couldn't stop being surprised at the transformation of Olivia from sweet, angelic little girl to surly, furious, secretive teenager. She'd dyed her beautiful blond curls black and pulled her hair dead straight, so she looked like Morticia from *The Addams Family*. "Who?" Olivia had sneered. You couldn't talk to her. Anything you said was likely to give offense. The slamming of her bedroom door reverberated throughout the house on a regular basis. "I hate my life!" she would scream, and Alice would be researching teenage suicide on the Net, when next thing she'd hear her shrieking with laughter with her friends on the phone. Drugs. Teenage pregnancy. Tattoos. It all seemed possible with Olivia. Alice was pretty sure she was going to need intense therapy when Olivia was studying for her HSC in two years' time. For herself.

It's just a stage, Madison told her. Just ride it out, Mum.

Madison had got all her teenage angst over and done with by the time she was fourteen. Now she was a joy. So beautiful to look at that it sometimes made Alice catch her breath in the morning when she saw her come down to breakfast, her hair tousled, her skin translucent. She was studying economics at uni and had a besotted boyfriend called Pete, whom Alice had begun to think of as a bonus son (which was unfortunate, because she had an awful feeling that Madison would be breaking his heart in the not too distant future). It had all gone so fast. One minute they were driving her home from the hospital, a tiny, wrinkled, squalling baby. The next she was all legs and cheekbones and opinions. *Whoosh*. It made Alice's head spin.

"It goes so fast," she told Elisabeth, but Elisabeth didn't really believe her. Anyway, she was the expert on all things mothering now. Even if she didn't have teenagers yet, she still knew best. Alice wanted to say, *Just you wait until your beautiful little Francesca is sleeping until noon and then slumps about the house, flying into a rage when you suggest she might want to get dressed before it's bedtime again.*

But Elisabeth was too busy to hear it. Busy, busy, busy.

She and Ben had ended up adopting three little boys from Vietnam after Francesca was born.

Two were brothers. The youngest was a severe asthmatic and was constantly in and out of hospital. One was in speech therapy for a stammer. Francesca was into swimming, which required early-morning training sessions. Elisabeth was involved with the Vietnamese expatriate community, a support group for adoptive parents, and of course she was treasurer of her school's Parents and Friends Committee. She'd also got back into rowing and was as thin as a rake.

She and Ben also had two dogs, a cat, three guinea pigs, and a fish tank. That quiet, neat little house Alice had visited all those years ago when Elisabeth was refusing to get out of the bed was now an absolute madhouse. Alice got a headache after five minutes.

Luckily they were all coming here today for a Mother's Day lunch, rather than Elisabeth's crazy house, and Madison, the precious girl, was going to cook.

Sleep, Alice. In a few hours the house will be filled with people.

Mum and Roger would be early. They'd be desperate to show them their photos from their recent holiday to the Latin Dance Convention in Las Vegas. Salsa dancing was still their passion.

As Frannie once said, "They've created a whole life around salsa dancing." Xavier had added, "Not like us. We've created a whole life around sex." Frannie hadn't spoken to him for a week, she had been so humiliated to hear him speak like that in front of the grandchildren.

Frannie and Xavier would be there today, together with Jess, one of Xavier's granddaughters, who had moved to Sydney a few years ago and made contact with her grandfather, to his everlasting joy. She was an extremely hip young Web designer who was also the lead singer in a band. Frannie and Xavier enjoyed going along to Jess's "gigs" and making knowledgeable comments afterward about the "crowd" and the "acoustics."

Alice worried sometimes that Frannie was overtiring herself, keeping up with all of Xavier's activities, but there was no denying her happiness.

She shifted in her bed. Sleep. As Frannie would certainly point out, she was quite old enough to take care of herself!

Hurry up and sleep.

She slept, and dreamed of Gina again.

She, Mike, Nick, and Alice were sitting around the dinner table after a long night of eating and drinking.

"I wonder what we'll all be doing in ten years' time," said Gina.

"We'll be grayer and fatter and wrinklier," said Nick, who was a bit drunk. "But hopefully the four of us will still be friends sitting around a table like this, talking about our memories."

"Awwww," said Gina, raising her glass. "You're so sweet, Nick."

"Preferably on a yacht," said Mike.

Was it a dream or a memory?

"Alice," said a voice in her ear.

Alice opened her eyes.

Nick's face was creased with sleep. "Were you dreaming about Gina?"

"Did I say her name?"

"Yes. And Mike's name."

Thankfully she hadn't said Dominick's name. He was still a bit strange about Dominick. Did Nick sometimes dream of that Megan? She looked at him suspiciously.

"What?" he said.

"Nothing."

"Happy Mother's Day."

"Thank you."

He said, "I'll go bring us up some coffee in a minute."

"Okay."

Nick closed his eyes and fell immediately back asleep.

Alice put her hands behind her head and considered her dream. Dominick had made an appearance because she'd seen him at the IGA yesterday. He was studying a packet of floss as if his life depended upon it. She had a feeling he'd seen her first and wasn't in the mood for one of their overly hearty, let's-pretend-this-isn't-awkward chats and so she'd obligingly darted into the next aisle.

It was so strange to think that she'd seriously considered spending her life with him. (He was married now to one of the other mothers from school; he probably thought the same thing about her.)

Madison had been asking Alice a lot of questions lately about the year they separated.

"If you hadn't lost your memory that time, do you think you and Dad would have still got back together?" she'd asked just yesterday.

It made Alice sick with guilt when she thought about what they had put the children through that year. She and Nick had been so *young*, so full of the earth-shattering importance of their own feelings.

"Do you think we damaged you?" she asked Madison anxiously.

"No need to get hysterical, Mum," Madison had sighed, worldly-wise.

Would they have got back together if she hadn't lost her memory?

Yes. No. Probably not.

She remembered that hot summer's afternoon a few months after Francesca was born. Nick had stopped by the house to return a school-bag Tom had left in his car. The children were out back, in the pool, and Alice, Dominick, and Nick were on the front lawn, reminiscing about their own childhood summers playing with water sprinklers on front lawns, before the days of water restrictions. Alice and Dominick were standing together, and Nick was standing a little way apart.

The conversation had led to Alice and Nick telling Dominick about how they'd painted the front veranda on a sweltering hot day. It had been a disaster. The paint had dried too quickly; it had all cracked and peeled.

"You were in such a bad mood that day," Nick said to Alice. "Stomping around. Blaming me." He imitated her stomping.

Alice gave him a shove. "You were in a bad mood, too."

"I poured a bucket of water over you to calm you down."

"And then I threw the tin of paint at you and you went *crazy*. You were running after me. You looked like Frankenstein."

They laughed at the memory. They couldn't stop laughing. Each time their eyes met they laughed harder.

Dominick smiled uneasily. "Guess you had to be there."

That just made them laugh harder.

When they finally stopped and wiped the tears from their eyes, the shadows on the lawn had lengthened and Alice saw that she was standing next to Nick and Dominick was standing apart, as if she and Nick were the couple and Dominick was the visitor. She looked at Dominick and his eyes were flat and sad. They all knew. Maybe they'd all known for the last few months.

Three weeks later, Nick moved back in.

The funny thing was that Nick didn't even remember that moment on the lawn. He thought she imagined it. For him, the significant moment had been at Madison's oratory competition.

"You turned around and looked at me and I thought, Yep, she wants me back."

Alice didn't remember that at all.

"What are you thinking about?"

Alice blinked. Nick stood at the foot of the bed, looking down at her. "Your face has gone all serious."

"Pancakes," said Alice. "I'm hoping they're seriously good pancakes."

"Ah. Well, they will be. Madison is cooking."

She watched him pull back the curtains and examine the day outside. He lifted the window and breathed in luxuriously. Obviously the weather had met with his approval. Then he went into the en suite bathroom, pulling up his T-shirt to scratch his stomach and yawning.

Alice closed her eyes and remembered those first few months after Nick moved back in.

Sometimes it was exhilaratingly easy to be happy again. Other times they found that they did have to "try," and the trying seemed stupid and pointless and Alice would wake up in the middle of the night thinking of all the times Nick had hurt her and wondering why she hadn't stayed with Dominick. But then there were the other times, unexpected quiet moments, where they'd catch each other's eyes, and all the years of hurt and joy, bad times and good times, seemed to fuse into a feeling that she knew was so much stronger, more complex and real, than any of those fledgling feelings for Dominick, or even the love she'd first felt for Nick in those early years.

She had always thought that exquisitely happy time at the beginning of her relationship with Nick was the ultimate, the feeling they'd always be trying to replicate, to get back, but now she realized that was wrong. That was like comparing sparkling mineral water to French champagne. Early love is exciting and exhilarating. It's light and bubbly. Anyone can love like that. But love after three children, after a separation and a near-divorce, after you've hurt each other and forgiven each other, bored each other and surprised each other, after you've seen the worst and the best—well, that sort of a love is ineffable. It deserves its own word.

And quite possibly she could have achieved that feeling with Dominick one day. It was never so much that Dominick was wrong for her and that Nick was right. She may have had a perfectly happy life with Dominick.

But Nick was Nick. He knew what she meant when she said, "Oh my dosh." They could look at an old photo together and travel back in time to the same place; they could begin a million conversations with "Do you remember when . . ."; they could hear the first chords of an old song on the radio and exchange glances that said everything without words. Each memory, good and bad, was another invisible thread that bound them together, even when they were foolishly thinking they could lead separate lives. It was as simple and complicated as that.

When Olivia started high school, Alice had begun work as a consultant for fund-raising events. Working seemed to give her relationship with Nick a new edge. Sometimes they would go out to dinner after they'd both been working, and she felt an entirely new attraction for him. Two professionals flirting across the table. It had the frisson of an affair. It was so good to find that their relationship could keep on changing, finding new edges.

Nick stopped suddenly beside the bed and looked down at her, his hand pressed to his chest.

"What?" Alice sat upright. "Chest pain? Are you feeling chest pain?"

She was obsessed with chest pain.

He removed his hand and smiled. "Sorry. No. I was just thinking."

"God," she said irritably, lying back down again. "You nearly gave *me* a heart attack."

He knelt on the bed next to her. She swatted him away. "I haven't cleaned my teeth."

"Oh, for heaven's sakes," he said. "I'm trying to say something profound."

"I prefer you to be profound when I've cleaned my teeth."

"I was just thinking," he said, "how grateful I am that you hit your head that day. Every day I say a little prayer thanking God for creating the spin class."

She smiled. "That's very profound. Very romantic."

"Thank you. I do my best."

He lowered his head, and she went to give him a friendly, perfunctory kiss (she hadn't cleaned her teeth; she was impatient for her coffee) but the kiss turned unexpectedly lovely and she felt that ticklish, teary feeling behind her eyes as a lifetime of kisses filled her head: from the very first brand-new-boyfriend kiss, to *"You may kiss the bride,"* to the unshaven, shell-shocked, red-eyed kiss after Madison was born, to that aching, beautiful kiss after she broke up with Dominick and told Nick (standing in the car park of McDonald's, the kids arguing in the backseat of the car), *"Will you please come back home now?"*

The bedroom door burst open and Nick jumped back to his side of the bed, grinning. Madison was balancing a tray set for breakfast, Tom was holding a huge bunch of sunflowers, and Olivia had a present.

"Happy Mother's Day to you," they sang, to the tune of "Happy Birthday."

"We're trying to redeem ourselves for last year," explained Madison as she placed the tray on Alice's lap.

"I should think so," said Alice. She picked up the fork, took a mouthful of pancake, and closed her eyes.

"Mmmmm."

They would think she was savoring the taste (blueberries, cinnamon, cream—excellent), but she was actually savoring the whole morning, trying to catch it, pin it down, keep it safe before all those precious moments became yet another memory.

Acknowledgments

A special thank-you to my lovely sisters, Jaclyn and Nicola Moriarty, for reading and commenting on my first drafts.

Thank you to my cousin, Penelope Lowe, for advice on medical matters, and my friend Rachel Gordon for patiently answering questions about life as a mother to school-aged children.

Thank you to my U.S. agent, Faye Bender, for all her support in finding the right home for this book.

Thank you to my wonderful editors around the world: Amy Einhorn in the United States, Cate Paterson and Julia Stiles in Australia, Melanie Blank-Schroeder in Germany, and Lydia Newhouse in the U.K. You all helped make *What Alice Forgot* a better book.

Readers Guide

what alice forgot

DISCUSSION QUESTIONS

1. Did you like the younger Alice best? Or did you relate more to the older Alice?

2. What would your younger self of ten years ago think of the person you are today?

3. What would surprise your younger self most about the life you're currently leading? What would disappoint you?

4. What would you think of your children? Are they how you imagined they would be? Are you the parent you envisioned? Why or why not?

5. Alice is shocked by many transformations—her gym-toned body, her clothes, her house. Are you more or less polished than you were a decade ago? And do you think there's any deeper significance to such change?

6. Do you think it was realistic that Alice ended up back with Nick? Were you happy with that ending? Do you think they would have ended up together if she hadn't lost her memory?

7. In order for Nick to be successful at his job, was it inevitable that he would spend less time with his family and thereby grow apart from Alice?

8. How did you feel about the sections written from the perspectives of Elisabeth and Frannie? Did they add to your enjoyment of the book, or would you have preferred to have it written entirely from Alice's point of view?

9. Do you think it was unavoidable that Elisabeth and Alice had grown apart, because of the tension caused by Elisabeth's infertility versus Alice's growing family? Or do you think their rift had more to do with the kind of people both of them had become?

10. It's not only Alice who changed over the last decade. Elisabeth changed, too. Do you think she would have been so accepting of the new Alice at the end if she herself didn't get pregnant?

11. Out of all the characters in the book, who do you think had changed the most over the past decade and why?

12. The film rights to the book have been sold to Fox 2000—who do you think would be good in the lead roles?

13. If you were to write a letter to your future self to be opened in ten years, what would you say?

And now, a special excerpt from
Liane Moriarty's new novel

Big Little Lies

Available in hardcover from
G. P. Putnam's Sons

Chapter 1

T hat doesn't sound like a school trivia night," said Mrs. Patty Ponder to Marie Antoinette. "That sounds like a riot."

The cat didn't respond. She was dozing on the couch and found school trivia nights to be trivial.

"Not interested, eh? Let them eat cake! Is that what you're thinking? They do eat a lot of cake, don't they? All those cake stalls. Goodness me. Although I don't think any of the mothers ever actually eat them. They're all so sleek and skinny, aren't they? Like you."

Marie Antoinette sneered at the compliment. The "let them eat cake" thing had grown old a long time ago, and she'd recently heard one of Mrs. Ponder's grandchildren say it was meant to be "let them eat brioche" and also that Marie Antoinette never said it in the first place.

Mrs. Ponder picked up her television remote and turned down the volume on *Dancing with the Stars*. She'd turned it up loud earlier because of the sound of the heavy rain, but the downpour had eased now.

She could hear people shouting. Angry hollers crashed through the quiet, cold night air. It was somehow hurtful for Mrs. Ponder to hear, as if all that rage were directed at her. (Mrs. Ponder had grown up with an angry mother.)

"Goodness me. Do you think they're arguing over the capital of Guatemala? Do you know the capital of Guatemala? No? I don't either. We should Google it. Don't sneer at me."

Marie Antoinette sniffed.

"Let's go see what's going on," said Mrs. Ponder briskly. She was feeling nervous and therefore behaving briskly in front of the cat, the same way she'd once done with her children when her husband was away and there were strange noises in the night.

Mrs. Ponder heaved herself up with the help of her walker. Marie Antoinette slid her slippery body comfortingly in between Mrs. Ponder's legs (she wasn't falling for the brisk act) as she pushed the walker down the hallway to the back of the house.

Her sewing room looked straight out onto the school yard of Pirriwee Public.

"Mum, are you mad? You can't live this close to a primary school," her daughter had said when she was first looking at buying the house.

But Mrs. Ponder loved to hear the crazy babble of children's voices at intervals throughout the day, and she no longer drove, so she couldn't care less that the street was jammed with those giant, truck-like cars they all drove these days, with women in big sunglasses leaning across their steering wheels to call out terribly urgent information about Harriett's ballet and Charlie's speech therapy.

Mothers took their mothering so seriously now. Their frantic little faces. Their busy little bottoms strutting into the school in their tight gym gear. Ponytails swinging. Eyes fixed on the mobile phones held in the palms of their hands like compasses. It made Mrs. Ponder laugh. Fondly though. Her three daughters, although older, were exactly the same. And they were all so pretty.

"How are you this morning?" she always called out if she was on the front porch with a cup of tea or watering the front garden as they went by.

"Busy, Mrs. Ponder! Frantic!" they always called back, trotting along, yanking their children's arms. They were pleasant and friendly and just a touch condescending because they couldn't help it. She was so old! They were so busy!

The fathers, and there were more and more of them doing the school run these days, were different. They rarely hurried, strolling past with a measured casualness. No big deal. All under control. That was the message. Mrs. Ponder chuckled fondly at them too.

But now it seemed the Pirriwee Public parents were misbehaving. She got to the window and pushed aside the lace curtain. The school had recently paid for a window guard after a cricket ball had smashed the glass and nearly knocked out Marie Antoinette. (A group of Year 3 boys had given her a hand-painted apology card, which she kept on her fridge.)

There was a two-story sandstone building on the other side of the playground with an event room on the second level and a big balcony with ocean views. Mrs. Ponder had been there for a few functions: a talk by a local historian, a lunch hosted by the Friends of the Library. It was quite a beautiful room. Sometimes ex-students had their wedding receptions there. That's where they'd be having the school trivia night. They were raising funds for SMART Boards, whatever they were. Mrs. Ponder had been invited as a matter of course. Her proximity to the school gave her a funny sort of honorary status, even though she'd never had a child or grandchild attend. She'd said no thank you to the school trivia night invitation. She thought school events without the children in attendance were pointless.

The children had their weekly school assembly in the same room. Each Friday morning, Mrs. Ponder set herself up in the sewing room with a cup of English Breakfast and a ginger-nut biscuit. The sound of the children singing floating down from the second floor of the building always made her weep. She'd never believed in God, except when she heard children singing.

There was no singing now.

Mrs. Ponder could hear a lot of bad language. She wasn't a prude about bad language—her eldest daughter swore like a trooper—but it was upsetting and disconcerting to hear someone maniacally screaming that particular four-letter word in a place that was normally filled with childish laughter and shouts.

"Are you all drunk?" she said.

Her rain-splattered window was at eye level with the entrance doors to the building, and suddenly people began to spill out. Security lights illuminated the paved area around the entrance like a stage set for a play. Clouds of mist added to the effect.

It was a strange sight.

The parents at Pirriwee Public had a baffling fondness for costume parties. It wasn't enough that they should have an ordinary trivia night; she knew from the invitation that some bright spark had decided to make it an "Audrey and Elvis" trivia night, which meant that the women all had to dress up as Audrey Hepburn and the men had to dress up as Elvis Presley. (That was another reason Mrs. Ponder had turned down the invitation. She'd always abhorred costume parties.) It seemed that the most popular rendition of Audrey Hepburn was the *Breakfast at Tiffany's* look. All the women were wearing long black dresses, white gloves and pearl chokers. Meanwhile, the men had mostly chosen to pay tribute to the Elvis of the latter years. They were all wearing shiny white jumpsuits, glittery gemstones and plunging necklines. The women looked lovely. The poor men looked perfectly ridiculous.

As Mrs. Ponder watched, one Elvis punched another across the jaw. He staggered back into an Audrey. Two Elvises grabbed him from behind and pulled him away. An Audrey buried her face in her hands and turned aside, as though she couldn't bear to watch. Someone shouted, "Stop this!"

Indeed. What would your beautiful children think?

"Should I call the police?" wondered Mrs. Ponder out loud, but then she heard the wail of a siren in the distance, at the same time as a woman on the balcony began to scream and scream.

Gabrielle: It wasn't like it was just the mothers, you know. It wouldn't have happened without the dads. I guess it *started* with the mothers. We were the main players, so to speak. The mums. I can't stand the word "mum." It's a frumpy word. "Mom" is better. With an *o*. It sounds skinnier. We should change to the American spelling. I have body-image issues, by the way. Who doesn't, right?

Bonnie: It was all just a terrible misunderstanding. People's feelings got hurt, and then everything just spiraled out of control. The way it does. All conflict can be traced back to someone's feelings getting hurt, don't you think? Divorce. World wars. Legal action. Well, maybe not every legal action. Can I offer you an herbal tea?

Stu: I'll tell you exactly why it happened: *Women don't let things go.* Not saying the blokes don't share part of the blame. But if the girls hadn't gotten their knickers in a knot . . . And that might sound sexist, but it's not, it's just a fact of life. Ask any man—not some new-age, artsy-fartsy, I-wear-moisturizer type, I mean a real man—ask a real man, then he'll tell you that women are like the Olympic athletes of grudges. You should see my wife in action. And she's not even the worst of them.

Miss Barnes: Helicopter parents. Before I started at Pirriwee Public, I thought it was an exaggeration, this thing about parents being overly involved with their kids. I mean, my mum and dad loved me, they were, like, *interested* in me when I was growing up in the nineties, but they weren't, like, *obsessed* with me.

Mrs. Lipmann: It's a tragedy, and deeply regrettable, and we're all trying to move forward. I have no further comment.

Carol: I blame the Erotic Book Club. But that's just me.

Jonathan: There was nothing erotic about the Erotic Book Club, I'll tell you that for free.

Jackie: You know what? I see this as a feminist issue.

Harper: Who said it was a feminist issue? What the heck? I'll tell you what started it: the *incident* at the kindergarten orientation day.

Graeme: My understanding was that it all goes back to the stay-at-home mums battling it out with the career mums. What do they call it? The Mummy Wars. My wife wasn't involved. She doesn't have time for that sort of thing.

Thea: You journalists are just loving the French-nanny angle. I heard someone on the radio today talking about the "French maid," which Juliette was certainly not. Renata had a housekeeper as well. Lucky for some. I have four children, and no staff to help out! Of course, I don't have a problem *per se* with working mothers, I just wonder why they bothered having children in the first place.

Melissa: You know what I think got everyone all hot and bothered? The head lice. Oh my gosh, don't let me get started on the head lice.

Samantha: The head lice? What did that have to do with anything? Who told you that? I bet it was Melissa, right? That poor girl suffered post-traumatic stress disorder after her kids kept getting reinfected. Sorry. It's not funny. It's not funny at all.

Detective-Sergeant Adrian Quinlan: Let me be clear: This is not a circus. This is a murder investigation.

Chapter 2

Six Months Before the Trivia Night

Forty. Madeline Martha Mackenzie was forty years old today.

"I am forty," she said out loud as she drove. She drew the word out in slow motion, like a sound effect. *"Fooorty."*

She caught the eye of her daughter in the rearview mirror. Chloe grinned and imitated her mother. "I am five. *Fiiiive.*"

"Forty!" trilled Madeline like an opera singer. "Tra la la la!"

"Five!" trilled Chloe.

Madeline tried a rap version, beating out the rhythm on the steering wheel. "I'm forty, yeah, forty—"

"That's enough now, Mummy," said Chloe firmly.

"Sorry," said Madeline.

She was taking Chloe to her kindergarten—"Let's Get Kindy Ready!"—orientation. Not that Chloe required any orientation before starting school next January. She was already very firmly oriented at Pirriwee Public. At this morning's drop-off Chloe had been busy taking charge of her brother, Fred, who was two years older but often seemed younger. "Fred, you forgot to put your book bag in the basket! That's it. In there. Good boy."

Fred had obediently dropped his book bag in the appropriate basket before running off to put Jackson in a headlock. Madeline had pretended not to see the headlock. Jackson probably deserved it. Jackson's mother, Renata, hadn't seen it either, because she was deep in conversation with Harper, both of them frowning earnestly over the stress of educating their gifted children. Renata and Harper attended the same weekly support group for parents of gifted children. Madeline imagined them all sitting in a circle, wringing their hands while their eyes shone with secret pride.

While Chloe was busy bossing the other children around at orientation (her gift was bossiness, she was going to run a corporation one day), Madeline was going to have coffee and cake with her friend Celeste. Celeste's twin boys were starting school next year too, so they'd be running amuck at orientation. (Their gift was shouting. Madeline had a headache after five minutes in their company.) Celeste always bought exquisite and very expensive birthday presents, so that would be nice. After that, Madeline was going to drop Chloe off with her mother-in-law, and then have lunch with some friends before they all rushed off for school pickup. The sun was shining. She was wearing her gorgeous new Dolce & Gabbana stilettos (bought online, thirty percent off). It was going to be a lovely, lovely day.

"Let the Festival of Madeline begin!" her husband, Ed, had said this morning when he brought her coffee in bed. Madeline was famous for her fondness of birthdays and celebrations of all kinds. Any excuse for champagne.

Still. Forty.

As she drove the familiar route to the school, she considered her magnificent new age. Forty. She could still feel "forty" the way it felt when she was fifteen. Such a colorless age. Marooned in the middle of your life. Nothing would matter all that much when you were forty. You wouldn't have real feelings when you were forty, because you'd be safely cushioned by your frumpy forty-ness.

Forty-year-old woman found dead. Oh dear.

Twenty-year-old woman found dead. Tragedy! Sadness! Find that murderer!

Madeline had recently been forced to do a minor shift in her head when she heard something on the news about a woman dying in her forties. *But, wait, that could be me! That would be sad! People would be sad if I was dead! Devastated, even. So there, age-obsessed world. I might be forty, but I am cherished.*

On the other hand, it was probably perfectly natural to feel sadder over the death of a twenty-year-old than a forty-year-old. The forty-year-old had enjoyed twenty years more of life. That's why, if there was a gunman on the loose, Madeline would feel obligated to throw her middle-aged self in front of the twenty-year-old. Take a bullet for youth. It was only fair.

Well, she would, if she could be sure it was a nice young person. Not one of those insufferable ones, like the child driving the little blue Mitsubishi in front of Madeline. She wasn't even bothering to hide the fact that she was using her mobile phone while she drove, probably *texting* or updating her Facebook status.

See! This kid wouldn't have even noticed the loose gunman! She would have been staring vacantly at her phone, while Madeline sacrificed her life for her! It was infuriating.

The little car appeared to be jammed with young people. At least three in the back, their heads bobbing about, hands gesticulating. Was that somebody's foot waving about? It was a tragedy waiting to happen. They all needed to concentrate. Just last week, Madeline had been having a quick coffee after her ShockWave class and was reading a

story in the paper about how all the young people were killing themselves by sending texts while they drove. *On my way. Nearly there!*
These were their last foolish (and often misspelled) words. Madeline
had cried over the picture of one teenager's grief-stricken mother, absurdly holding up her daughter's mobile phone to the camera as a
warning to readers.

"Silly little idiots," she said out loud as the car weaved dangerously
into the next lane.

"Who is an idiot?" said her daughter from the backseat.

"The girl driving the car in front of me is an idiot because she's
driving her car and using her phone at the same time," said Madeline.

"Like when you need to call Daddy when we're running late?" said
Chloe.

"I only did that one time!" protested Madeline. "And I was very
careful and very quick! And I'm *forty* years old!"

"Today," said Chloe knowledgeably. "You're forty years old today."

"Yes! Also, I made a quick call, I didn't send a text! You have to
take your eyes off the road to text. Texting while driving is illegal
and naughty, and you must promise to never ever do it when you're a
teenager."

Her voice quivered at the thought of Chloe being a teenager and
driving a car.

"But you're allowed to make a quick phone call?" checked Chloe.

"No! That's illegal too," said Madeline.

"So that means you broke the law," said Chloe with satisfaction.
"Like a *robber*."

Chloe was currently in love with the idea of robbers. She was definitely going to date bad boys one day. Bad boys on motorcycles.

"Stick with the nice boys, Chloe!" said Madeline after a moment.
"Like Daddy. Bad boys don't bring you coffee in bed, I'll tell you that
for free."

"What are you babbling on about, woman?" sighed Chloe. She'd picked this phrase up from her father and imitated his weary tone perfectly. They'd made the mistake of laughing the first time she did it, so she'd kept it up, and said it just often enough, and with perfect timing, so that they couldn't help but keep laughing.

This time Madeline managed not to laugh. Chloe currently trod a very fine line between adorable and obnoxious. Madeline probably trod the same line herself.

Madeline pulled up behind the little blue Mitsubishi at a red light. The young driver was *still* looking at her mobile phone. Madeline banged on her car horn. She saw the driver glance in her rearview mirror, while all her passengers craned around to look.

"Put down your phone!" she yelled. She mimicked texting by jabbing her finger in her palm. "It's illegal! It's dangerous!"

The girl stuck her finger up in the classic up-yours gesture.

"Right!" Madeline pulled on her emergency brake and put on her hazard lights.

"What are you doing?" said Chloe.

Madeline undid her seat belt and threw open the car door.

"But we've got to go to orientation!" said Chloe in a panic. "We'll be late! Oh, *calamity*!"

"Oh, calamity" was a line from a children's book that they used to read to Fred when he was little. The whole family said it now. Even Madeline's parents had picked it up, and some of Madeline's friends. It was a very contagious phrase.

"It's all right," said Madeline. "This will only take a second. I'm saving young lives."

She stalked up to the girl's car on her new stilettos and banged on the window.

The window slid down, and the driver metamorphosed from a shadowy silhouette into a real young girl with white skin, sparkly nose ring and badly applied, clumpy mascara. She looked up at Madeline with a mixture of aggression and fear. "What is your *problem*?" Her mobile phone was still held casually in her left hand.

"Put down that phone! You could kill yourself and your friends!" Madeline used the exact same tone she used on Chloe when she was being extremely naughty. She reached in the car, grabbed the phone and tossed it to the openmouthed girl in the passenger seat. "OK? Just stop it!"

She could hear their gales of laughter as she walked back to her SUV. She didn't care. She felt pleasantly stimulated. A car pulled up behind hers. Madeline smiled, lifted her hand apologetically and hurried back to be in her car before the lights changed.

Her ankle turned. One second it was doing what an ankle was meant to do, and the next it was flipping out at a sickeningly wrong angle. She fell heavily on one side. Oh, calamity.

That was almost certainly the moment the story began.

With the ungainly flip of an ankle.

Chapter 3

J ane pulled up at a red light behind a big shiny SUV with its hazard
lights blinking and watched a dark-haired woman hurry along the
side of the road back to it. She wore a floaty, blue summer dress and
high strappy heels, and she waved apologetically, charmingly at Jane.
The morning sun caught one of the woman's earrings, and it shone as
if she'd been touched by something celestial.

A glittery girl. Older than Jane but definitely still glittery. All her
life Jane had watched girls like that with scientific interest. Maybe a
little awe. Maybe a little envy. They weren't necessarily the prettiest,
but they decorated themselves so affectionately, like Christmas trees,
with dangling earrings, jangling bangles and delicate, pointless scarves.
They touched your arm a lot when they spoke. Jane's best friend at
school had been a glittery girl. Jane had a weakness for them.

Then the woman fell, as if something had been pulled out from
underneath her.

"Ouch," said Jane, and she looked away fast to save the woman's dignity.

"Did you hurt yourself, Mummy?" asked Ziggy from the backseat. He was always very worried about her hurting herself.

"No," said Jane. "That lady over there hurt herself. She tripped."

She waited for the woman to get up and get back in her car, but she was still on the ground. She'd tipped back her head to the sky, and her face had that compressed look of someone in great pain. The traffic light turned green, and a little blue Mitsubishi that had been in front of the SUV zoomed off with a squeal of tires.

Jane put her signal on to drive around the car. They were on their way to Ziggy's orientation day at the new school, and she had no idea where she was going. She and Ziggy were both nervous and pretending not to be. She wanted to get there in plenty of time.

"Is the lady OK?" said Ziggy.

Jane felt that strange lurch she sometimes experienced when she got distracted by her life, and then something (it was often Ziggy) made her remember just in time the appropriate way for a nice, ordinary, well-mannered grown-up to behave.

If it weren't for Ziggy she would have driven off. She would have been so focused on her goal of getting him to his kindergarten orientation that she would have *left a woman sitting on the road, writhing in pain.*

"I'll just check on her," said Jane, as if that were her intention all along. She flicked on her own hazard lights and opened the car door, aware as she did of a selfish sense of resistance. *You are an inconvenience, glittery lady!*

"Are you all right?" she called.

"I'm fine!" The woman tried to sit up straighter and whimpered, her hand on her ankle. "Ow. Shit. I've rolled my ankle, that's all. I'm such an *idiot*. I got out of the car to go tell the girl in front of me to stop texting. Serves me right for behaving like a school prefect."

Jane crouched down next to her. The woman had shoulder-length, well-cut dark hair and the faintest sprinkle of freckles across her nose. There was something aesthetically pleasing about those freckles, like a childhood memory of summer, and they were very nicely complemented by the fine lines around her eyes and the absurd swinging earrings.

Jane's resistance vanished entirely.

She liked this woman. She wanted to help her.

(Although, what did that say? If the woman had been a toothless, warty-nosed crone she would have continued to feel resentful? The injustice of it. The cruelty of it. She was going to be nicer to this woman because she liked her freckles.)

The woman's dress had an intricately embroidered cutout pattern of flowers all along the neckline. Jane could see tanned freckly skin through the petals.

"We need to get some ice on it straightaway," said Jane. She knew about ankle injuries from her netball days and she could see this woman's ankle was already beginning to swell. "And keep it elevated." She chewed her lip and looked about hopefully for someone else. She had no idea how to handle the logistics of making this actually happen.

"It's my birthday," said the woman sadly. "My fortieth."

"Happy birthday," said Jane. It was sort of cute that a woman of *forty* would even bother to mention that it was her birthday.

She looked at the woman's strappy shoes. Her toenails were painted a lustrous turquoise. The stiletto heels were as thin as toothpicks and perilously high.

"No wonder you did your ankle," said Jane. "No one could walk in those shoes!"

"I know, but aren't they gorgeous?" The woman turned her foot at an angle to admire them. "Ouch! *Fuck*, that hurts. Sorry. Excuse my language."

"Mummy!" A little girl with dark curly hair, wearing a sparkling tiara, stuck her head out the window of the car. "What are you doing? Get up! We'll be late!"

Glittery mother. Glittery daughter.

"Thanks for the sympathy, darling!" said the woman. She smiled ruefully at Jane. "We're on our way to her kindergarten orientation. She's very excited."

"At Pirriwee Public?" said Jane. She was astonished. "But that's where I'm going. My son, Ziggy, is starting school next year. We're moving here in December." It didn't seem possible that she and this woman could have anything in common, or that their lives could intersect in any way.

"Ziggy! Like Ziggy Stardust? What a great name!" said the woman. "I'm Madeline, by the way. Madeline Martha Mackenzie. I always mention the Martha for some reason. Don't ask me why." She held out her hand.

"Jane," said Jane. "Jane no-middle-name Chapman."

> **Gabrielle:** The school ended up split in two. It was, like, I don't know, a civil war. You were either on Team Madeline or Team Renata.

> **Bonnie:** No, no, that's awful. That never happened. There were no *sides*. We're a very close-knit community. There was too much alcohol. Also, it was a full moon. Everyone goes a little crazy when it's a full moon. I'm serious. It's an actual verifiable phenomenon.

> **Samantha:** Was it a full moon? It was pouring rain, I know that. My hair was all boofy.

> **Mrs. Lipmann:** That's ridiculous and highly defamatory. I have no further comment.

Carol: I know I keep harping on about the Erotic Book Club, but I'm sure something happened at one of their little quote-unquote meetings.

Harper: Listen, I *cried* when we learned Emily was gifted. I thought, *Here we go again!* I'd been through it all before with Sophia, so I knew what I was in for! Renata was in the same boat. *Two* gifted children. Nobody understands the stress. Renata was worried about how Amabella would settle in at school, whether she'd get enough stimulation and so on. So when that child with the ridiculous name, that Ziggy, did what he did, and it was only the orientation morning! Well, she was understandably very distressed. That's what started it all.